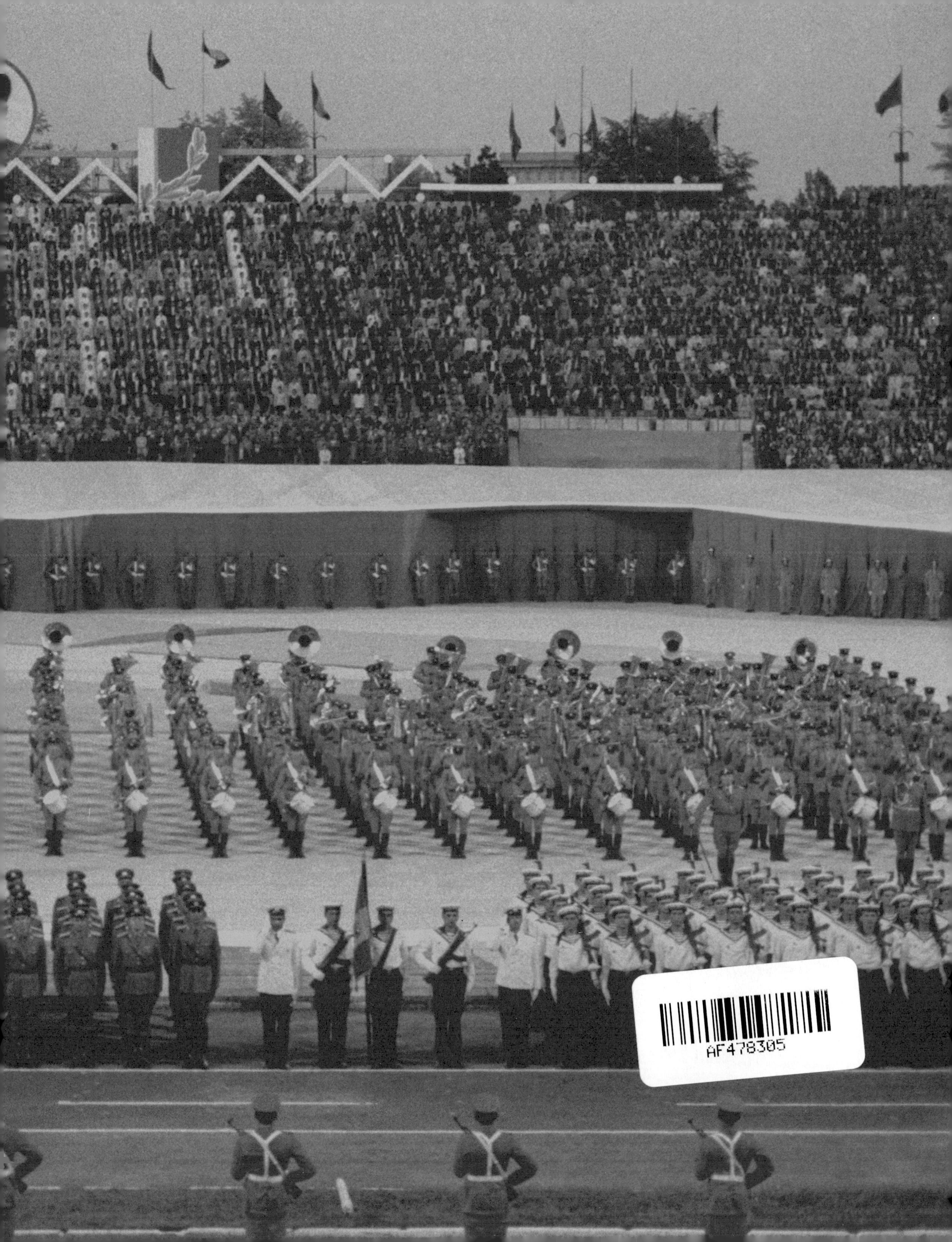

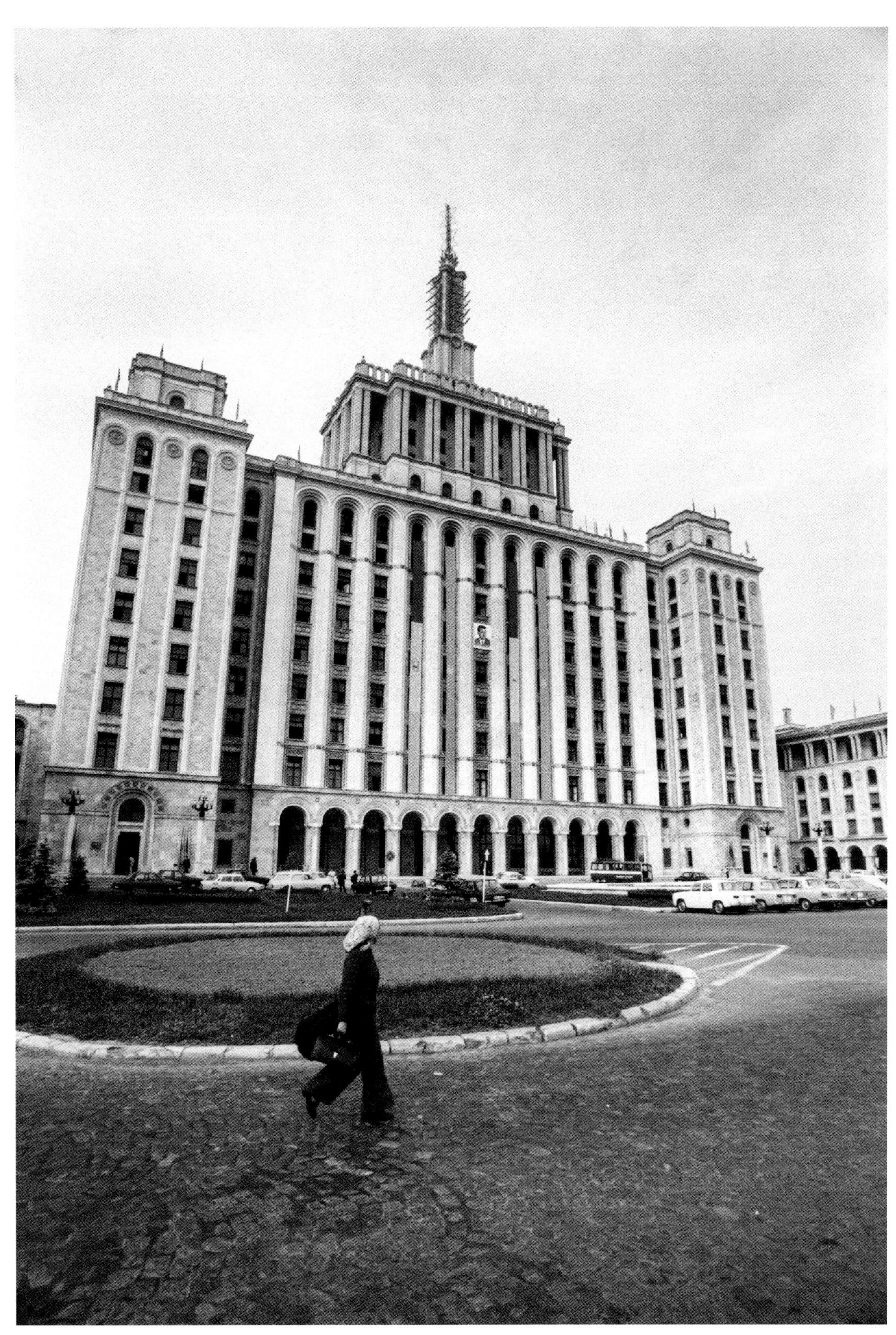

COMMUNISM(S):
A COLD WAR ALBUM

ARTHUR GRACE

"Those who cannot remember the past are condemned to repeat it."

- George Santayana

When I landed at West Berlin's Tempelhof Airport just over forty-three years ago, it marked the beginning of a twelve-year exploration of life behind the Iron Curtain. As a photojournalist for Western news outlets, I had unique access to both daily life and historic events across what was then known as the Soviet Bloc.

In those days and in those places, "access" took on a very different meaning for people in my line of visual work. I learned quickly that often while I was busy observing what was in front of me, someone from state security was busy observing me. This person might be the amiable representative from the State press office who was required to accompany me on my rounds, or it might be a more sinister and covert presence in the form of a plainclothes secret police officer who would appear at times as if out of nowhere.

Once I understood the obstacles I faced in pursuit of reality-based photographs - whether of everyday life or of more newsworthy people and events - I soon adopted the countermeasures necessary to do my job: misdirection, distraction, or outright evasion. Although I was occasionally reprimanded by my State-provided "minder," and in a few instances detained by authorities, I was able for the most part to photograph what was actually happening on the ground and capture what a given situation really looked like. This necessarily evasive pursuit of factual imagery became the ongoing challenge of my photographic coverage in autocratic countries during the 1970s and 1980s.

Due to limited visa accreditations, very few Western photojournalists gained entry into these countries at any one time. As a result, most of my photographs were unique for the simple reason that I was the only photographer present. Since only a tiny fraction of the images taken on assignment ever make it to the printed page, I filed away the unpublished negatives and transparencies, preserved in archival sheets and stored in binders waiting for me to return to them.

The reawakening in recent years of autocratic behavior in some of the countries I covered decades ago made me realize that many of my photographs from the Cold War era could have renewed relevance. Images once considered "outtakes" have acquired new meaning or importance with the passage of time. This volume contains a selection of my most representative pictures from that period organized in a way that helps provide context to the multi-dimensional reality of those times.

Even though these photographs offer only the merest glimpse of the Cold War from one photographer's perspective, I hope they will serve as a historical reminder of what autocracy looked like then, and could look like again in the not-too-distant future.

Arthur Grace

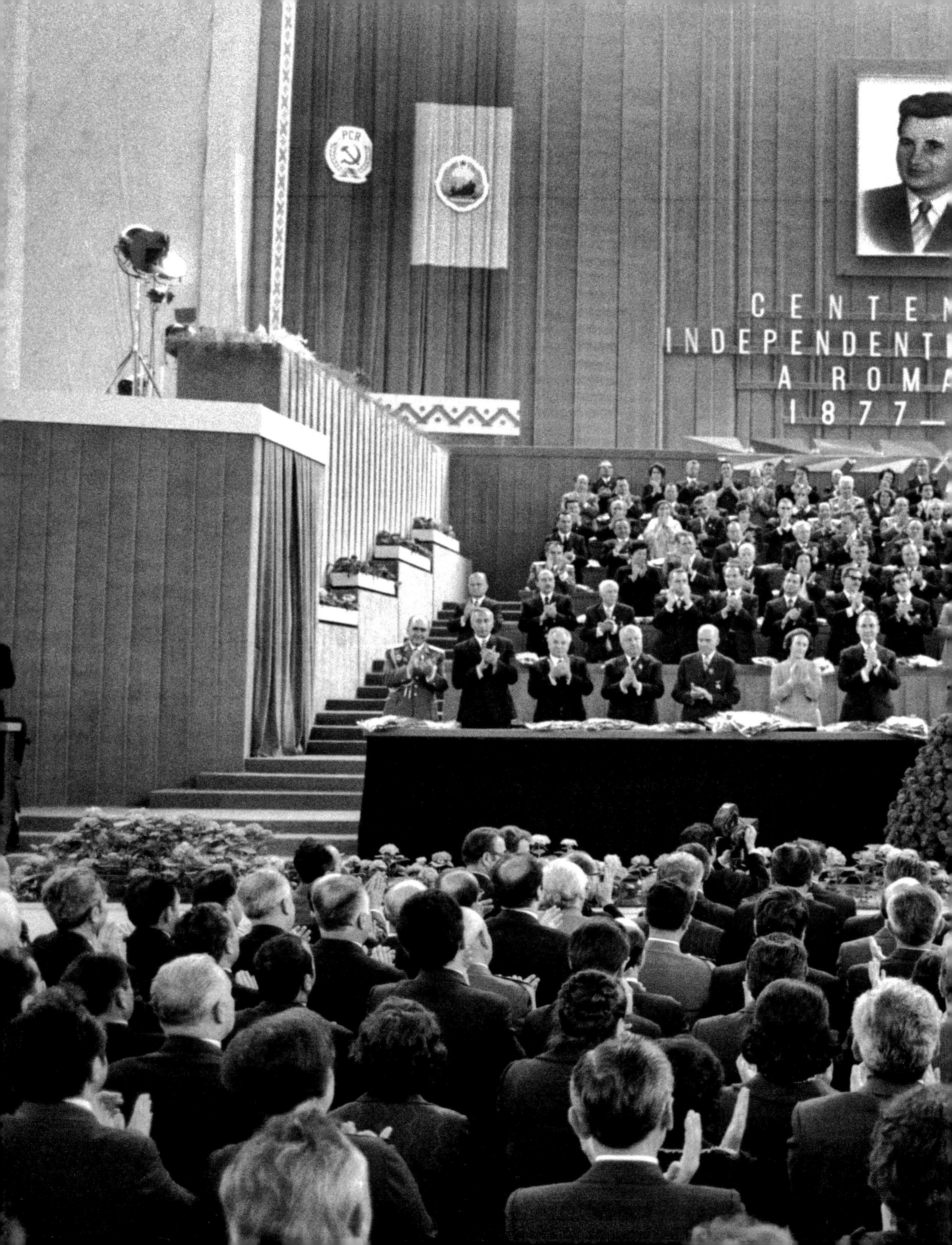
PCR
CENTEN
INDEPENDENT
A ROMA
1877

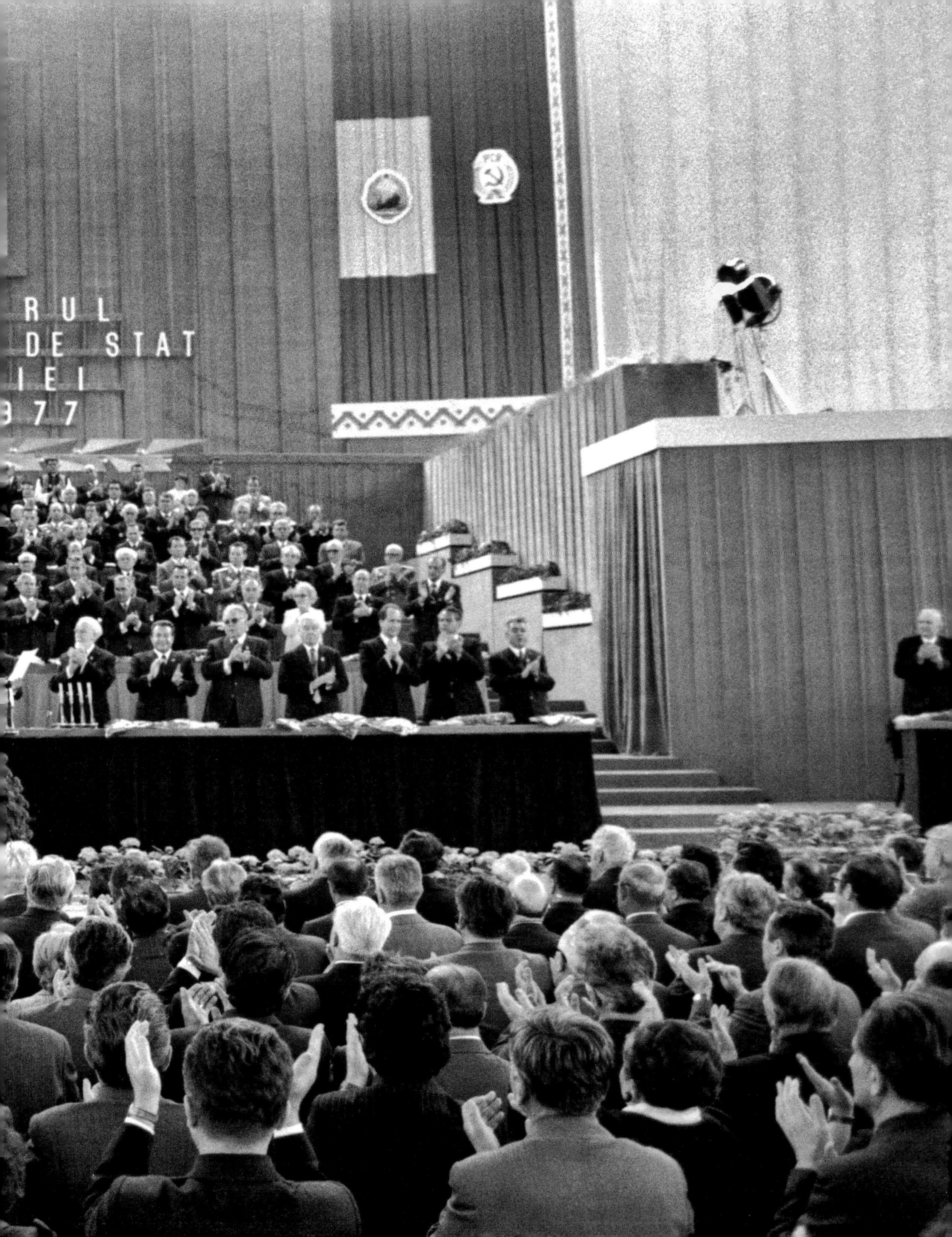
RUL
DE STAT
IEI
77

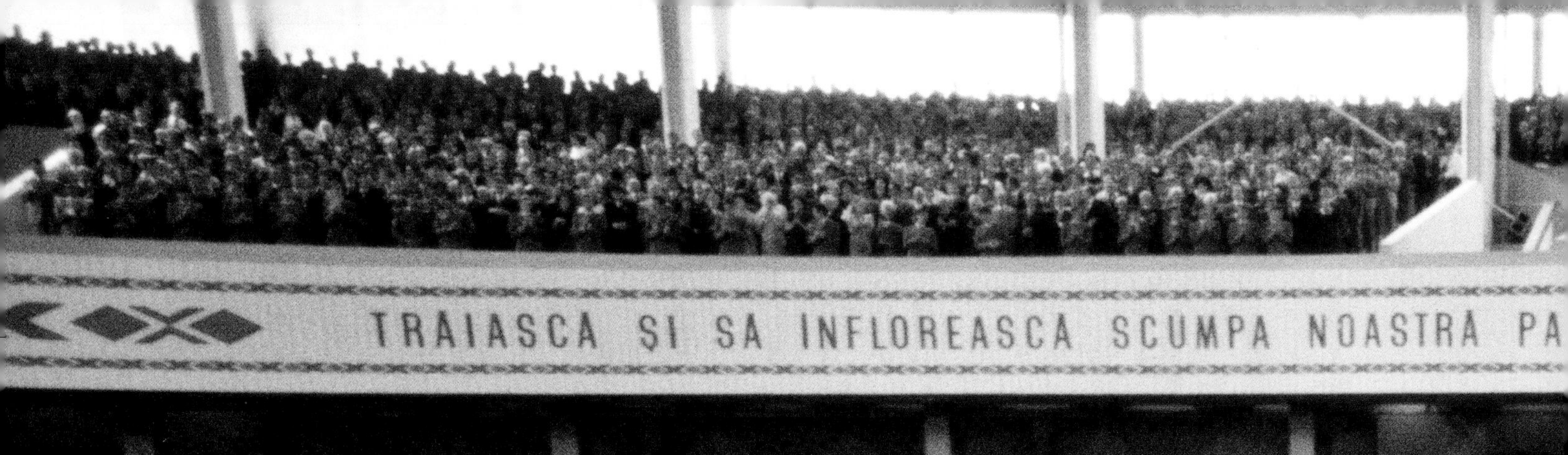
TRAIASCA ŞI SA INFLOREASCA SCUMPA NOASTRĂ PA

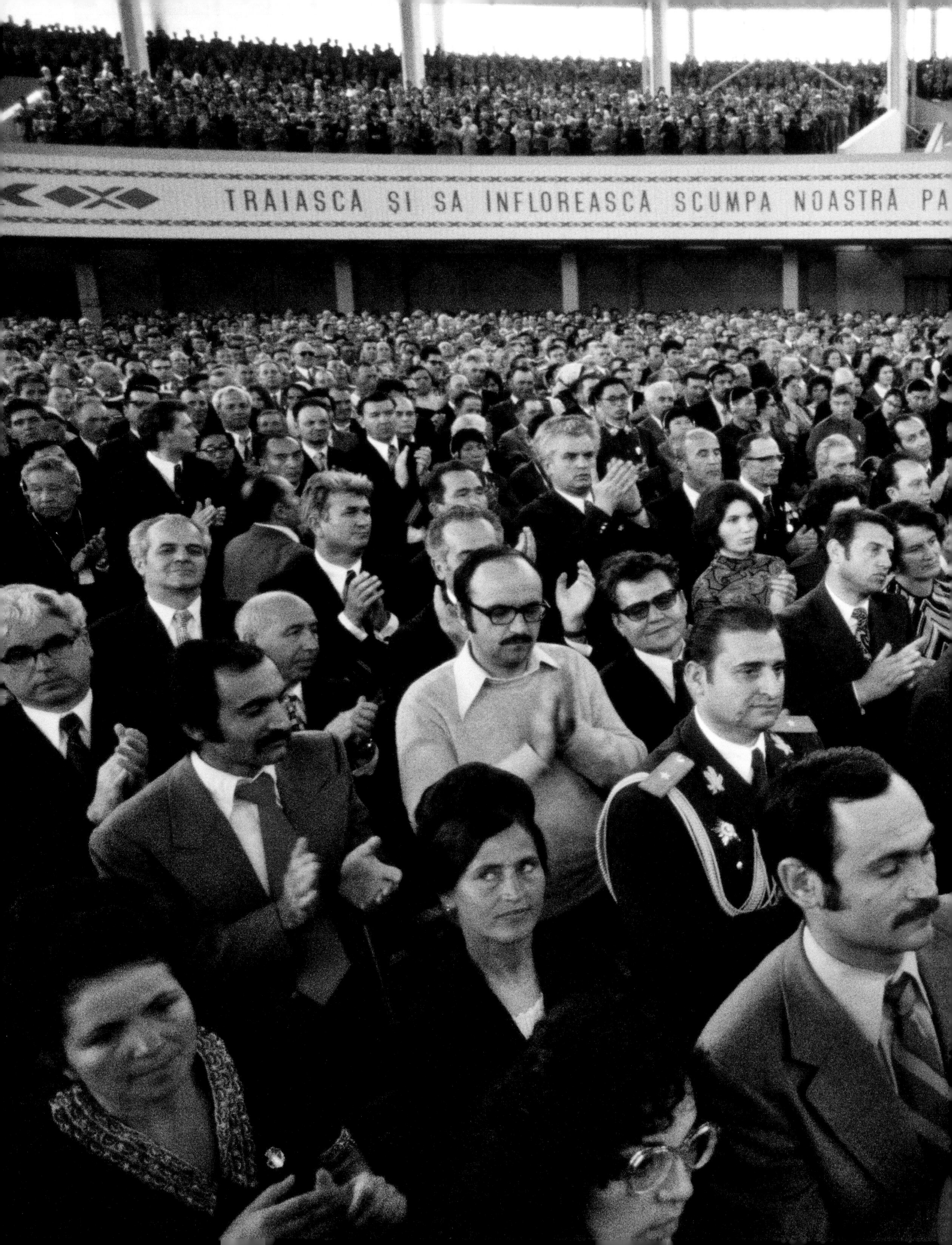

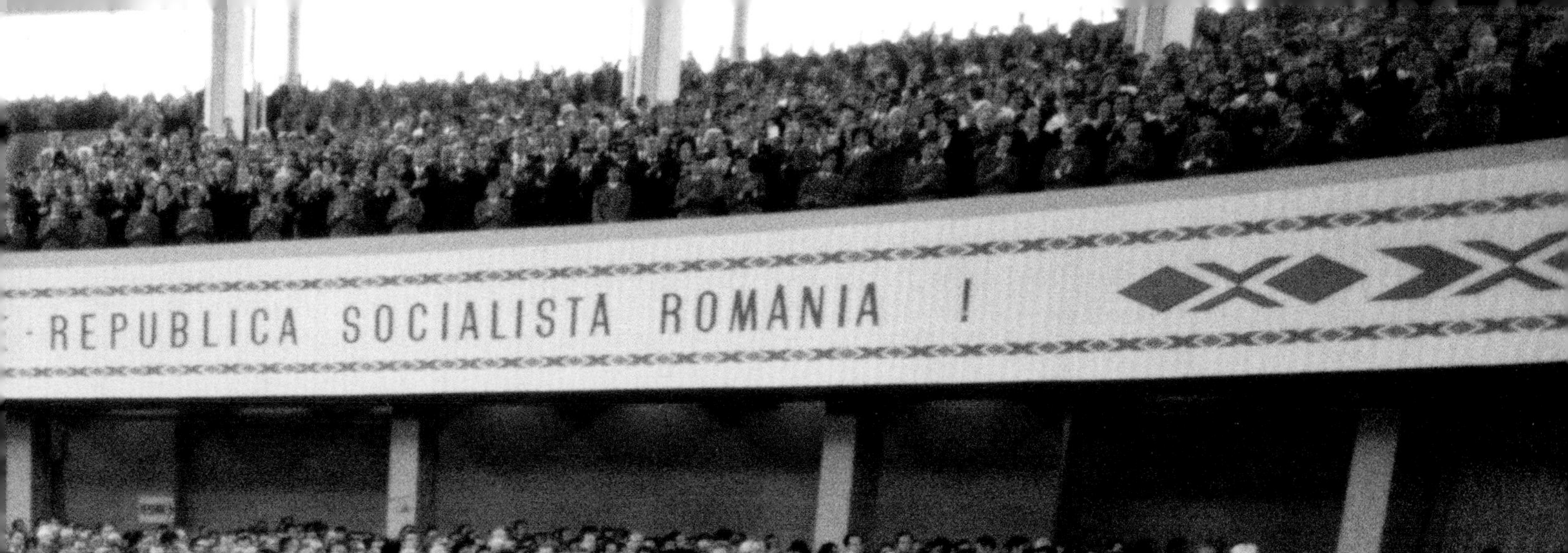
REPUBLICA SOCIALISTA ROMANIA !

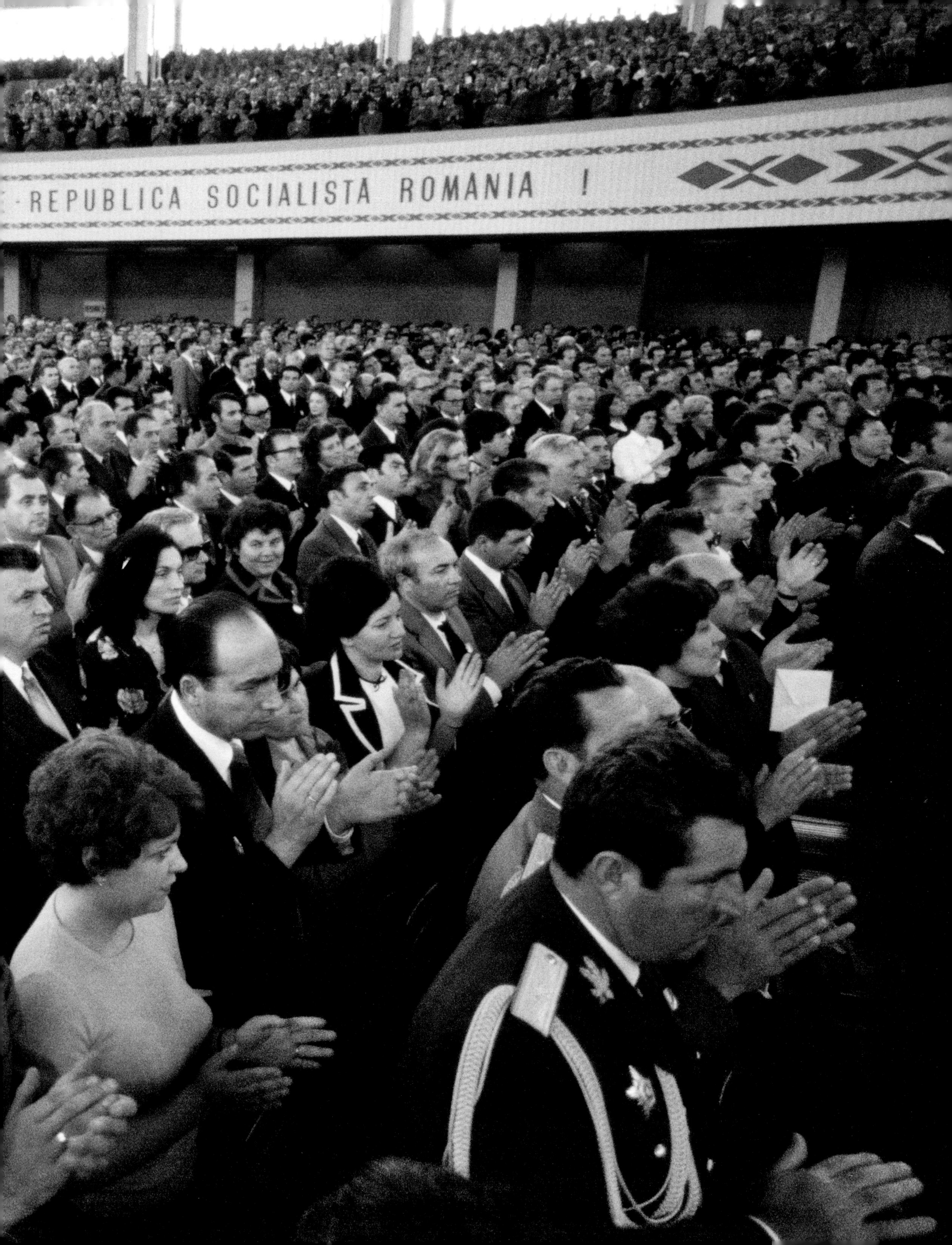

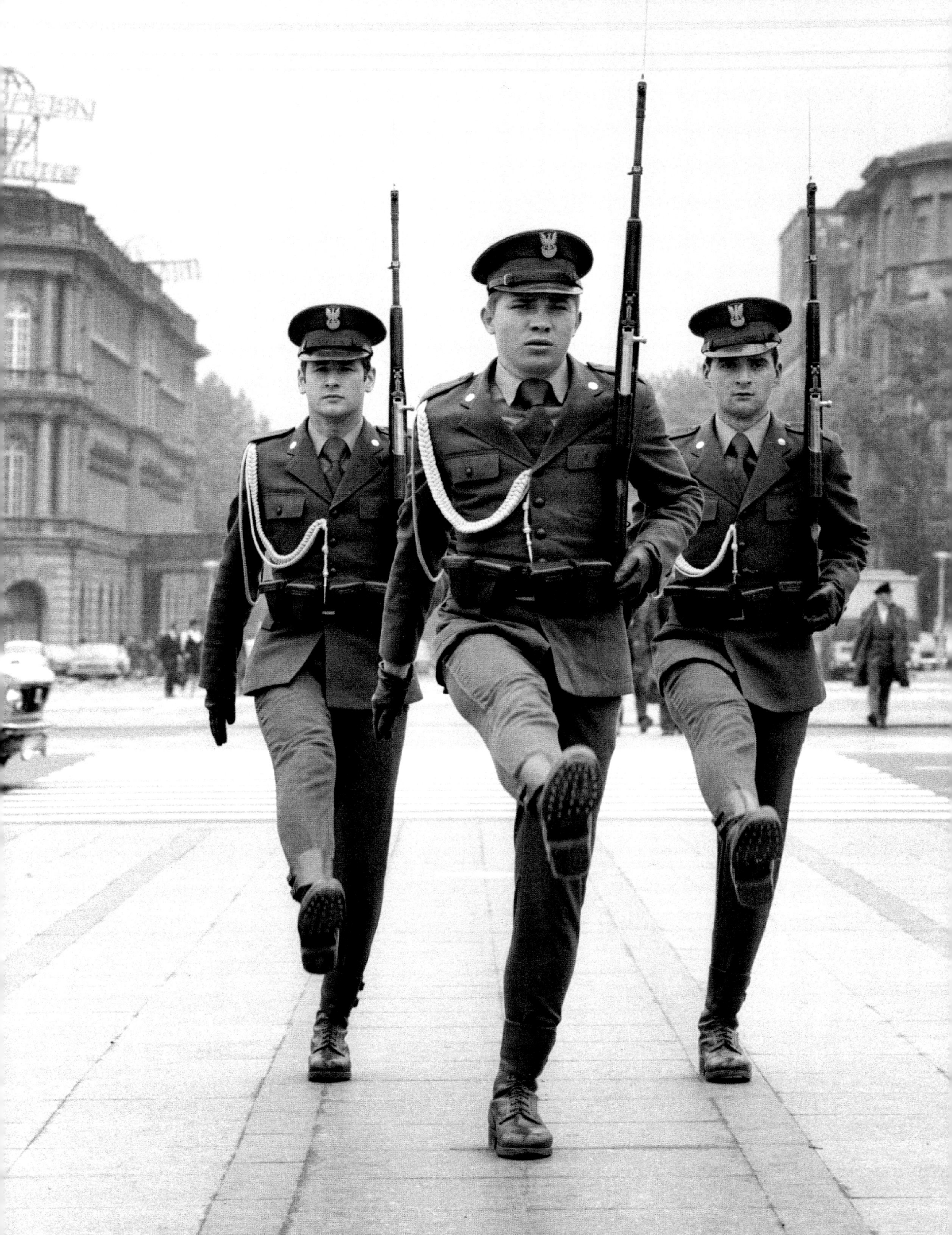

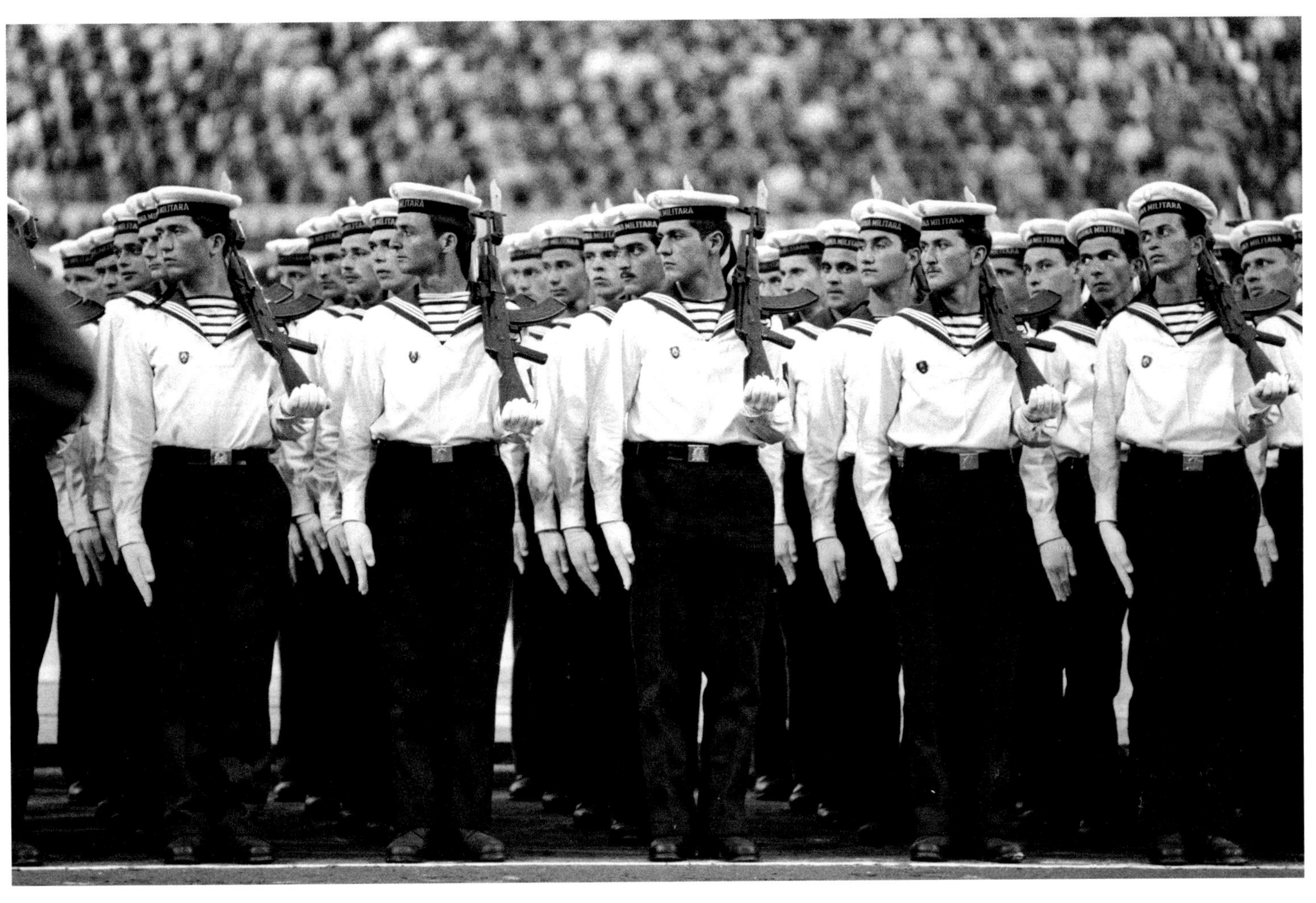

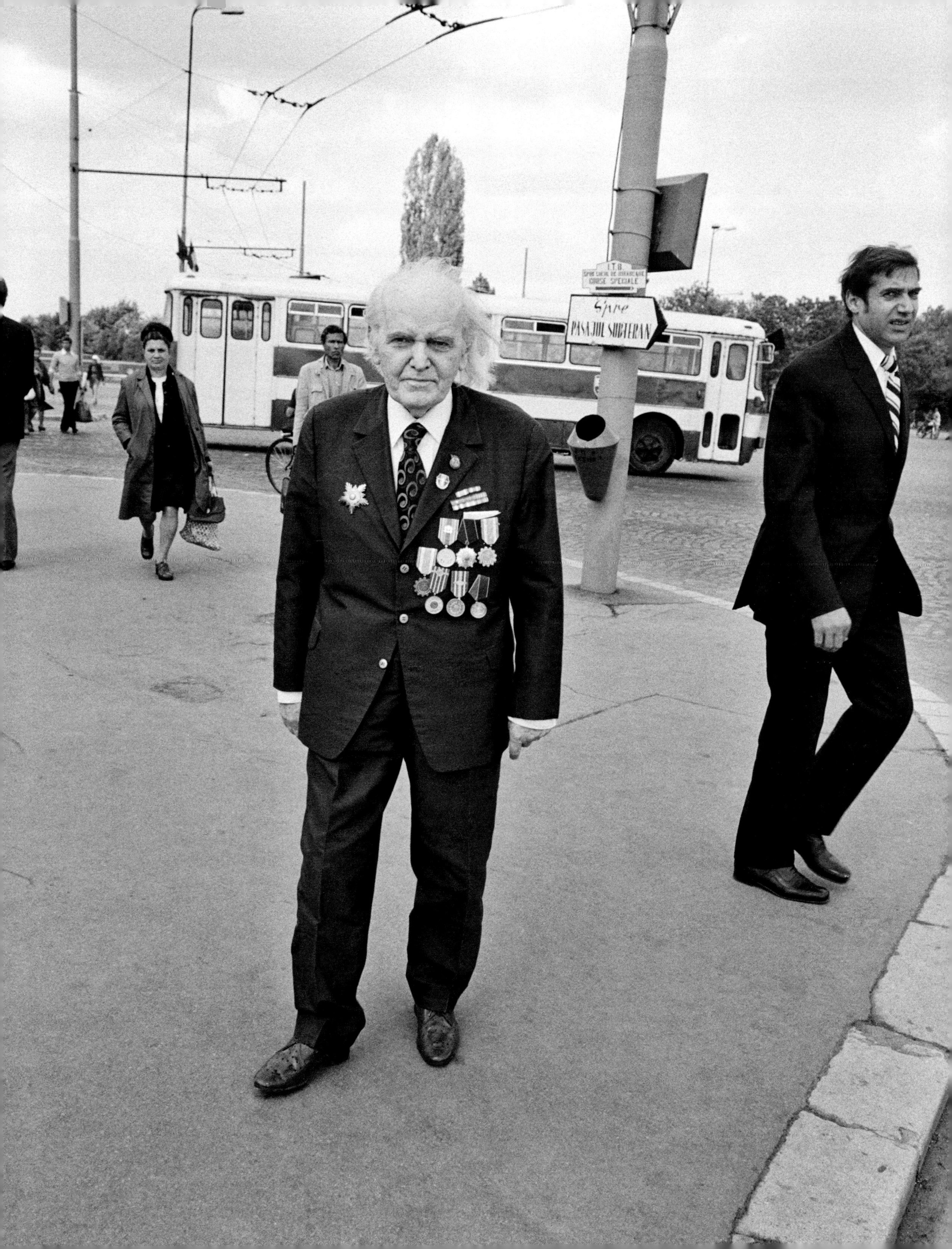
I.T.B.
CURSE SPECIALE
Spre
PASAJUL SUBTERAN

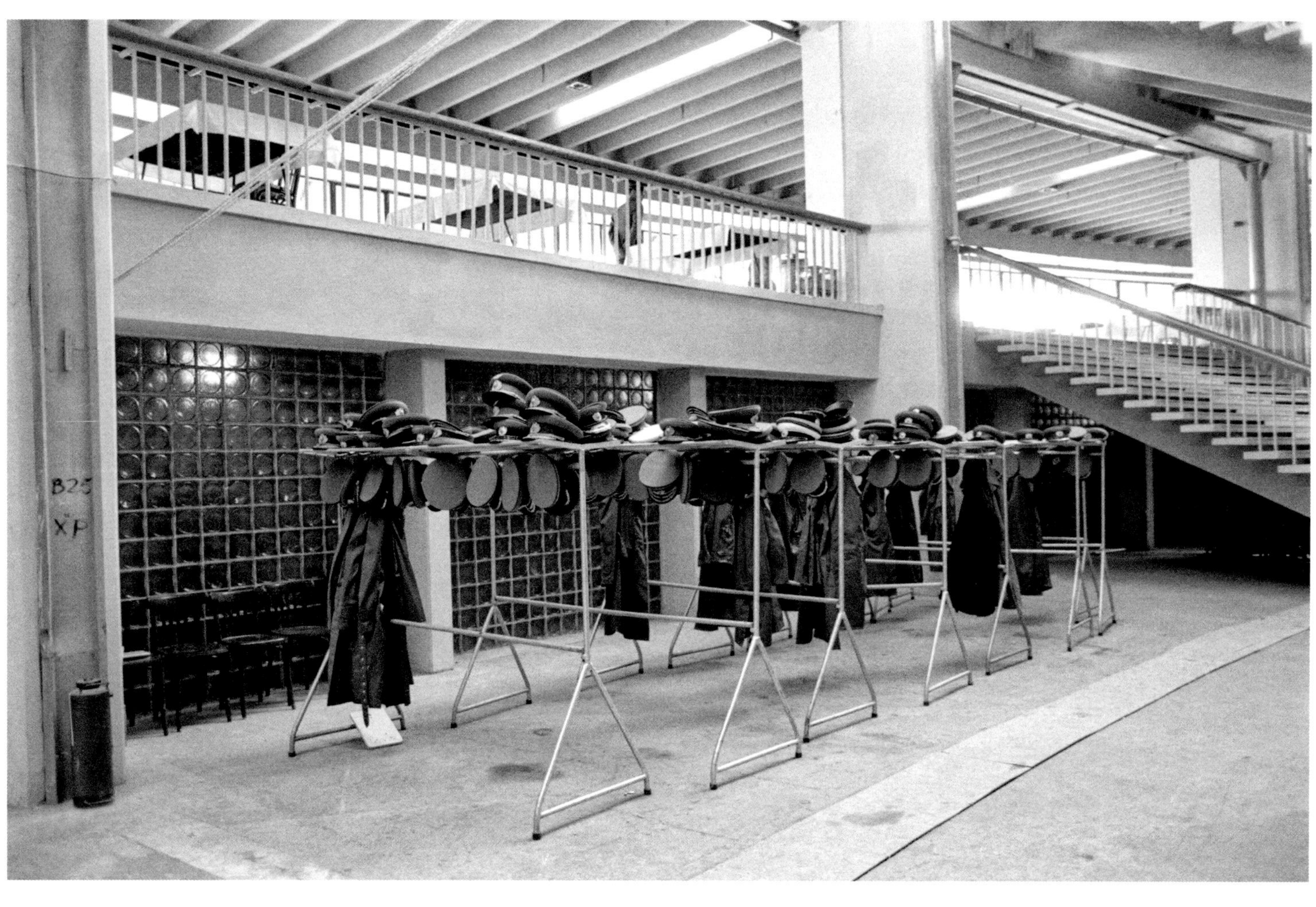
B25
XP

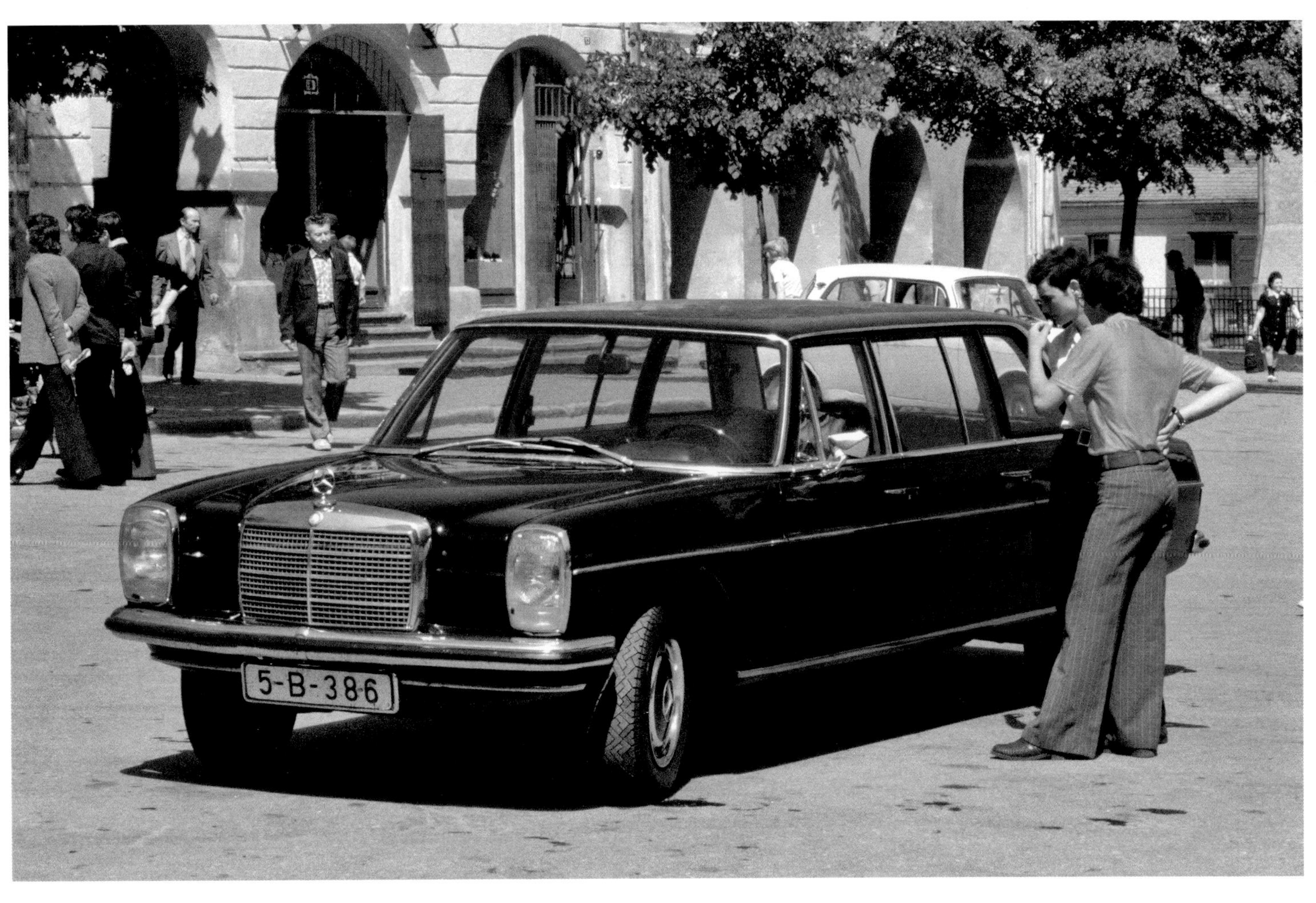
5-B-386

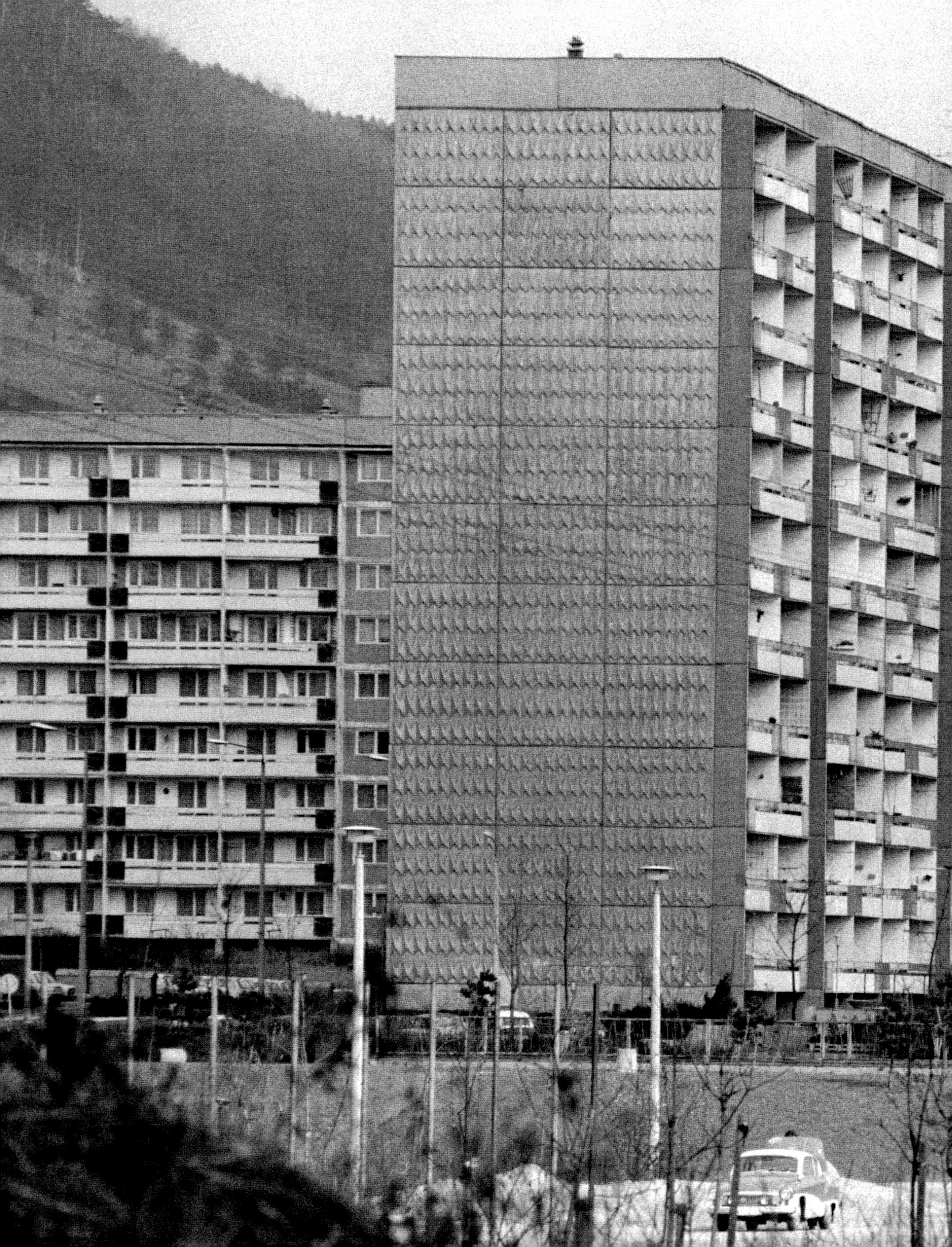

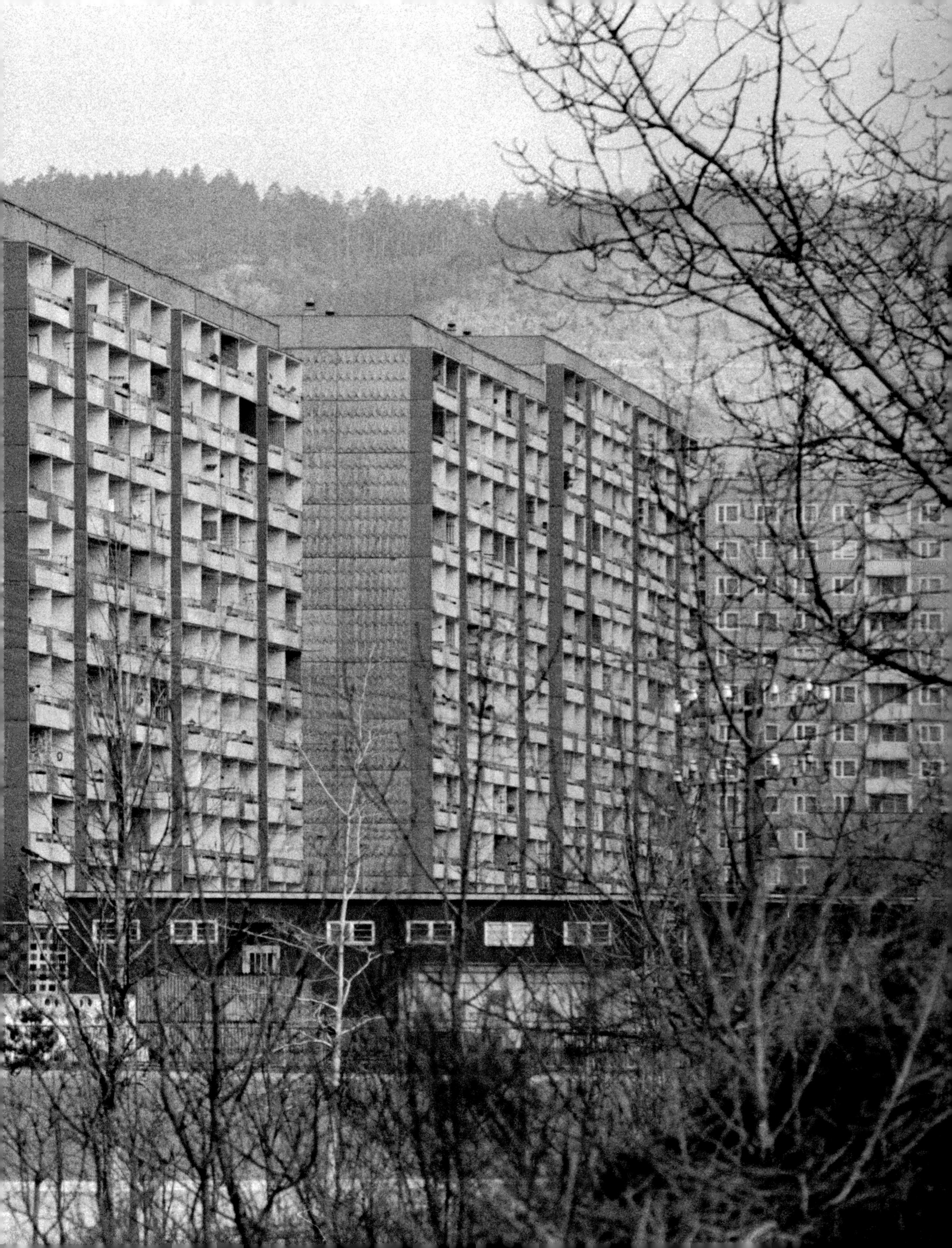

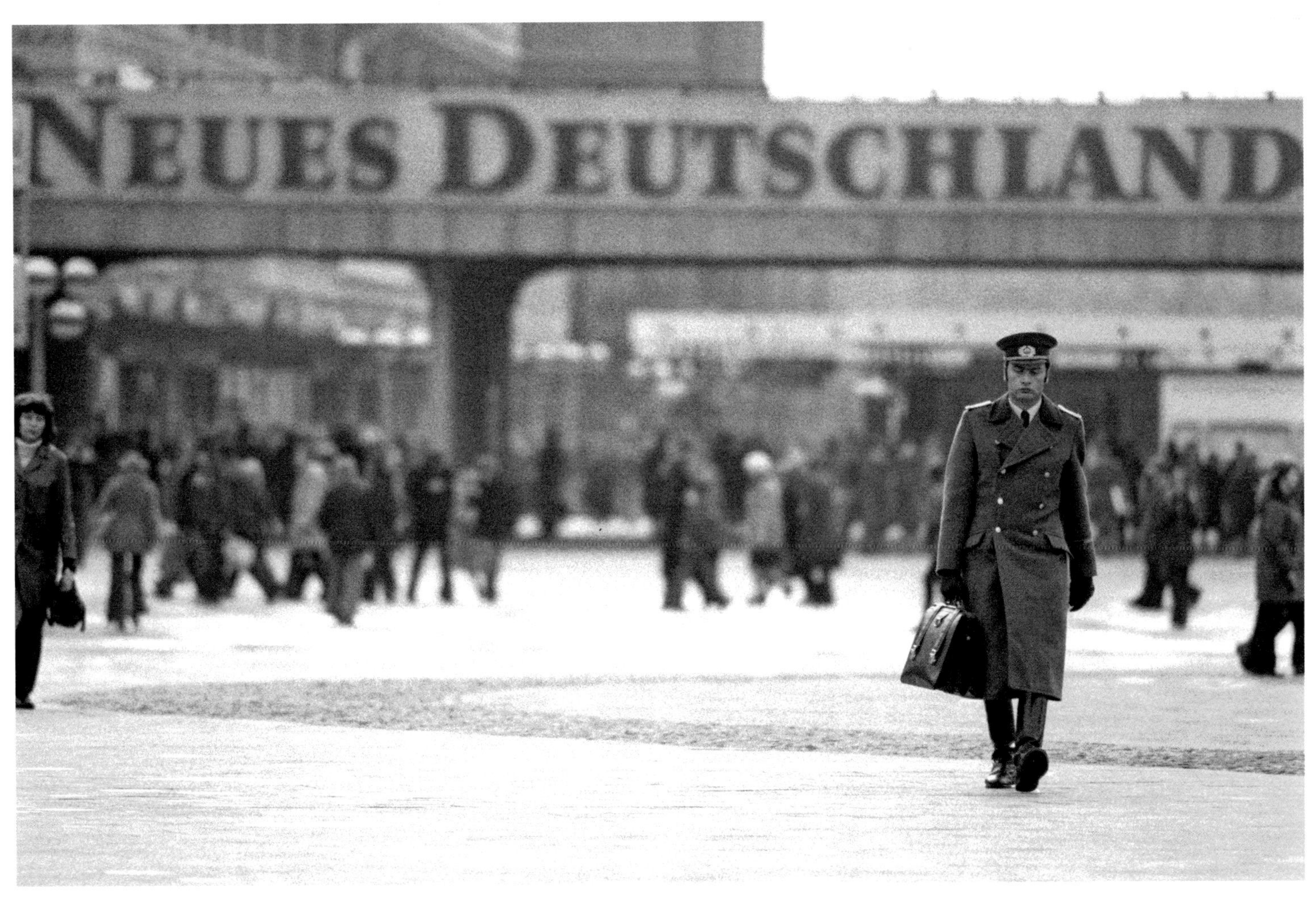
NEUES DEUTSCHLAND

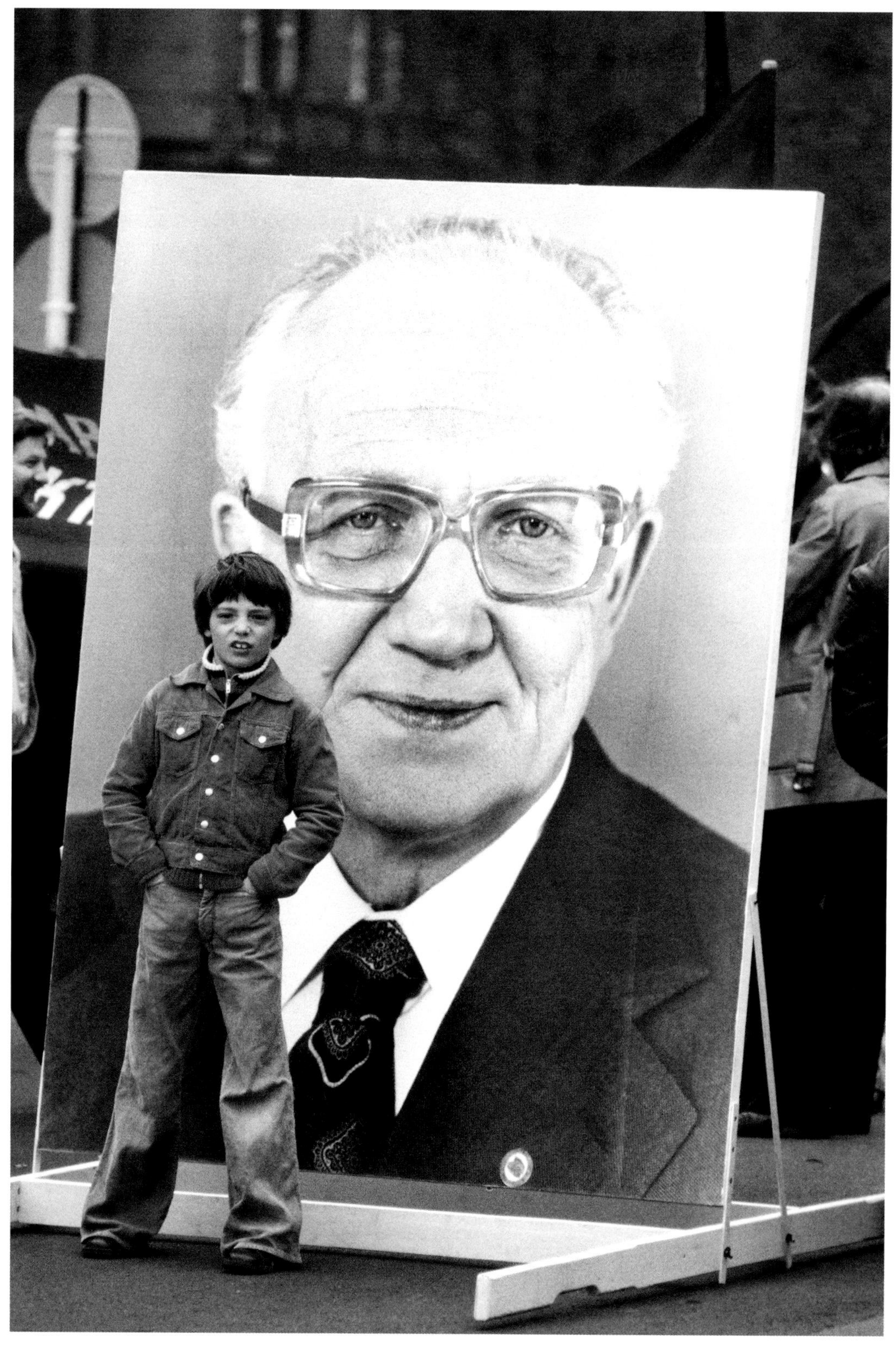

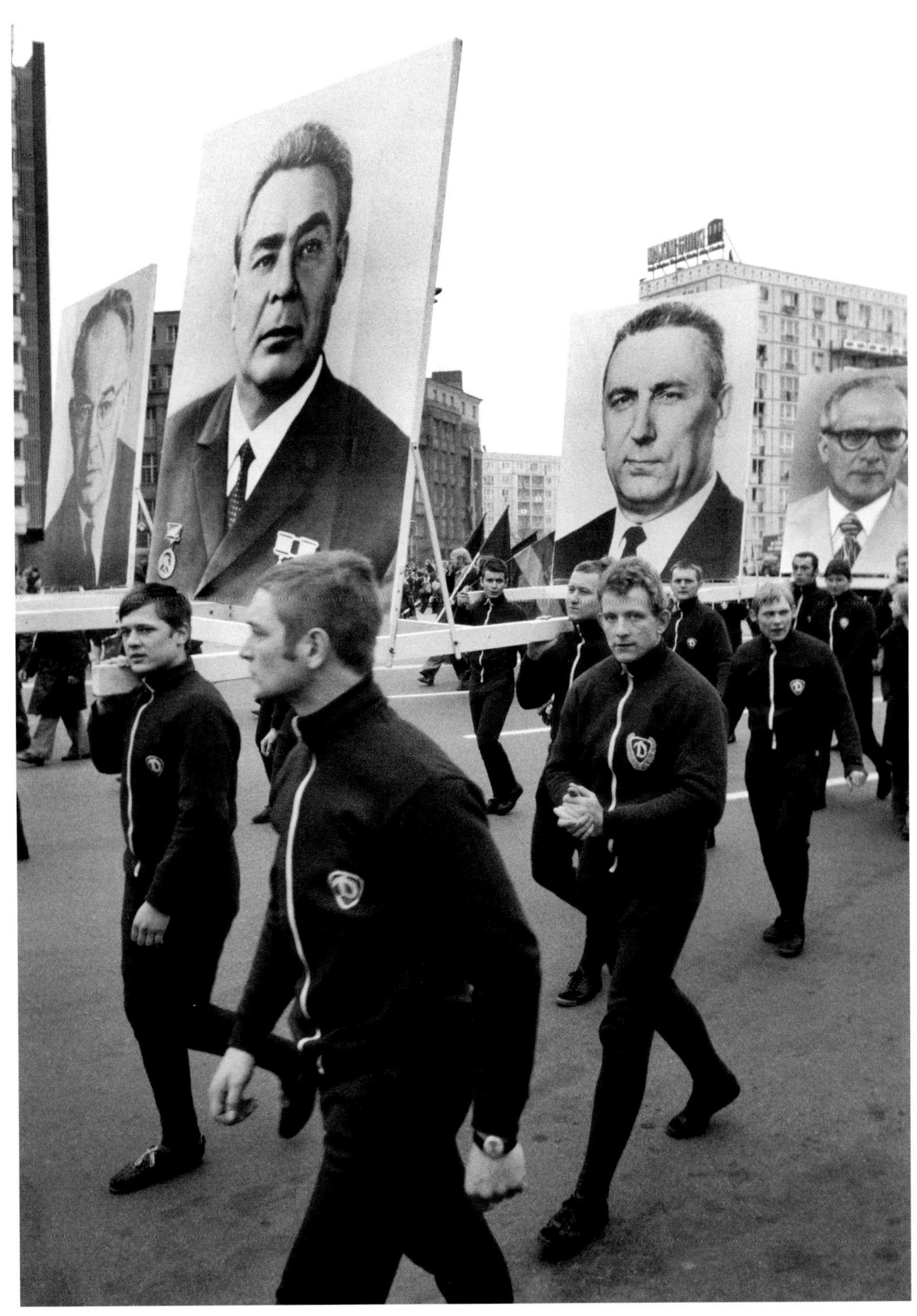

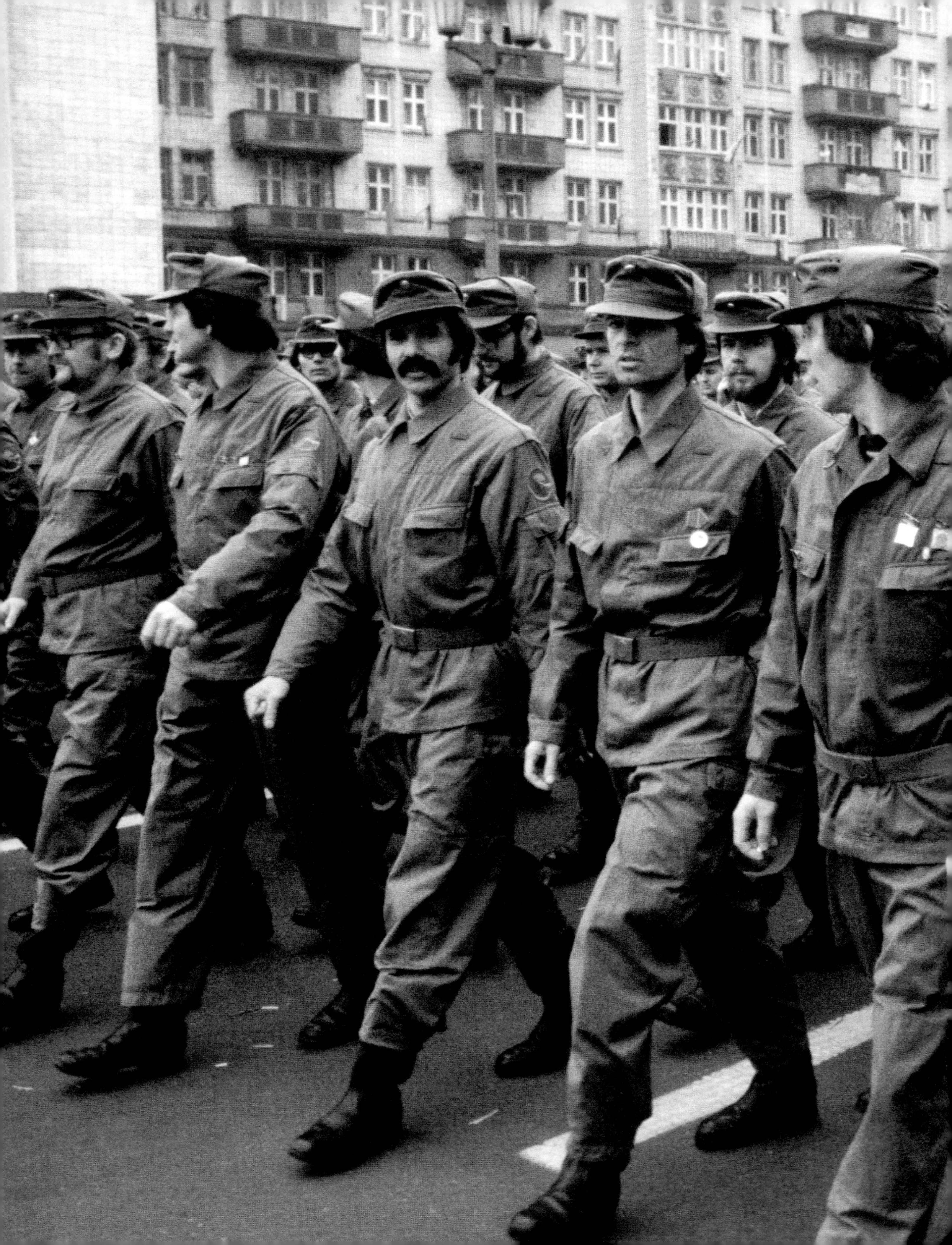

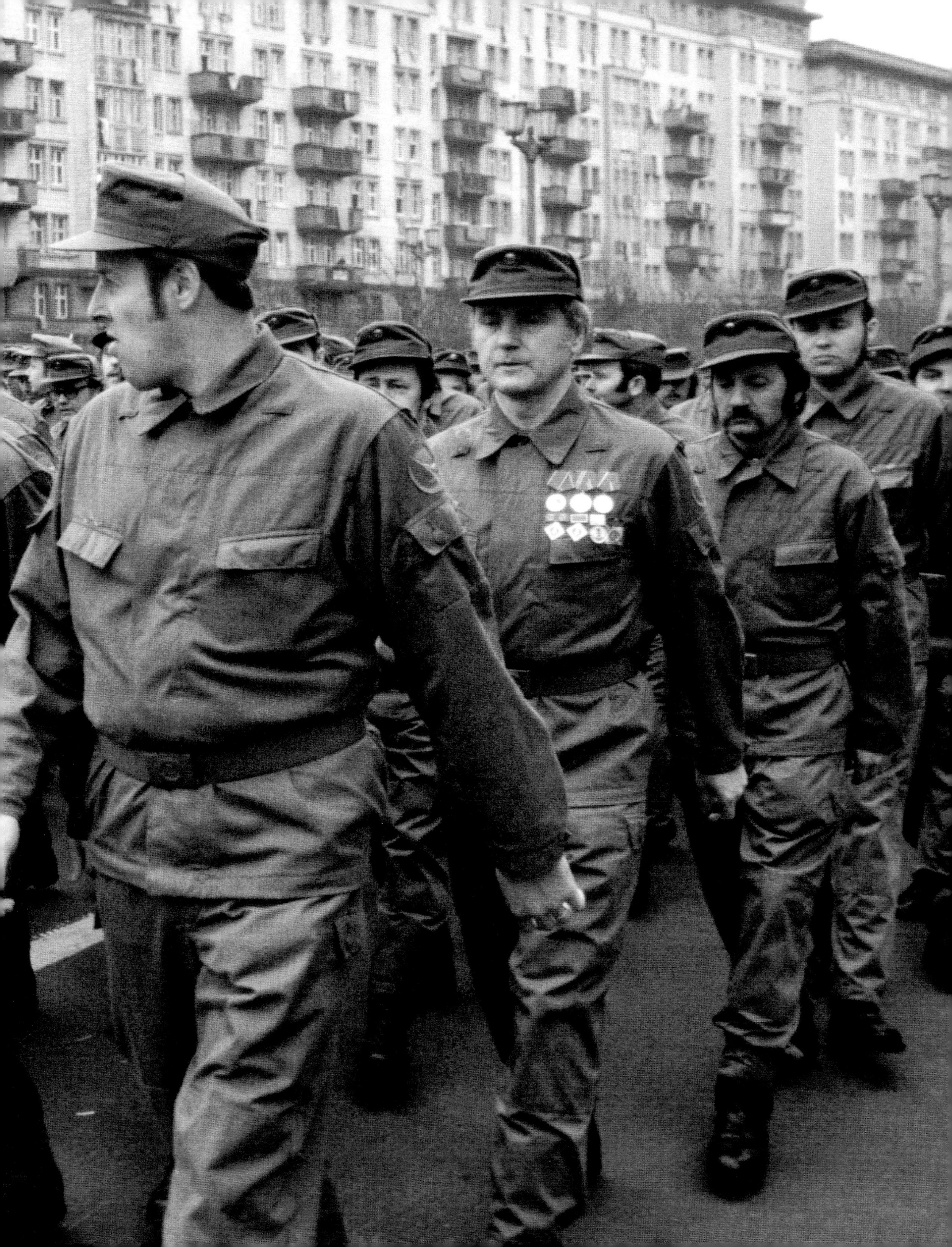

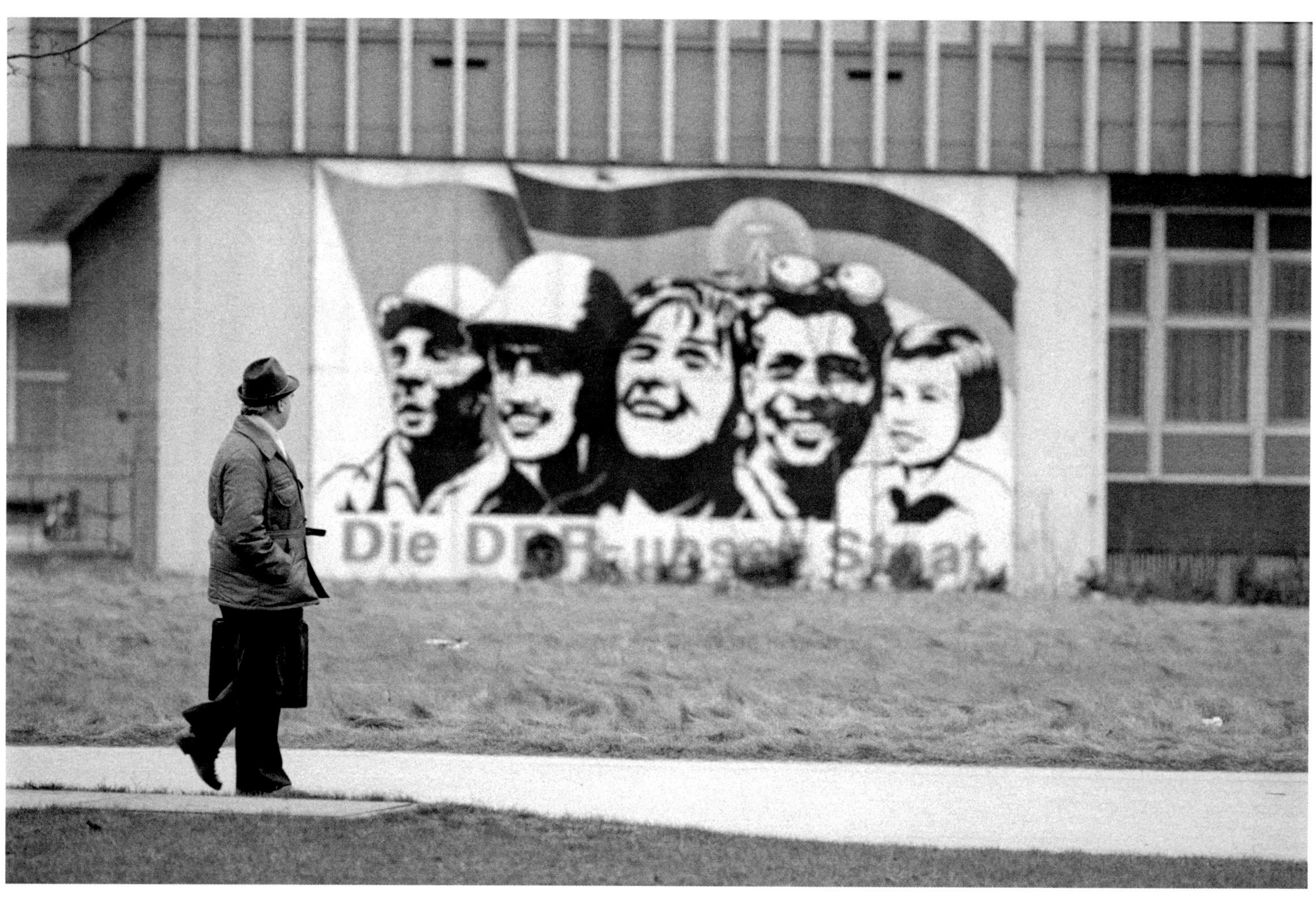
Die

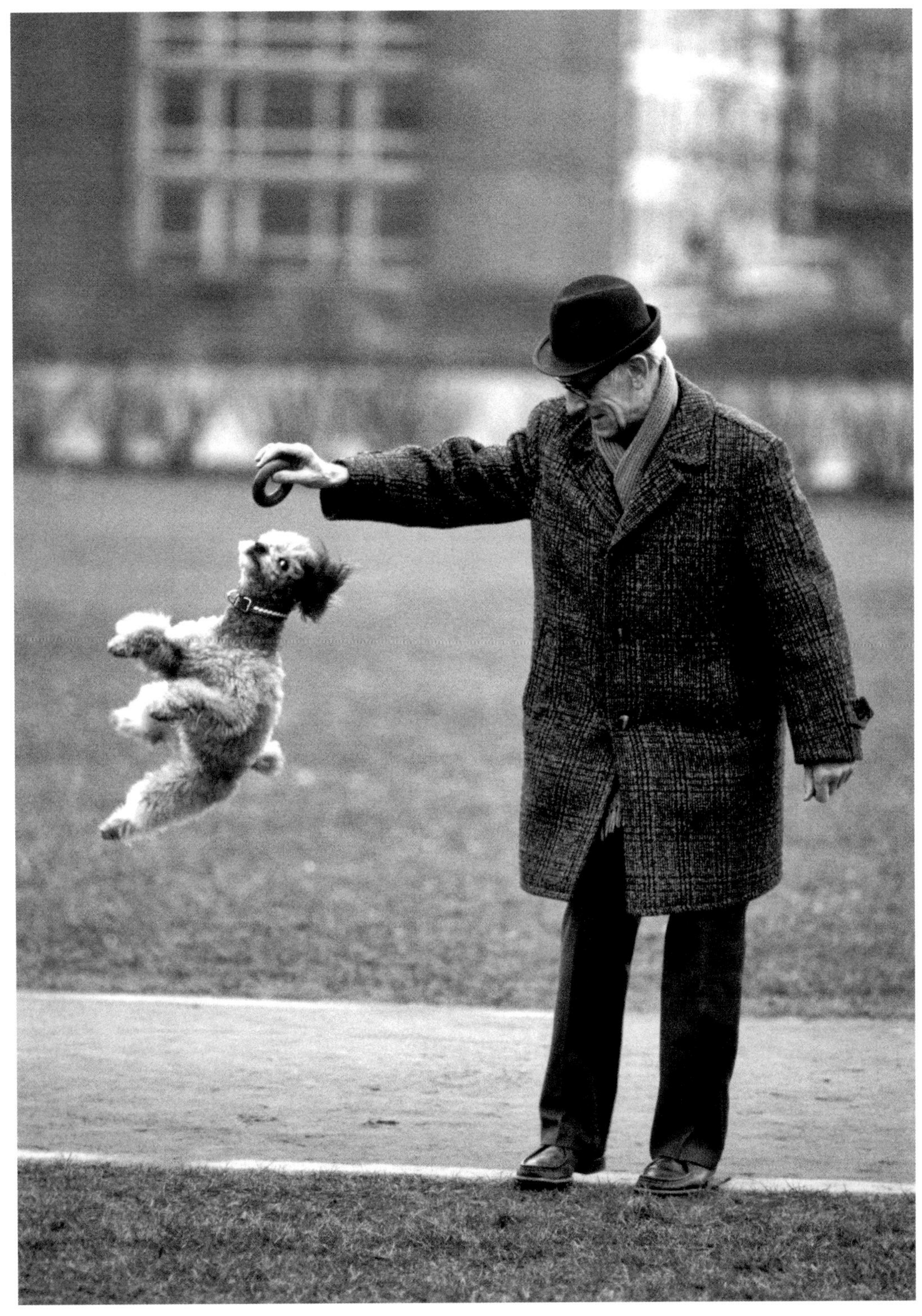

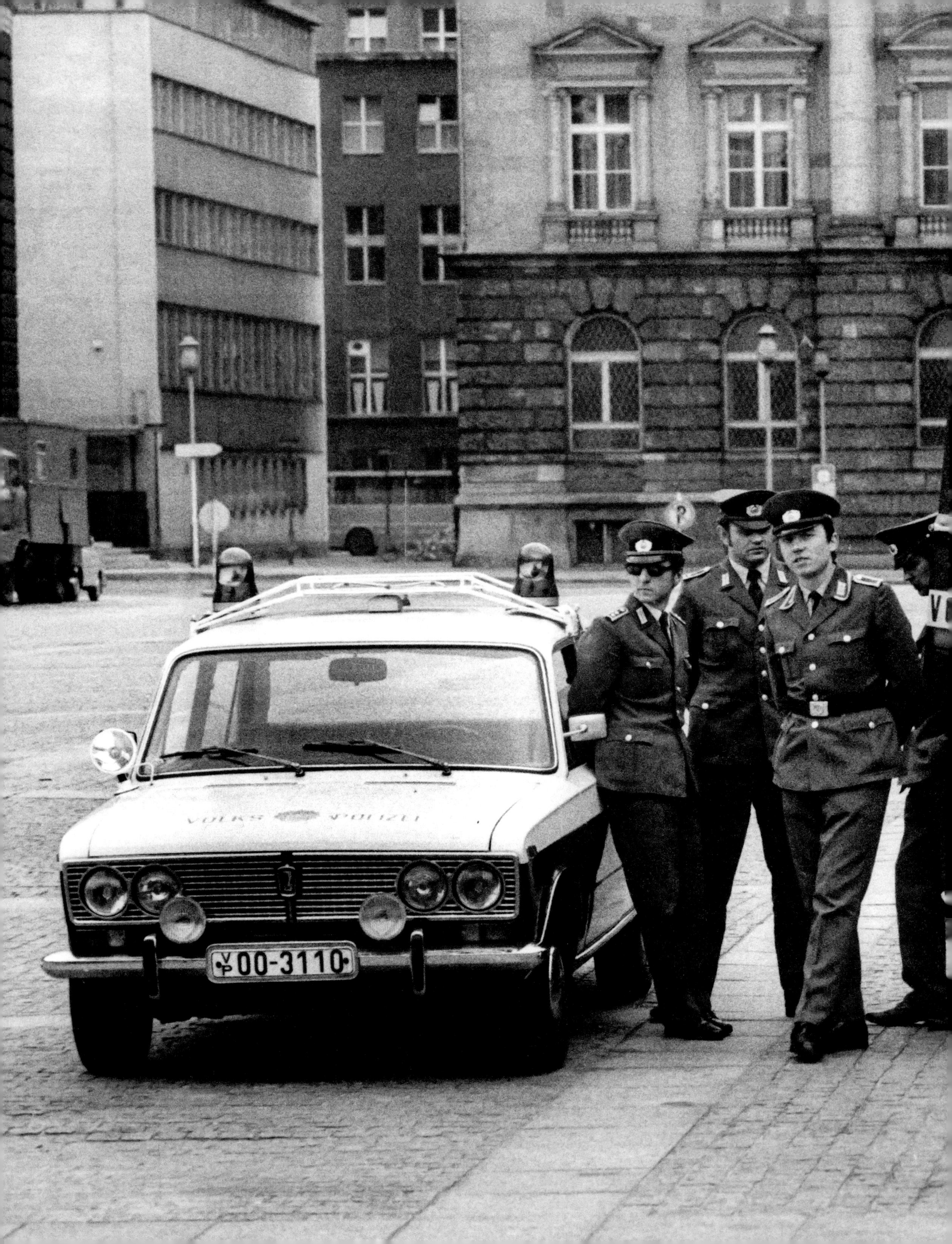
VOLKS POLIZEI
VP 00-3110

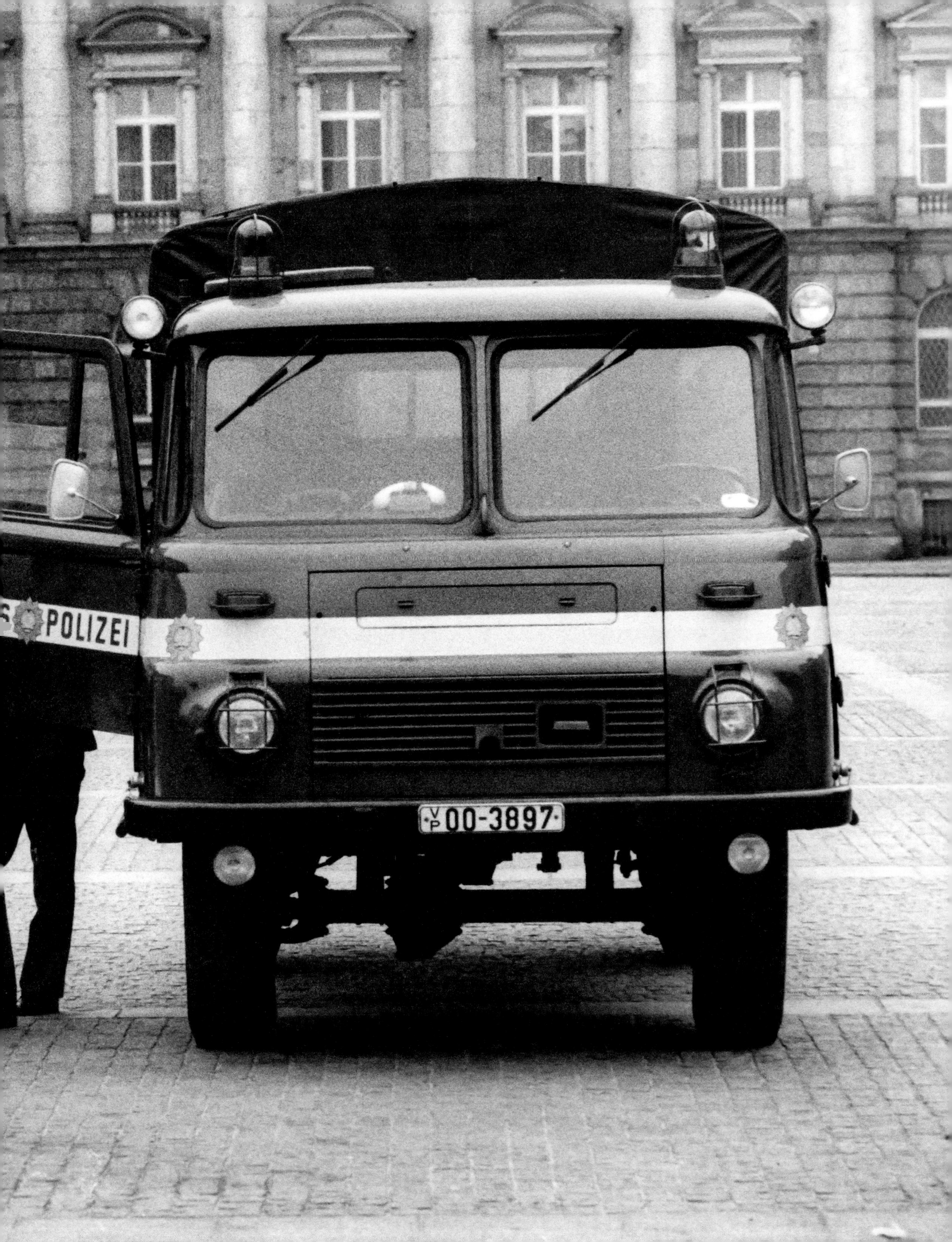
POLIZEI
VP 00-3897

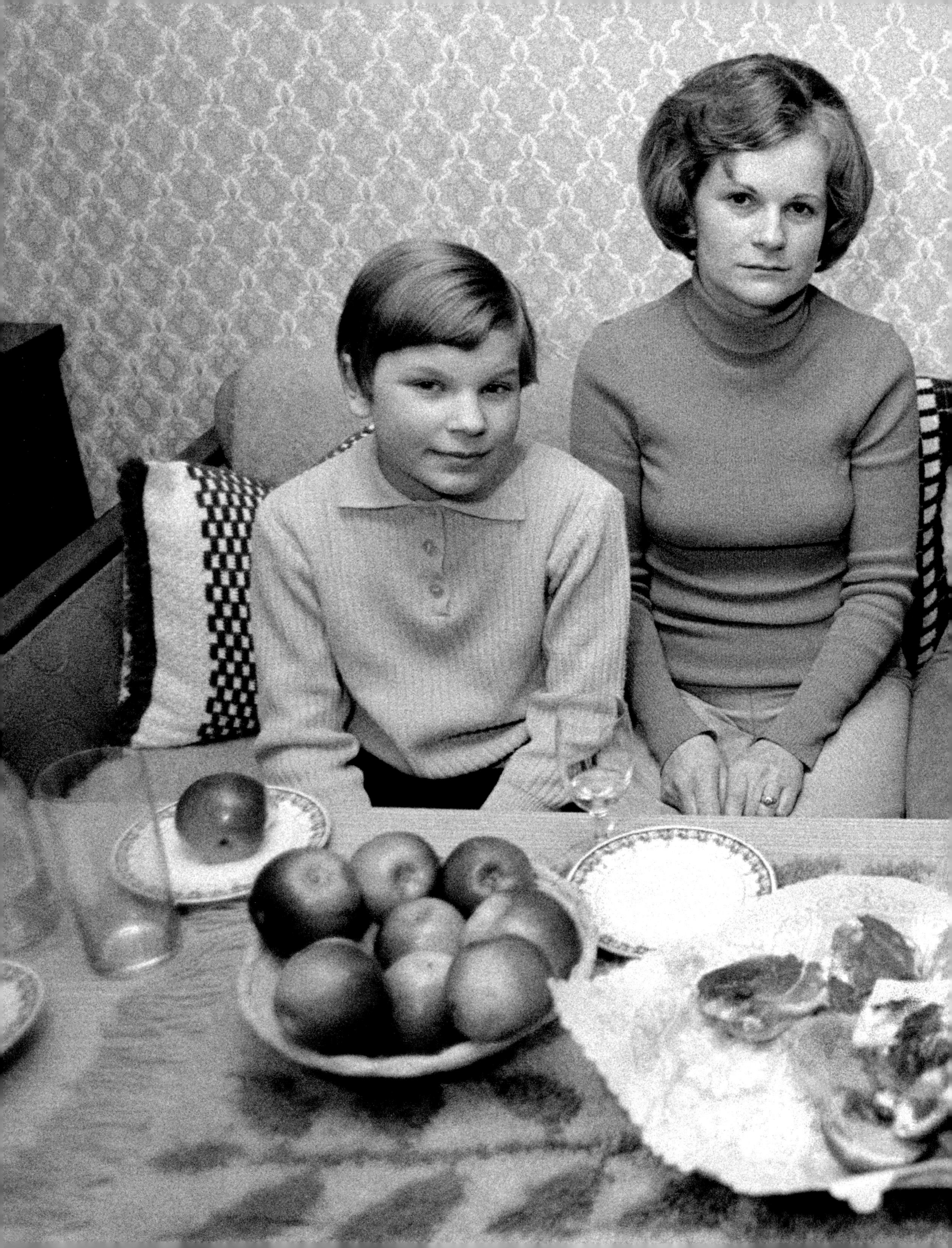

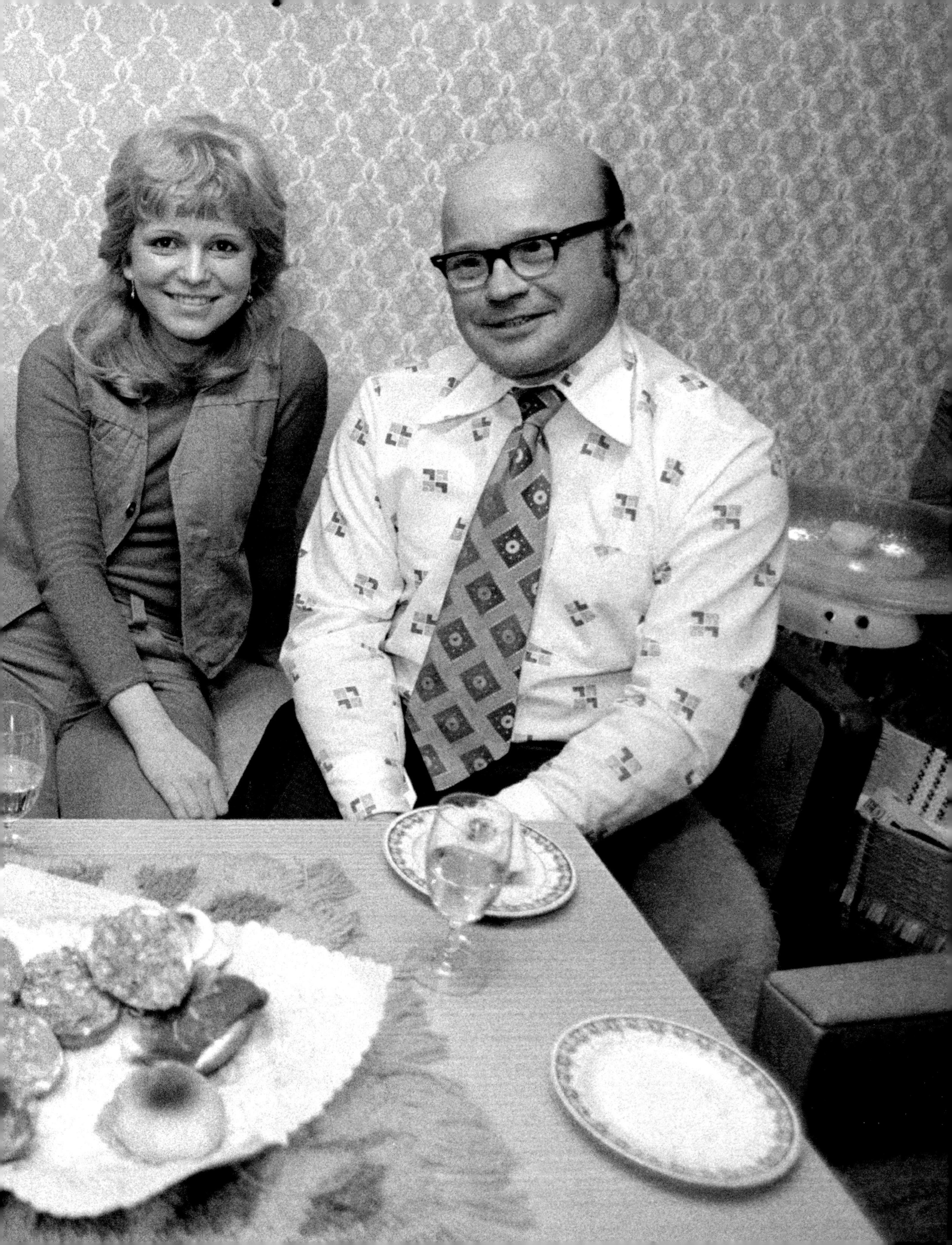

It is now more than three decades since the fall of the Berlin Wall and the collapse of one of the most dehumanizing forms of government the modern world has known. The Soviet method of governance, also known as Marxism-Leninism, promised its citizens a predictable if boring life in return for their acquiescence if not support. The threat of imprisonment, loss of work and the accompanying benefits made it possible to enforce an atomization of society in which even good friends feared sharing their inner thoughts. The result was a highly regimented, monochromatic society that was easy to categorize, over-simplify, and, eventually, forget.

The reality of the Soviet Bloc was far more complex and difficult to penetrate. The official version was a cartoon-like propaganda of posters, films, songs, mass meetings, and military parades accompanied by heartwarming scenes of the proletariat devoting themselves to their work for the state and living lives of limited but relative comfort.

The officials in charge of handling the few prying journalists admitted from the West were very good at arranging visits to the Potemkin villages they had created and equally adept at thwarting any efforts to peer through the façade of the Workers' Paradise. This was particularly true for photojournalists – and even more so for videographers. But the best of the visual journalists applied their talent for observation and their patience to see through that outer layer of enforced conformity.

The passage of time has clouded our collective memories of that place and that era. If people think of the Soviet Bloc at all these days, they think of the political repression, economic deprivation, and the uprisings with their inevitable crackdowns. But those images do an injustice to the people who lived through those times and leave us with a dangerous miscomprehension of history. Marxism-Leninism in both the Soviet Union and Eastern Europe was not simply forced down the throats of an unwilling public. Particularly in the aftermath of World War II, the political Left was viewed as both a necessary antidote to fascism and as an efficient way to mobilize society for the massive efforts that would be required to rebuild their shattered countries.

There was little illusion that these regimes were democratically elected, but most wrapped themselves in a concocted national identity and did their best to deliver economic benefits and a much-desired social stability. The leaders offered the public an implicit social contract: We will provide jobs, food, housing, education, medical care and a modicum of entertainment. You will stay silent.

Although there were violent uprisings through the first thirty years – East Germany in 1953, Hungary in 1956, Czechoslovakia in 1968, Poland in 1970 – for most citizens for most of the time that compact was grudgingly accepted. Life wasn't great, but it could be almost comfortable and, as long as you were apolitical, stress free. The proof of this is that there are to this day people in the former Soviet Bloc who long for the good old bad days when everyone had a job and a home and free medical care.

The political dissidents who opposed this system were remarkably brave and talented. They played an essential role in keeping the embers of independent life, belief, and thought alive. But they were almost all outliers – intellectuals, clerics, poorly-educated firebrands – who made little connection with the general public. That all changed in 1980 when an unknown, uneducated electrician clambered over the iron gates of the Lenin Shipyard in Gdansk to rally the workers there who were demanding the formation of a union independent of official oversight.

This was an impossible demand in any Marxist-Leninist society because ideologically only the communist party could serve the needs of the proletariat. Again, it is easy to simplify and glamorize this chapter in Soviet Bloc history, but the context in which Lech Wałęsa rose to lead Poland's workers is complex. Those intellectual and clerical dissidents, who had been so isolated from the public for so long throughout Eastern Europe, had spent the previous decade working to understand the needs of ordinary people and to devise ways of educating workers in the ways of self-help.

Perhaps more importantly, Poland's Catholic Church had remained the most vibrant in the region, drawing on its history as an icon of national identity. The election in October 1978 of Karol Wojtyla to become Pope John Paul II turned the Church into the most powerful unifying force in the country. His official visit to Poland in June 1979 drew millions of people and instantly destroyed thirty years of regime efforts to atomize the population into scared, wary individuals. That sense of unity gave the people of Poland palpable hope for the first time in decades. That hope was realized when Wałęsa and the workers of the Lenin Shipyard succeeded in extracting from the regime the right to form the first free and independent trade union in any communist country. Solidarity – Solidarność in Polish – spread rapidly in the fall of 1980, organizing chapters across the country and becoming a parallel center of power. Unfortunately, along with the exhilaration of that moment came what turned out to be insurmountable challenges.

Poland faced daunting economic problems that the regime could not solve on its own and which Solidarity was unable to help the government address. The Soviet economic model largely adopted in Poland had ignored and papered over market forces for thirty years. Everything was in short supply – the windows of food stores were filled with pyramids of empty tea boxes. But shoppers, waiting in long lines to buy practically anything, did not understand the link between prices and supply and demand. Why should they? Communist propaganda also denied that link. The only solution was to raise prices, but Solidarity's two key demands were stable prices and higher wages, a circle that was impossible to square.

In October 1981, the regime took the unprecedented step in the Soviet Bloc of putting an army general in charge of the country, and then the communist party itself. Poland's army had managed to maintain a high level of respect among the population, and its then-leader, Wojciech Jaruzelski was widely considered an improvement over the incompetents who had led Poland for the past decade. But within weeks it became clear the Jaruzelski had no magic wand. And Wałęsa's influence over the regional chapters of Solidarity was slipping by the day. In early December of 1981 the situation had become untenable. Factories across the country were on perpetual strike. Farmers were refusing to sell their produce for an increasingly worthless currency. Supply shortages were outstripping the government's ability to ration essential foodstuffs. Citizens were reduced to selling their belongings at impromptu flea markets that popped up all over the country.

On the night of December 13th, 1981, Jaruzelski imposed Martial Law. All domestic and international telephone and telegraph lines were cut. Wałęsa and thousands of other Solidarity officials and allies were arrested. A strict 9:00 PM to 6:00 AM curfew was imposed, and military units set up checkpoints at major intersections across the country. The military took over supervision of significant economic institutions, and the junta imposed a six-day workweek and price increases that resulted in a twenty percent drop in real wages.

And yet, Poles coped. Alcoholism initially surged, but most people found ways to survive and to keep their dignity. Journalists who refused to bow to the Army found other work. One of Poland's best-known TV hosts became a taxi driver. A remarkable underground press published not only diatribes against the regime, but also educational tracts on economics and politics. Because these were forbidden, the public soaked them up, and over time became one of Europe's best-informed citizenry.

The Church became a center of national resistance. Ordinary parishes turned religious events into political protests rich with symbolism. Priests like Father Jerzy Popiełuszko – later assassinated by the Secret Police – acted as intermediaries between the resistance and average citizens.

On the 13th of each month, demonstrations marking the imposition of Martial Law exploded across the country. The junta deployed tear gas, water cannons, and paramilitary police with long white truncheons (or 'blondes') to suppress the demonstrators in running skirmishes. And every day, Poles carried out small acts of defiance, like ostentatiously taking a stroll every night at the precise time when the government broadcast the official evening news program.

Over time, Poles began to understand that as the Czech dissident and eventual president Václav Havel had written, "Hope is not the conviction that something will turn out well but the certainty that something makes sense, regardless of how it turns out." That understanding not only enabled Poles to survive the deprivation and depression of the 1980s, it also prepared them to lead the rest of the Soviet Bloc out of communist repression in 1989.

Poland's transition from an impoverished police state to one of Europe's most vibrant economies and democracies is often cast as some miraculous intervention overseen by Pope John Paul II and/or Ronald Reagan. In fact, it was the result of hard work and great courage by both political leaders and ordinary Poles.

Tragically, their accomplishments are in danger of possibly fatal backsliding toward a twenty-first century version of soft authoritarianism. Part of the reason for the degradation of Poland's democracy lies in the amnesia many Poles have developed over the years about just how dehumanizing their country was before 1989. The only remedy for such willful forgetfulness is to confront the realities through film and images and verbal recollections.

Richard Hornik
Eastern Europe Bureau Chief
TIME Magazine
1981-1983

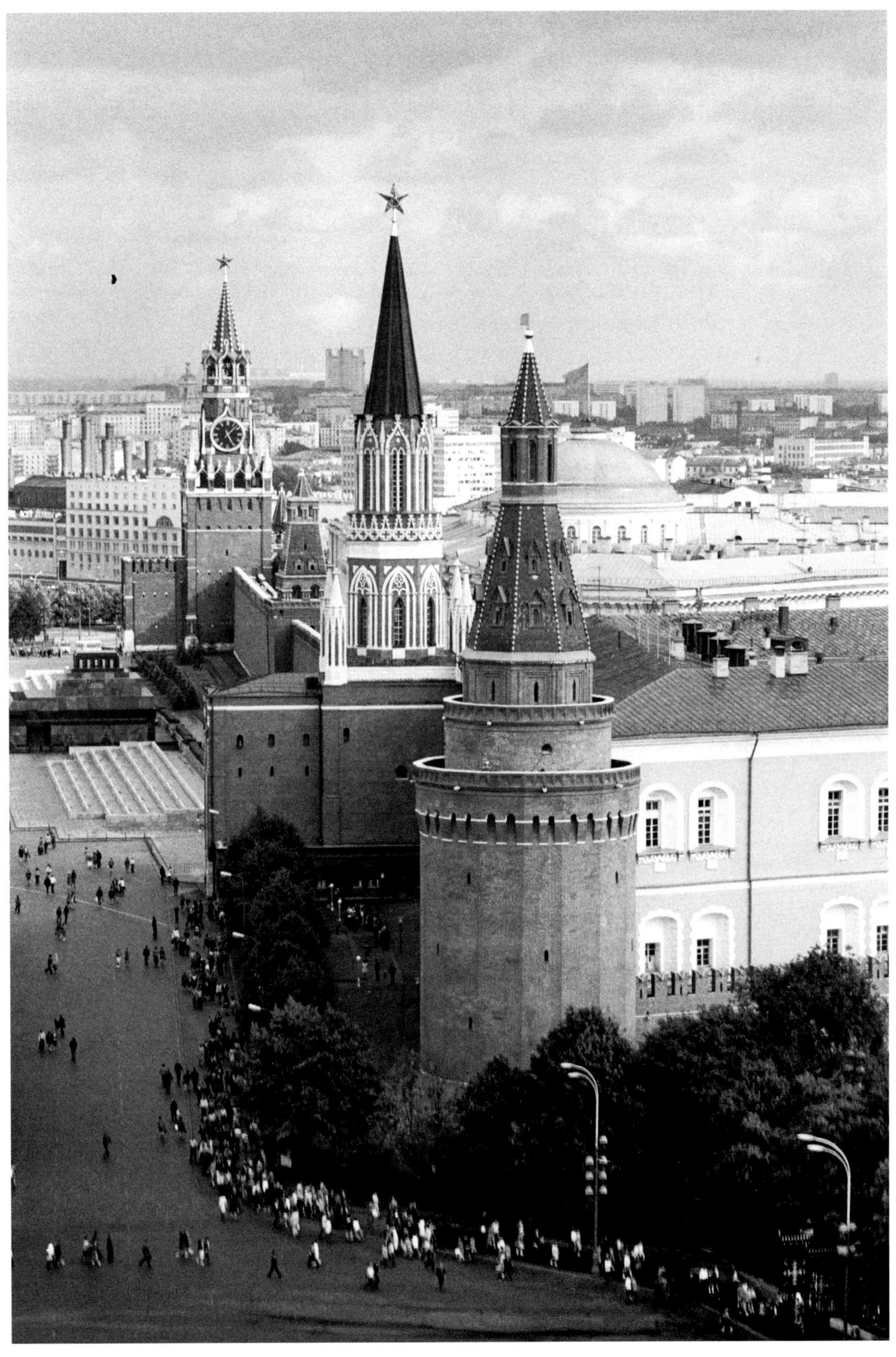

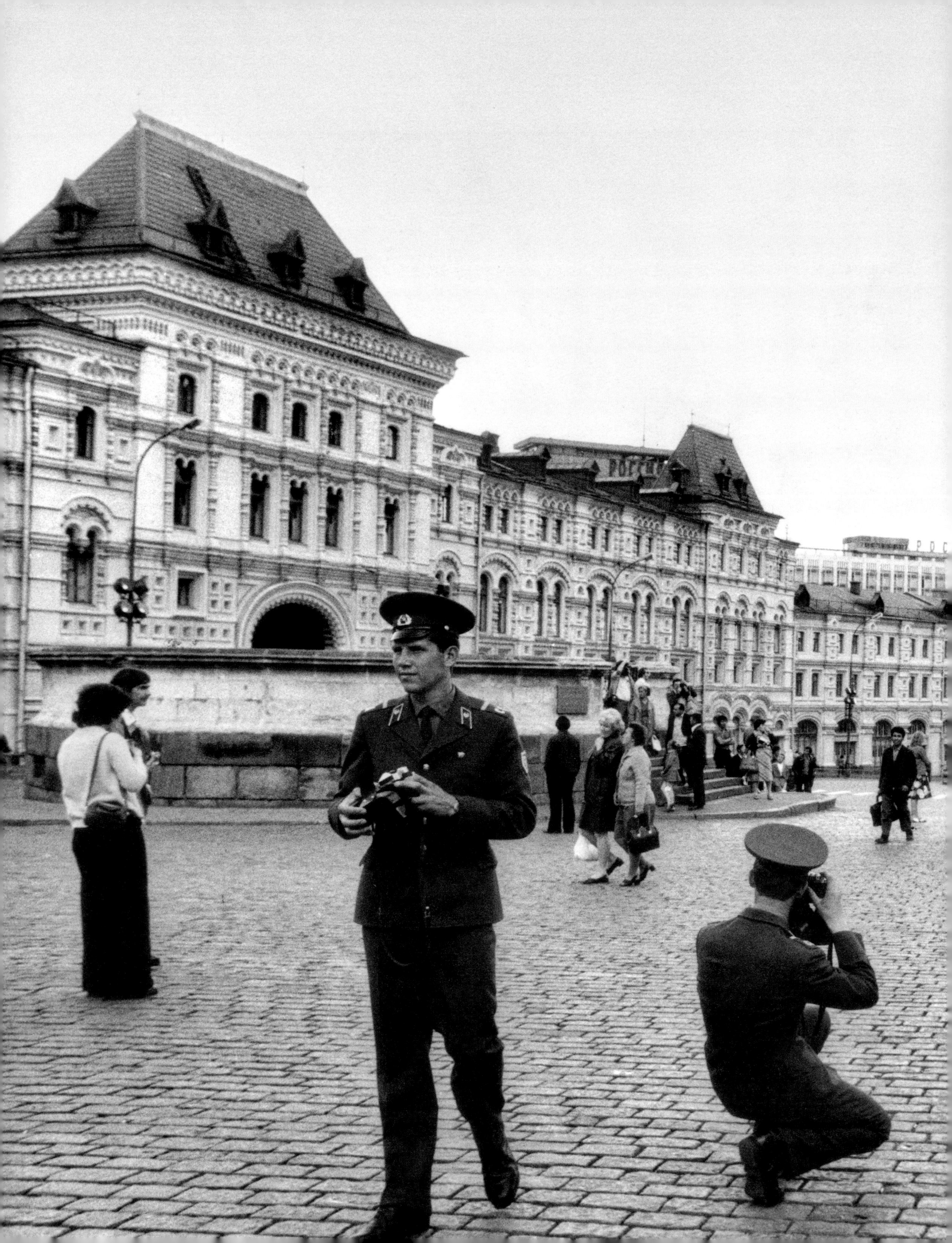

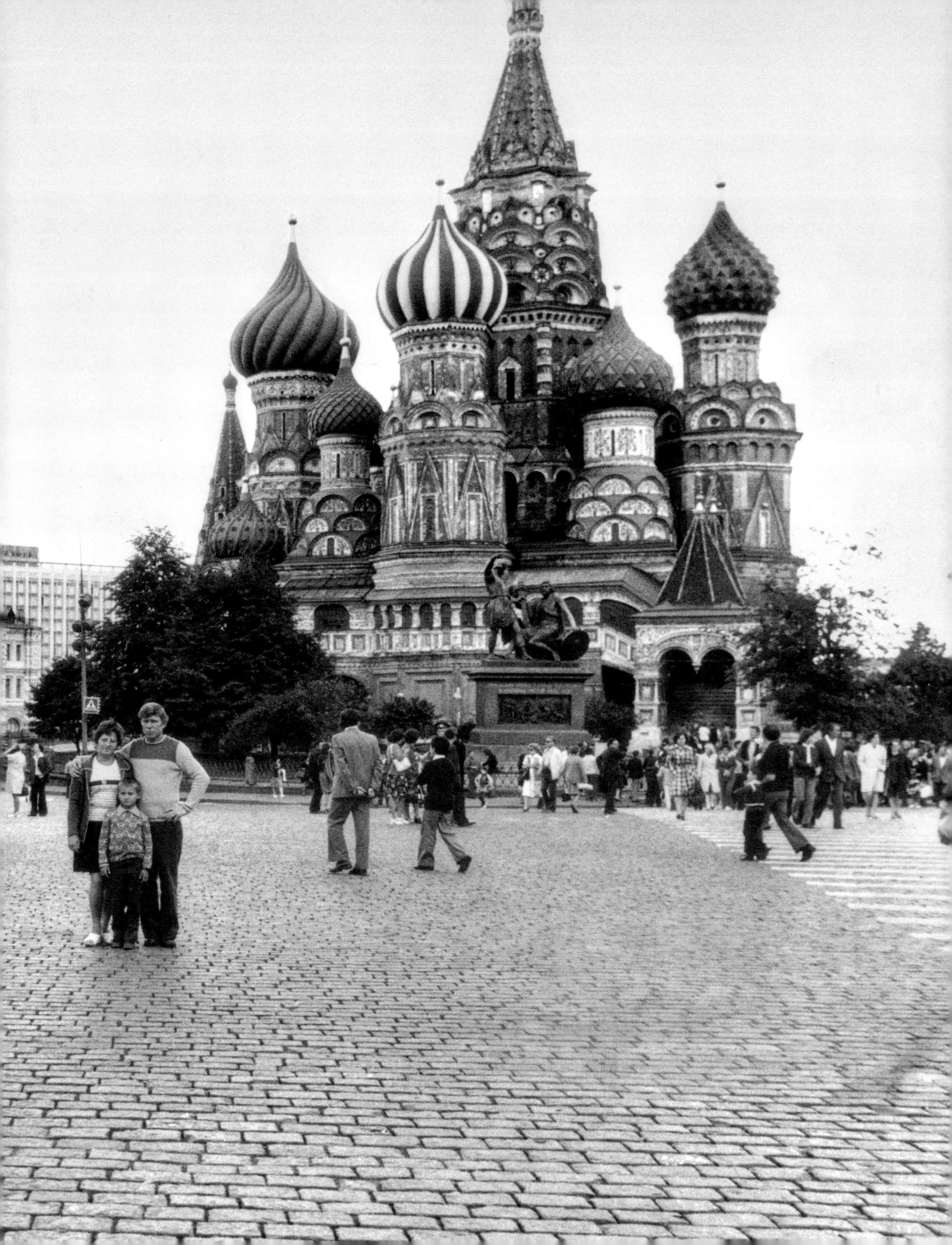

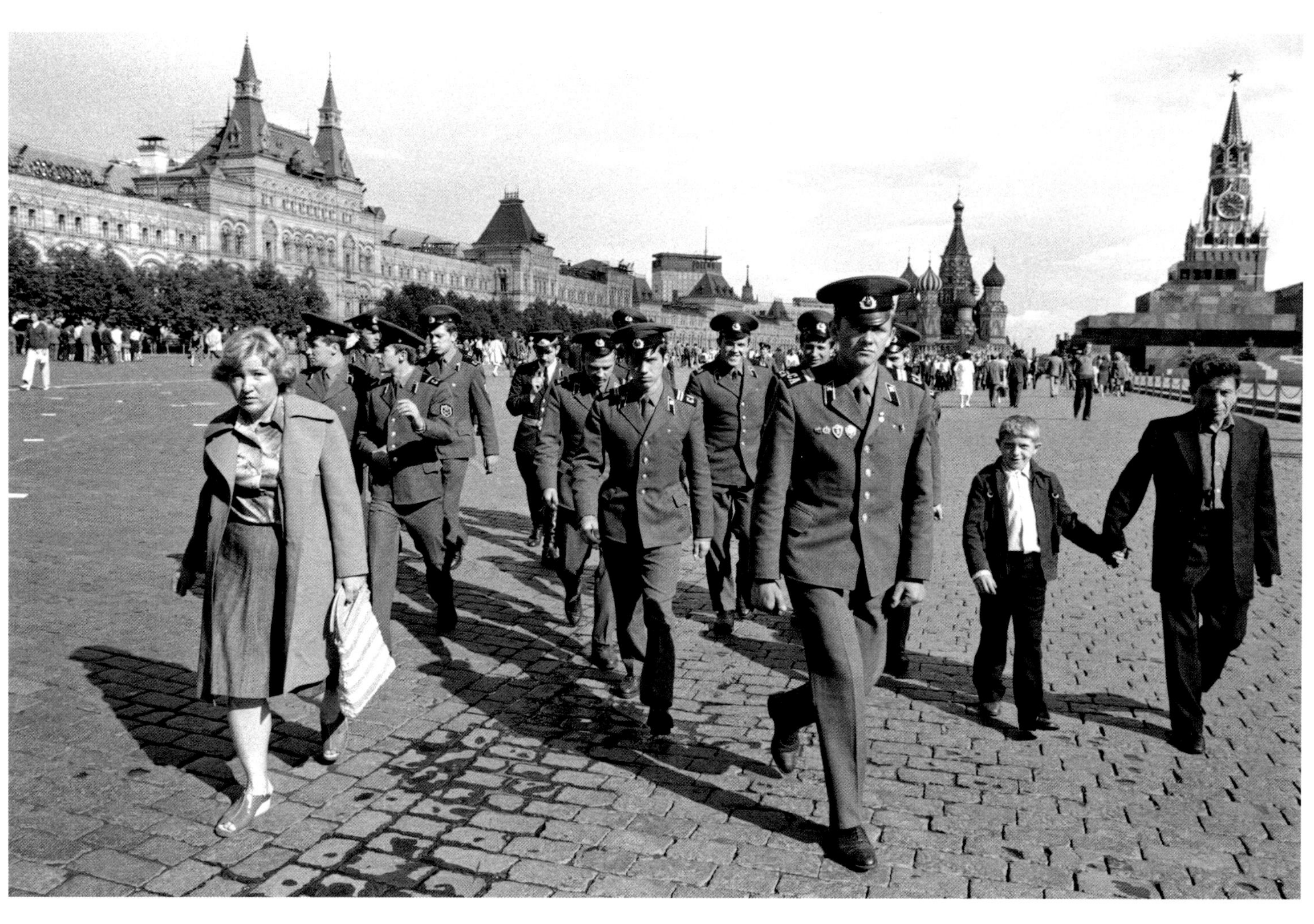

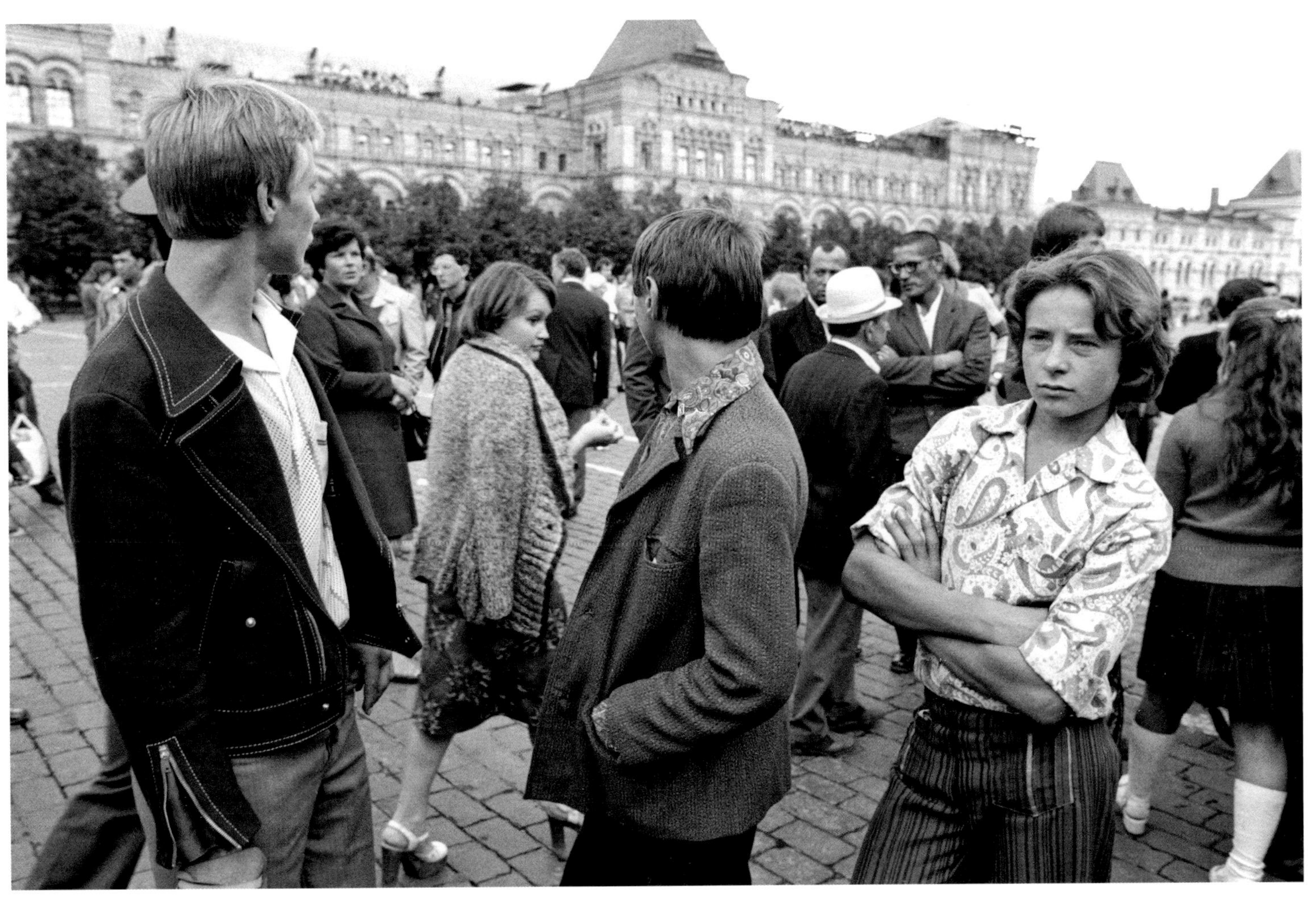

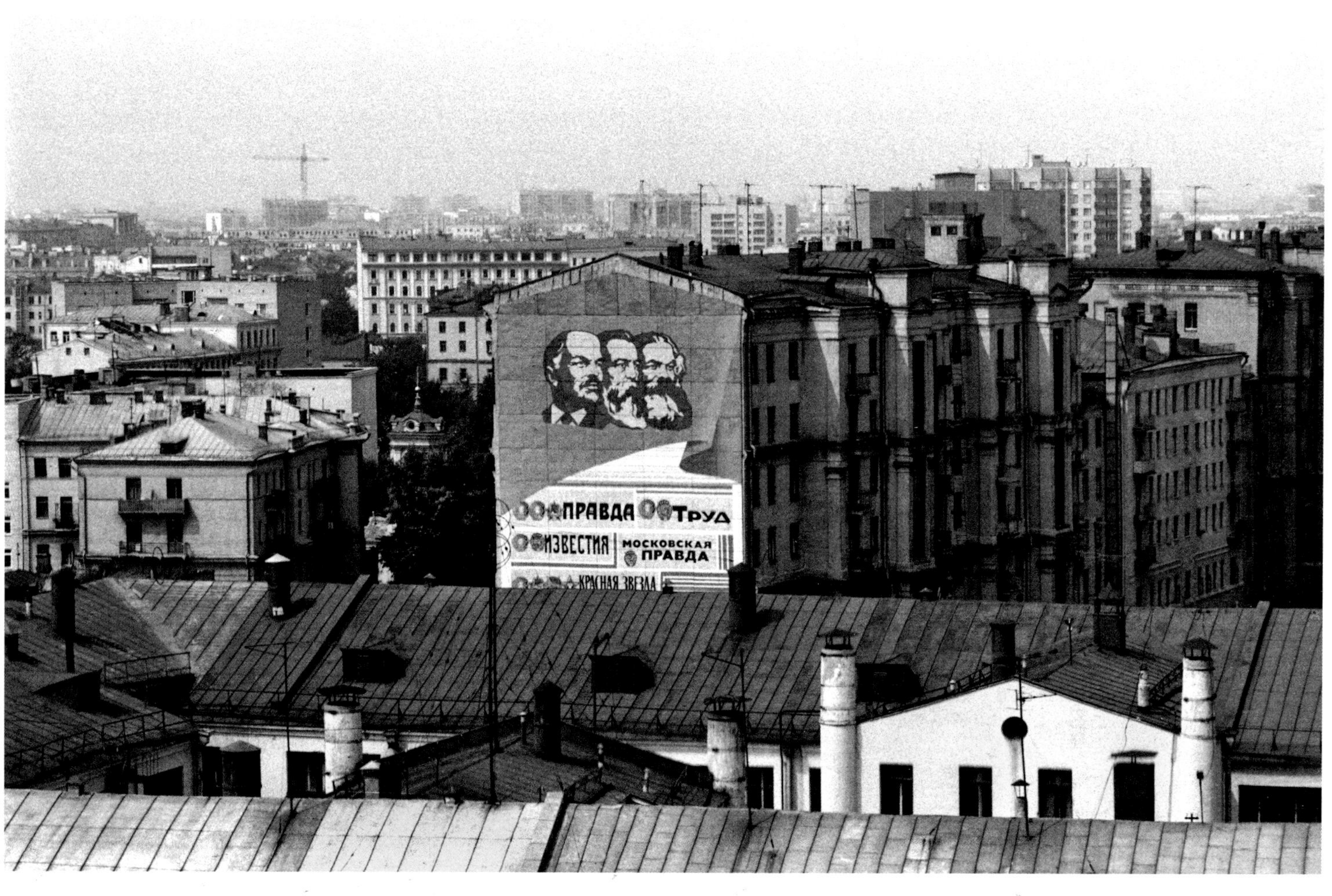
ПРАВДА
ТРУД
ИЗВЕСТИЯ
МОСКОВСКАЯ ПРАВДА
КРАСНАЯ ЗВЕЗДА

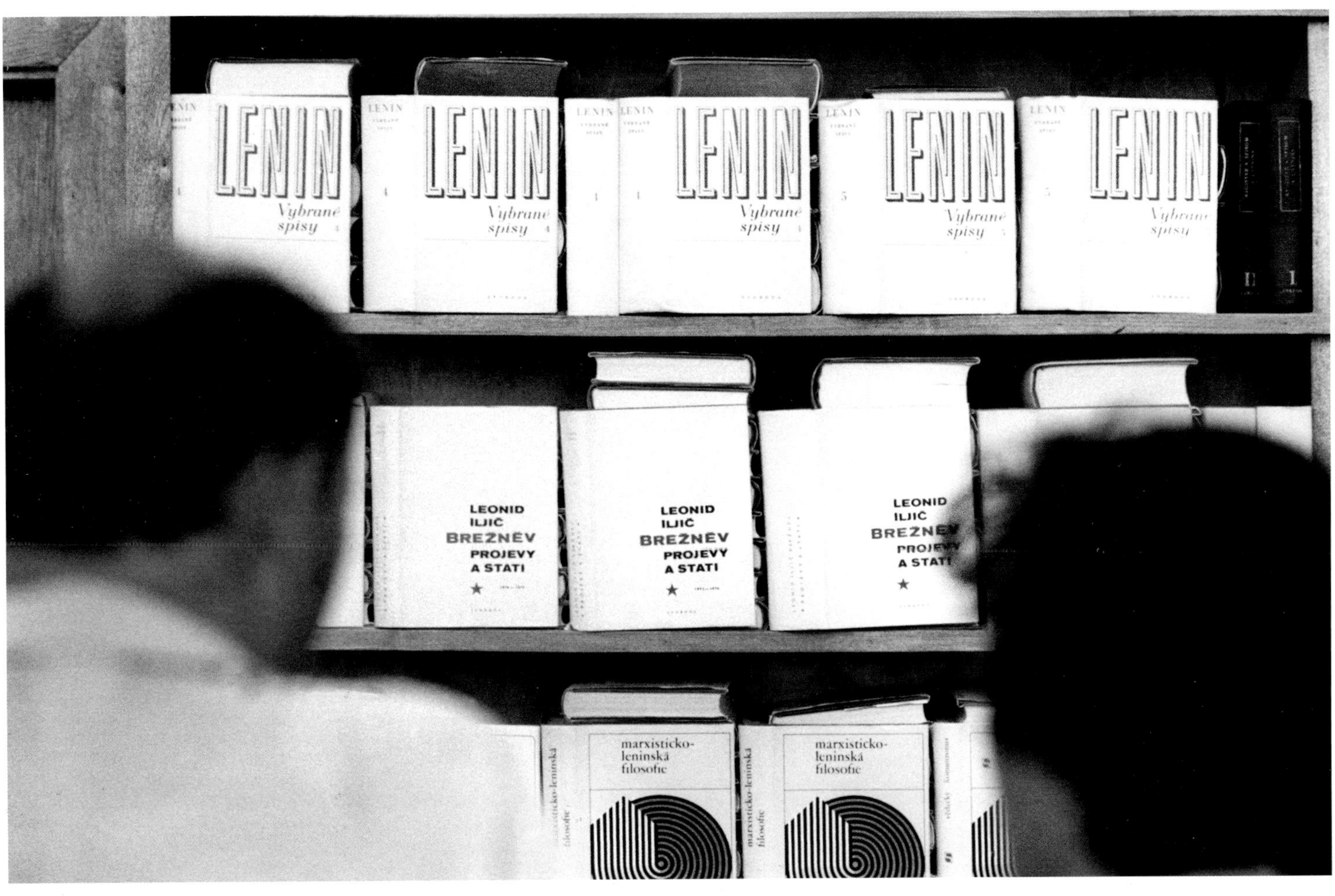
LENIN
Vybrané spisy
LEONID ILJIČ BREŽNĚV
PROJEVY A STATI
marxisticko-leninská filosofie

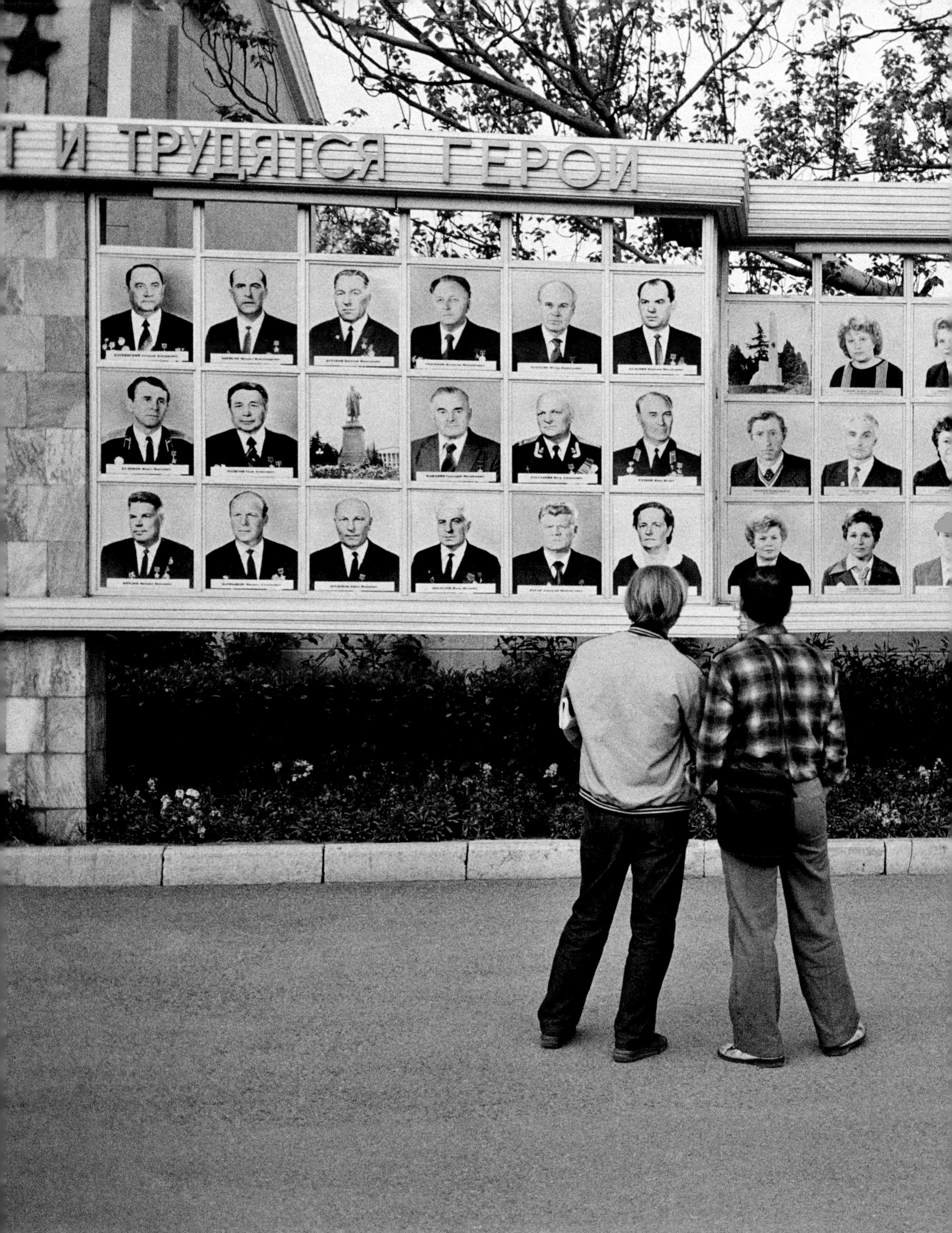
Т И ТРУДЯТСЯ ГЕРОИ

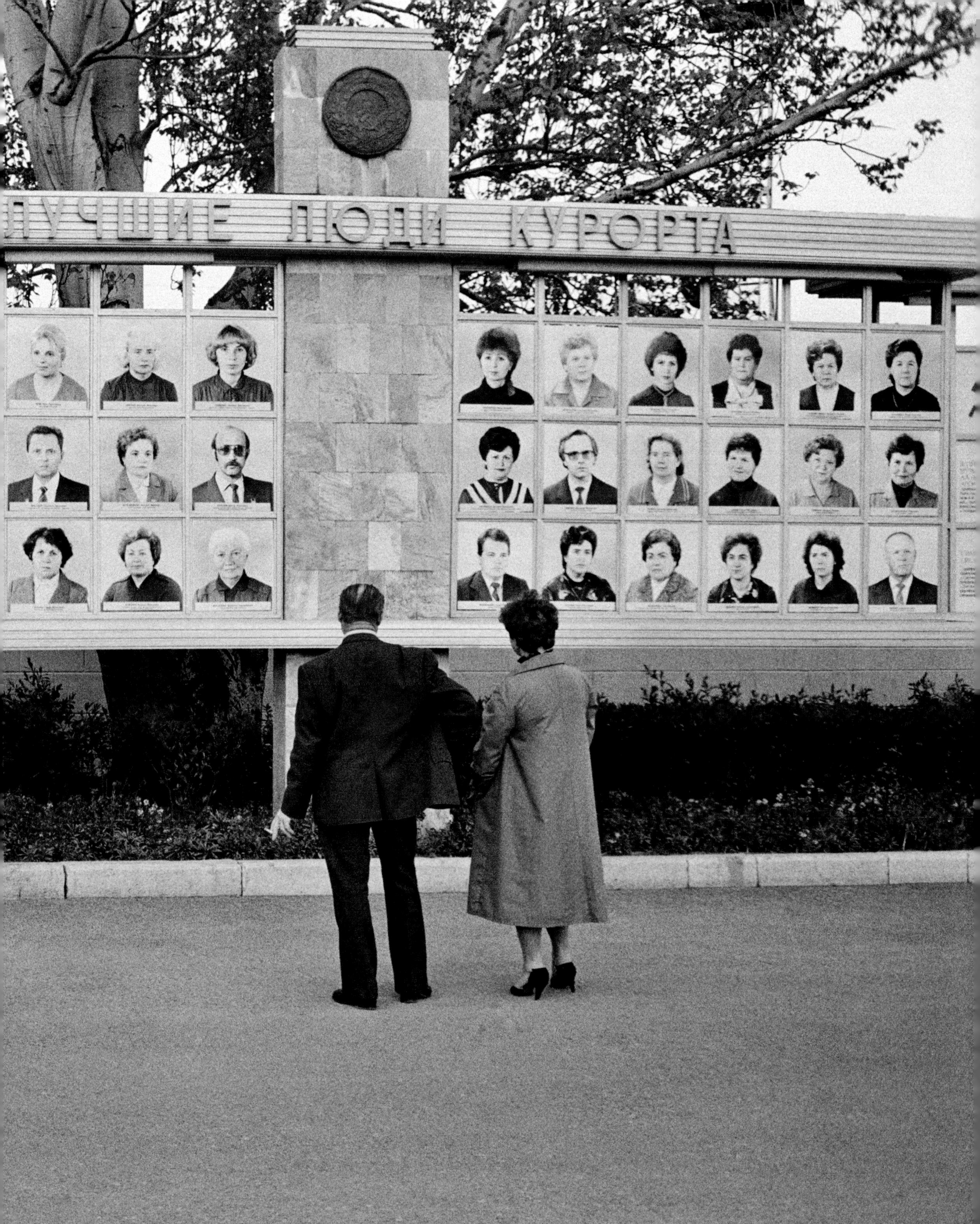
ЛУЧШИЕ ЛЮДИ КУРОРТА

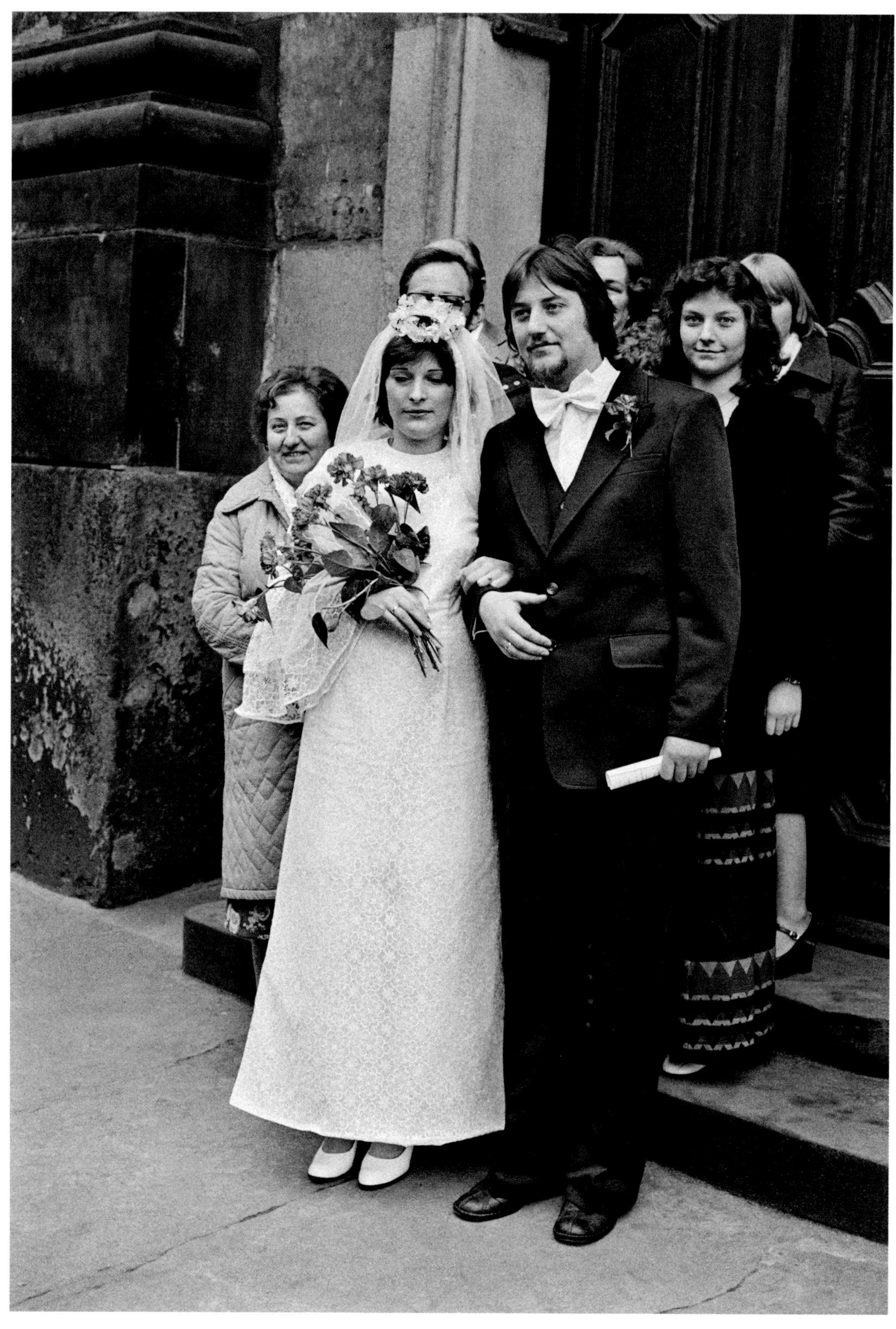

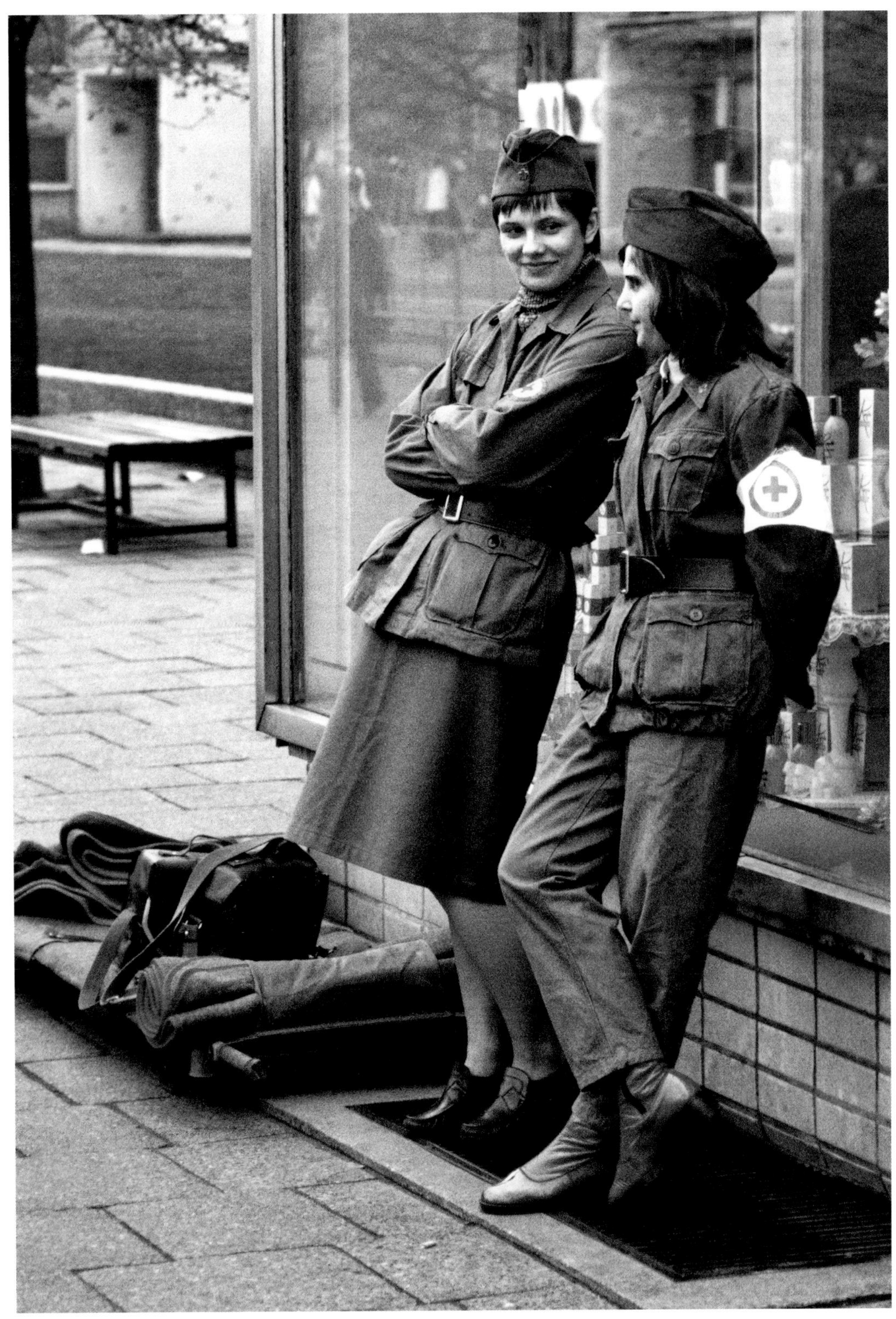

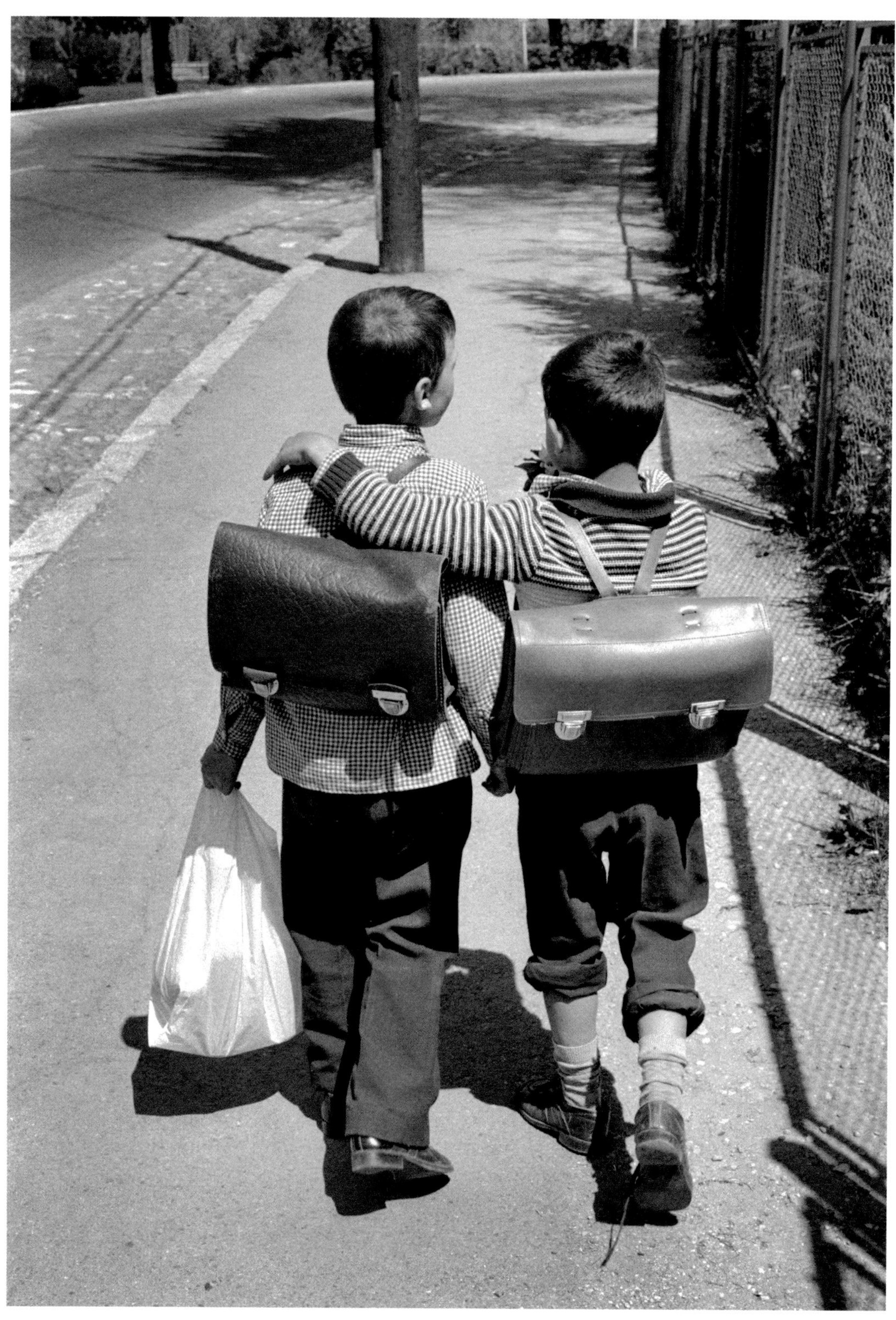

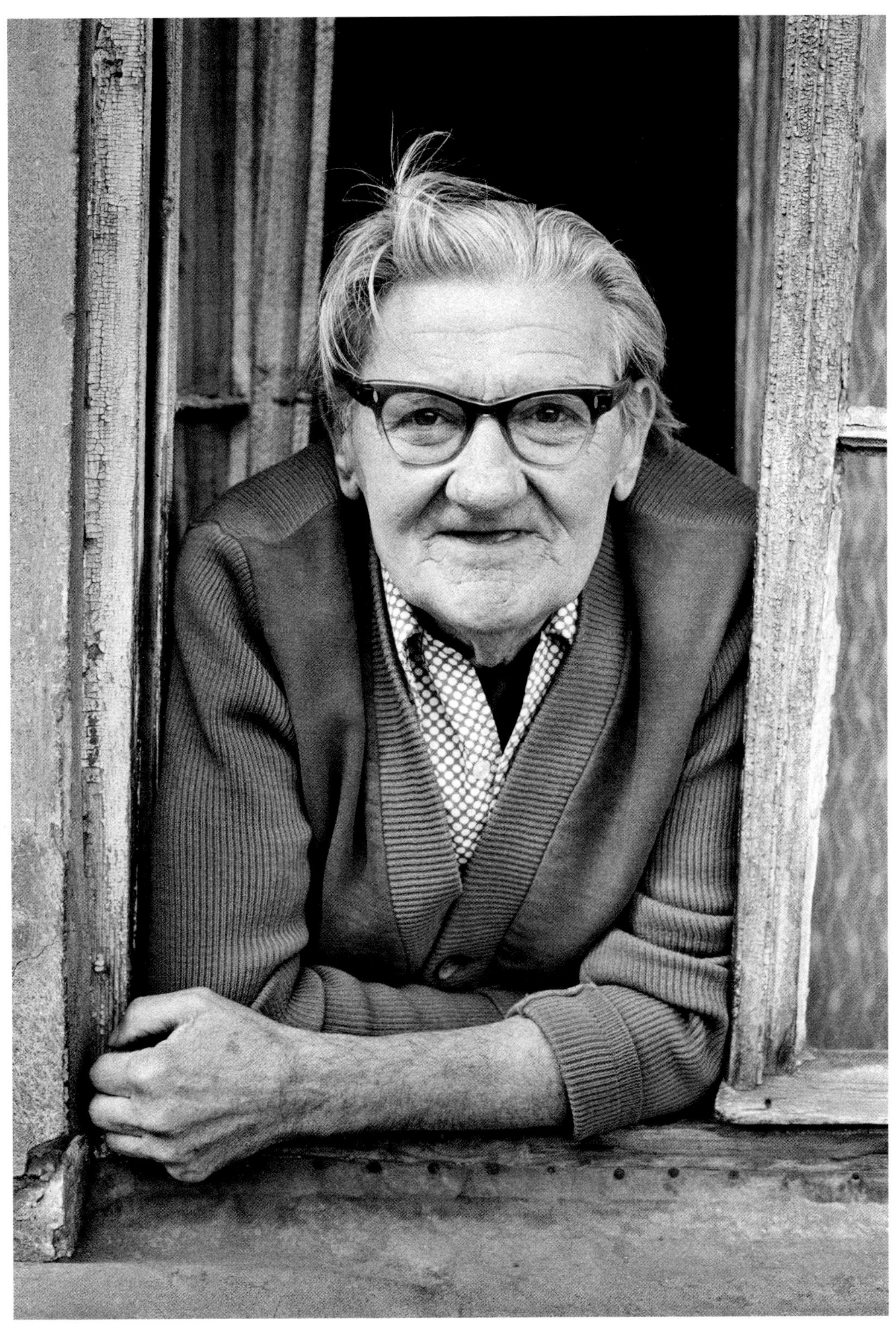

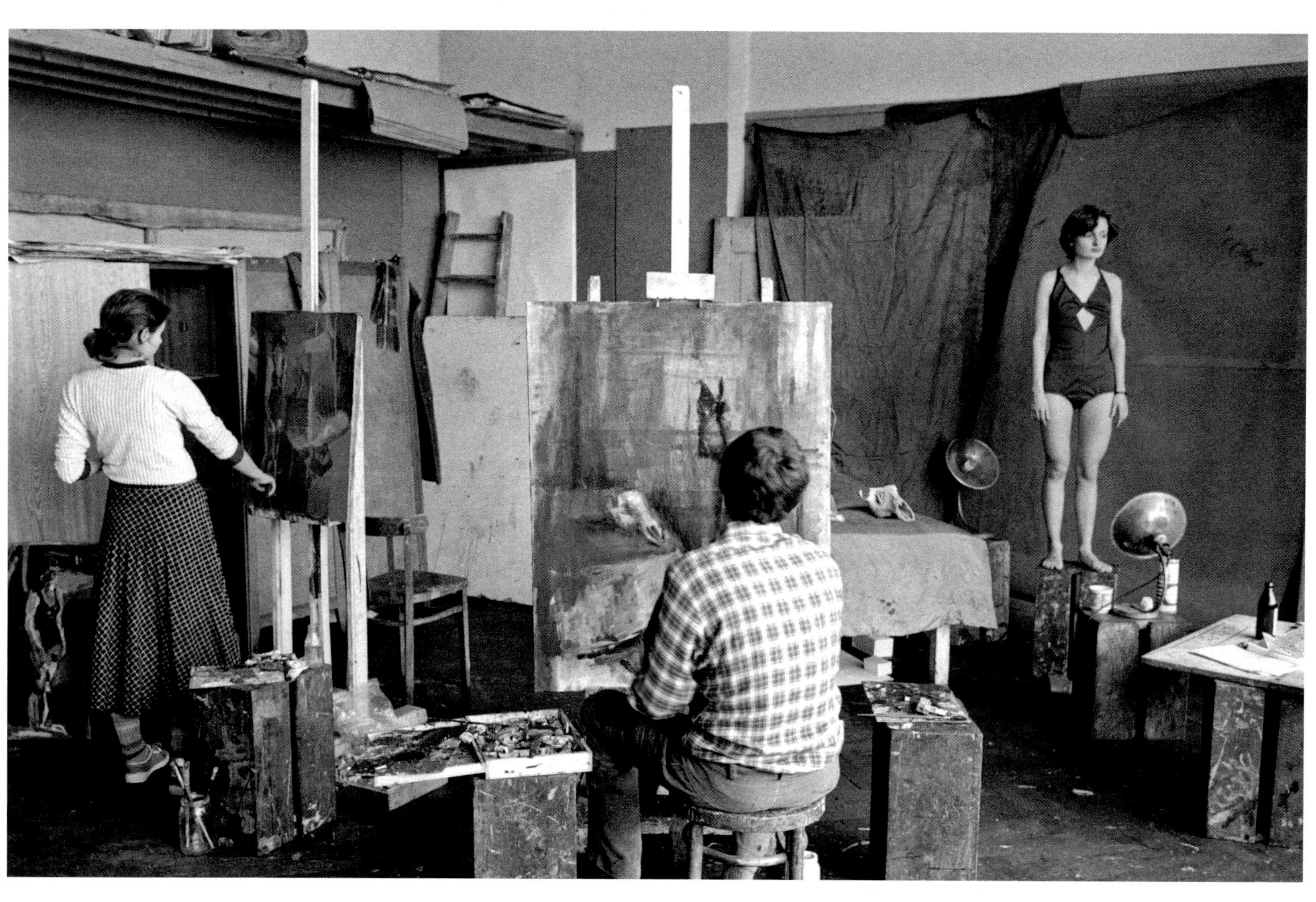

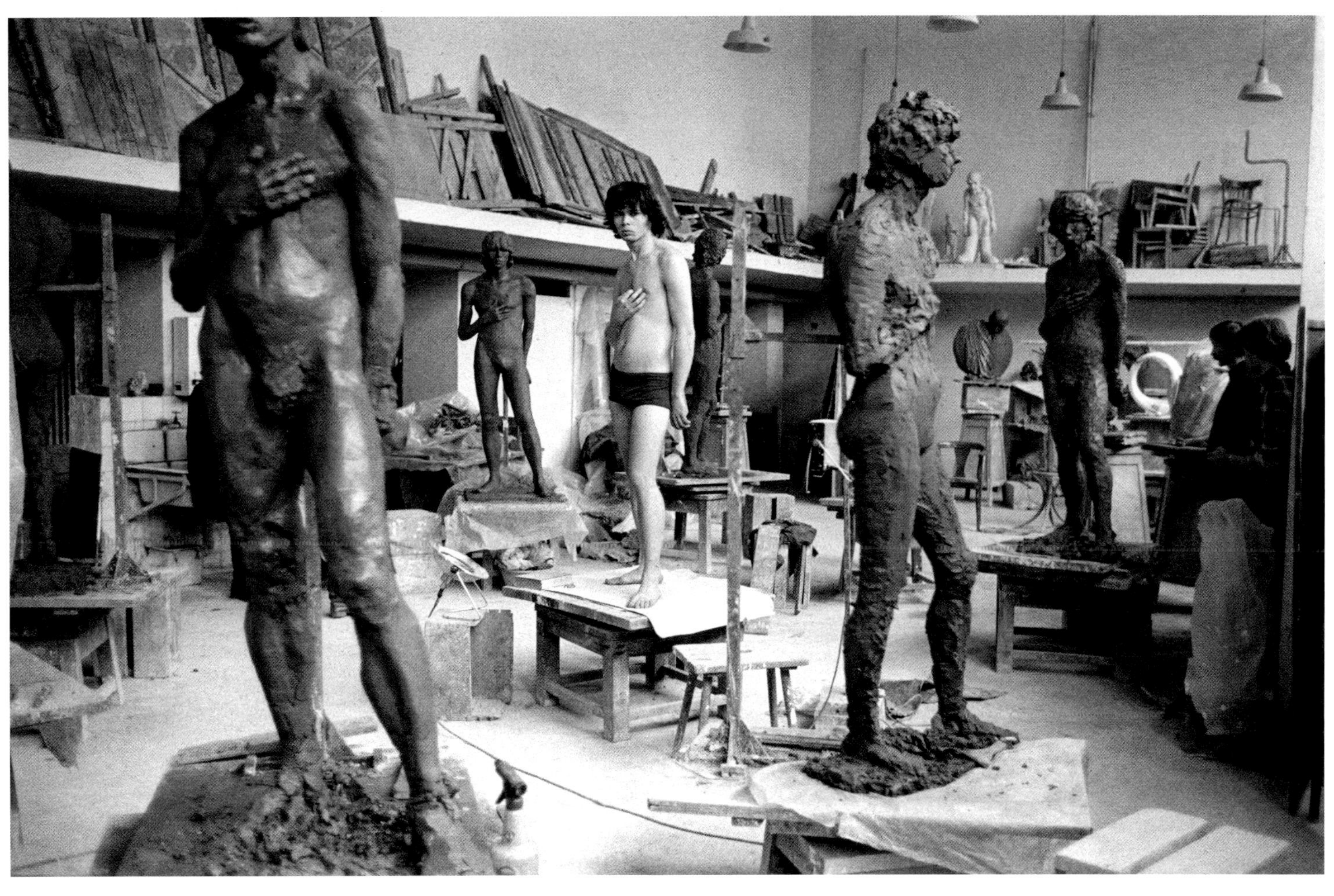

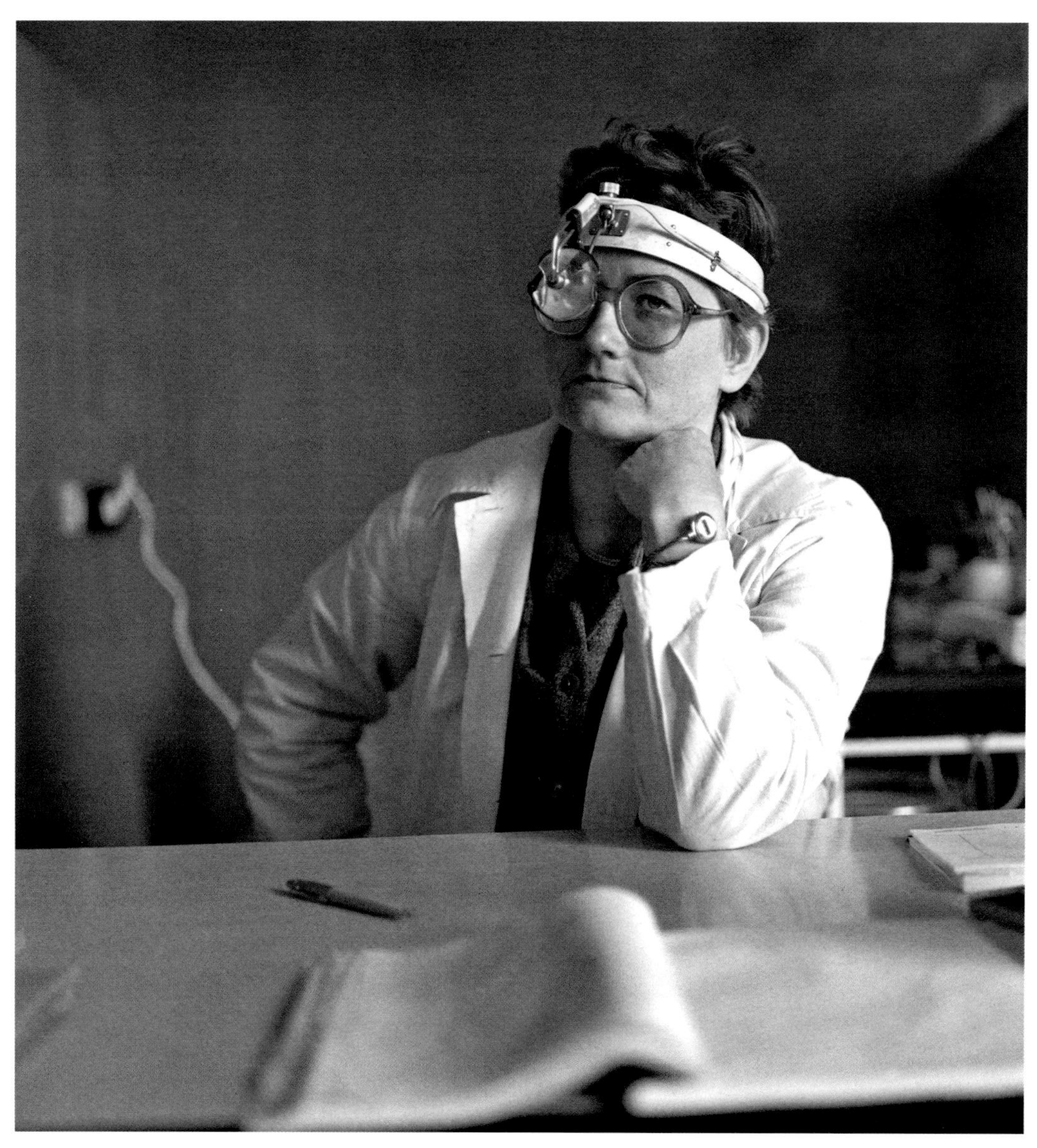

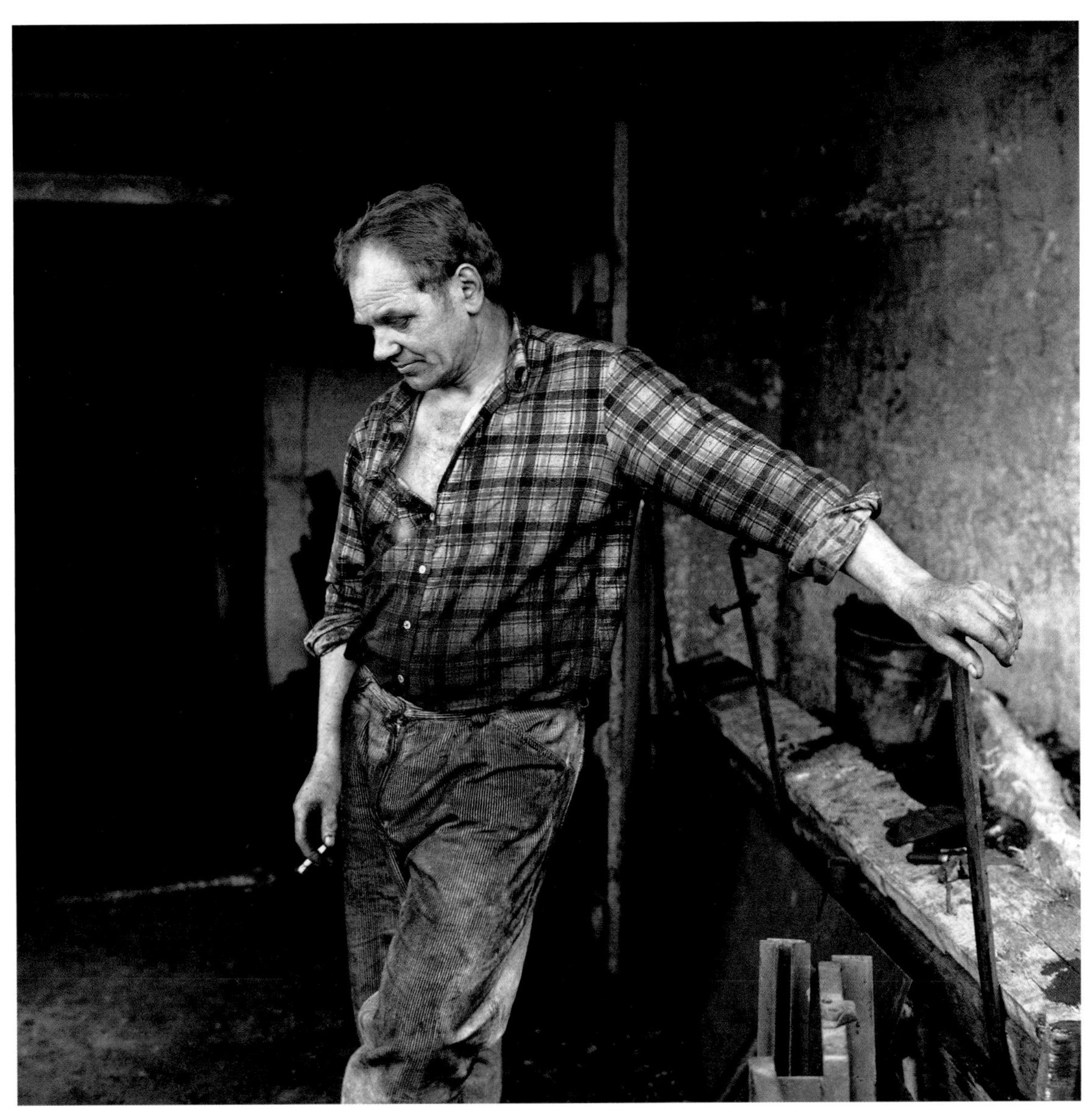

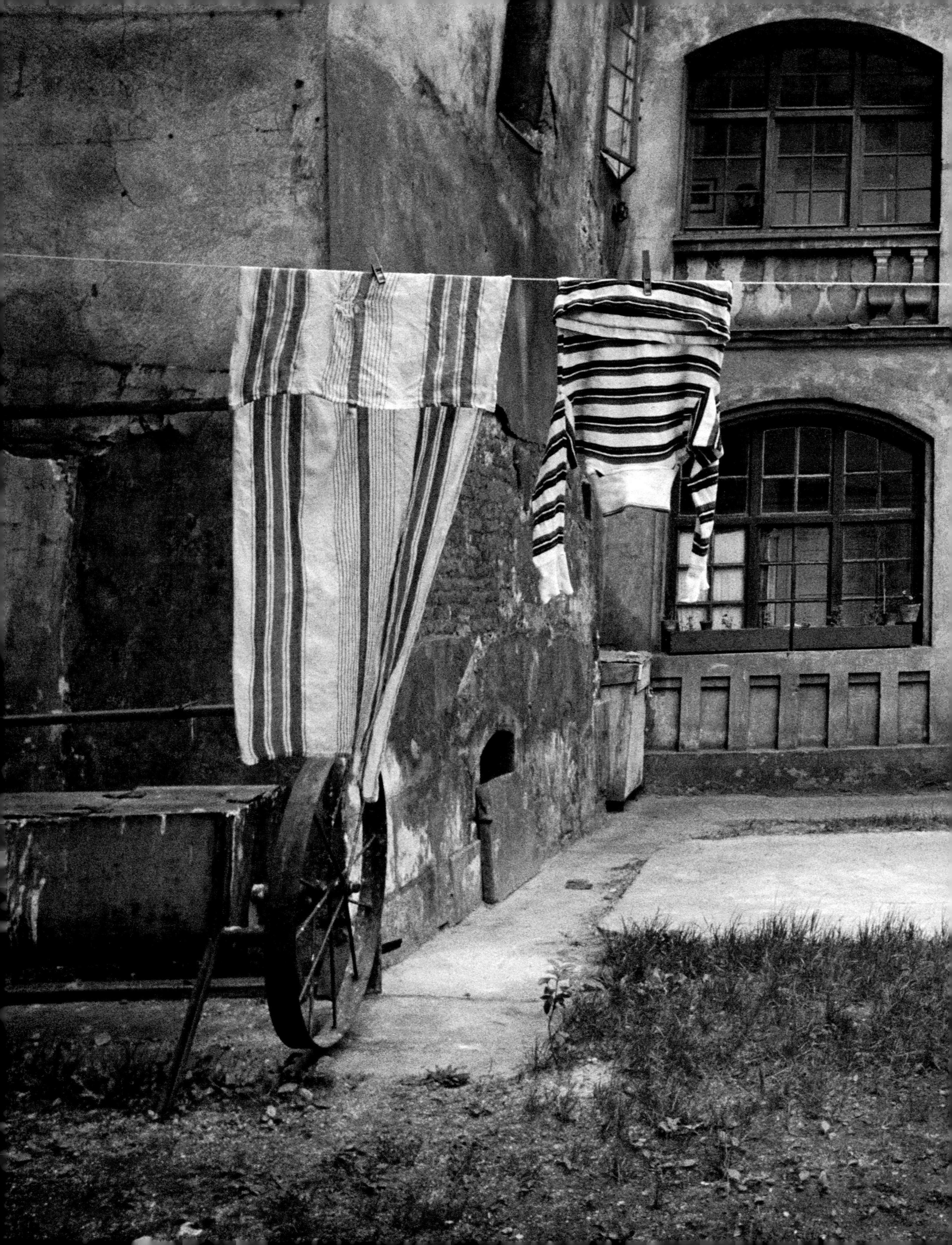

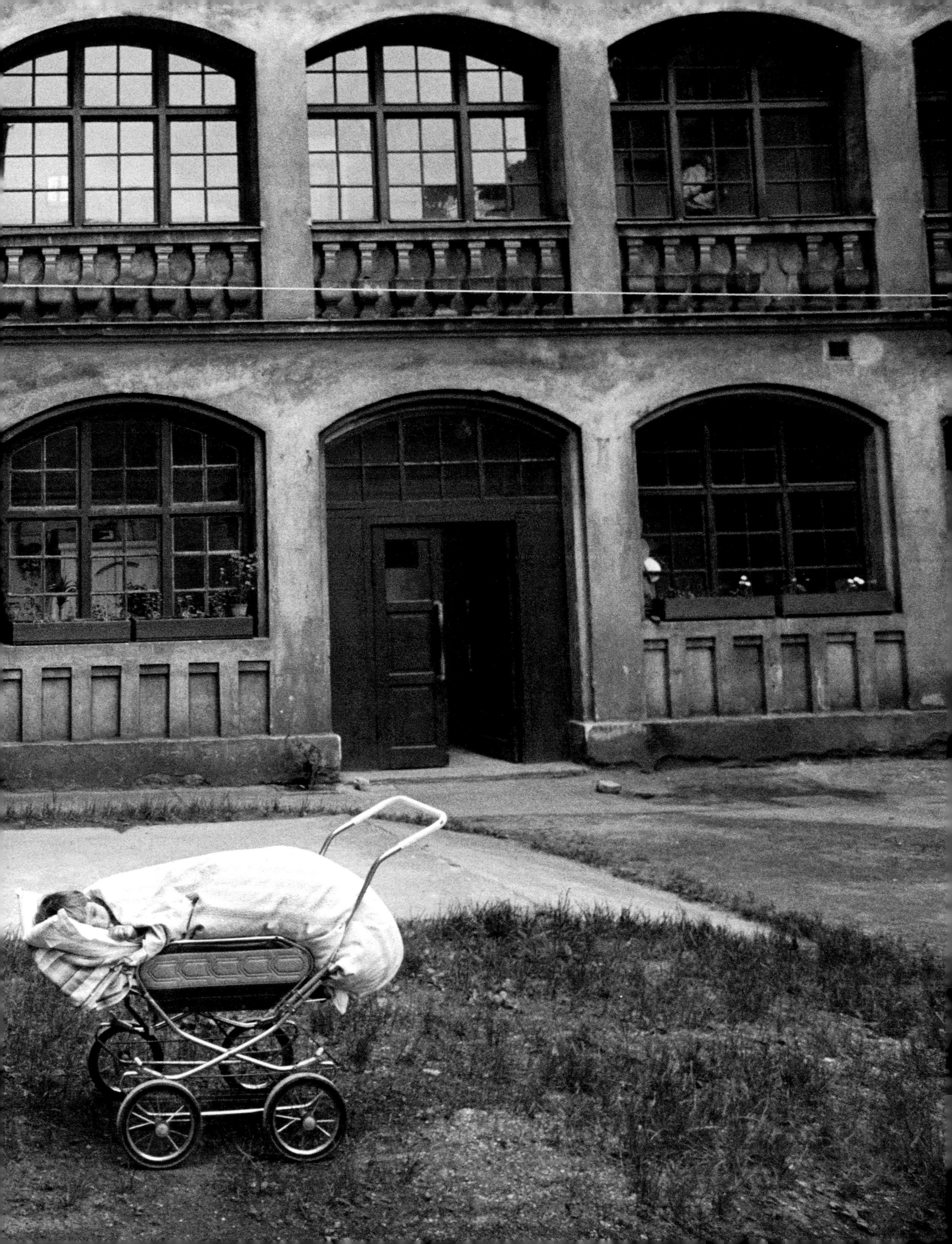

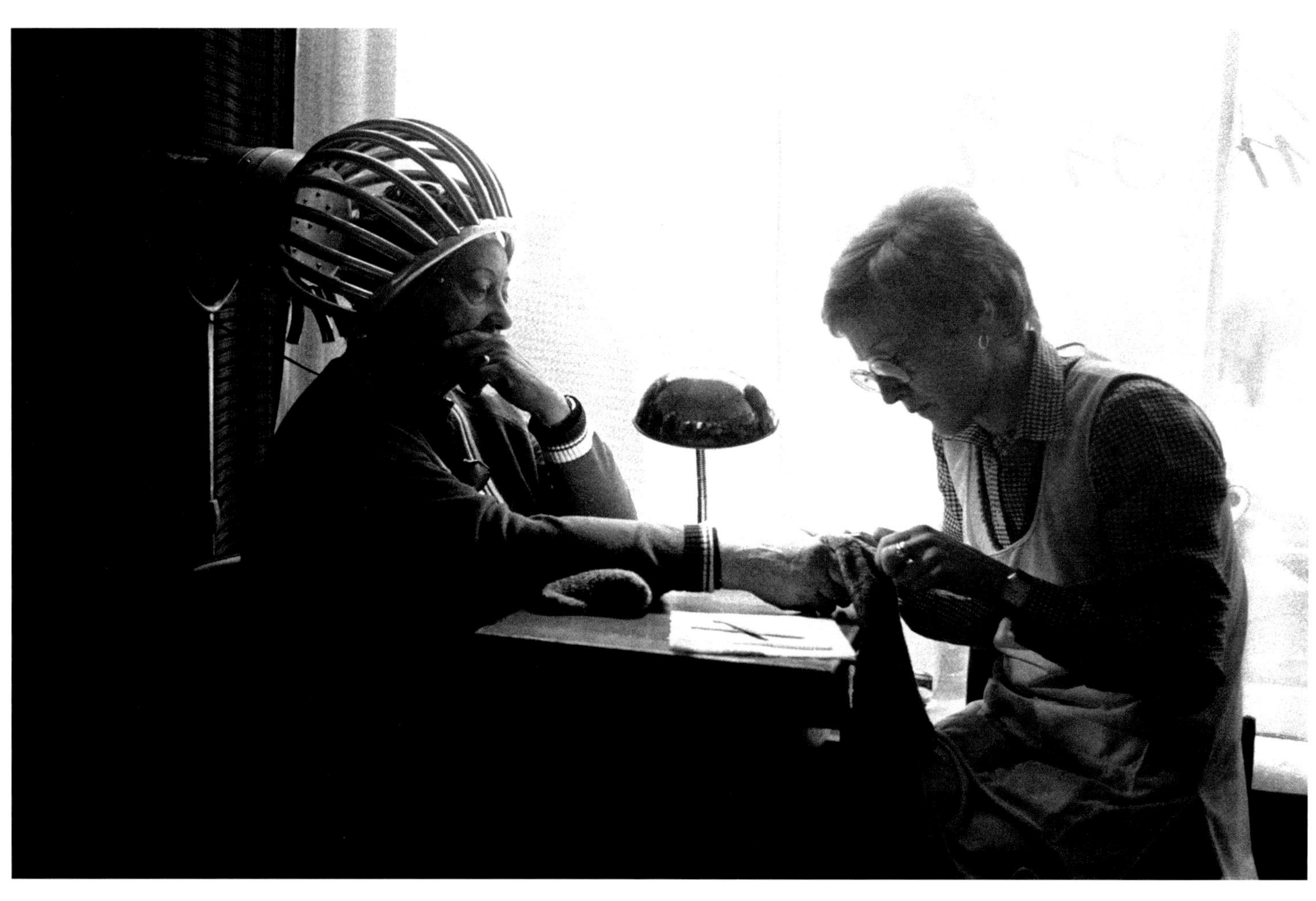

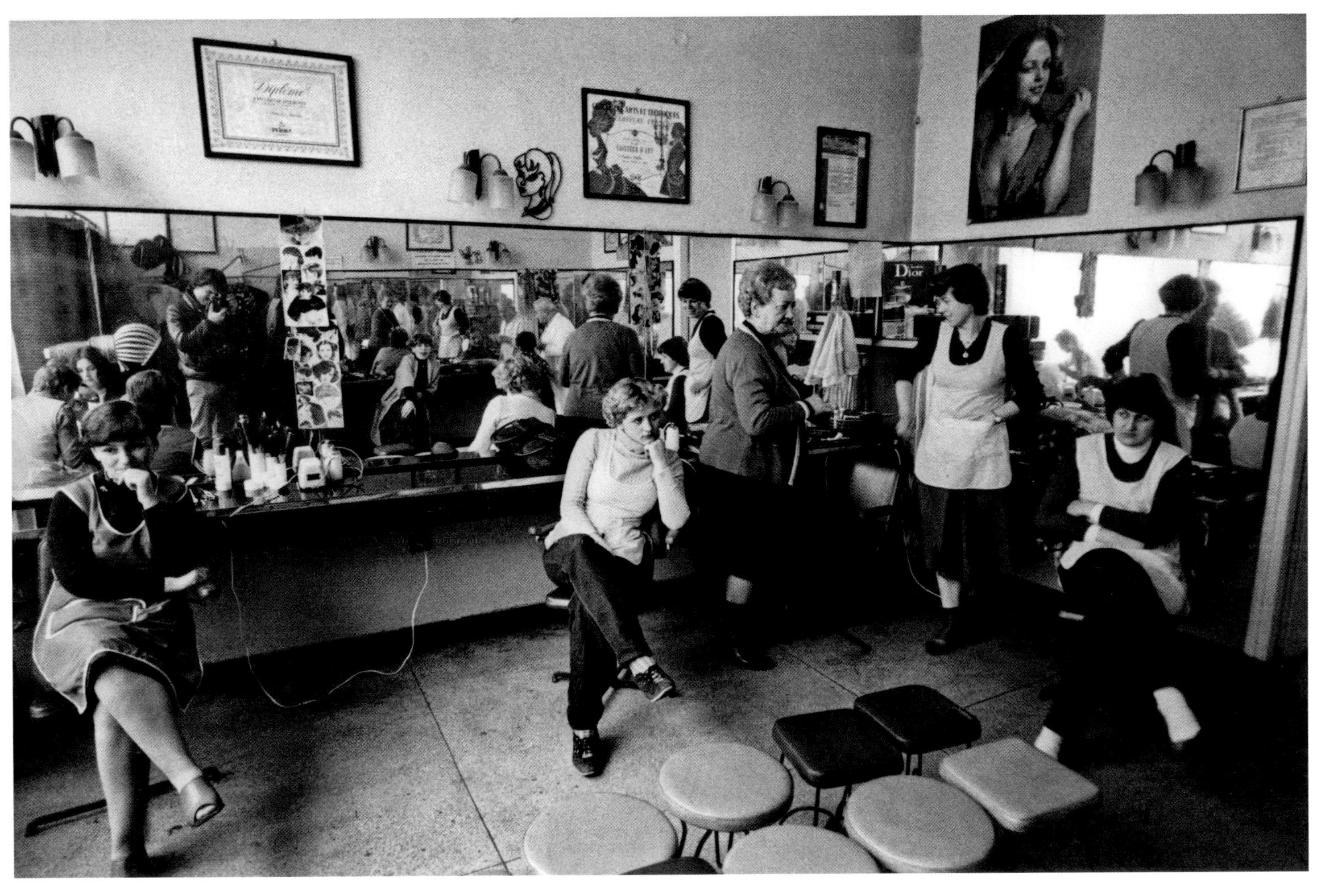
Diplôme
Dior

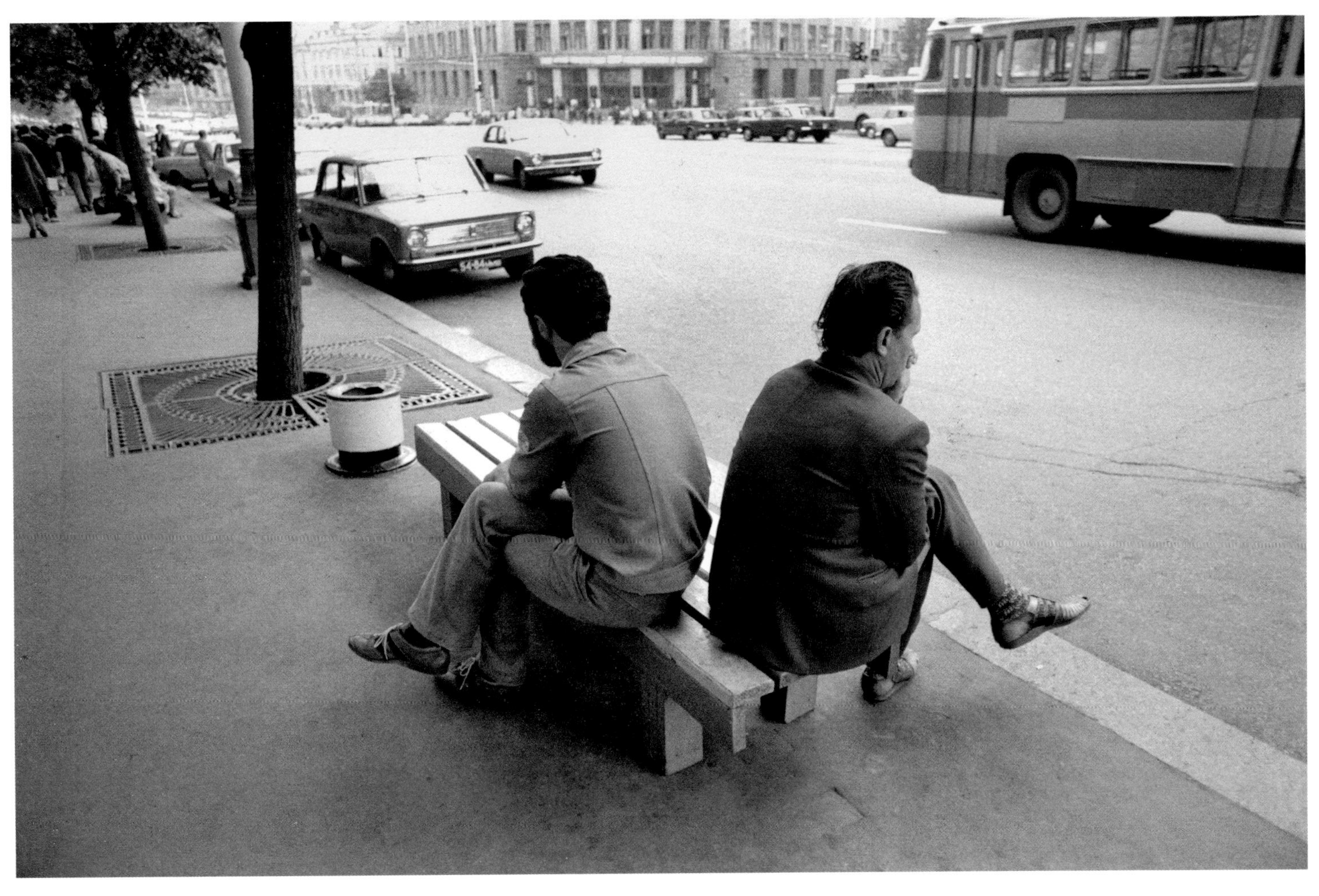

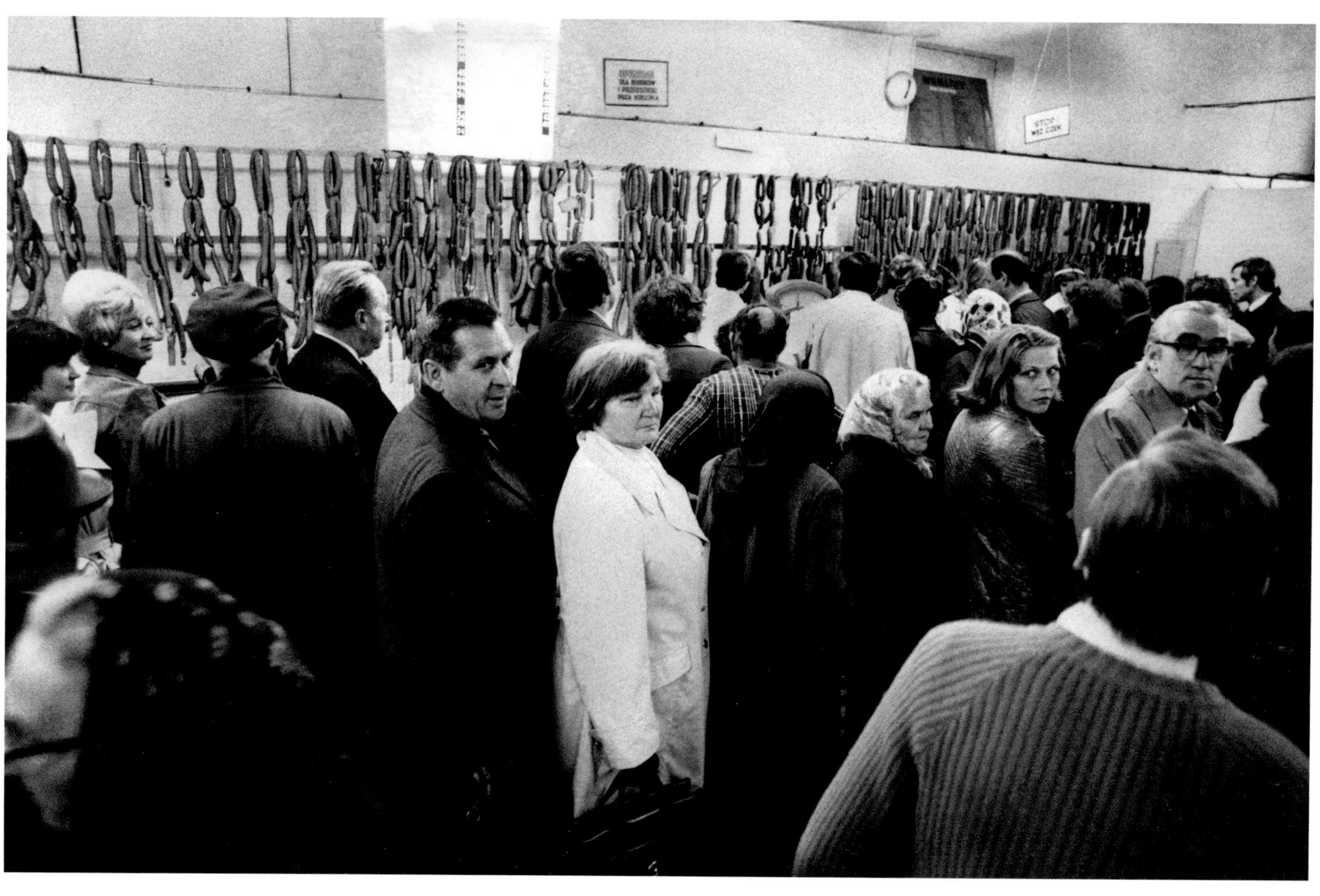
STOP

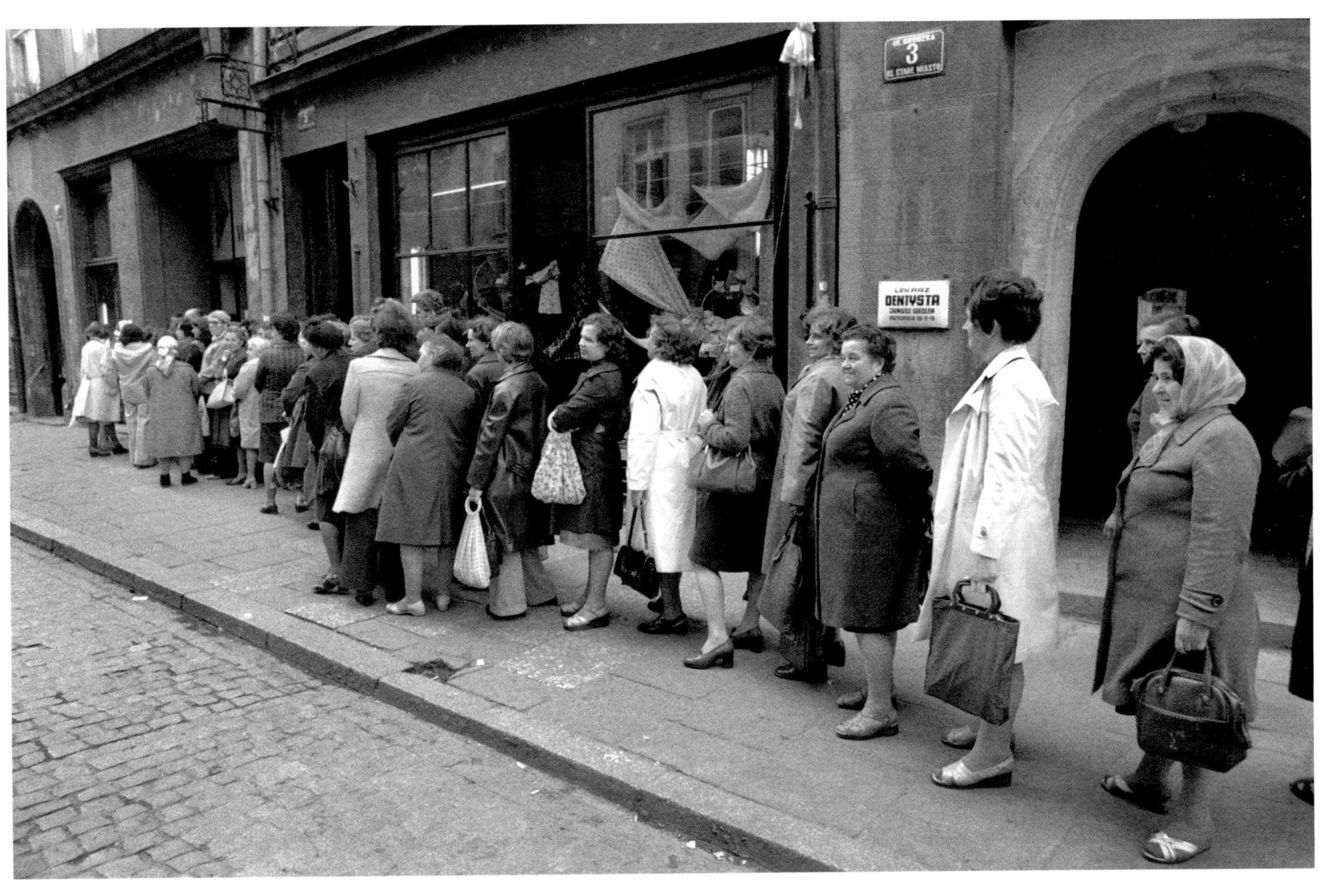
UL. GRODZKA
3
STARE MIASTO
LEKARZ
DENTYSTA

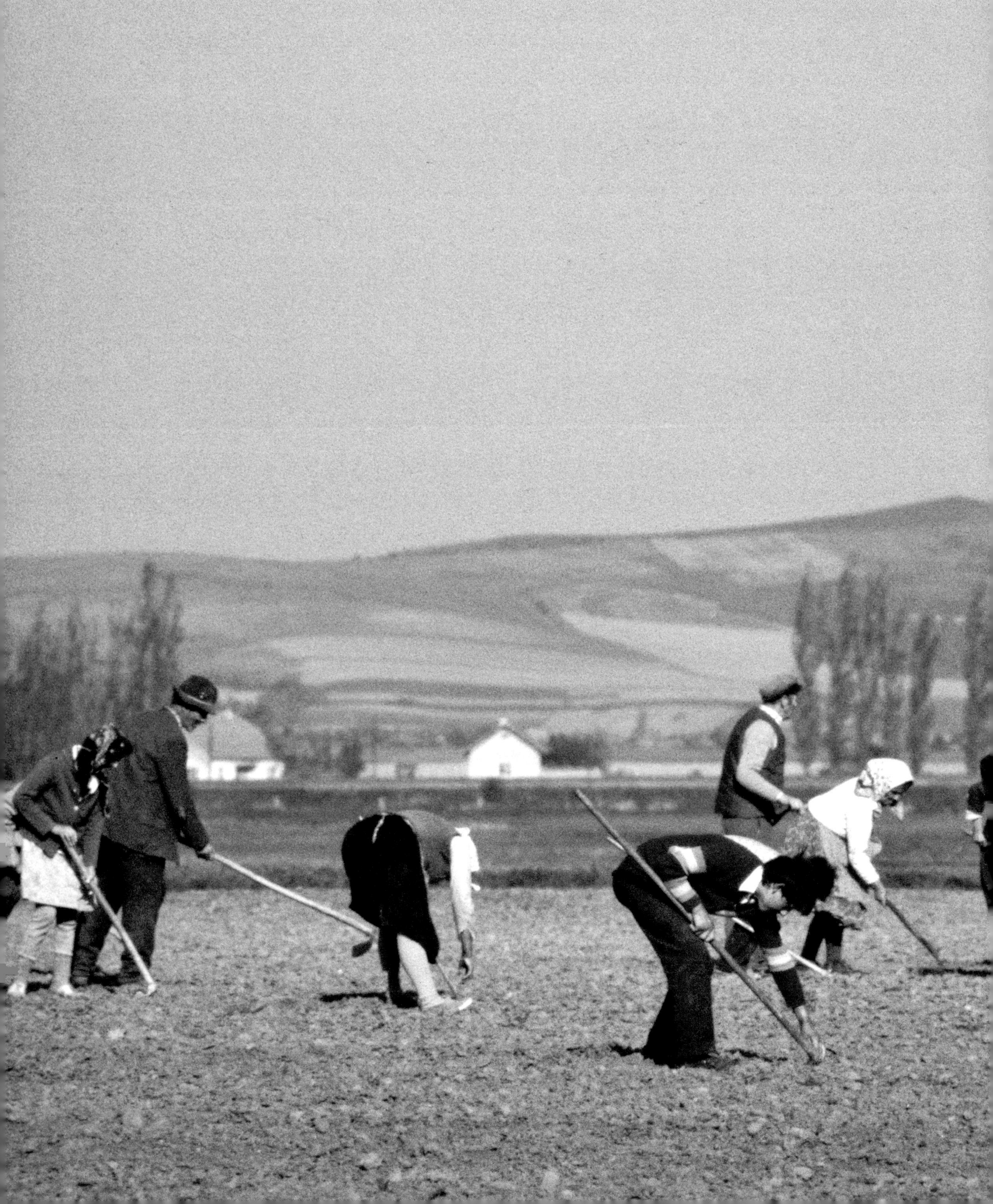

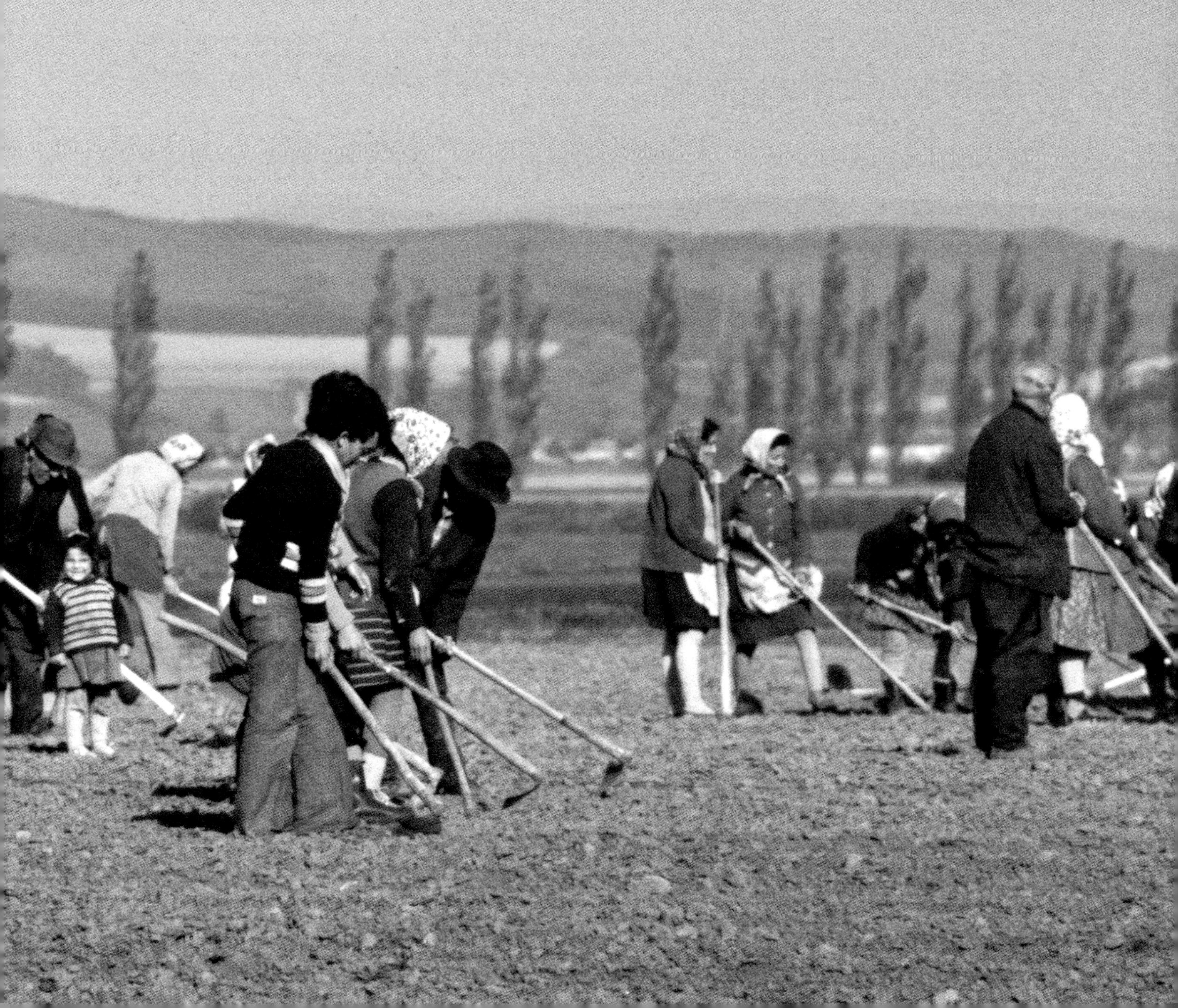

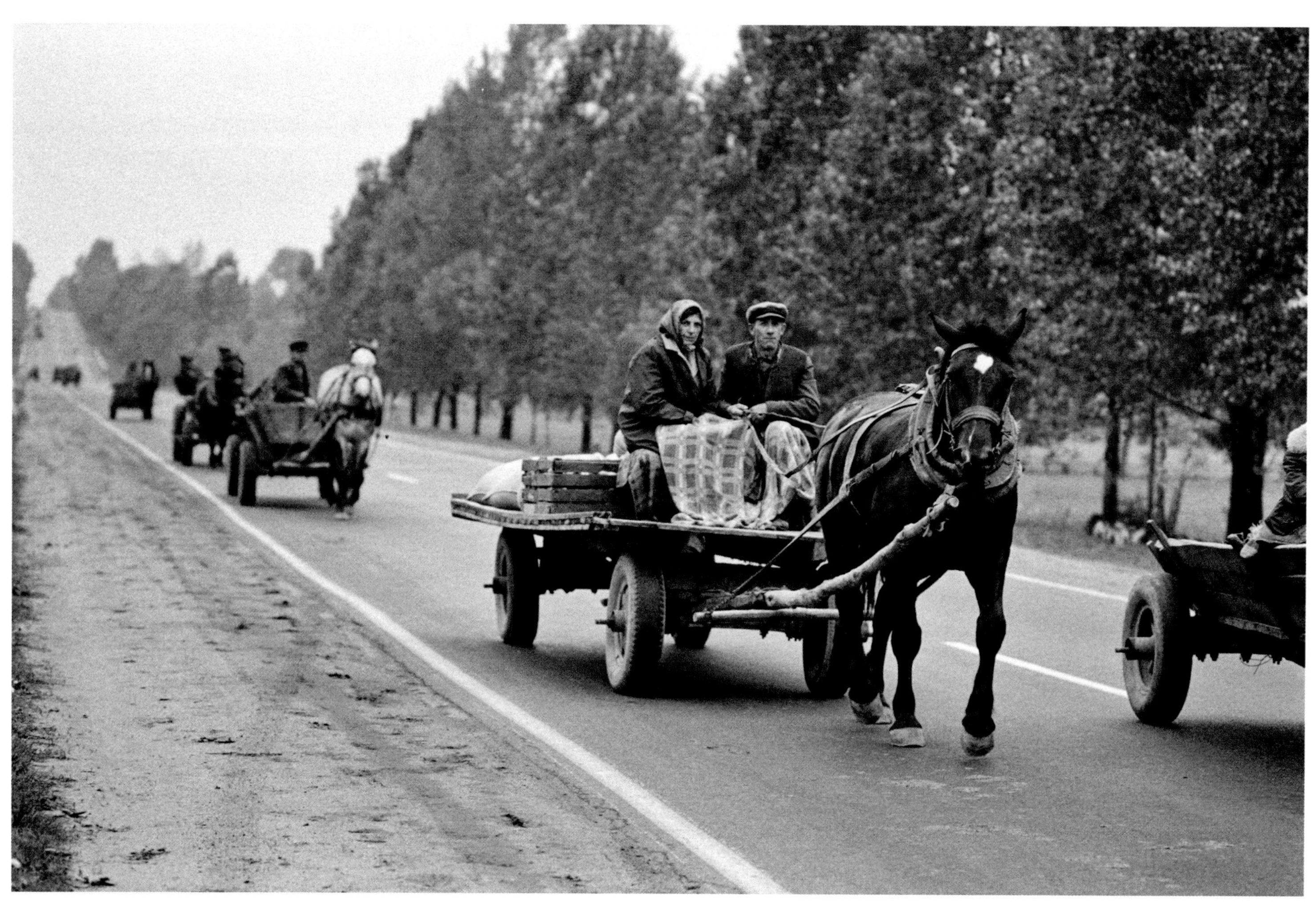

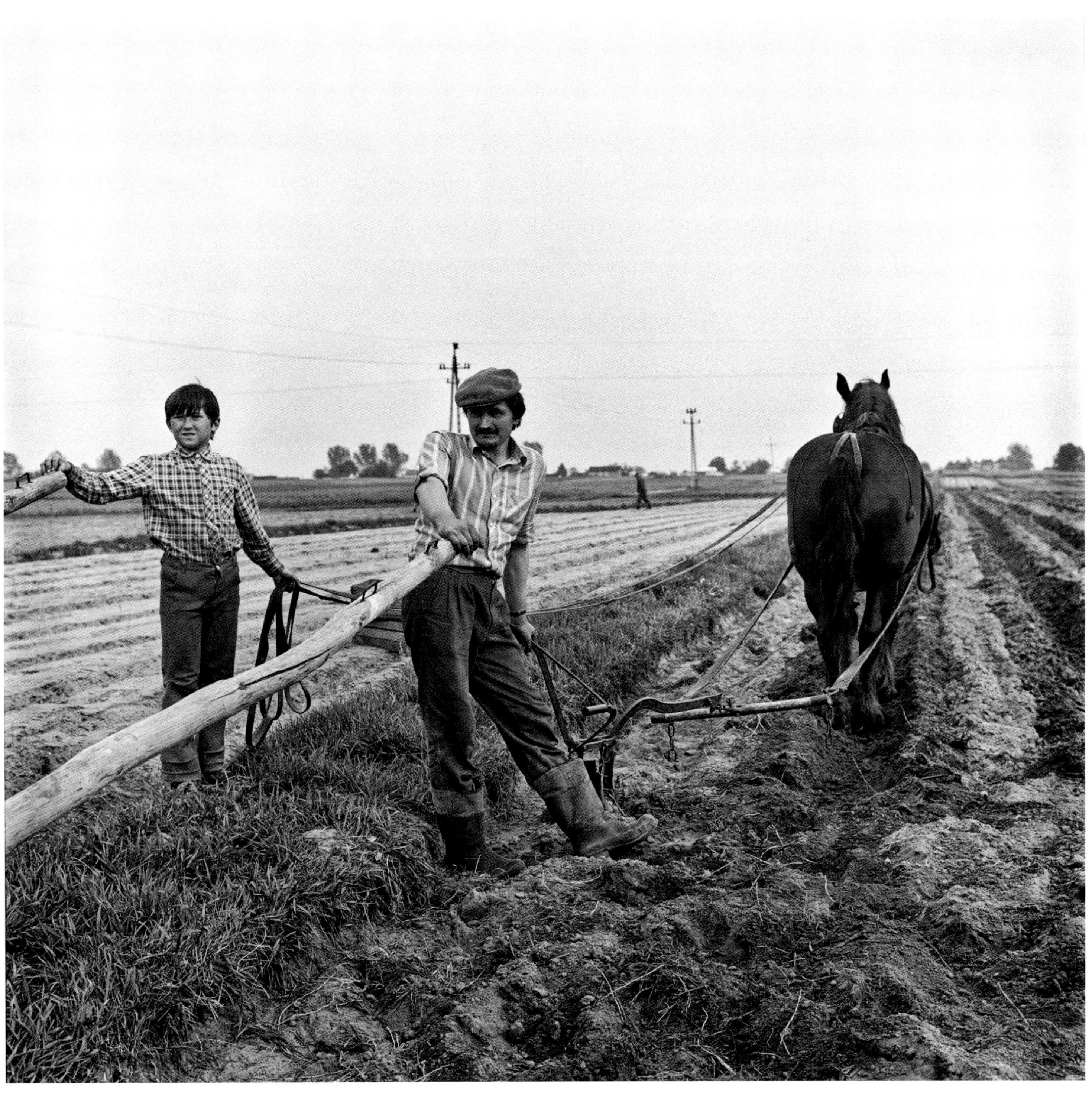

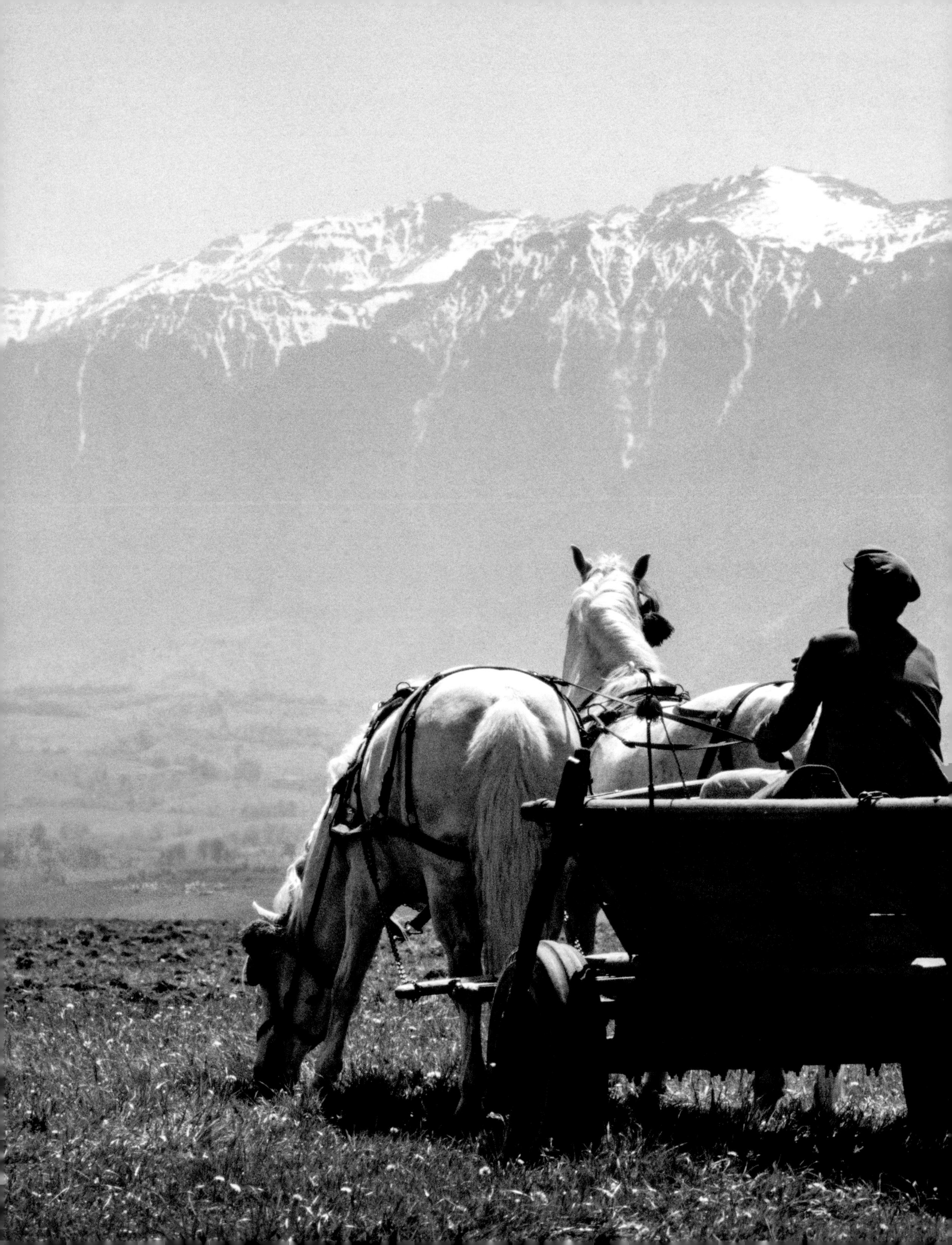

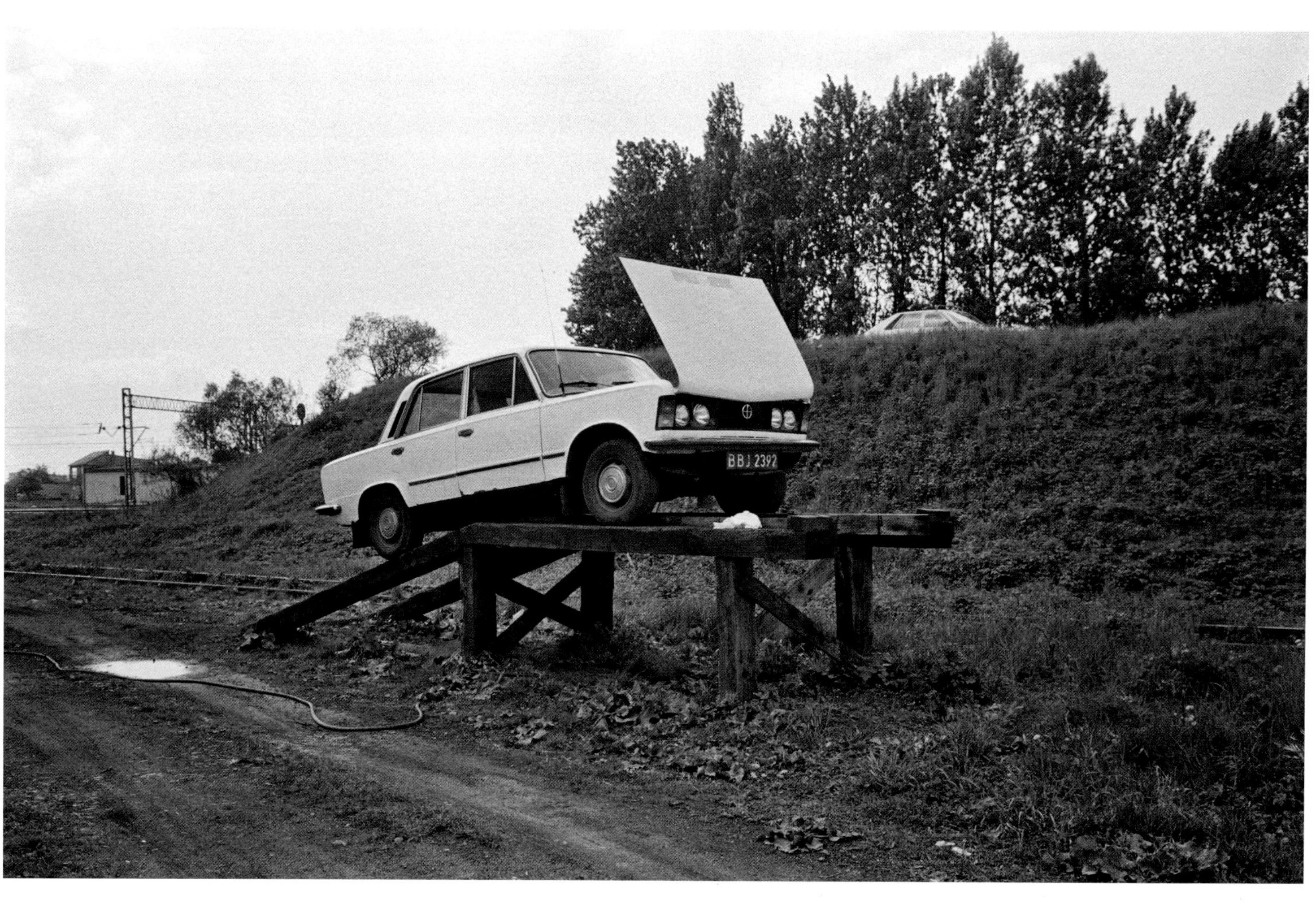
BBJ 2392

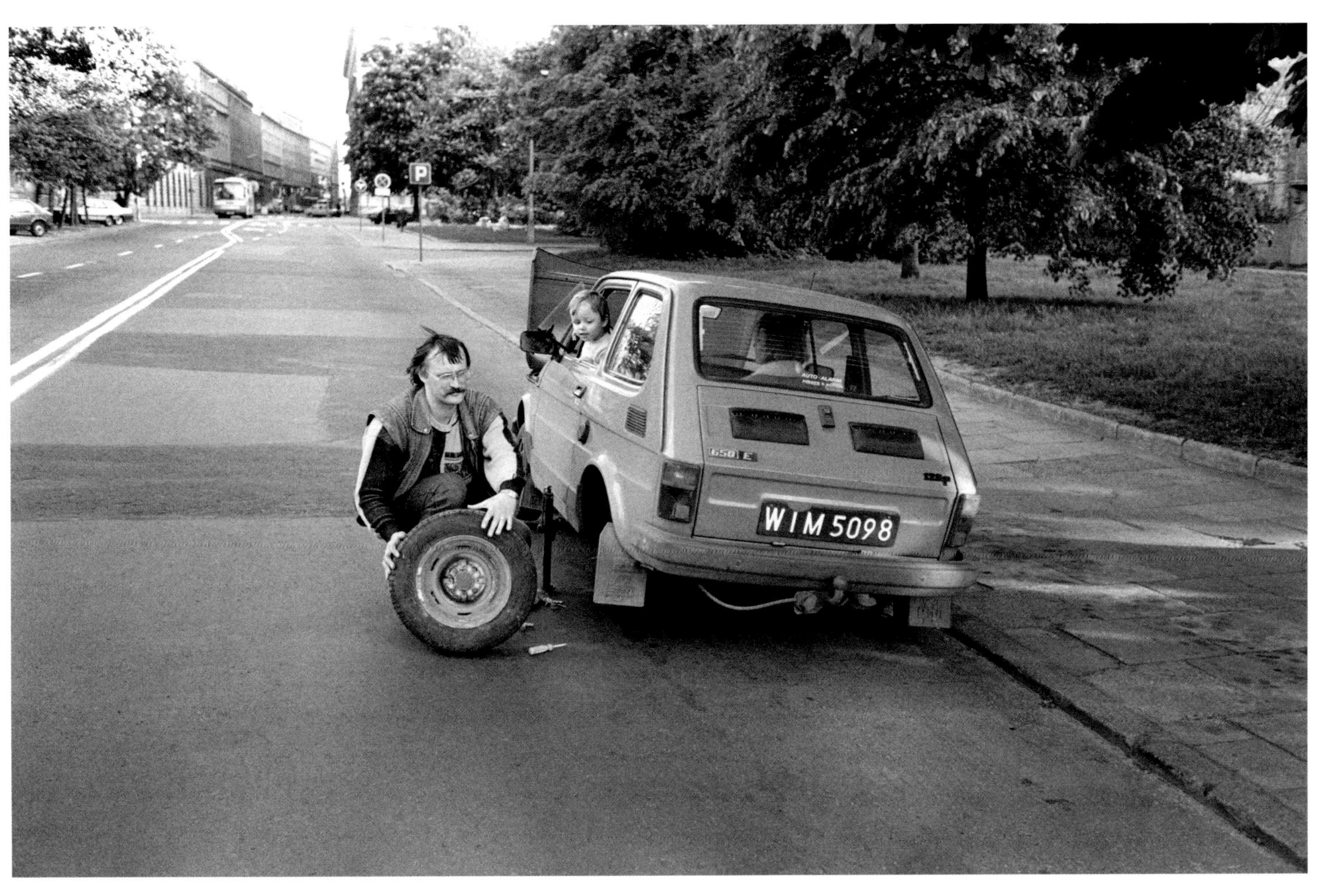
P
WIM 5098

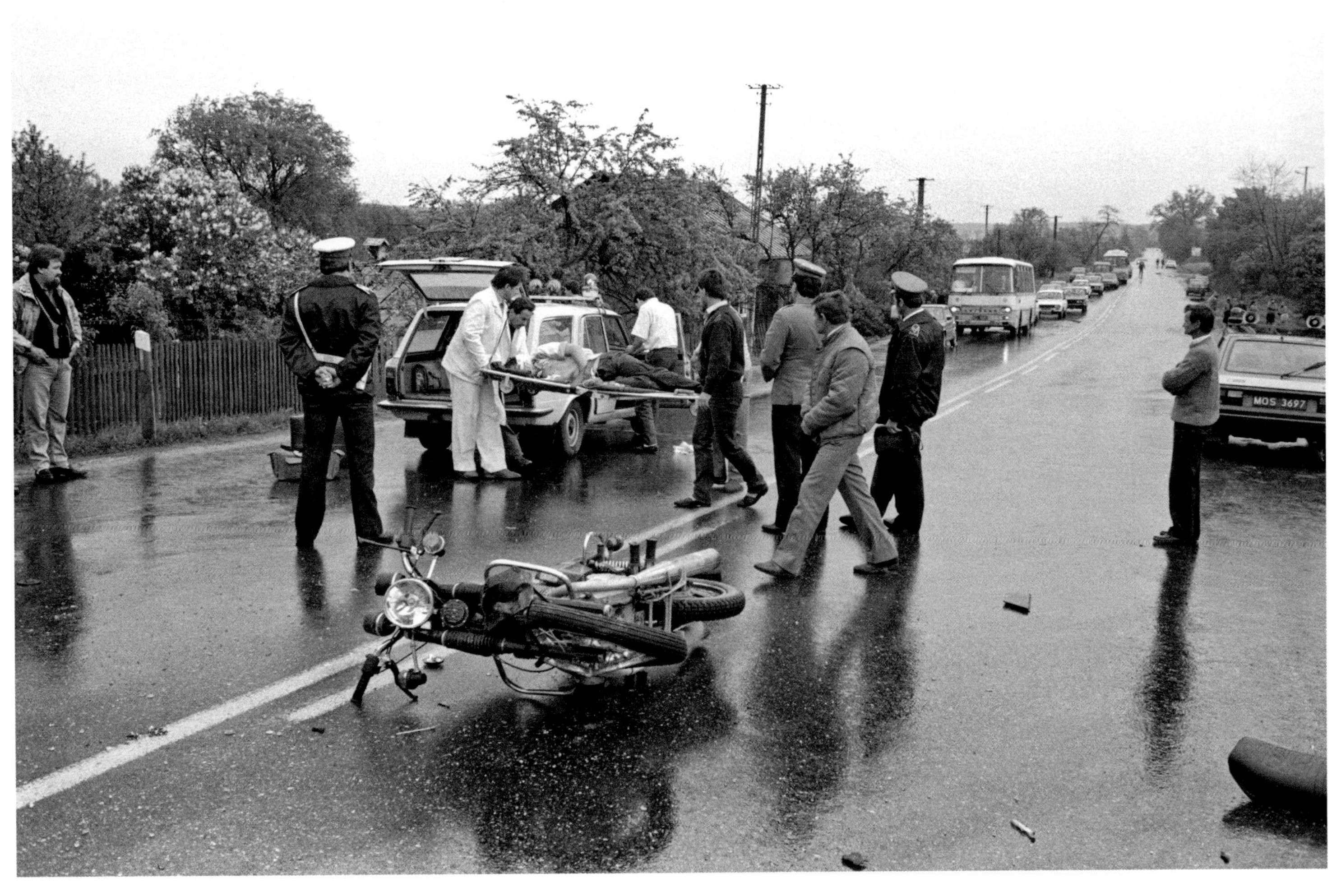
MOS 3697

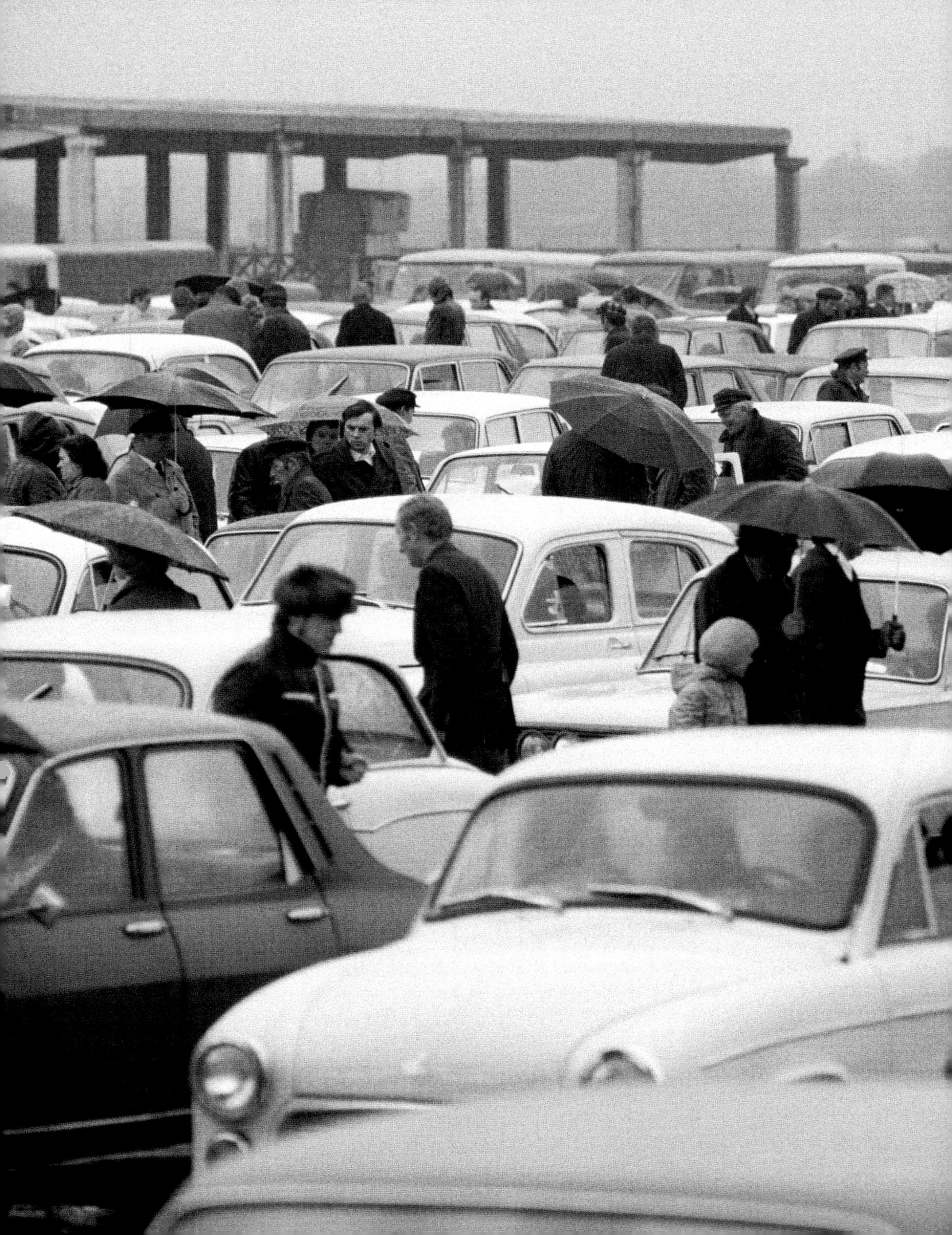

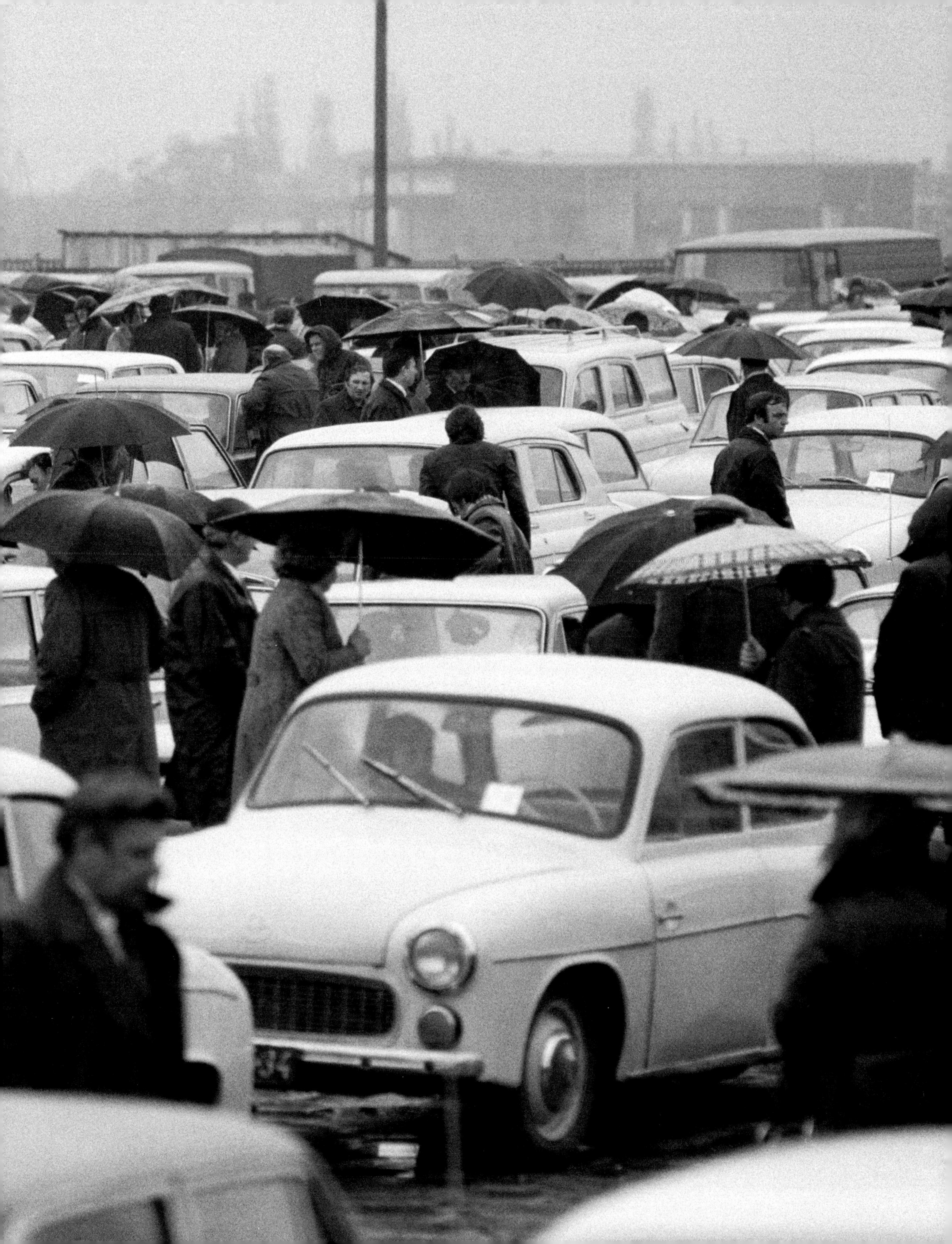

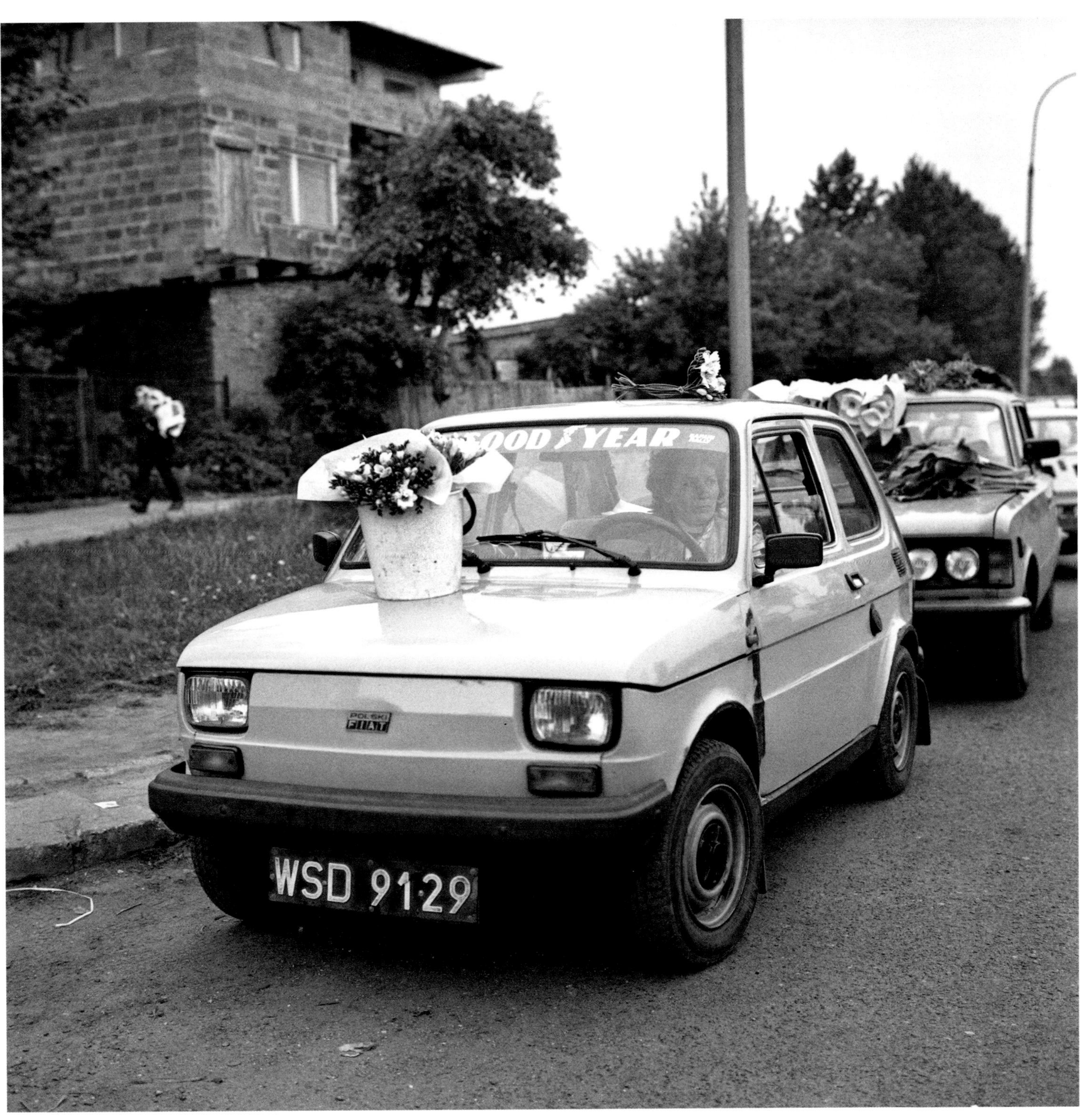
POLSKI FIAT
WSD 9129

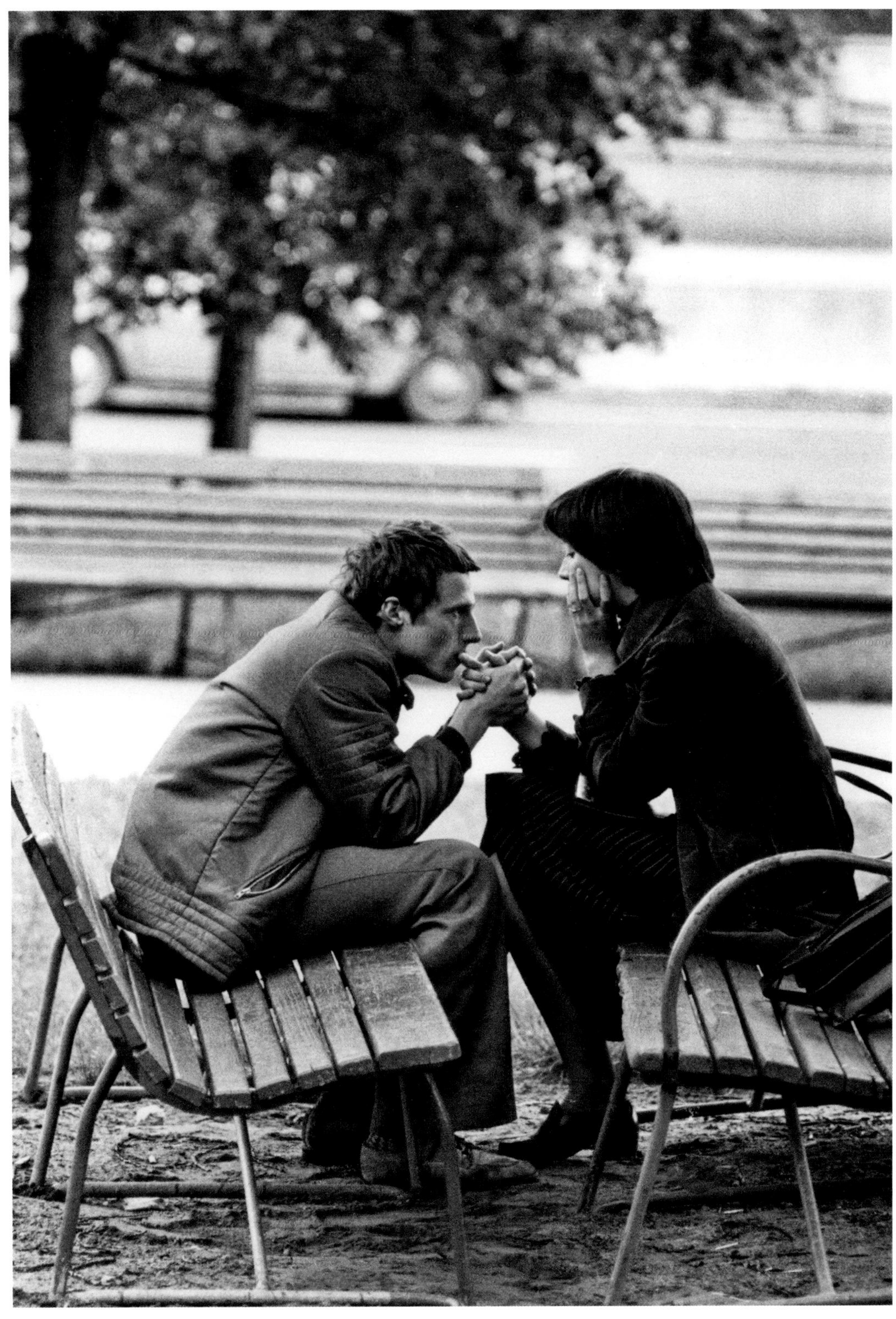

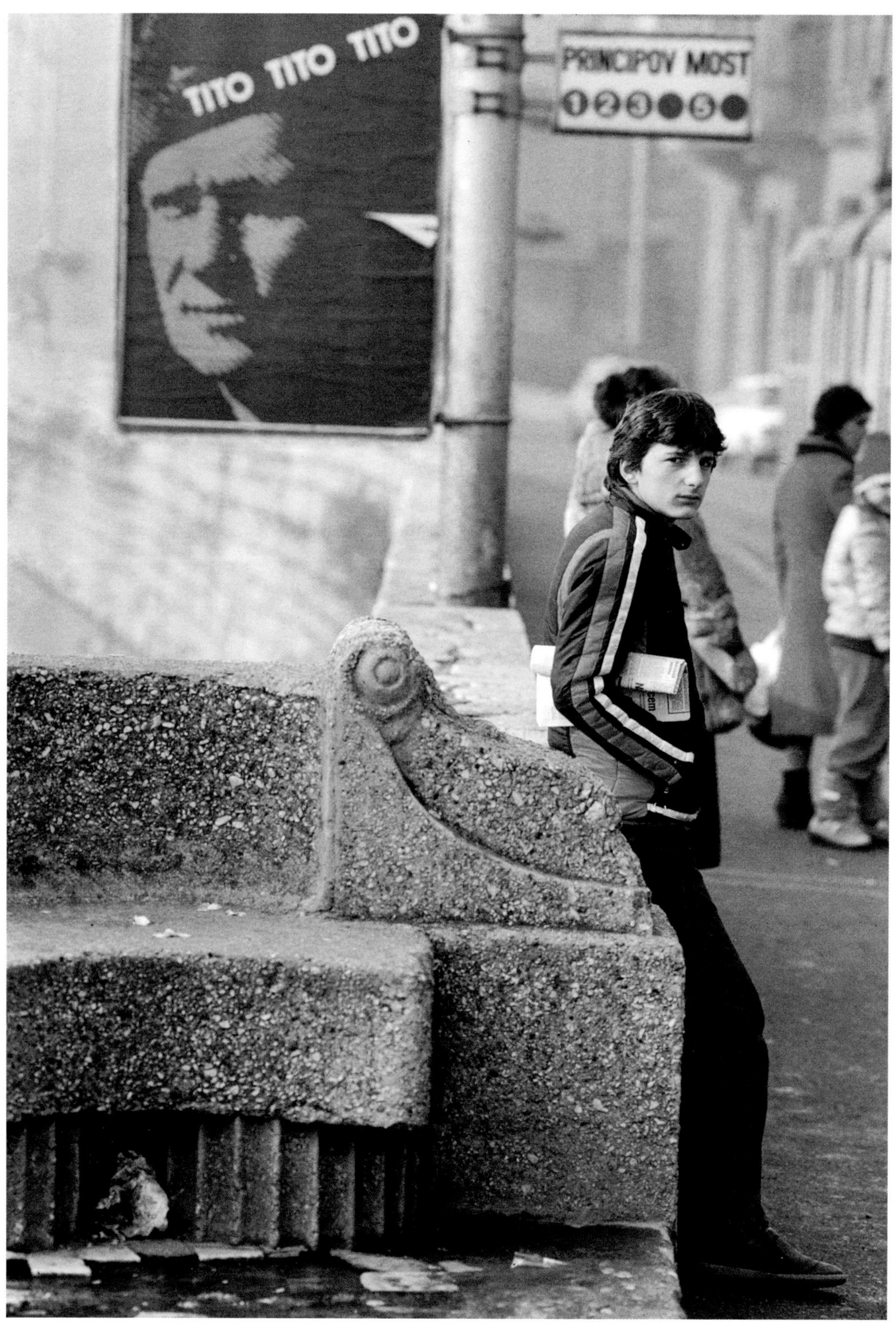
TITO TITO TITO
PRINCIPOV MOST

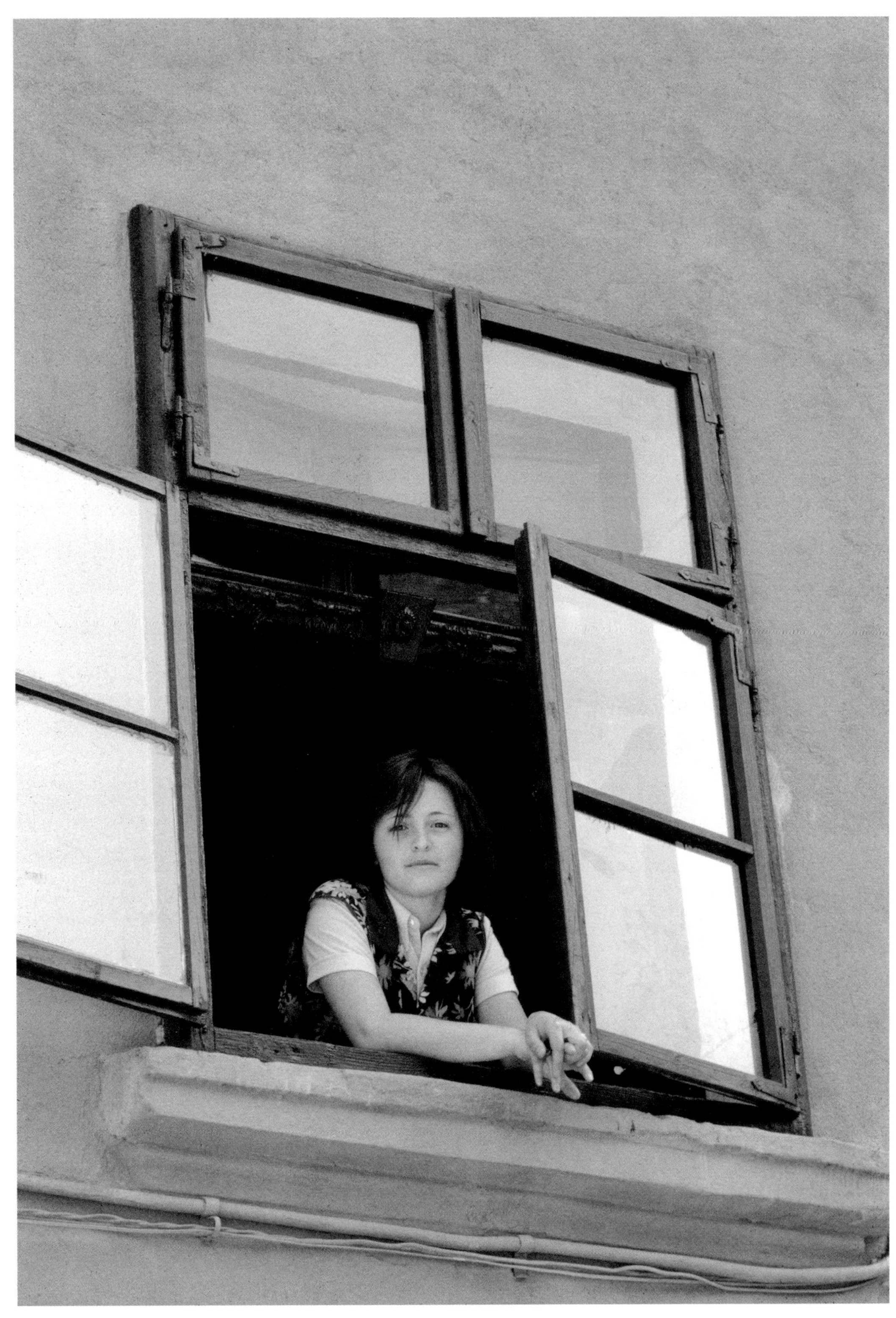

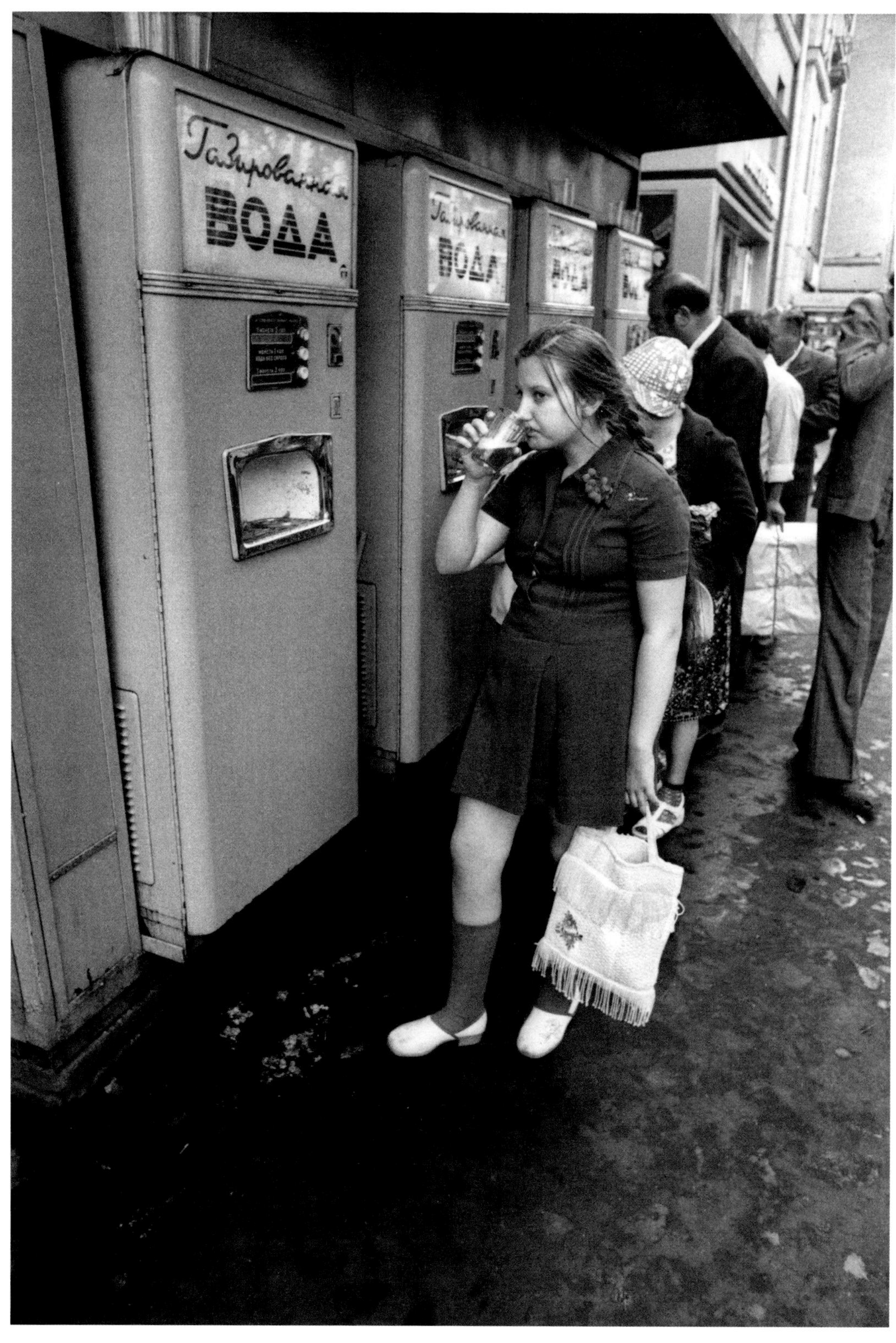
Газированная
ВОДА
Газированная
ВОДА

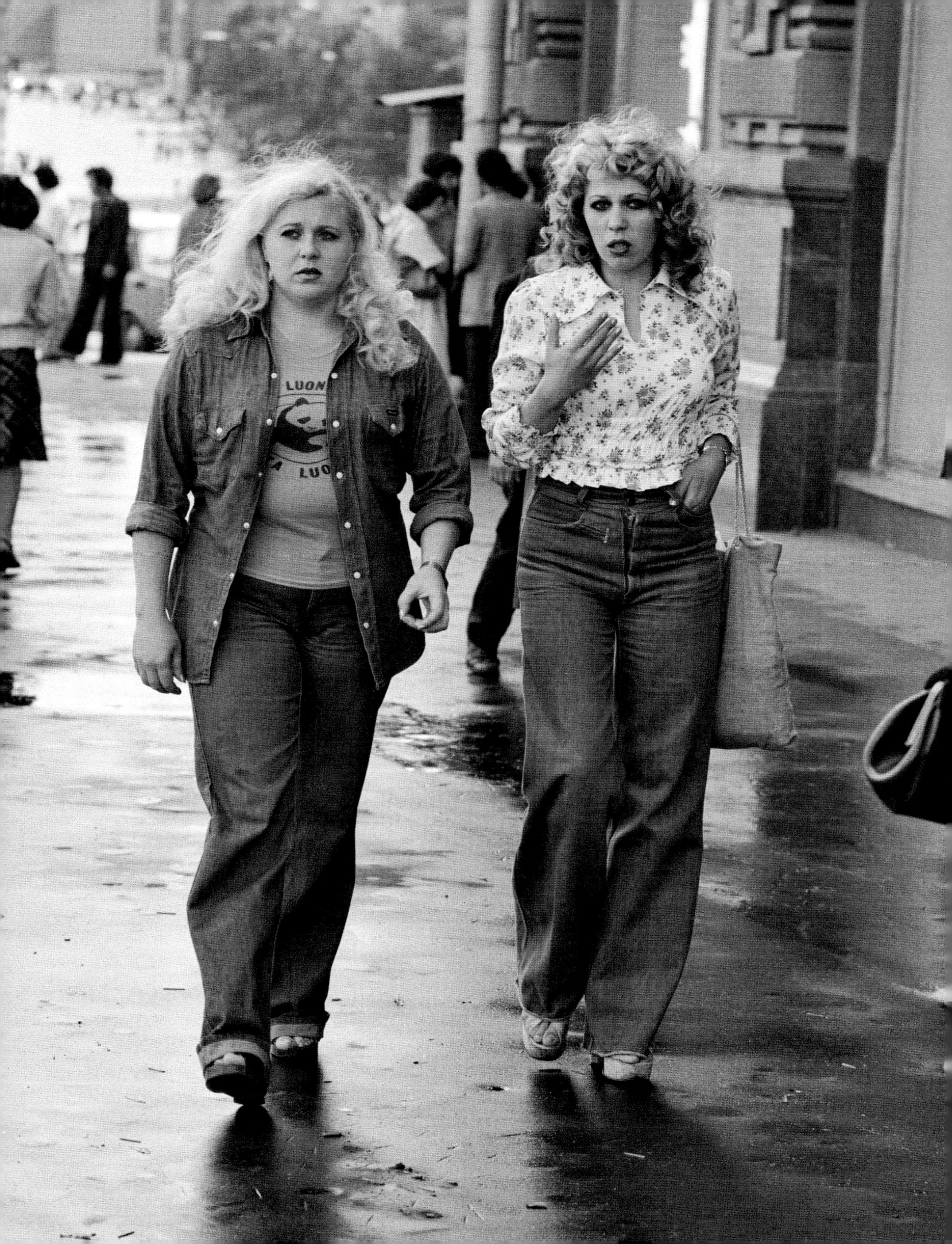

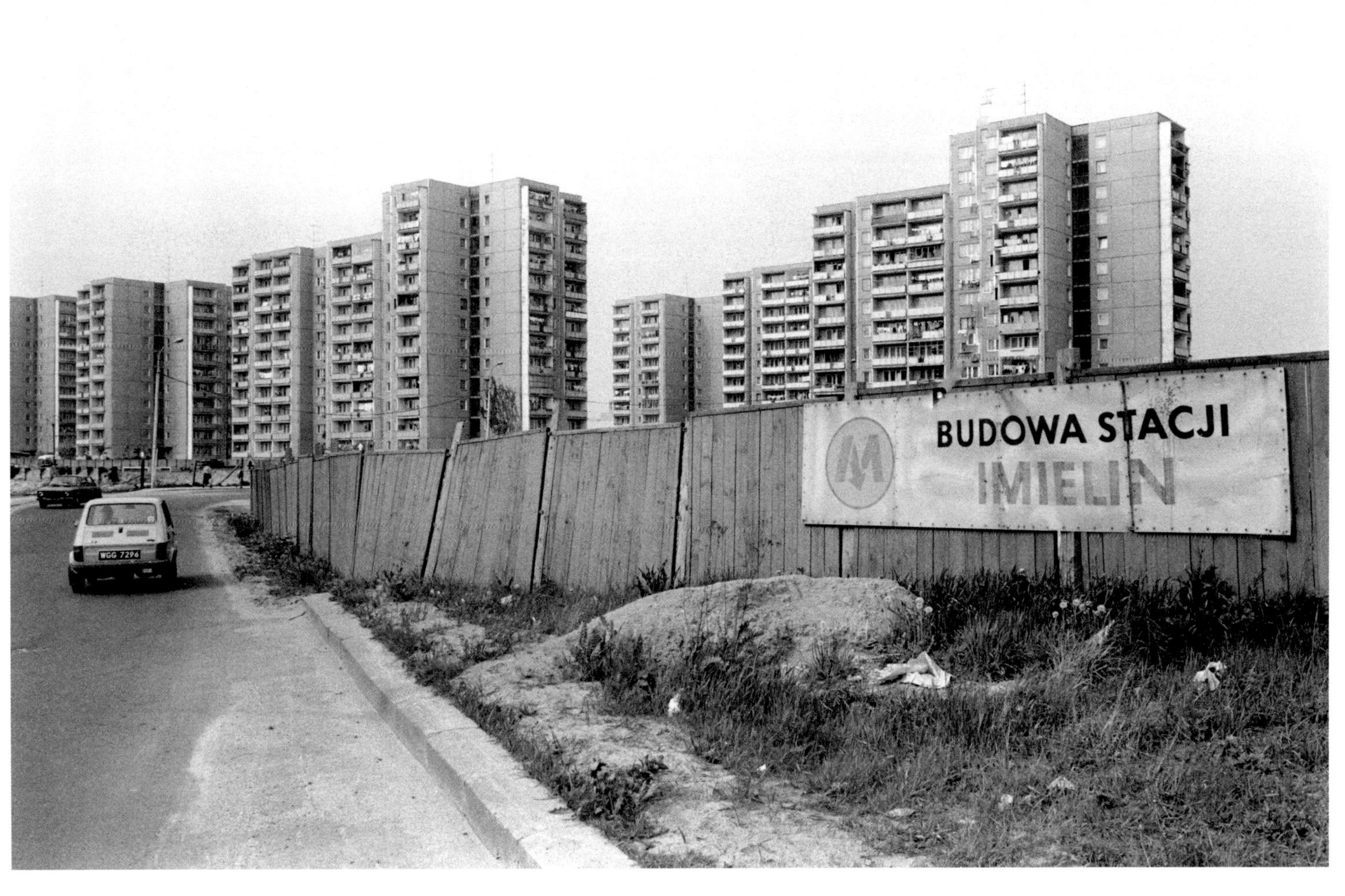
BUDOWA STACJI
IMIELIN

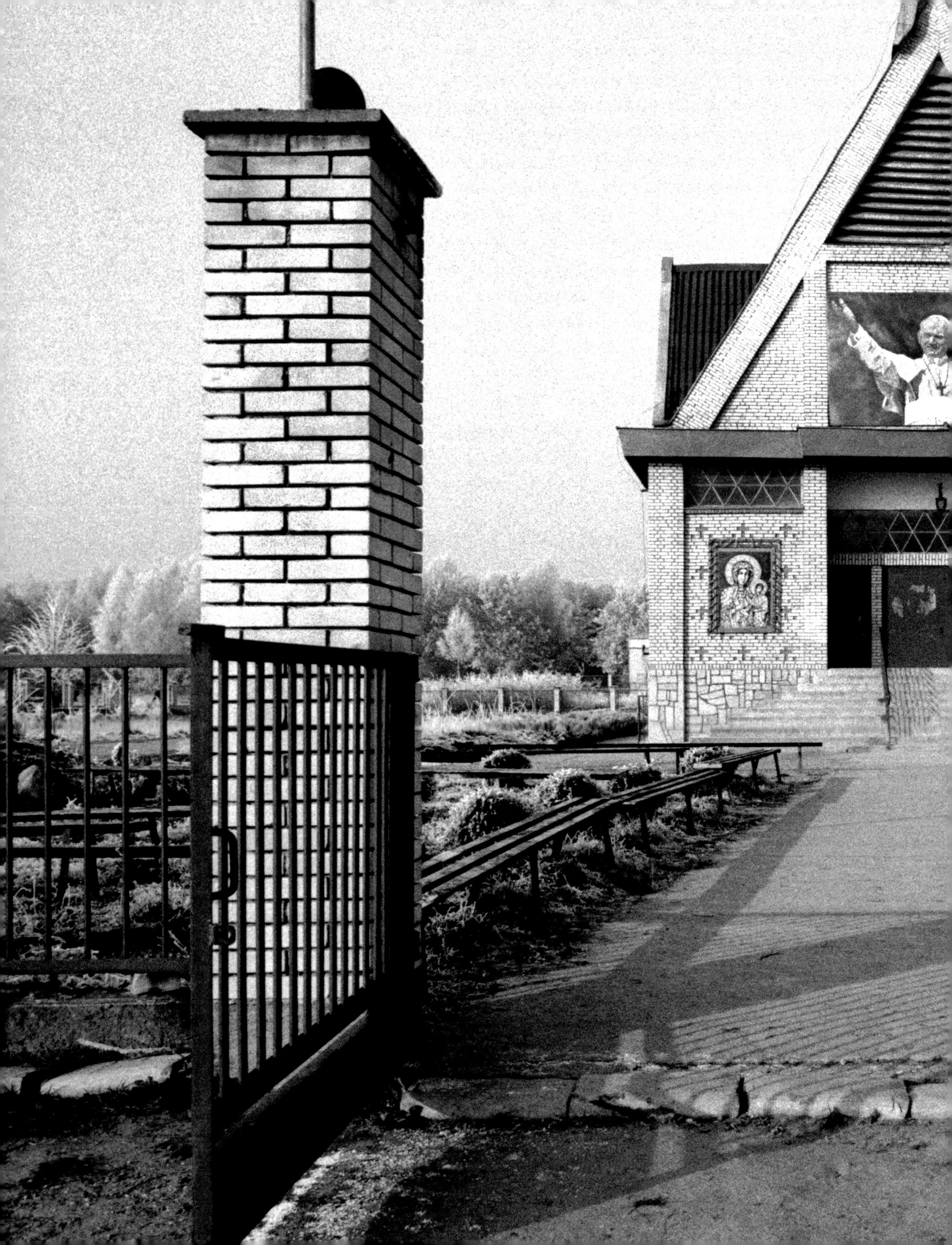

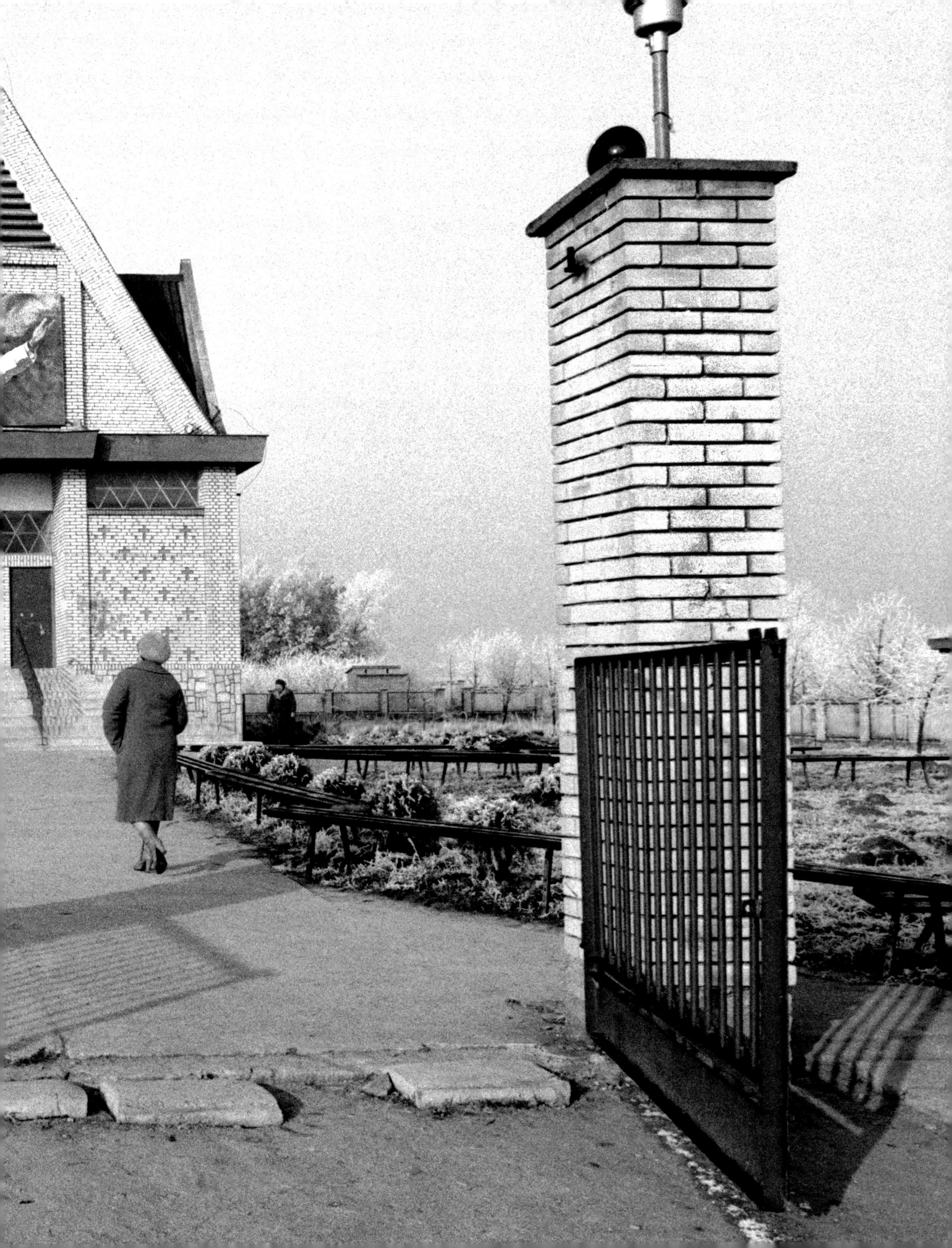

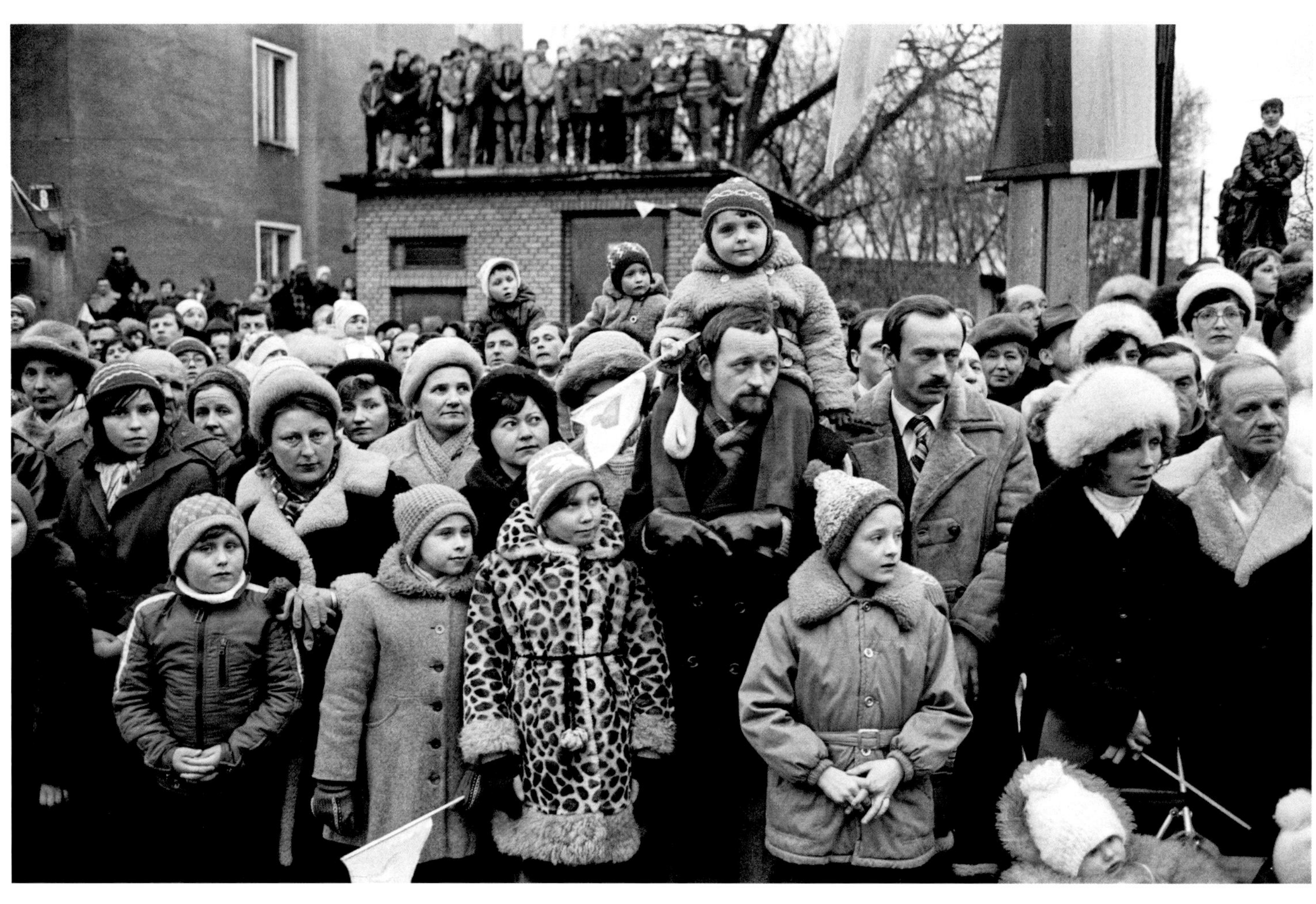
8

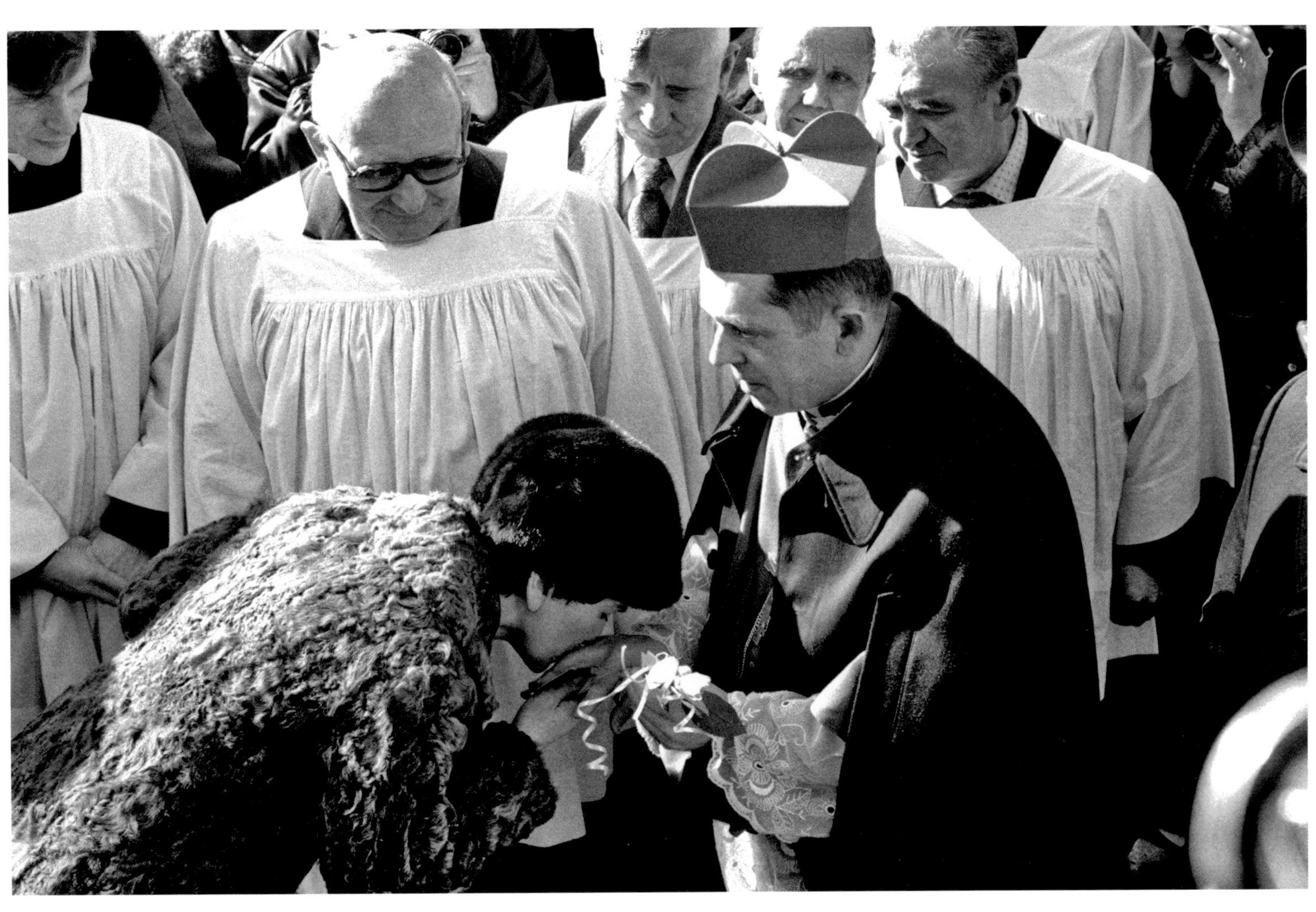

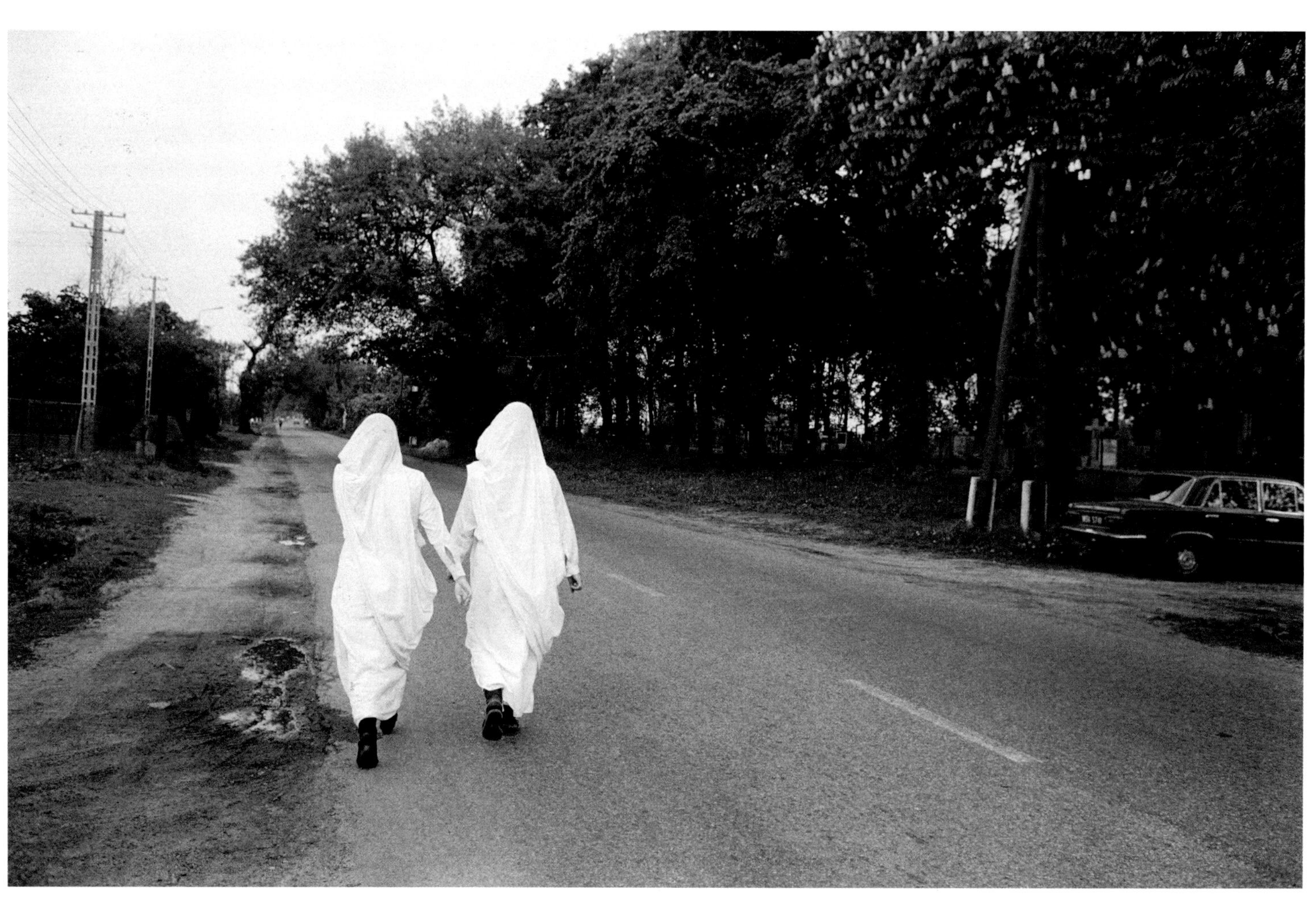

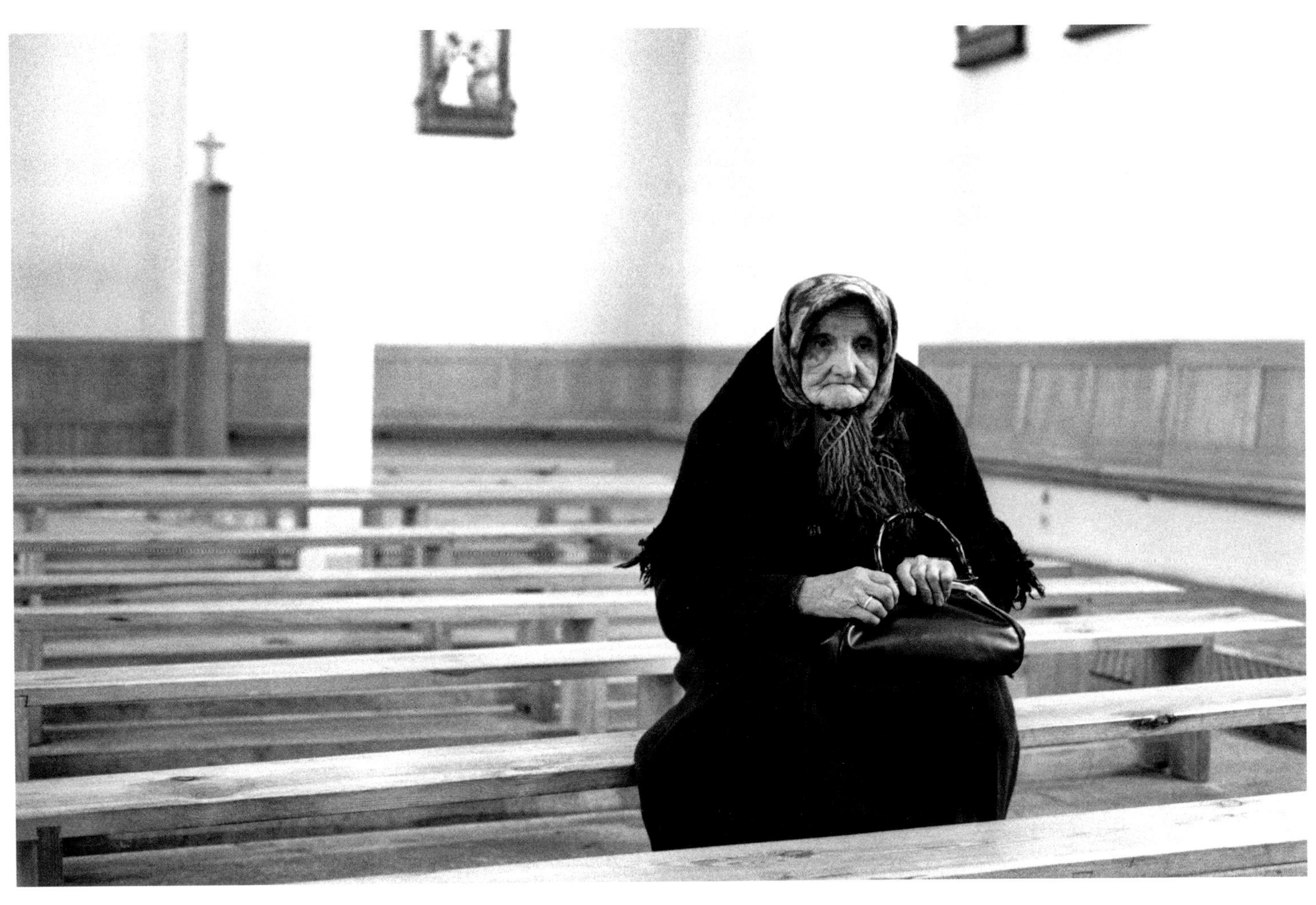

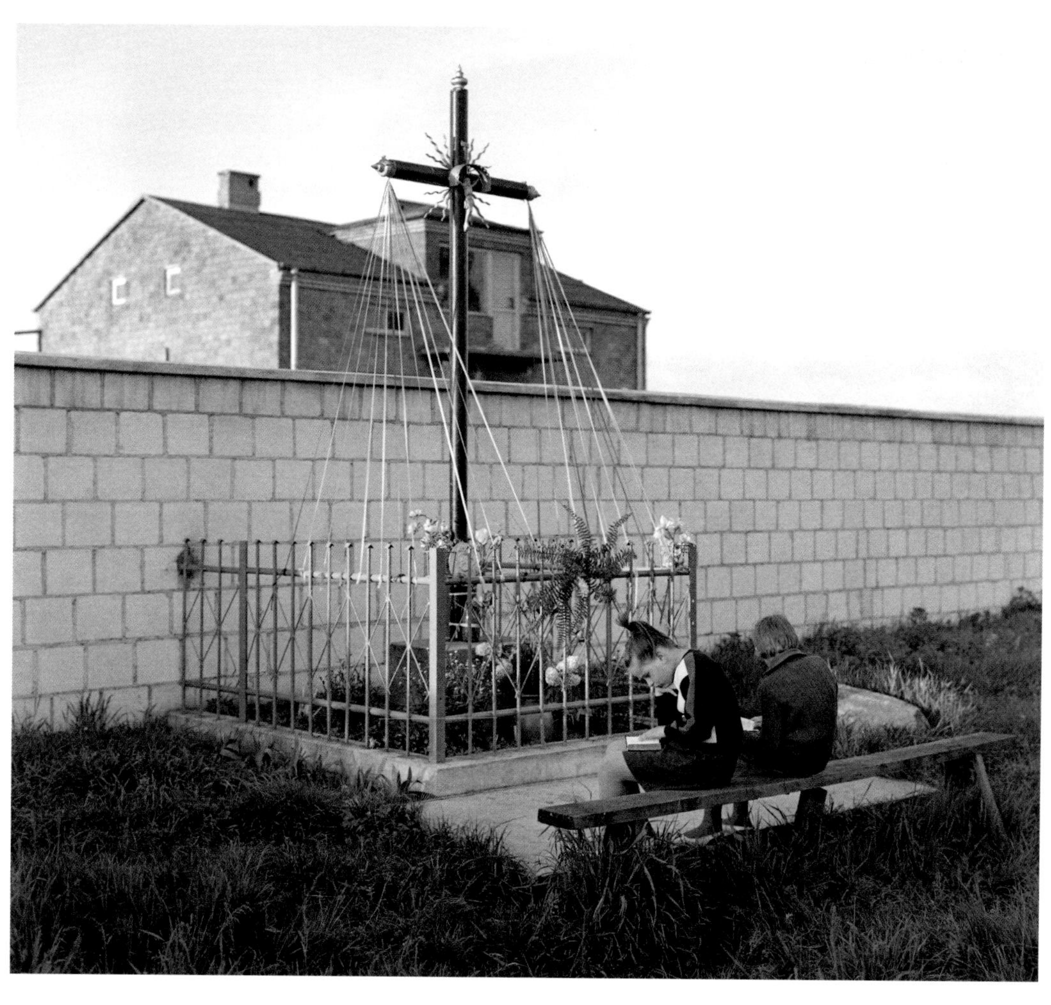

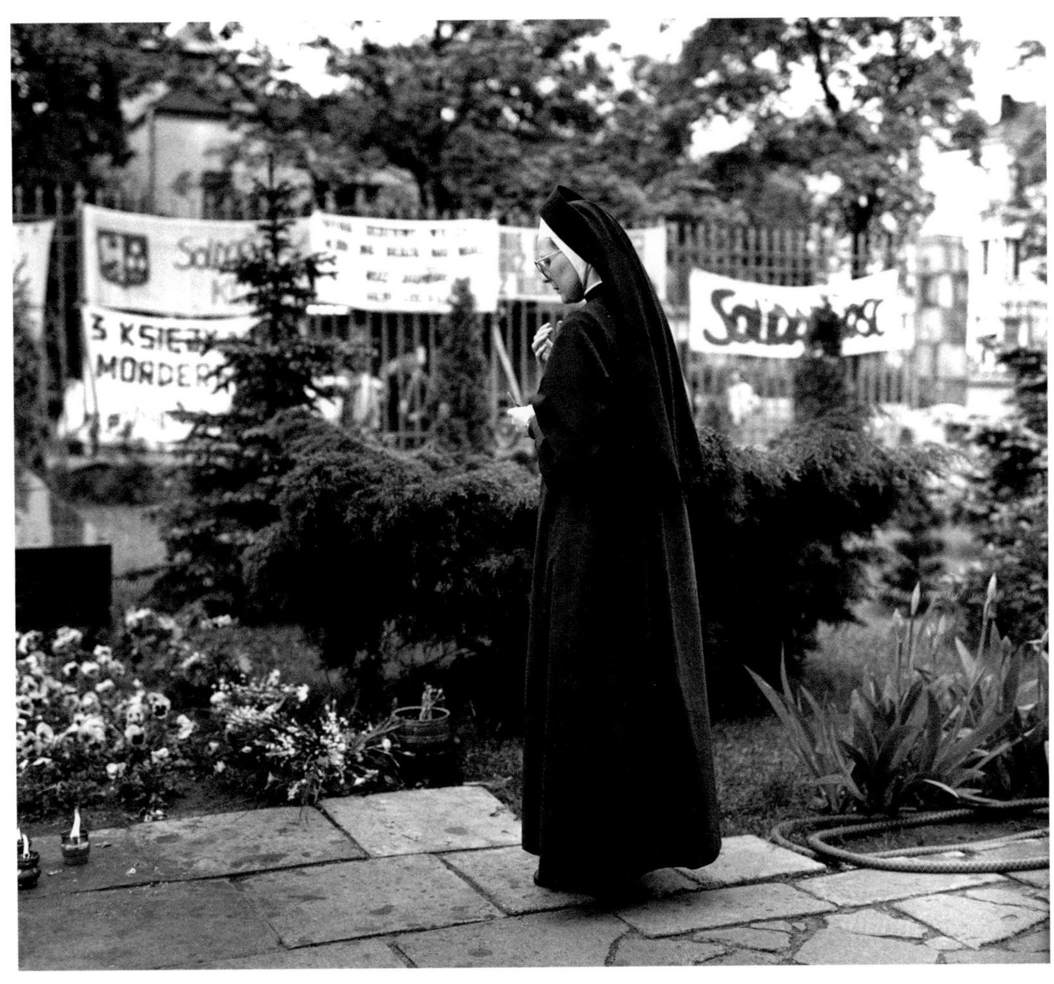

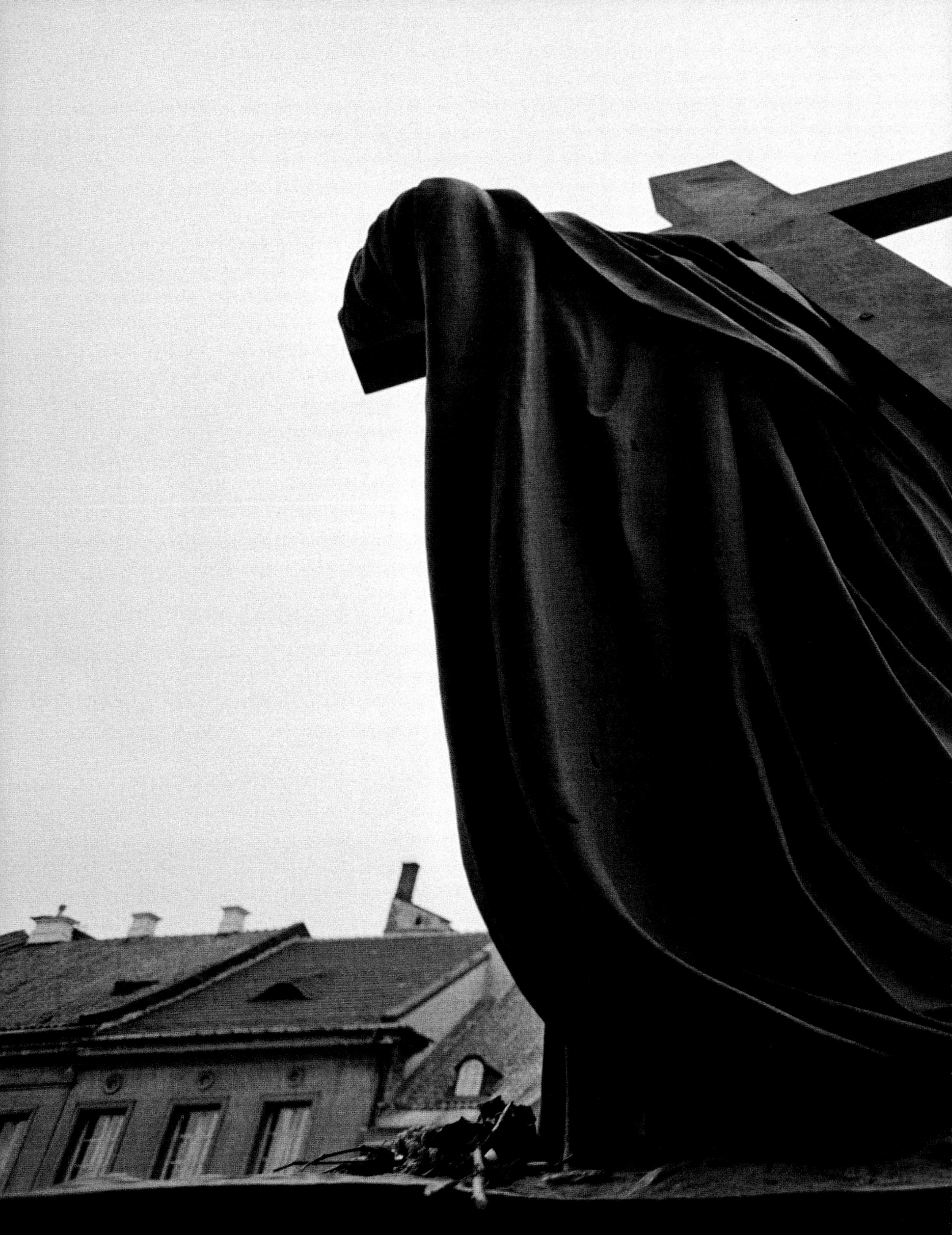

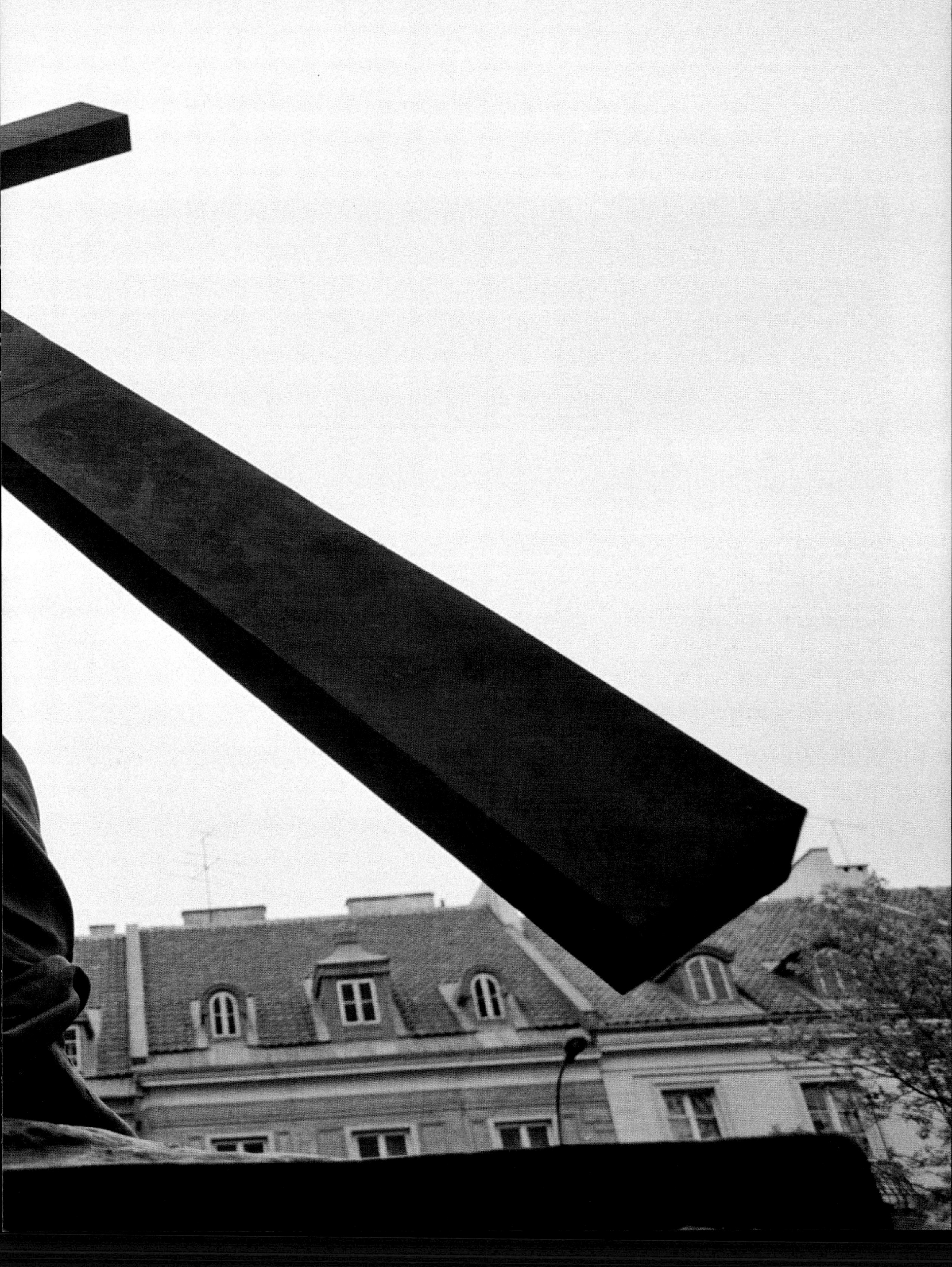

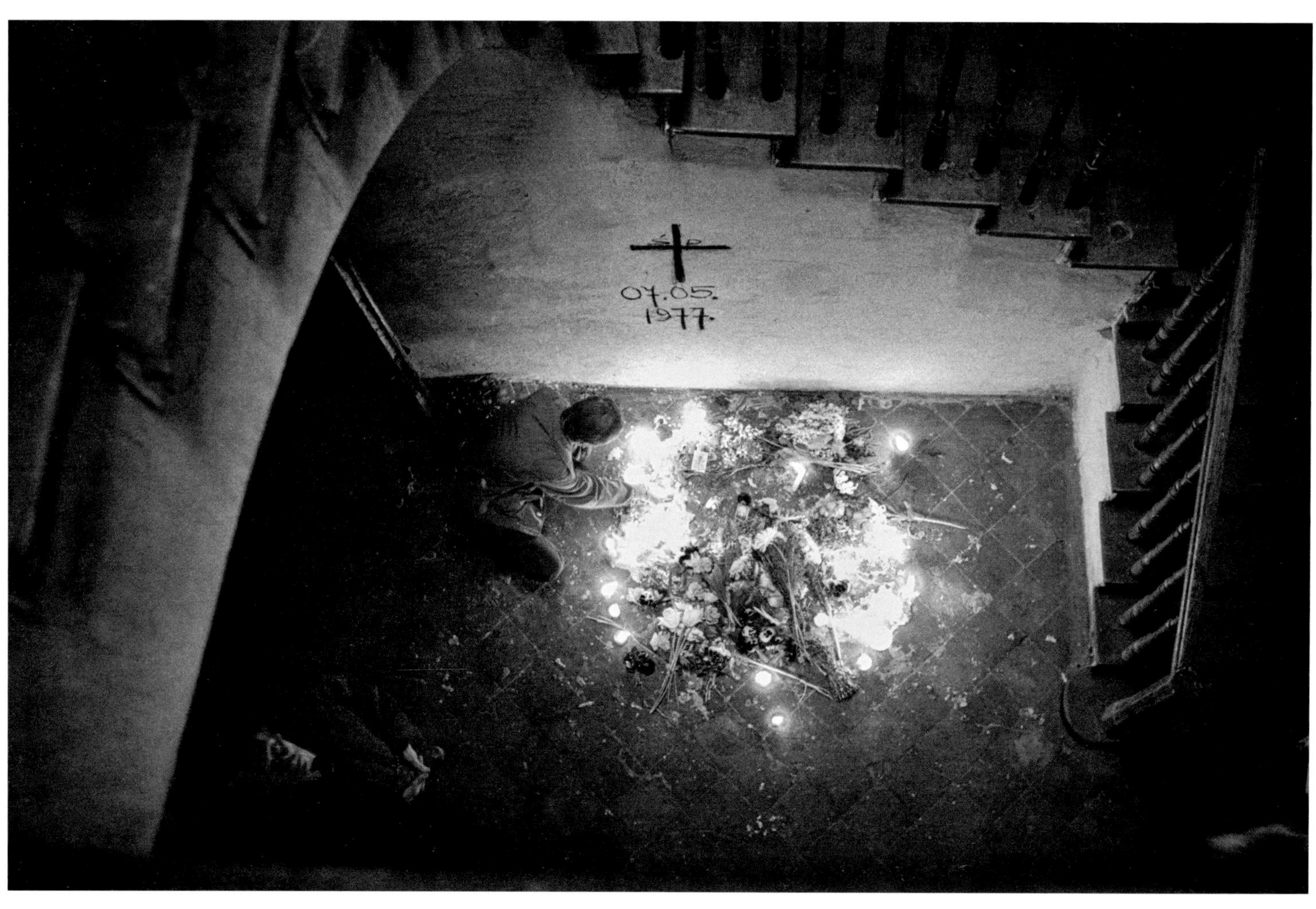
07.05.
1977.

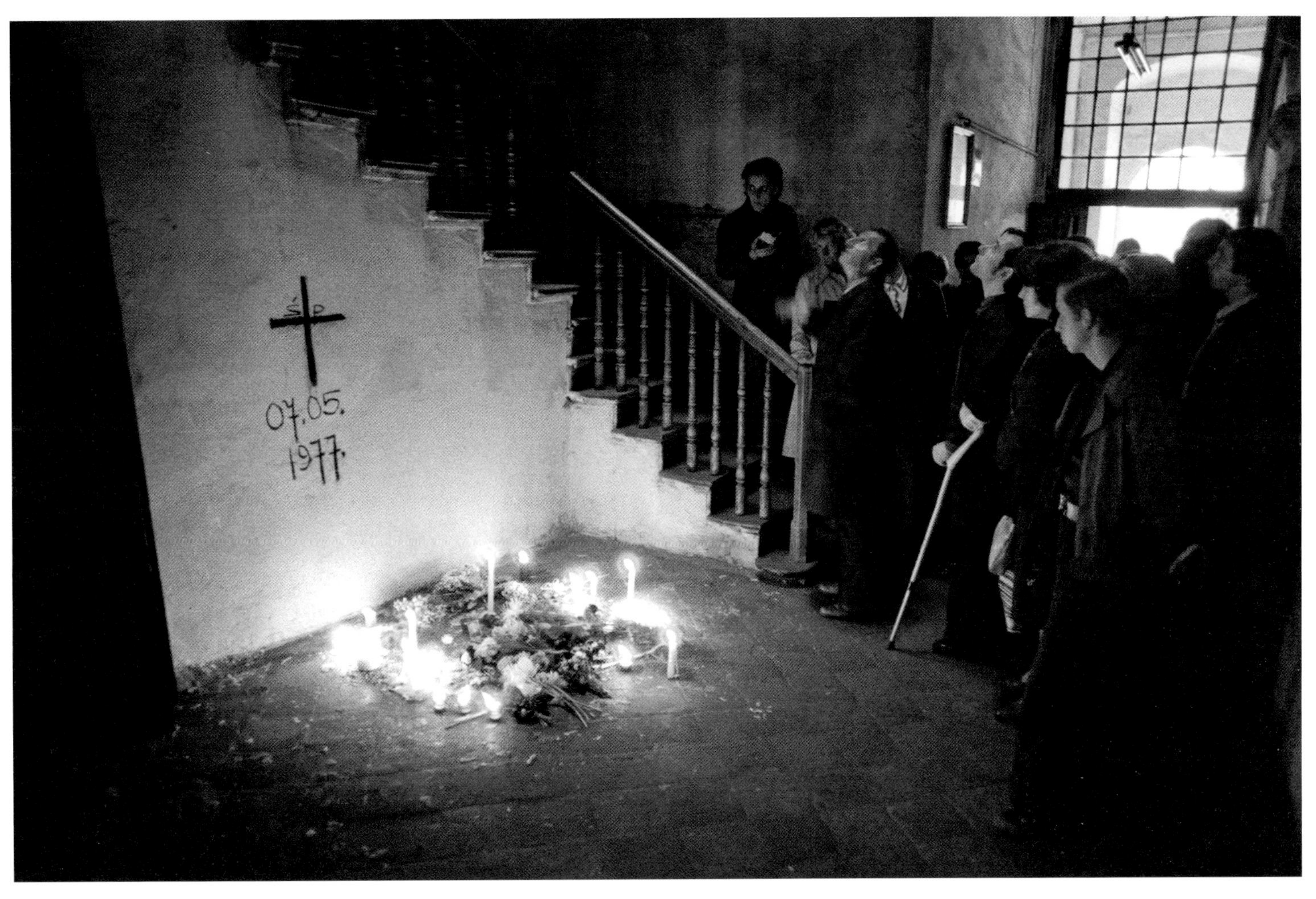
ŚP
07.05.
1977.

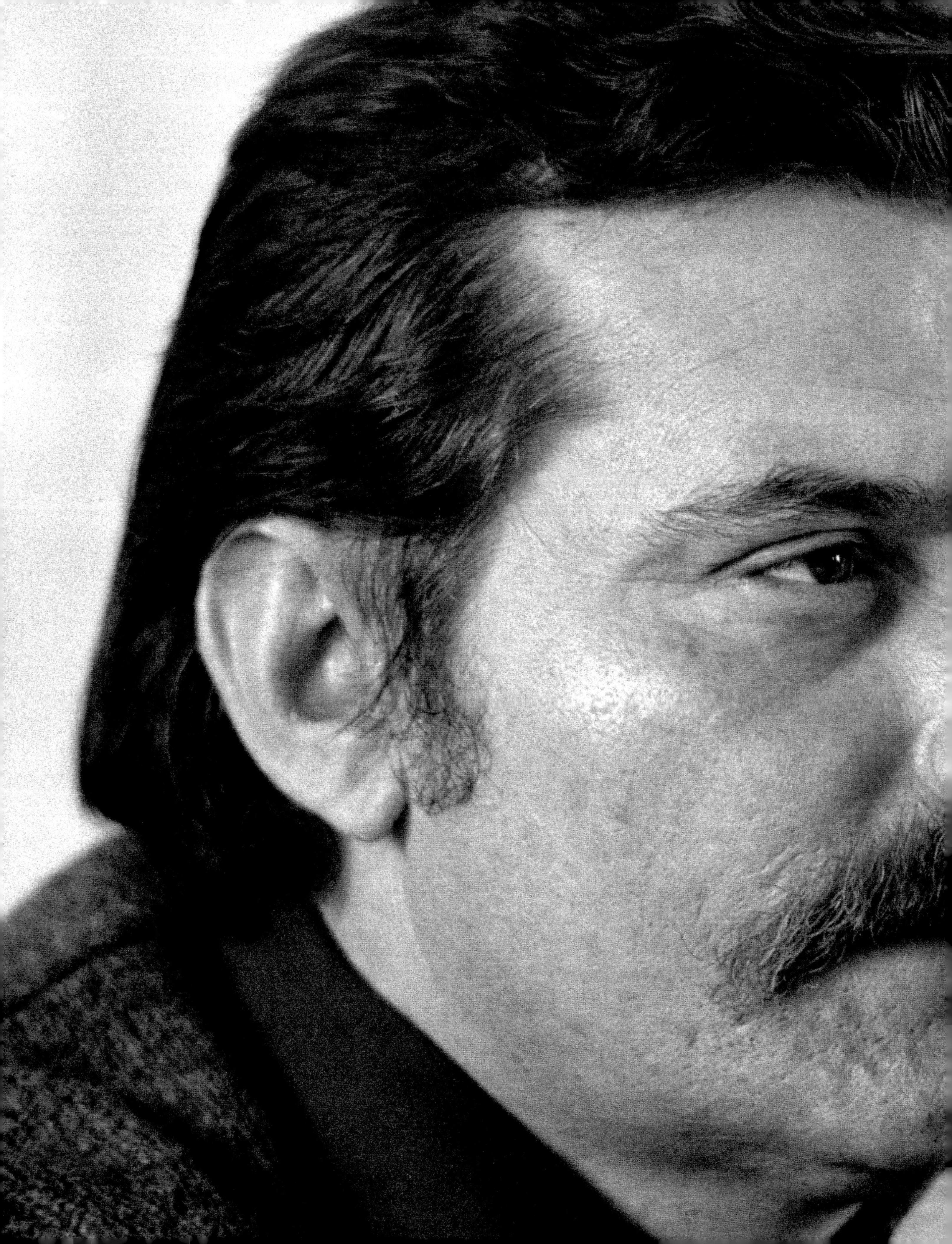

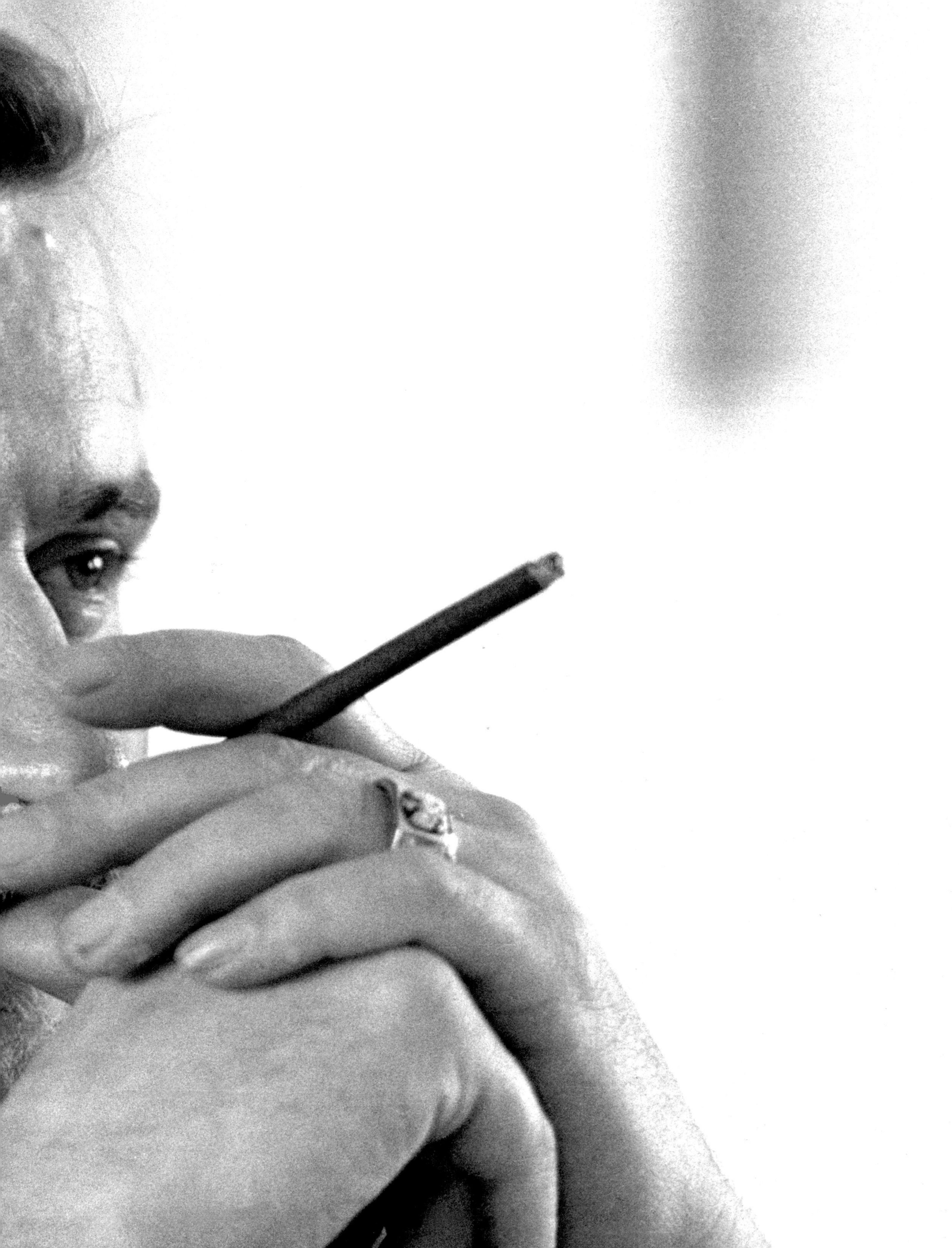

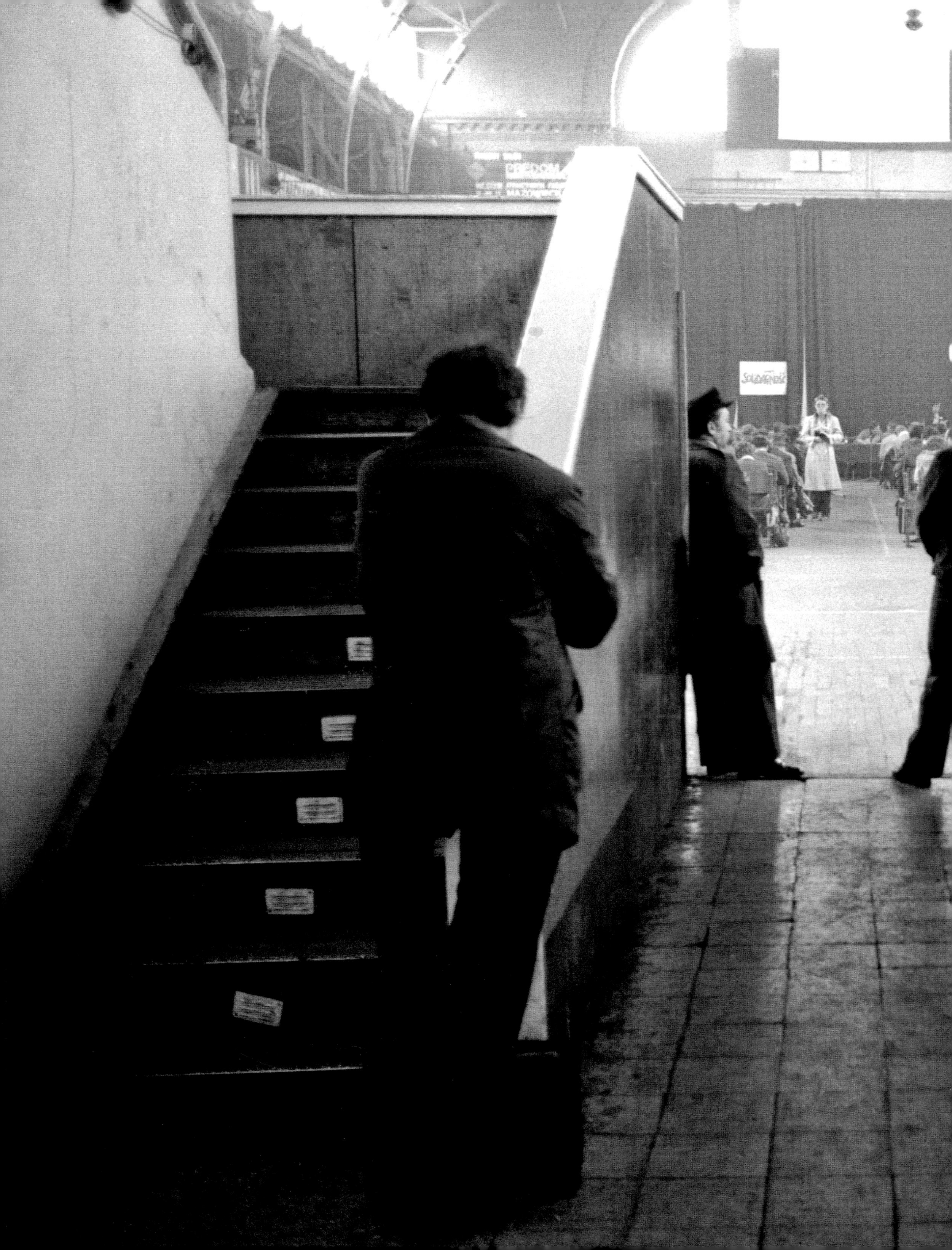

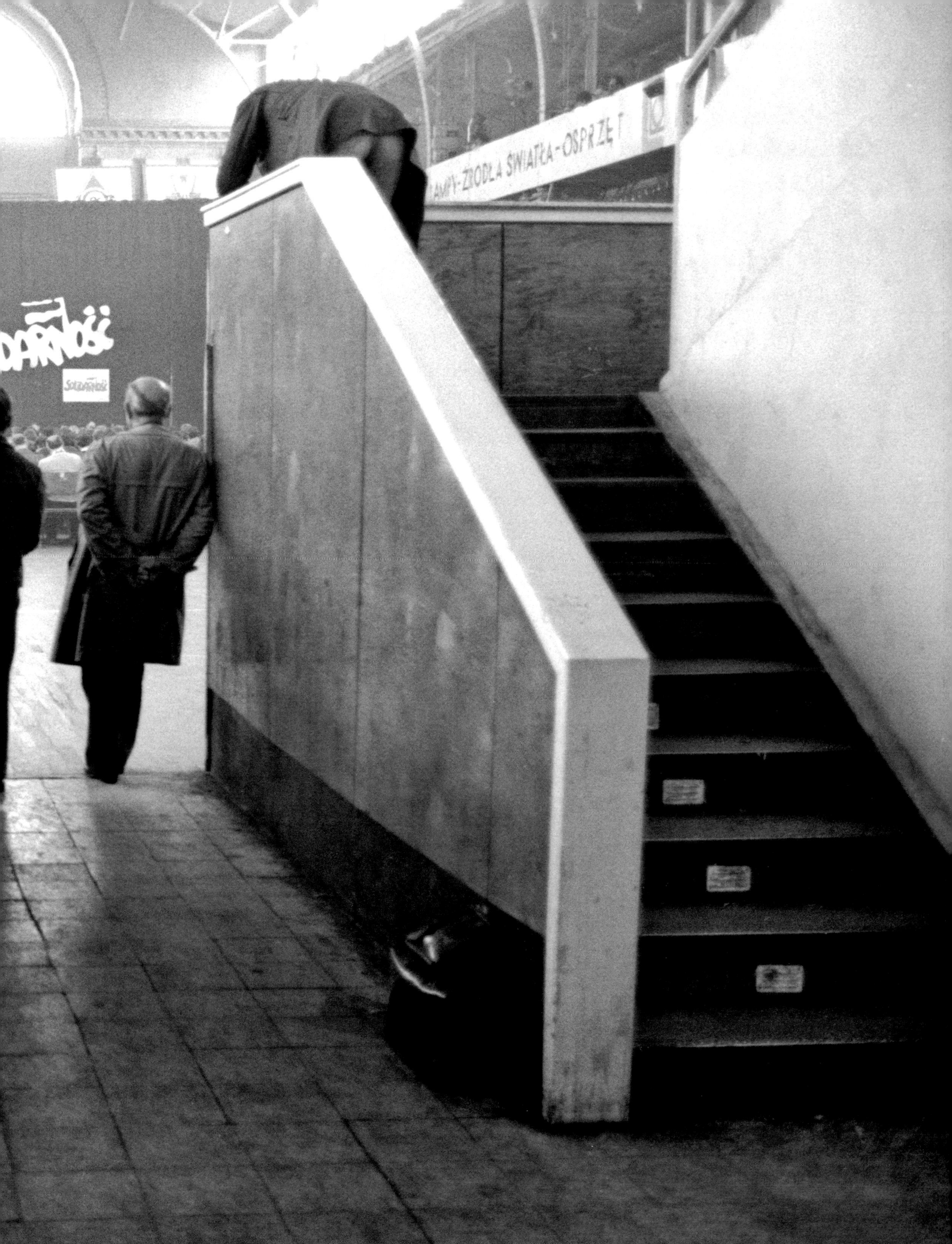
AMPY-ŹRÓDŁA ŚWIATŁA-OSPRZĘT
DARNOŚĆ

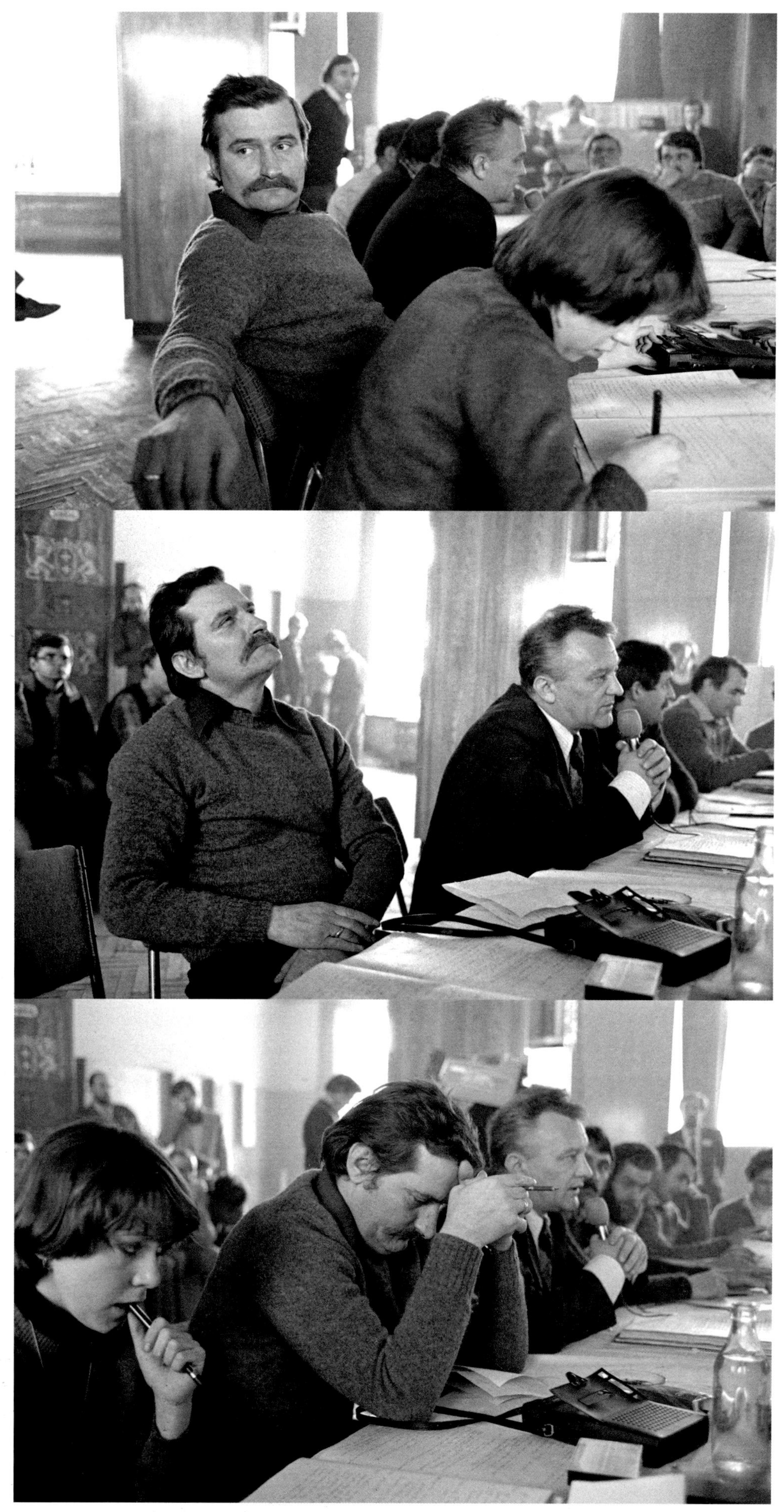

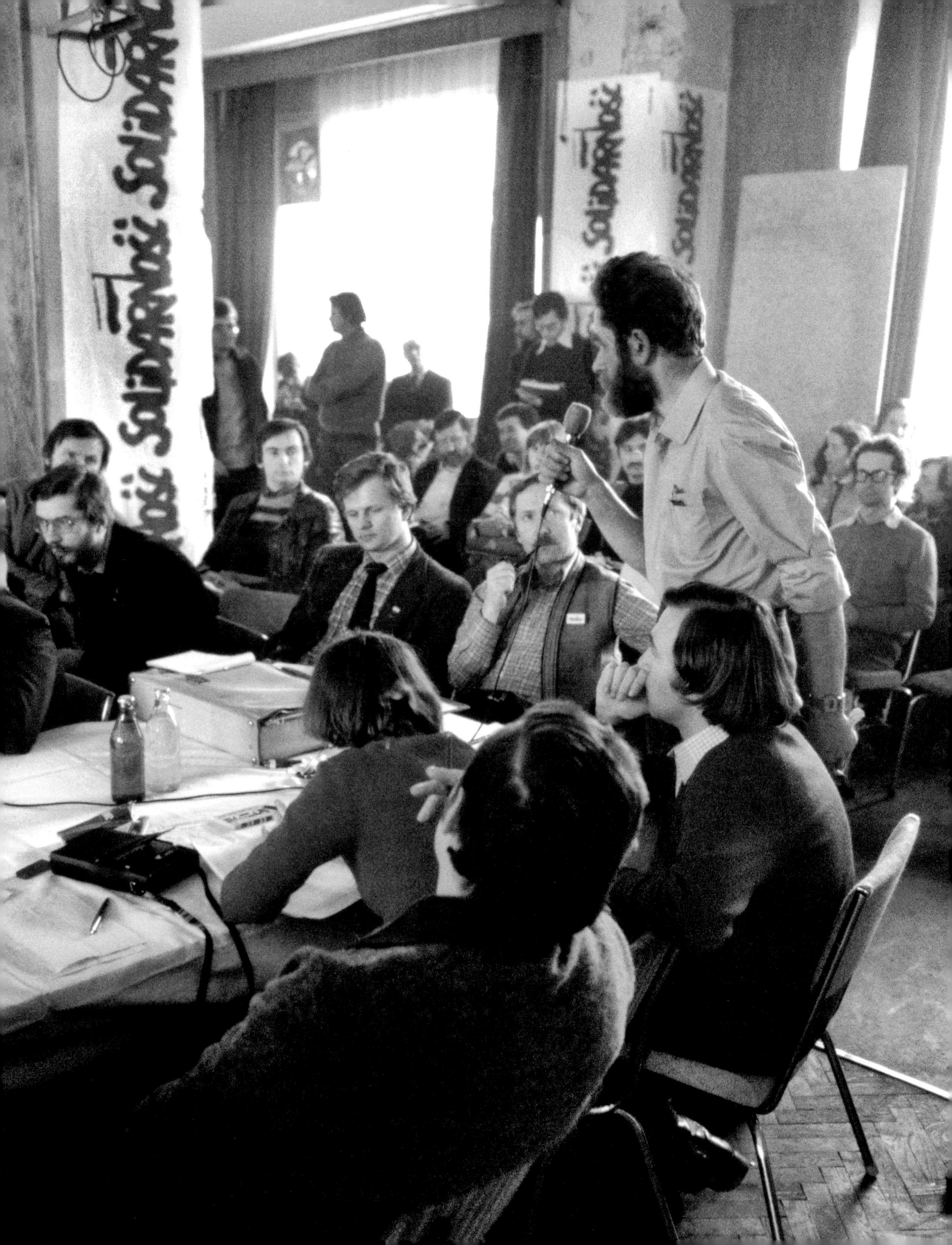
Solidarność Solidarność
Solidarność
Solidarność

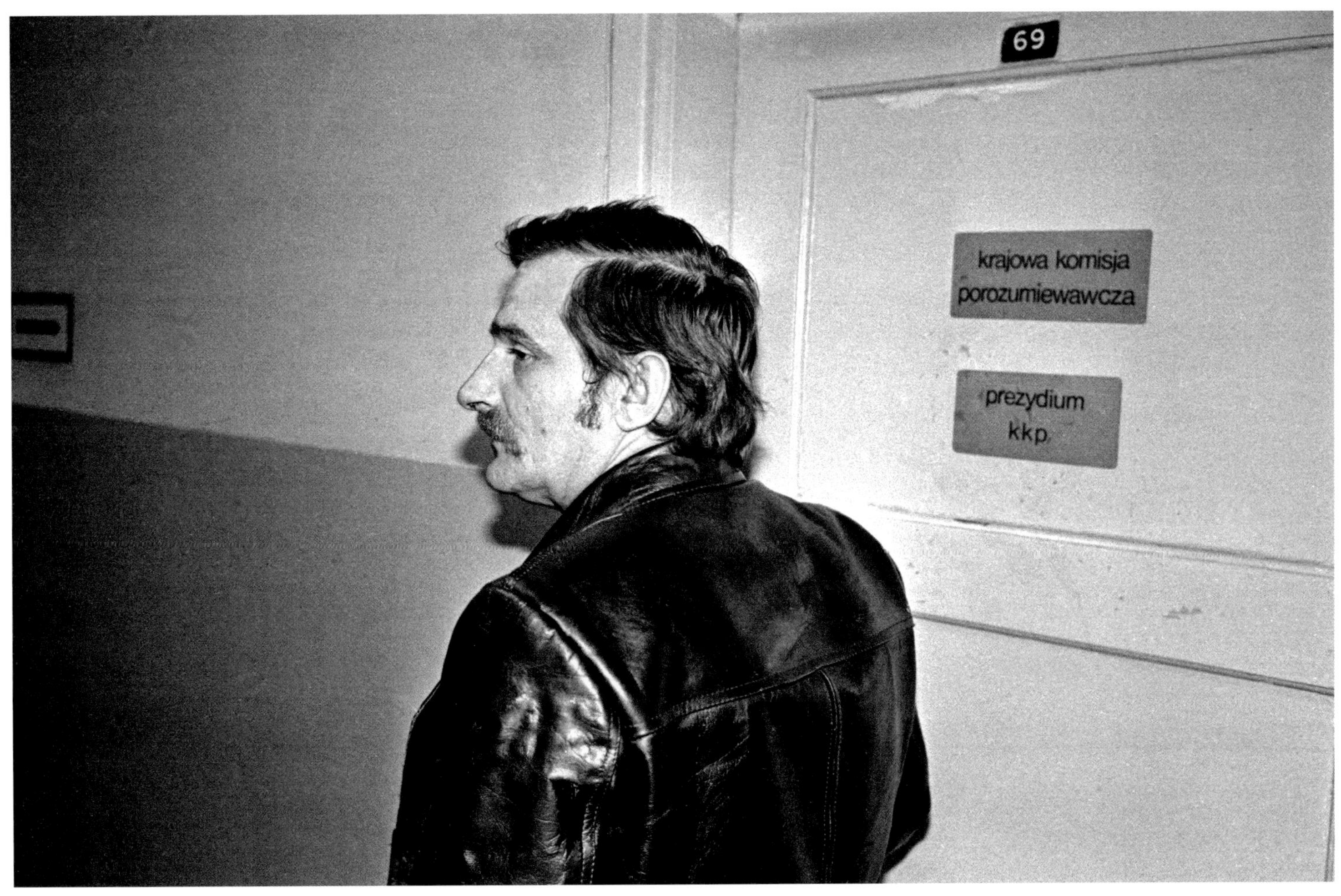
69
krajowa komisja
porozumiewawcza
prezydium
kkp

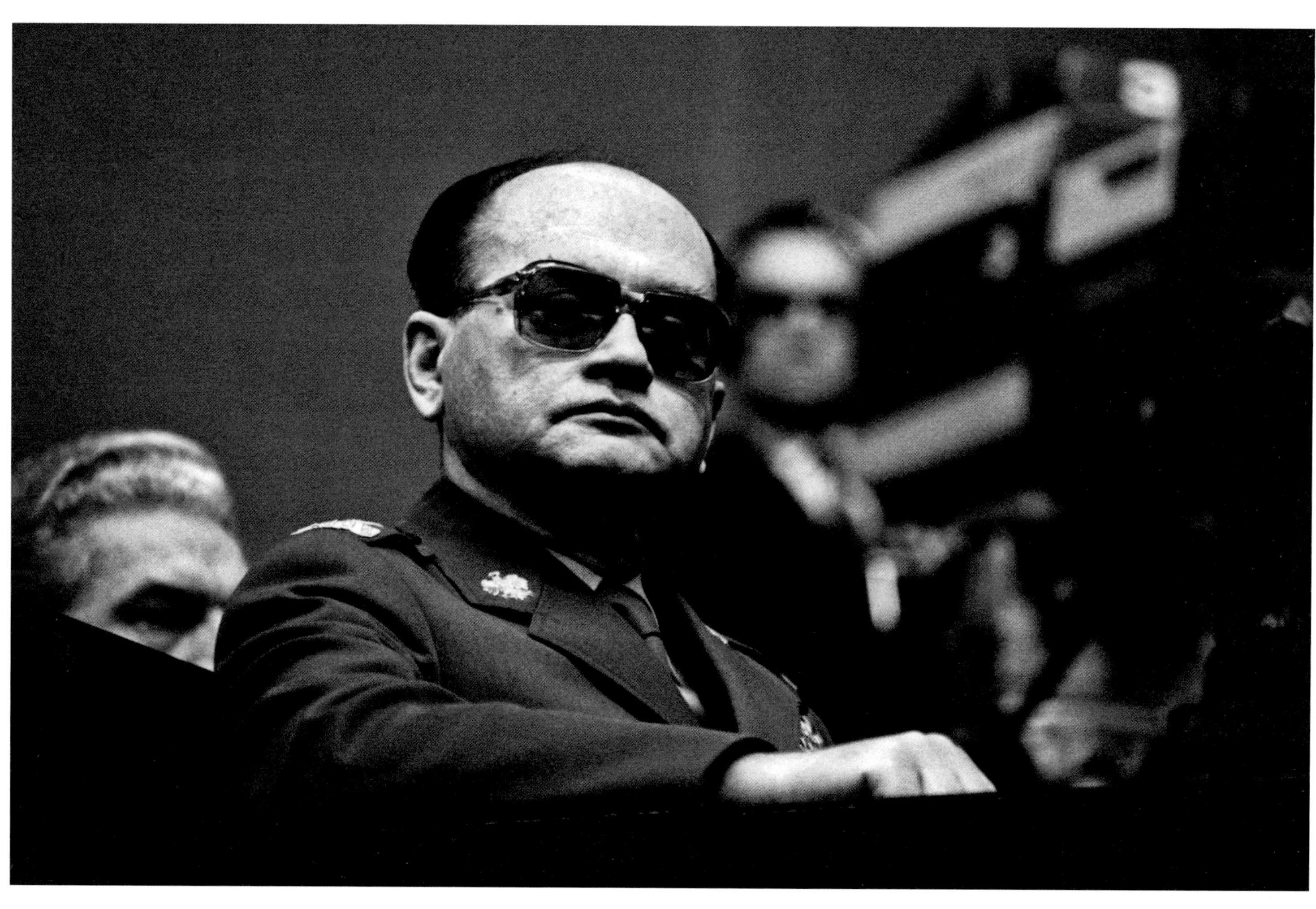

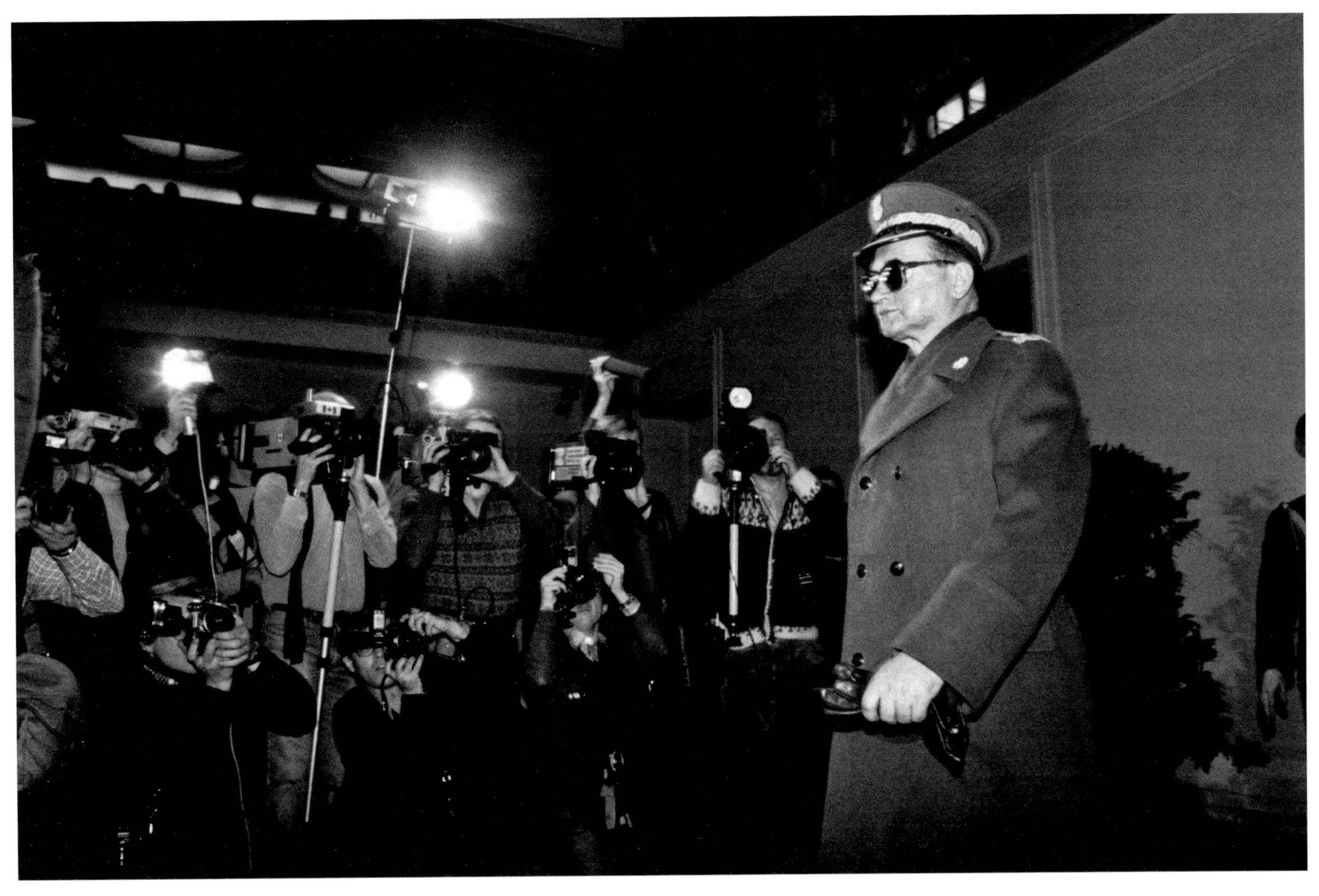

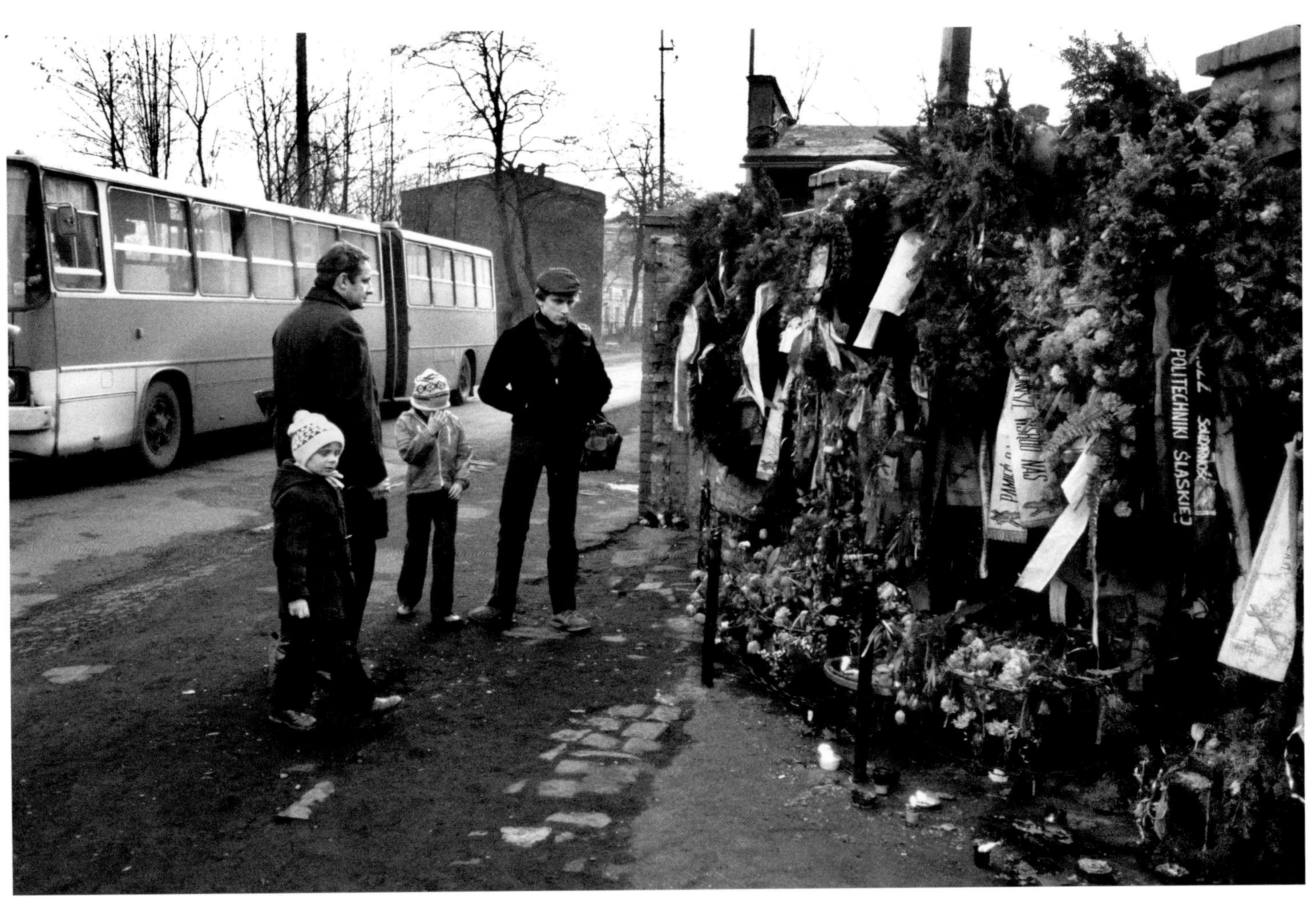
POLITECHNIKI ŚLĄSKIEJ

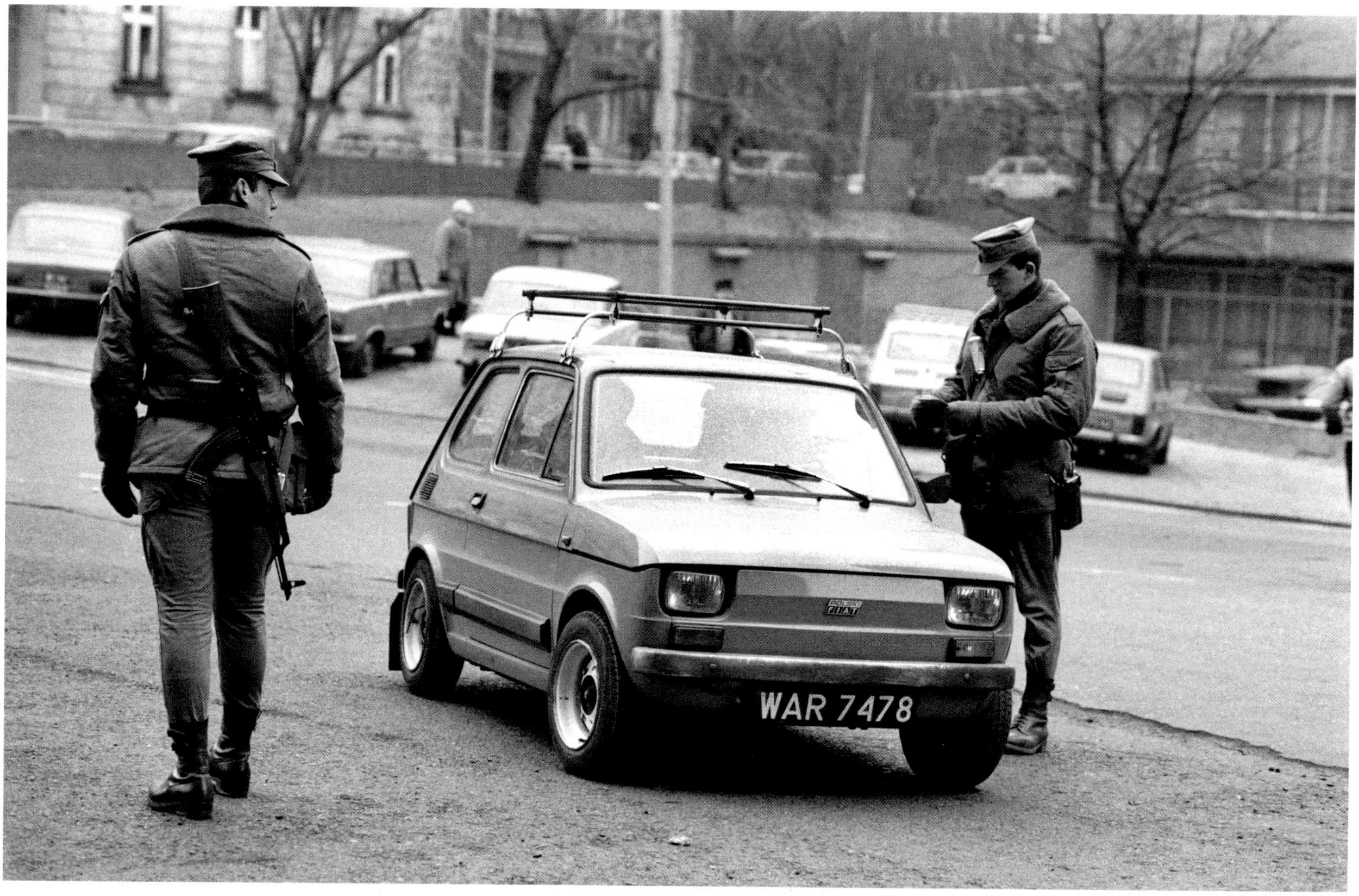

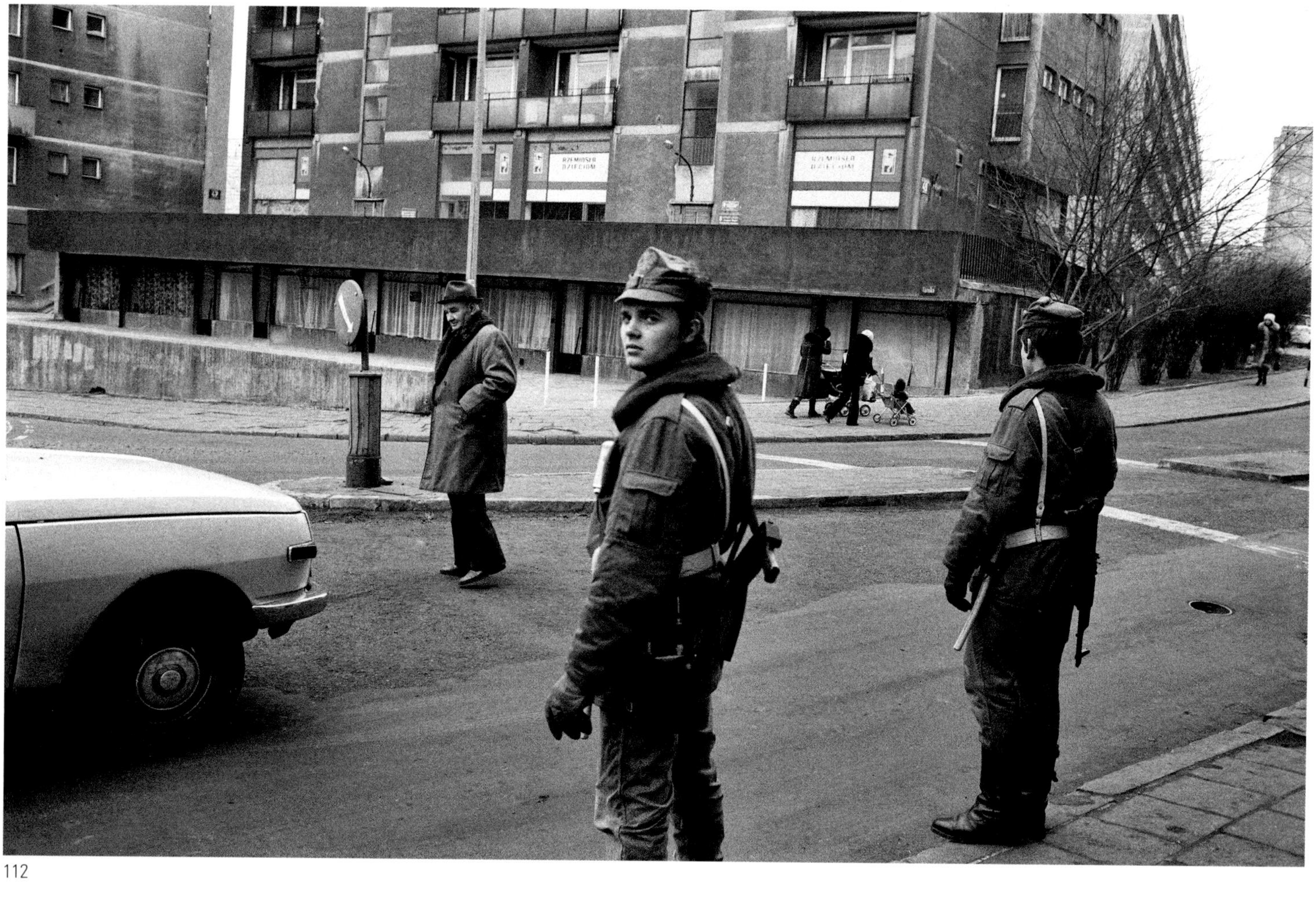

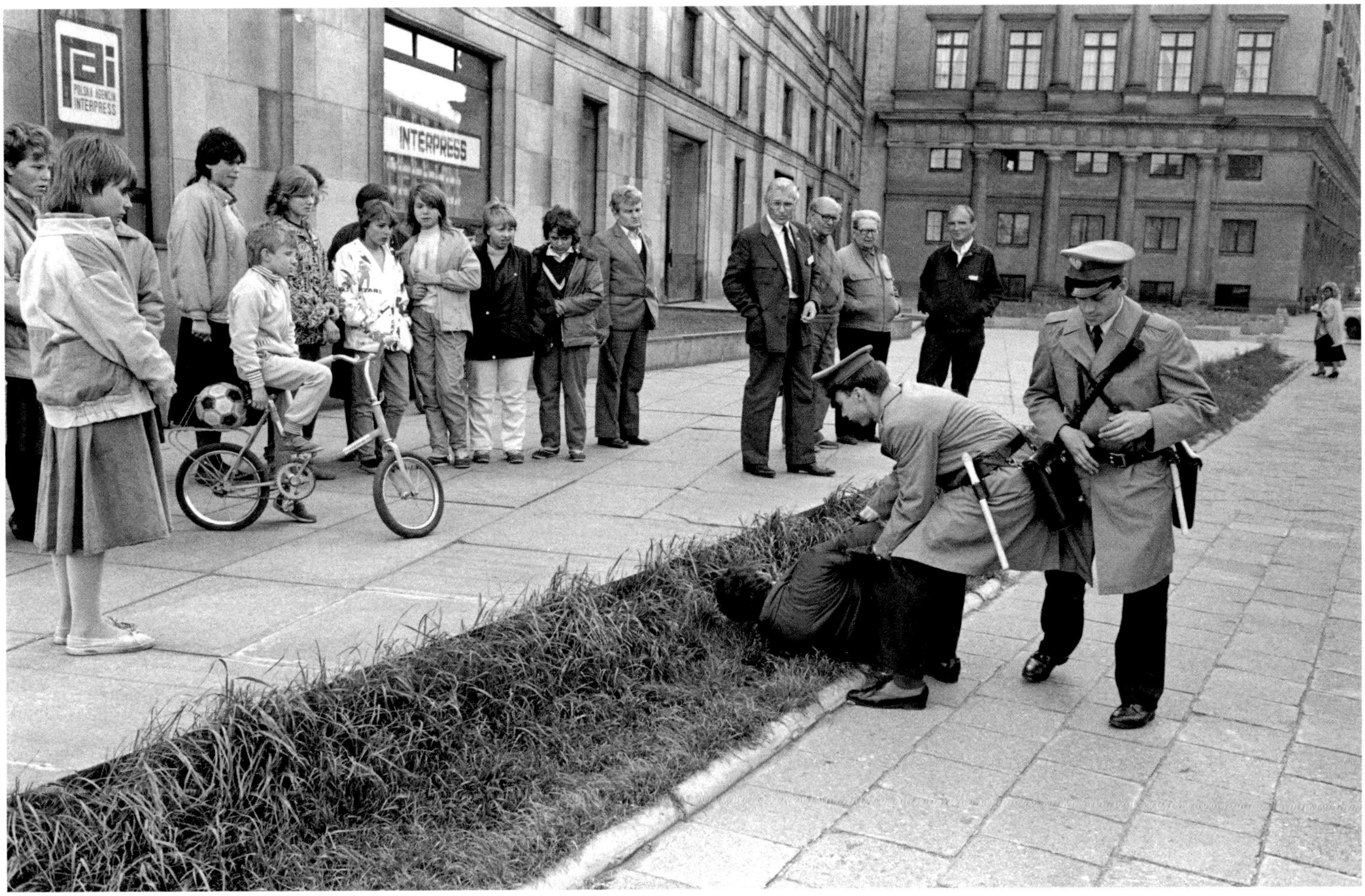

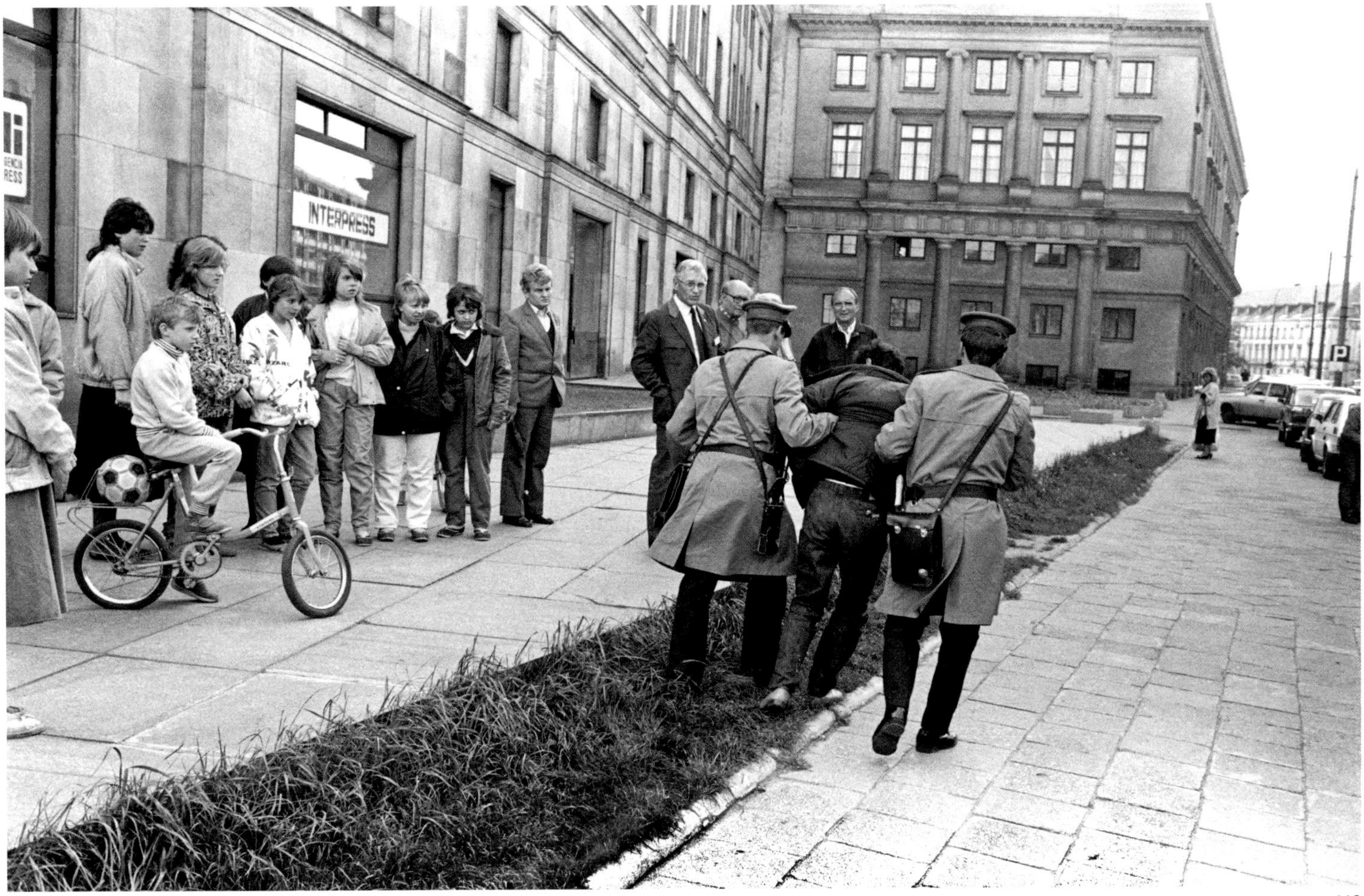

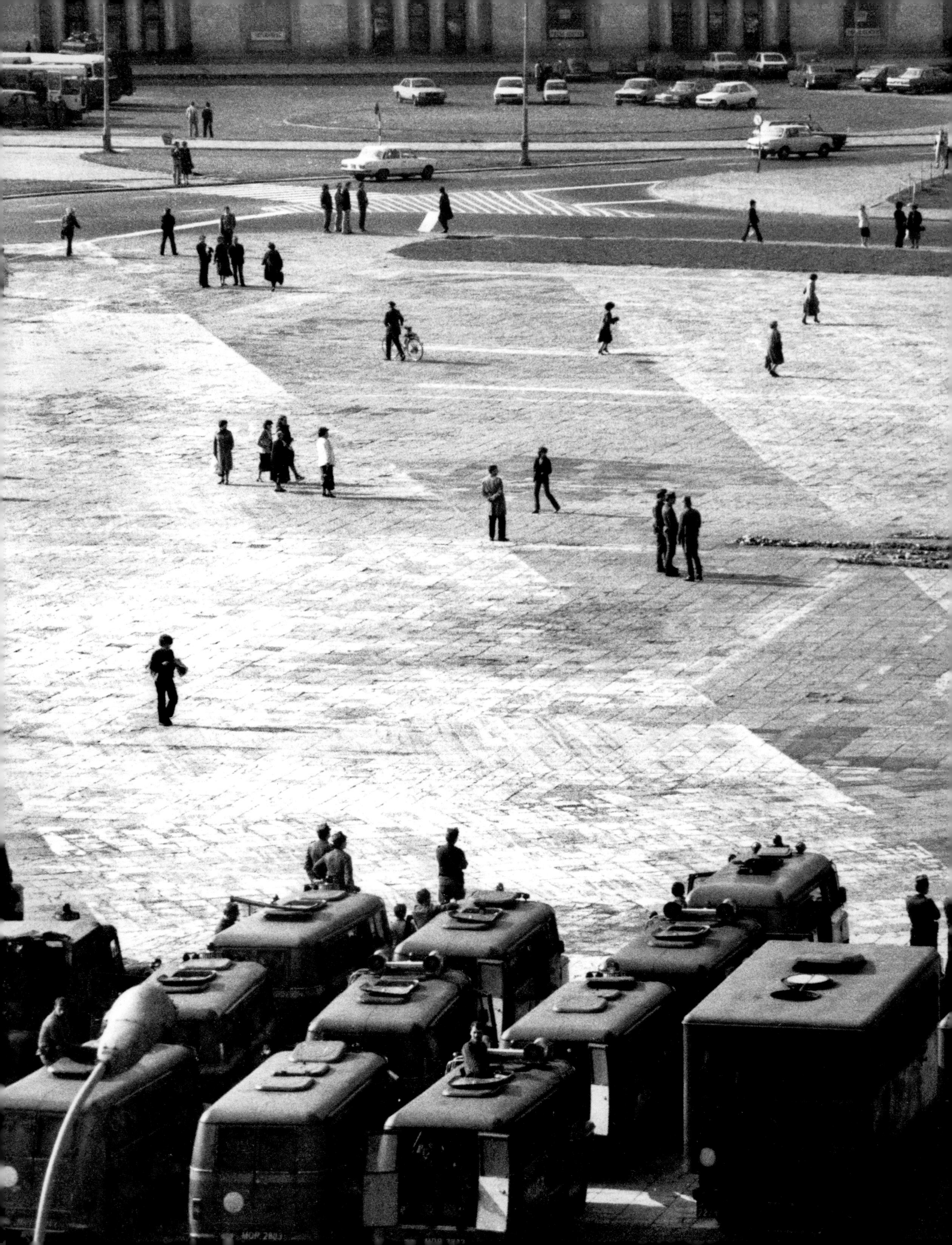

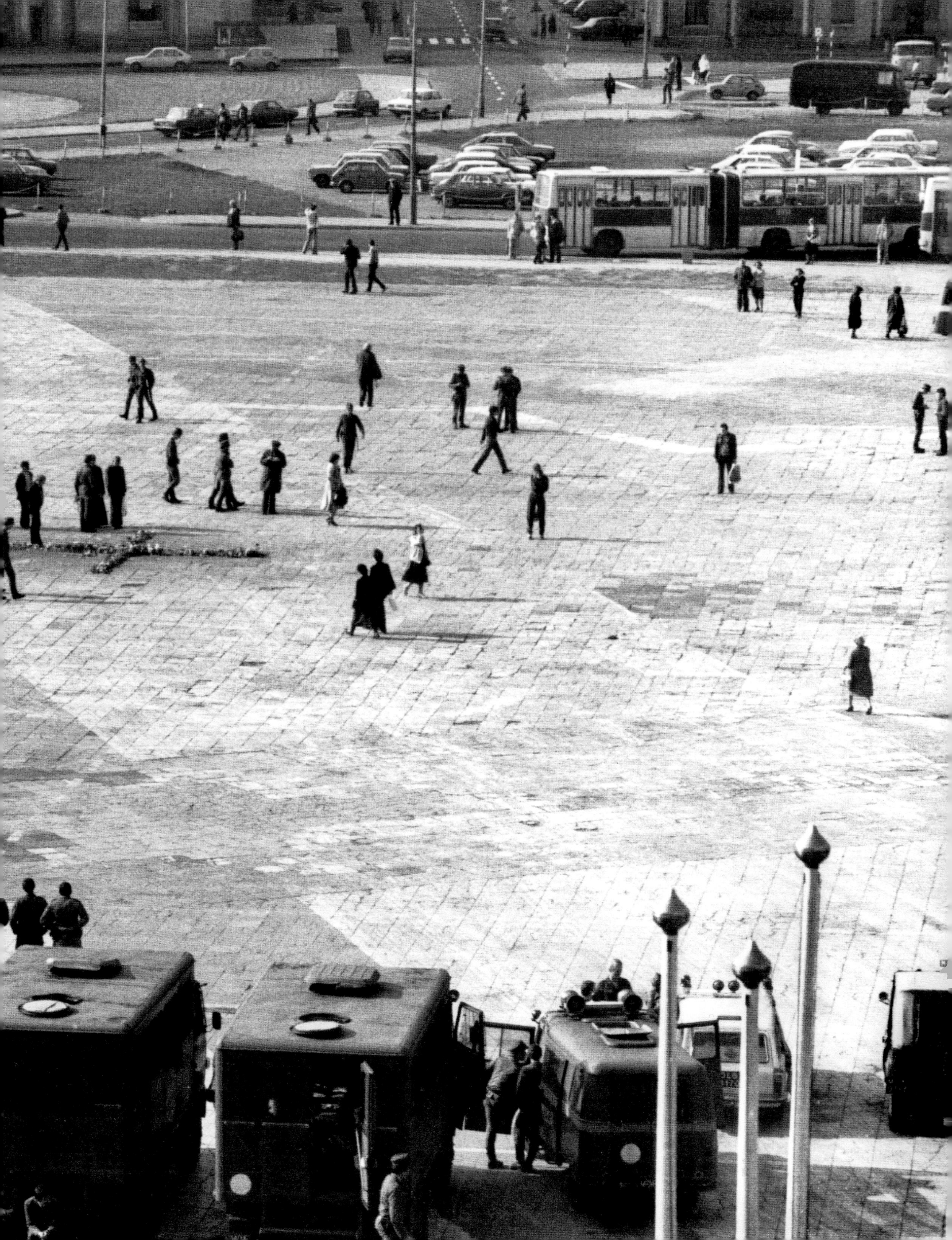

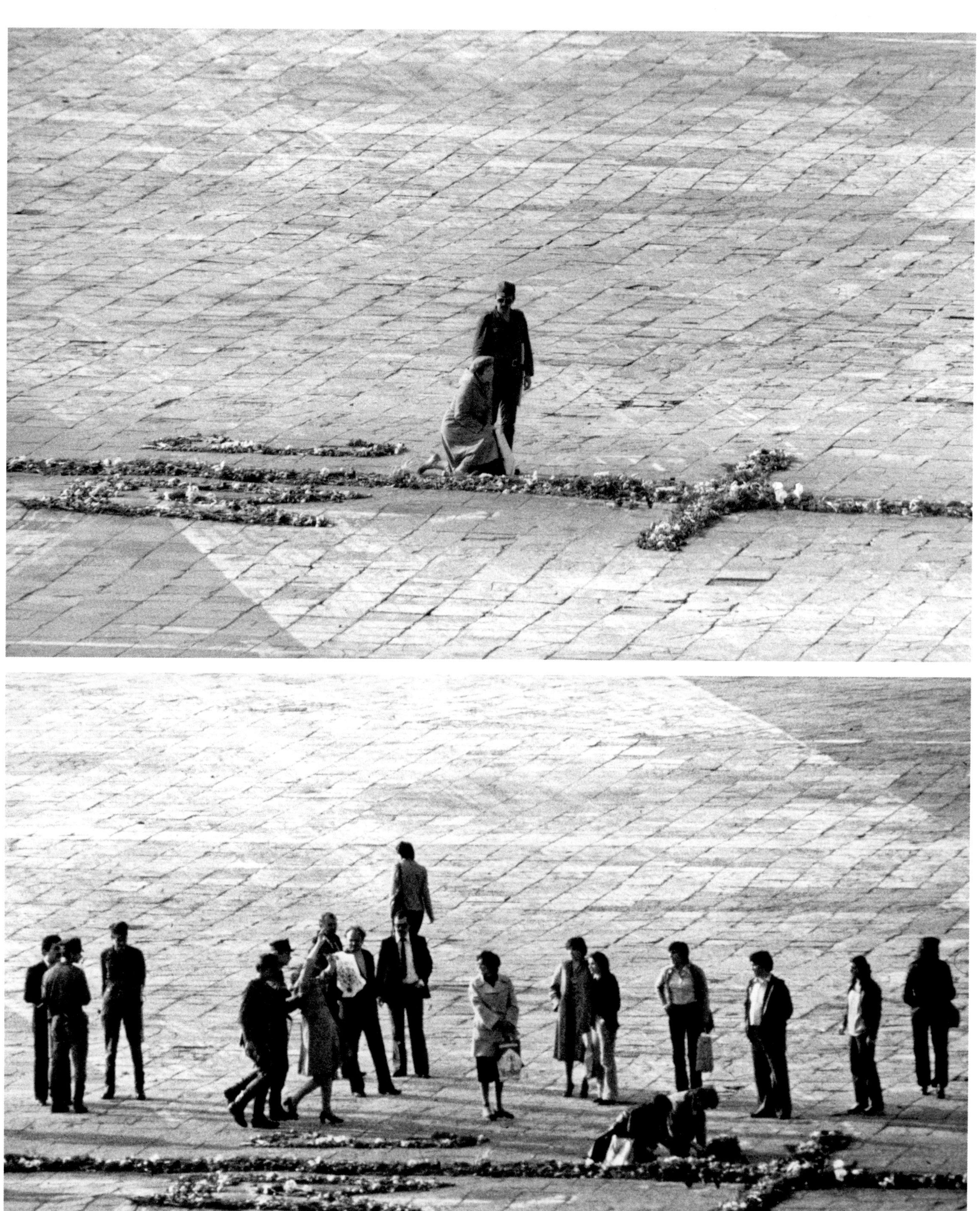

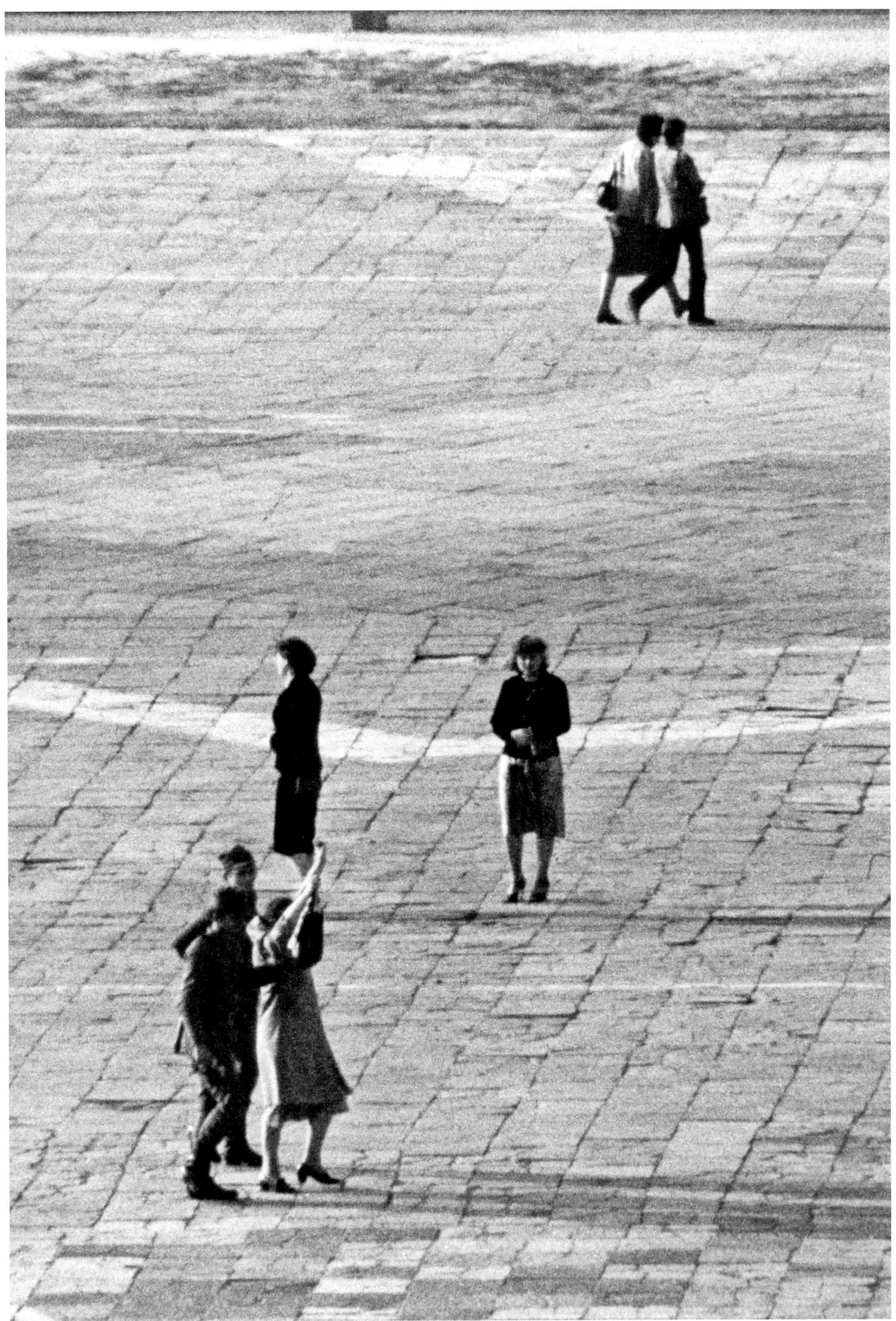

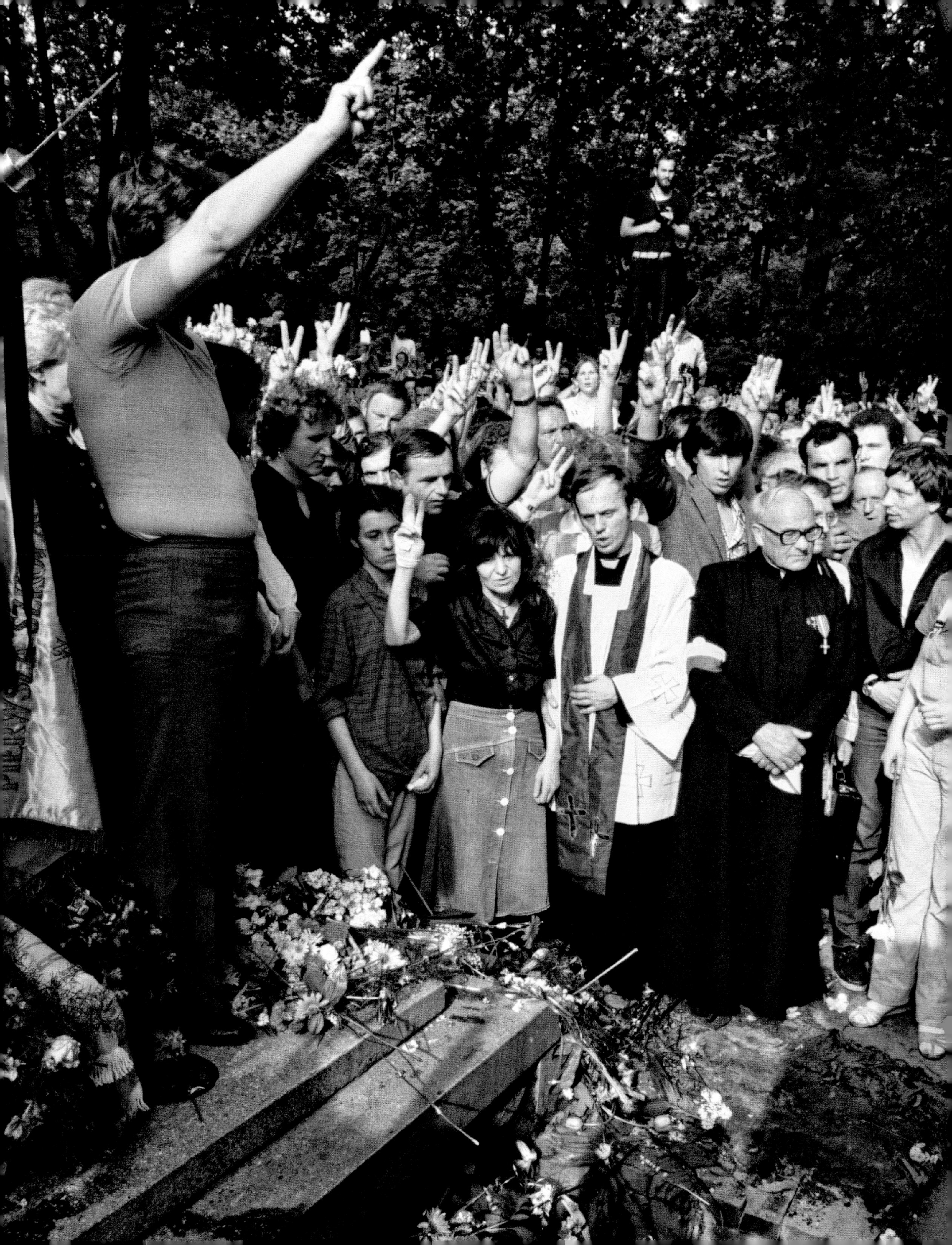

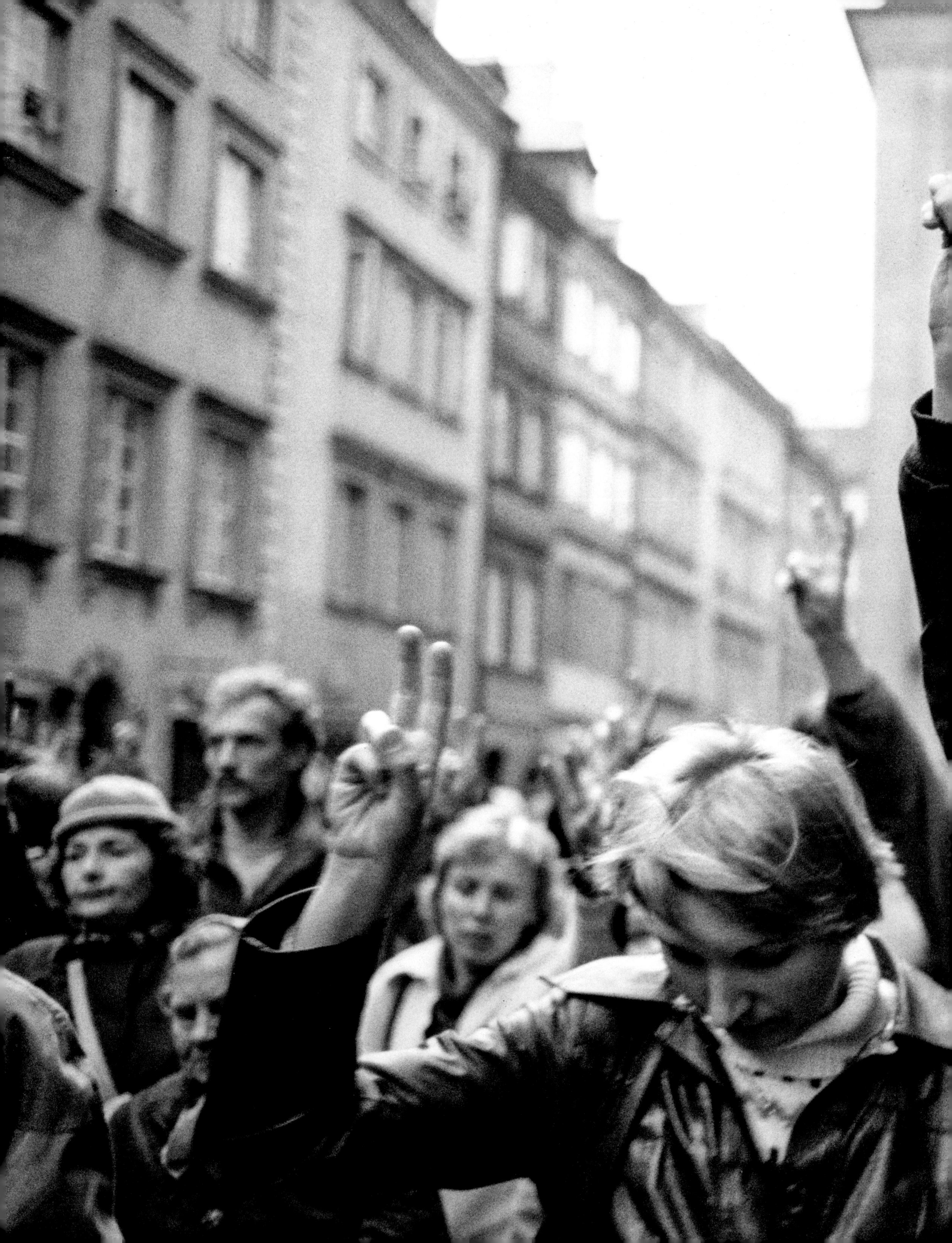

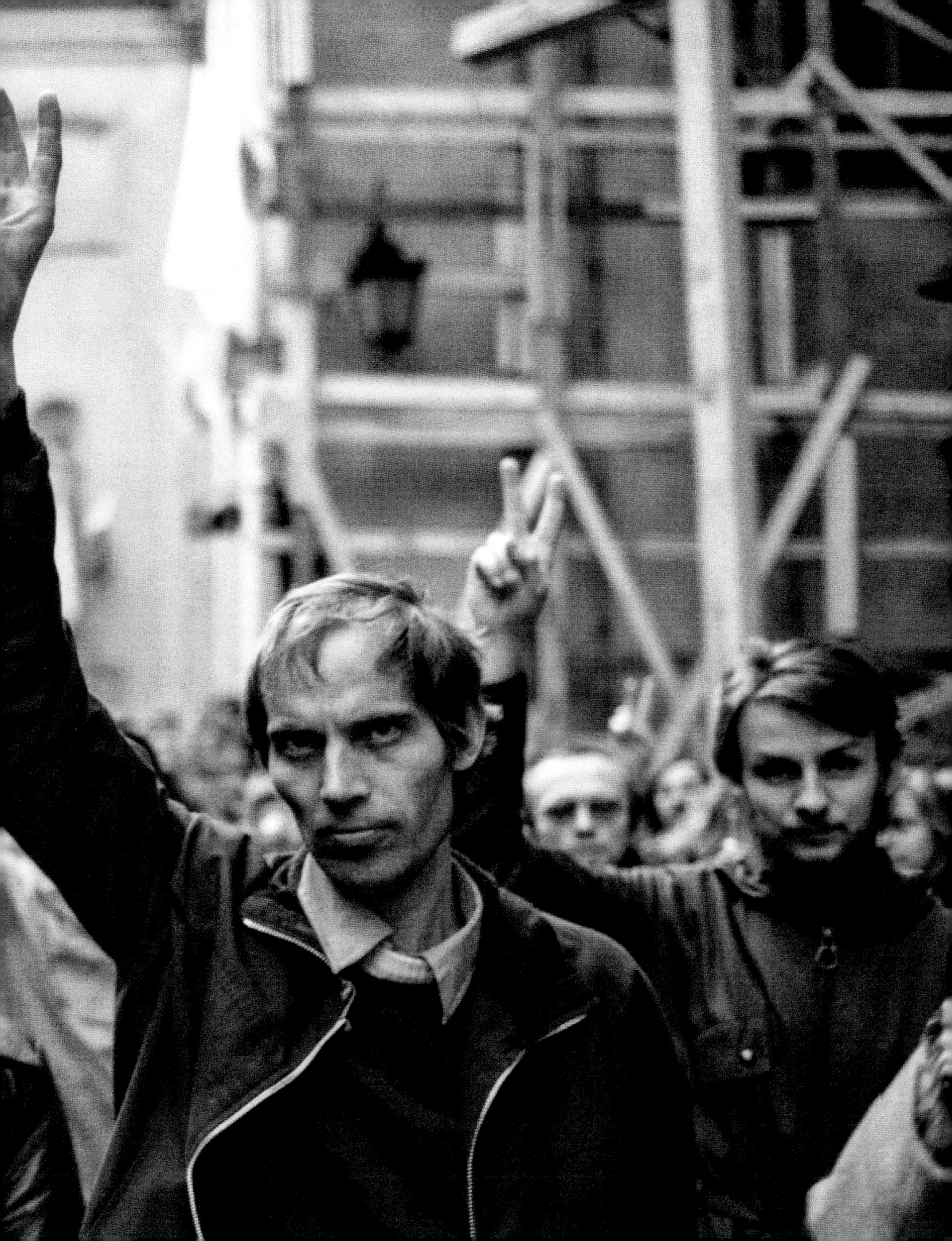

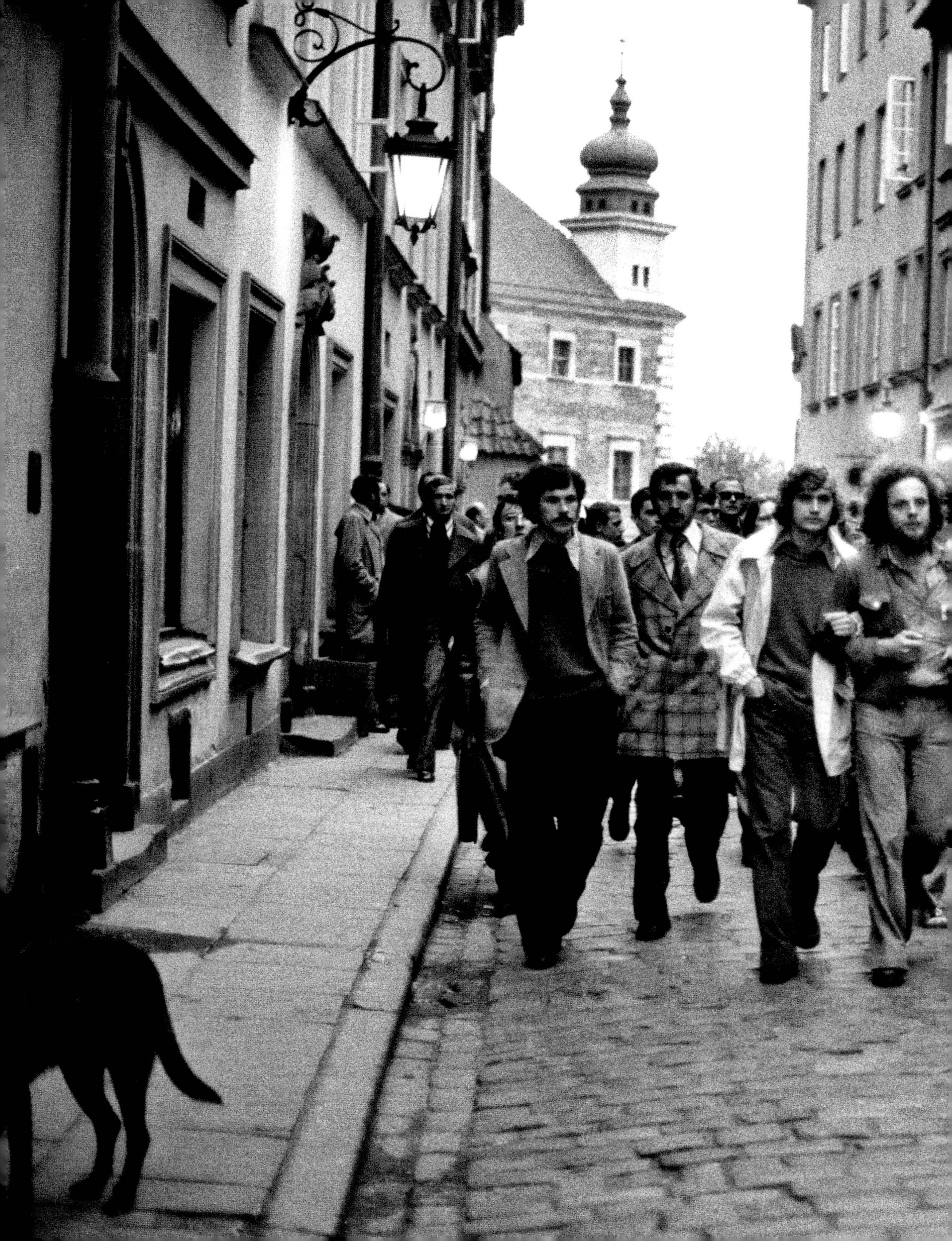

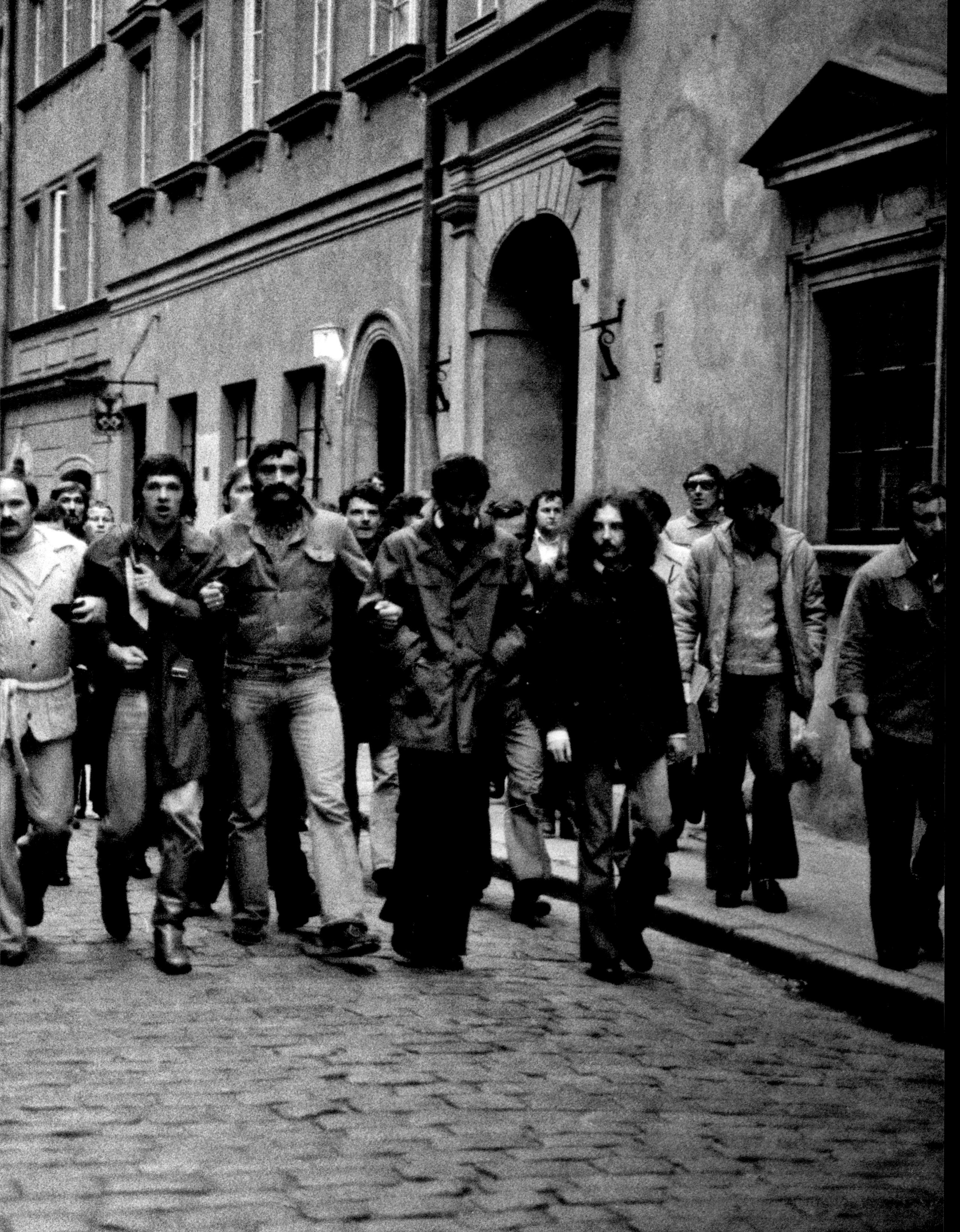

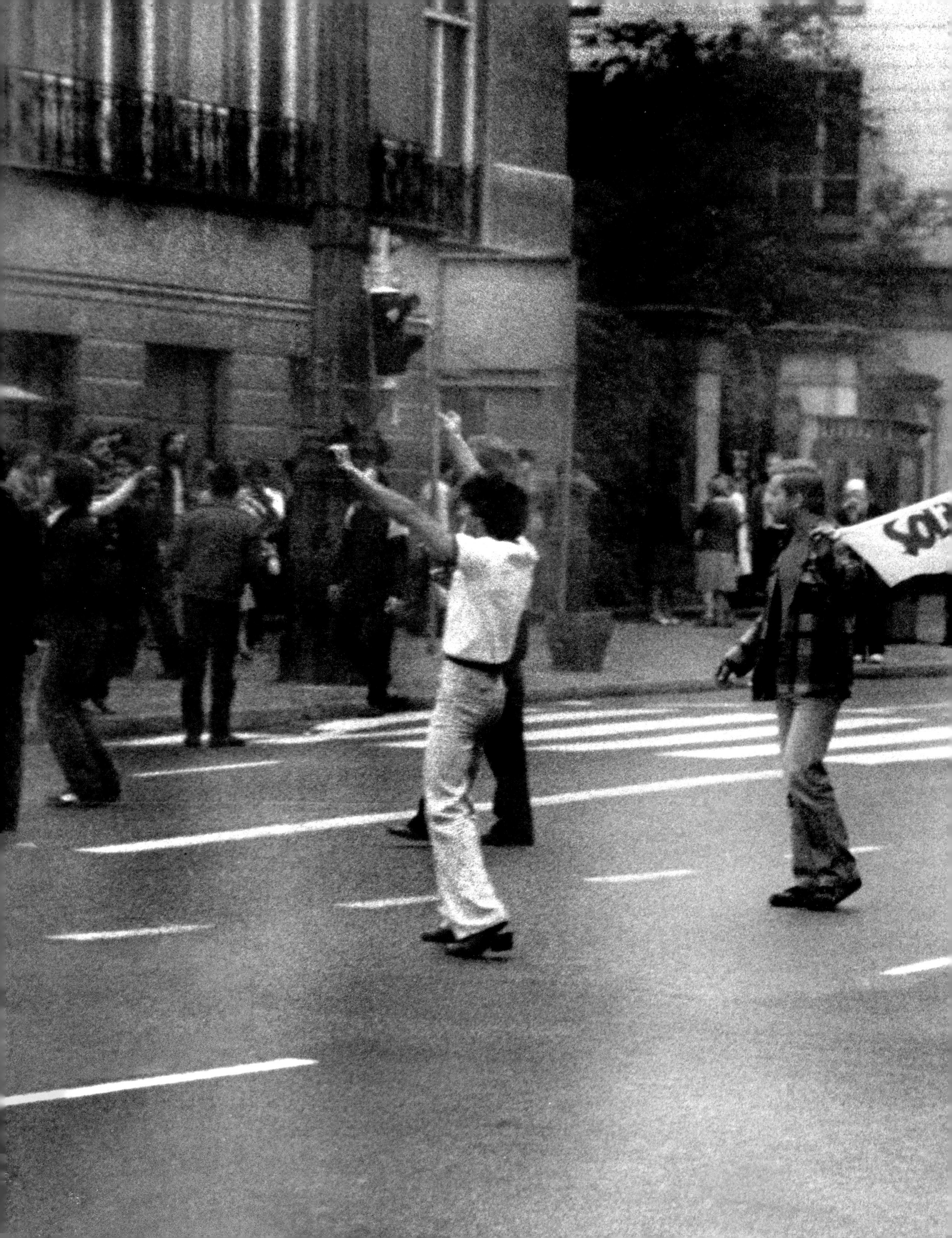

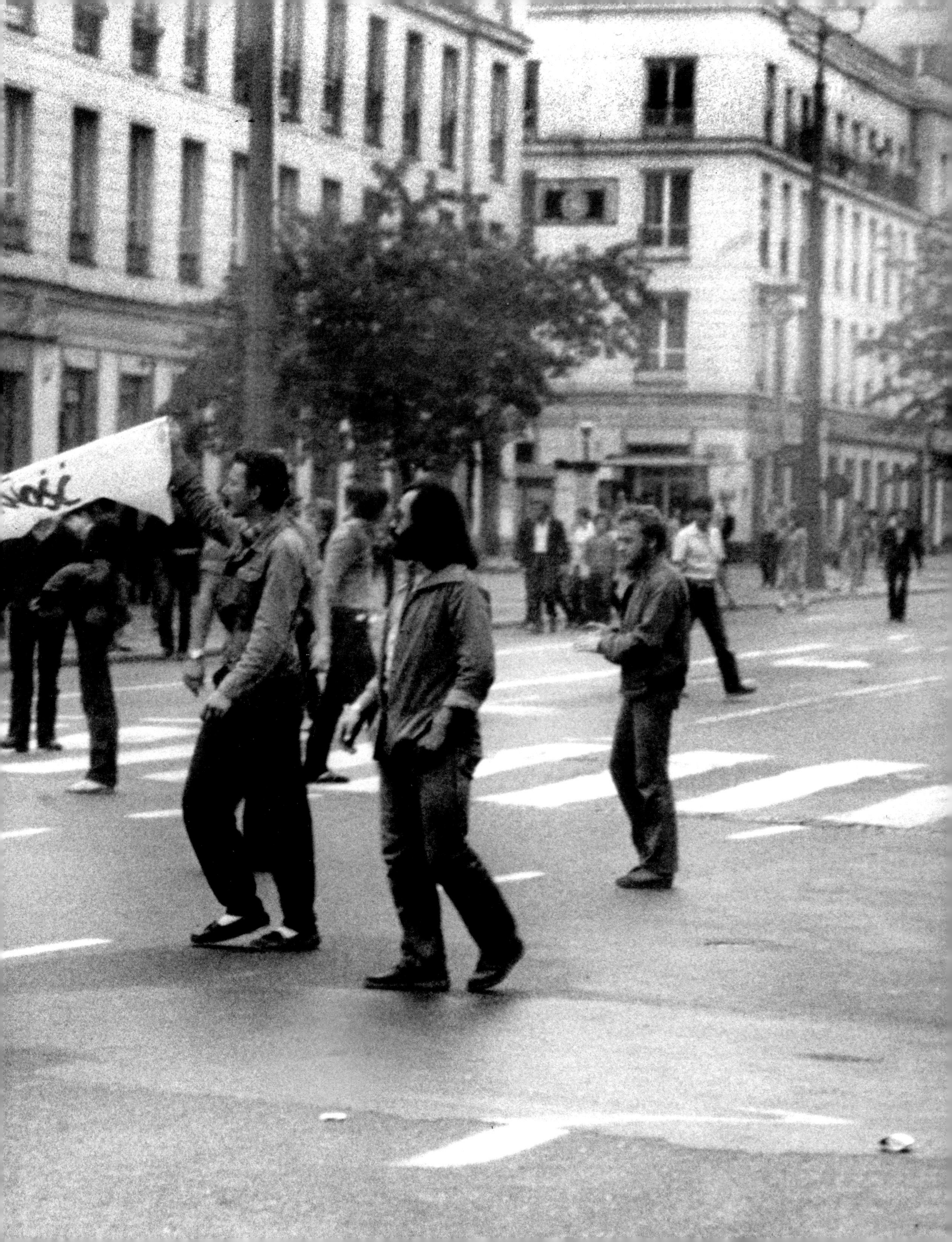

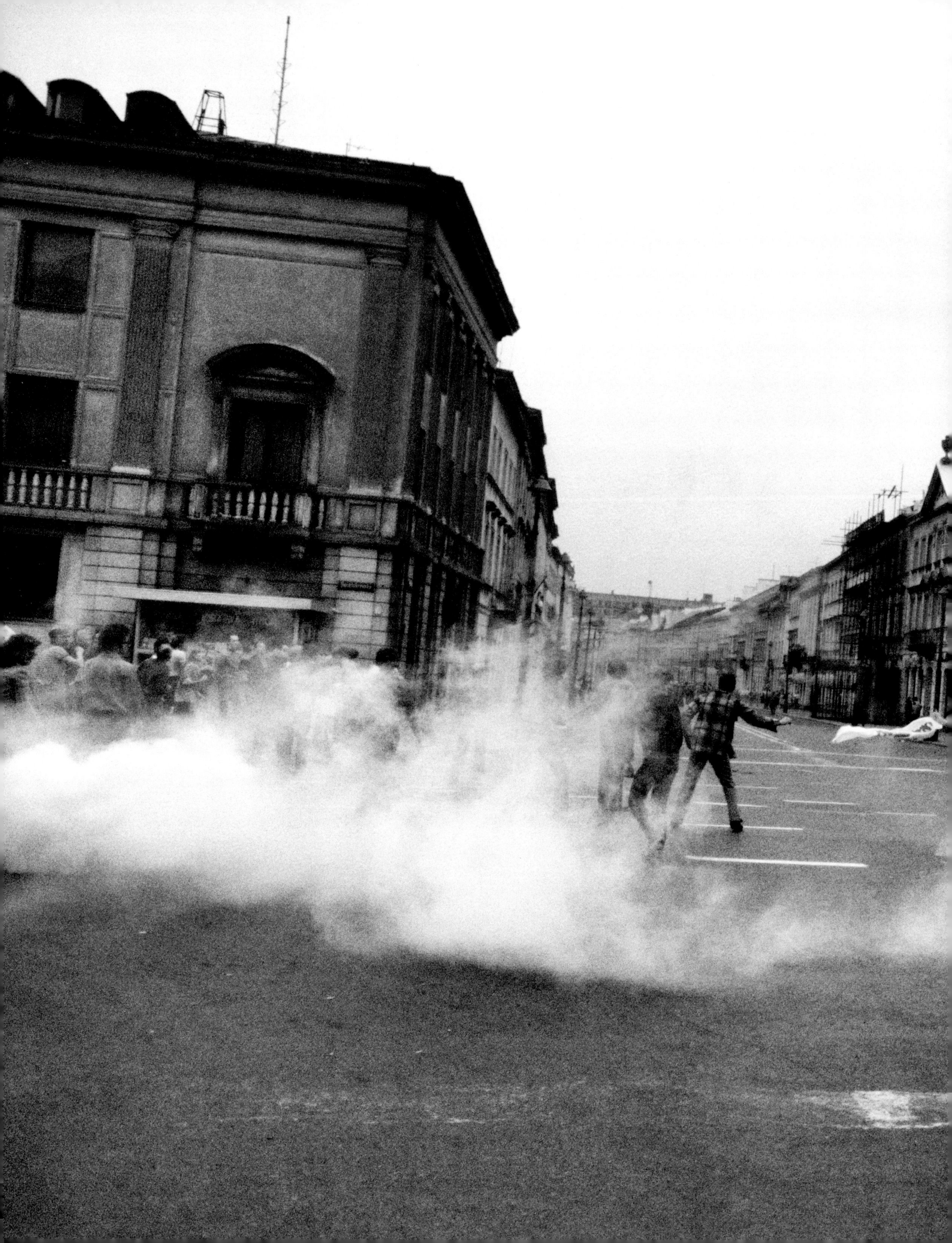

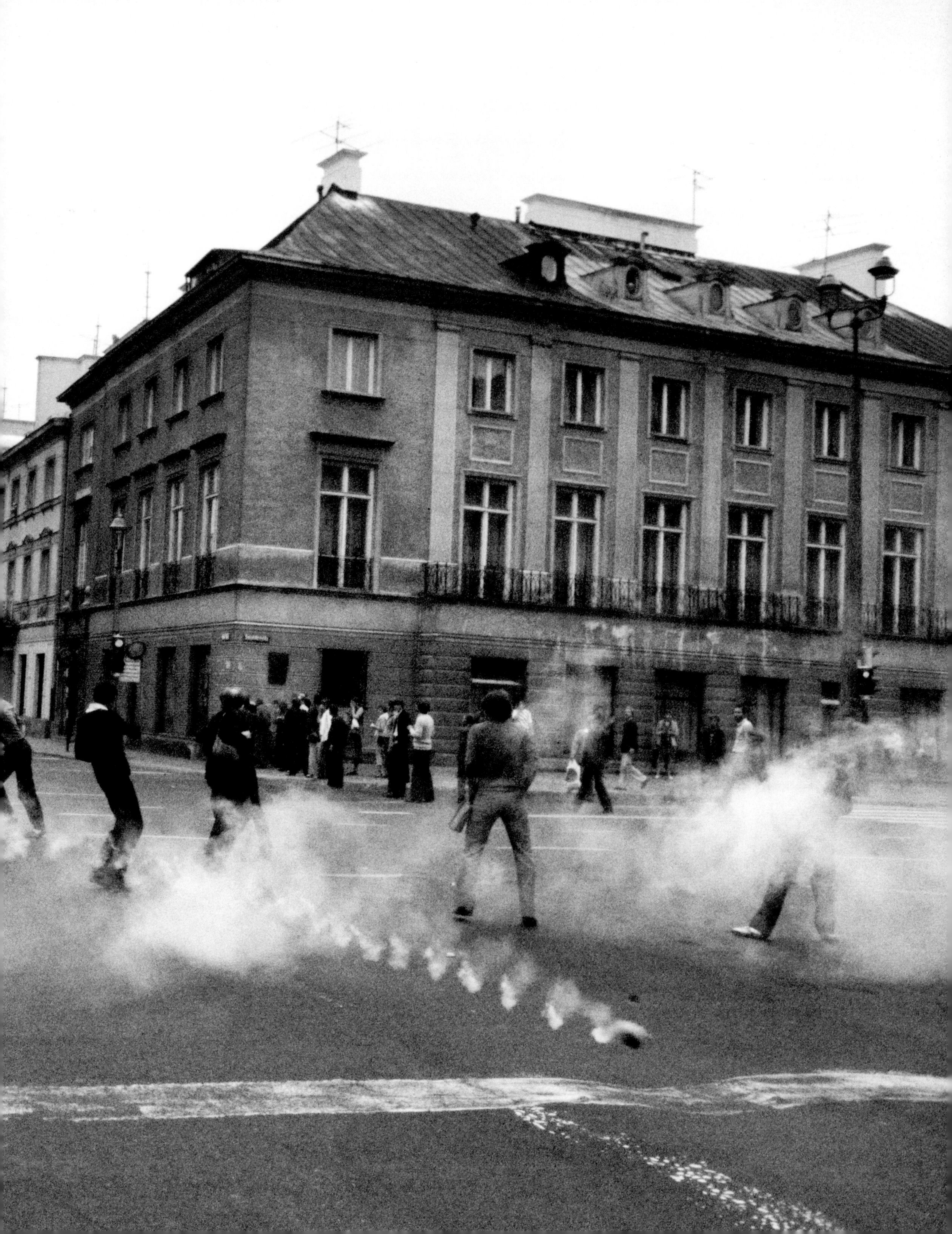

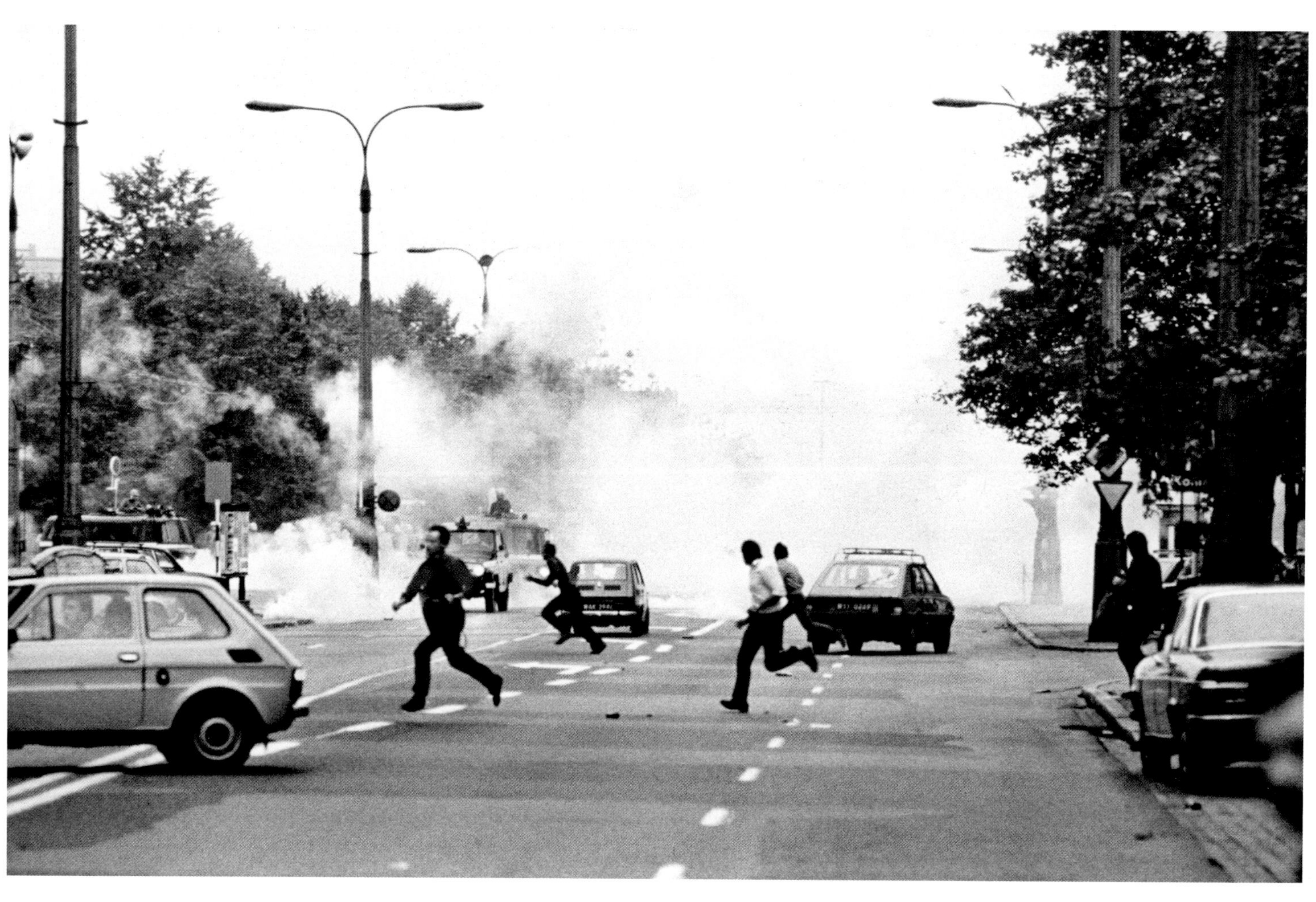

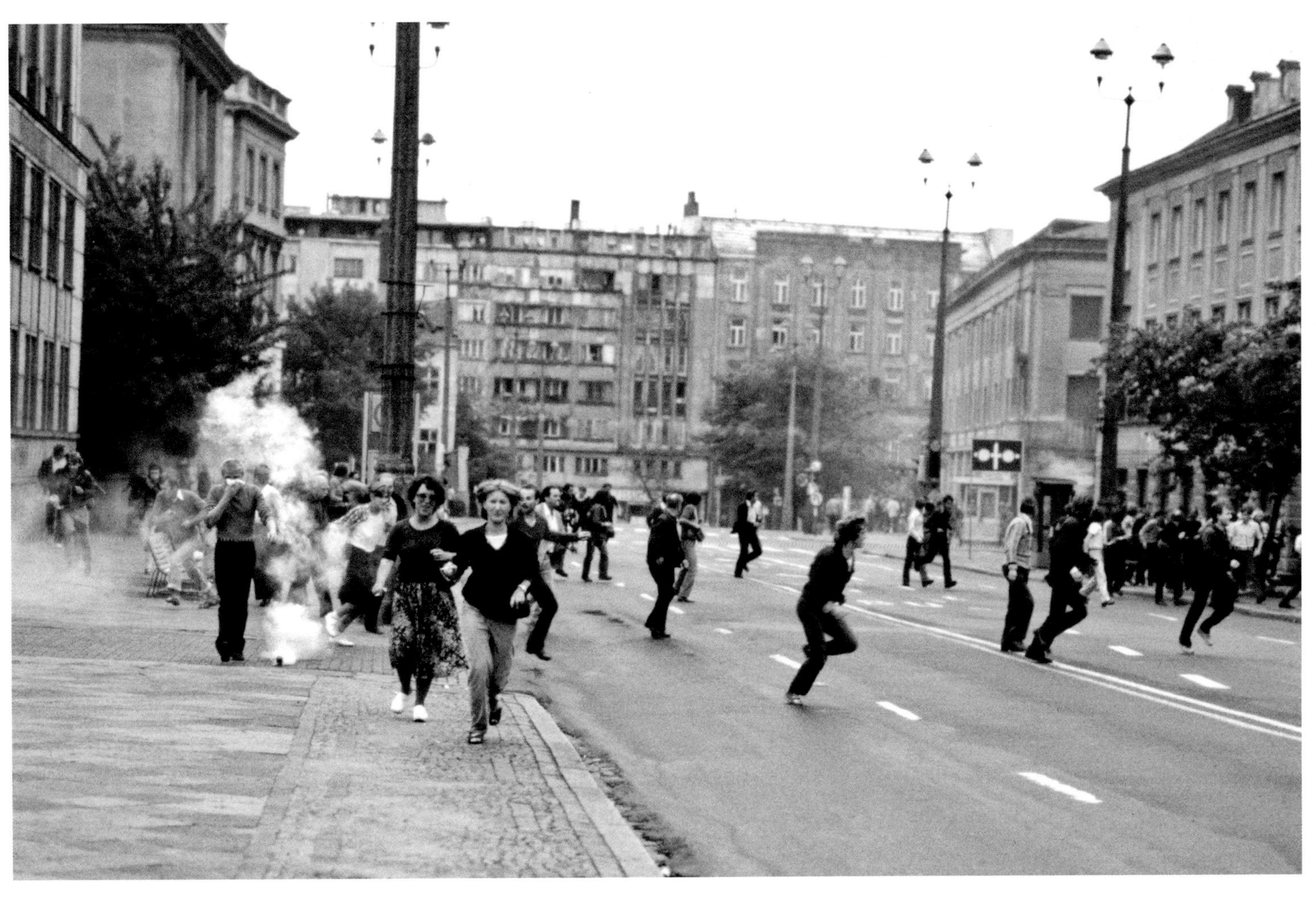

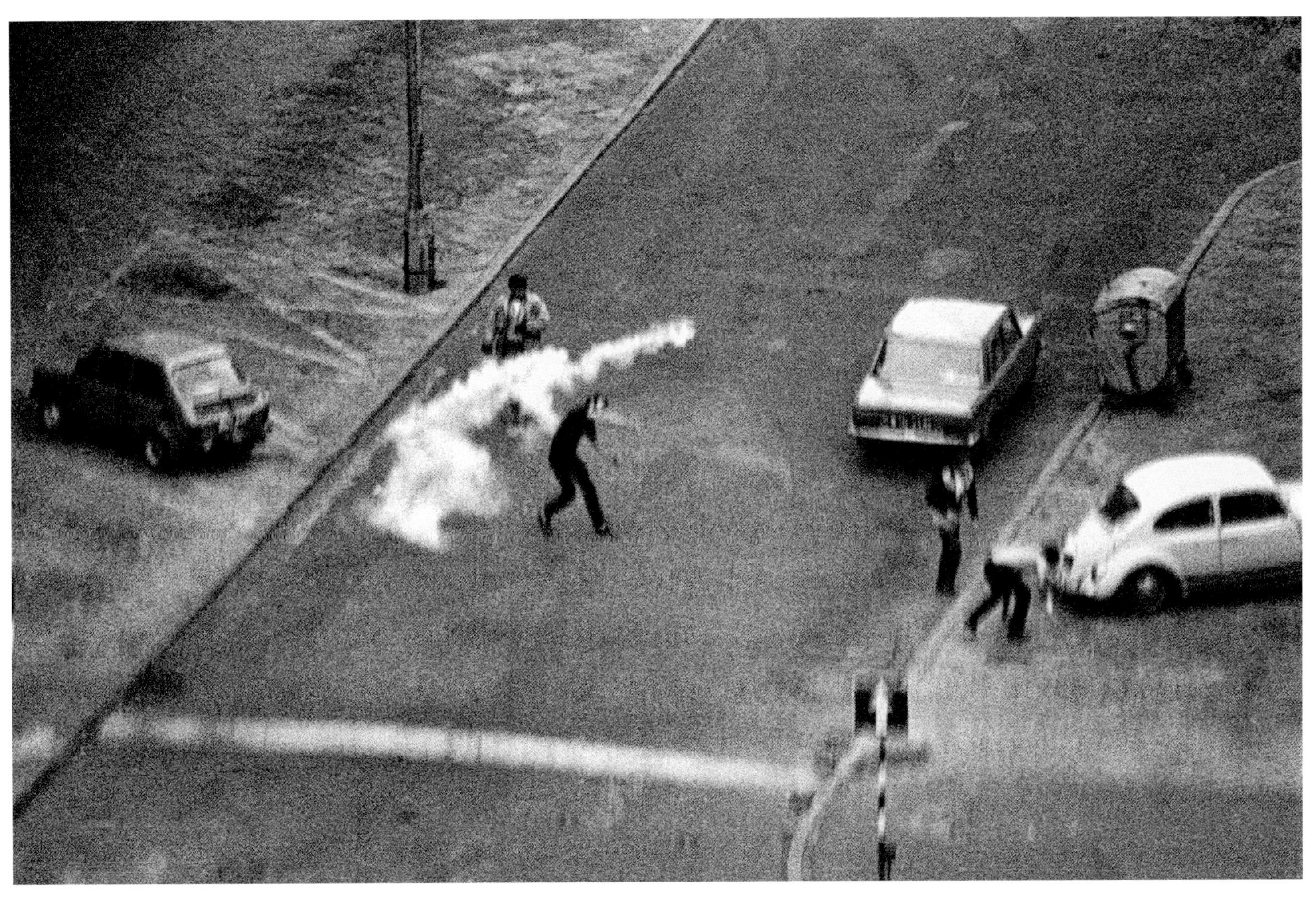

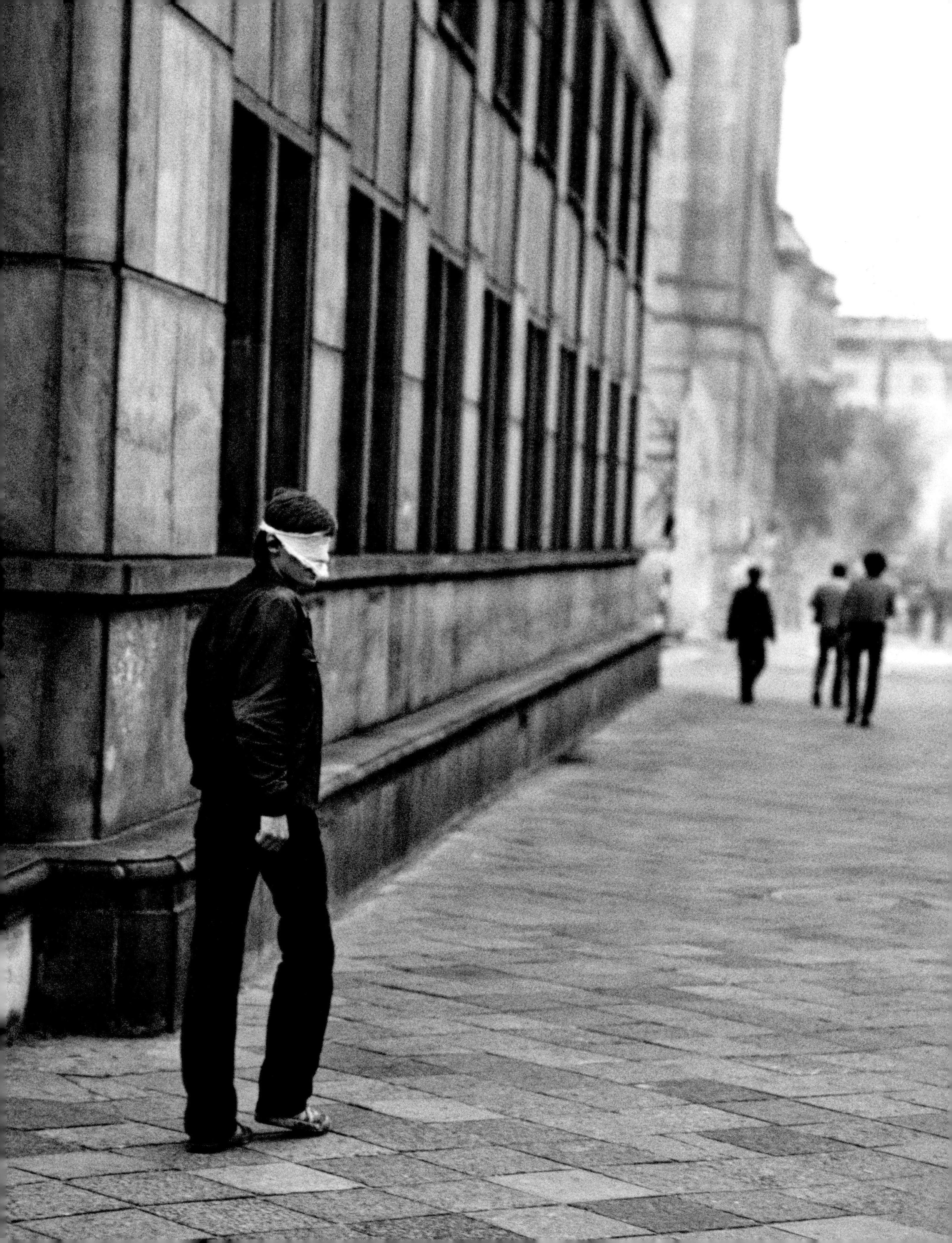

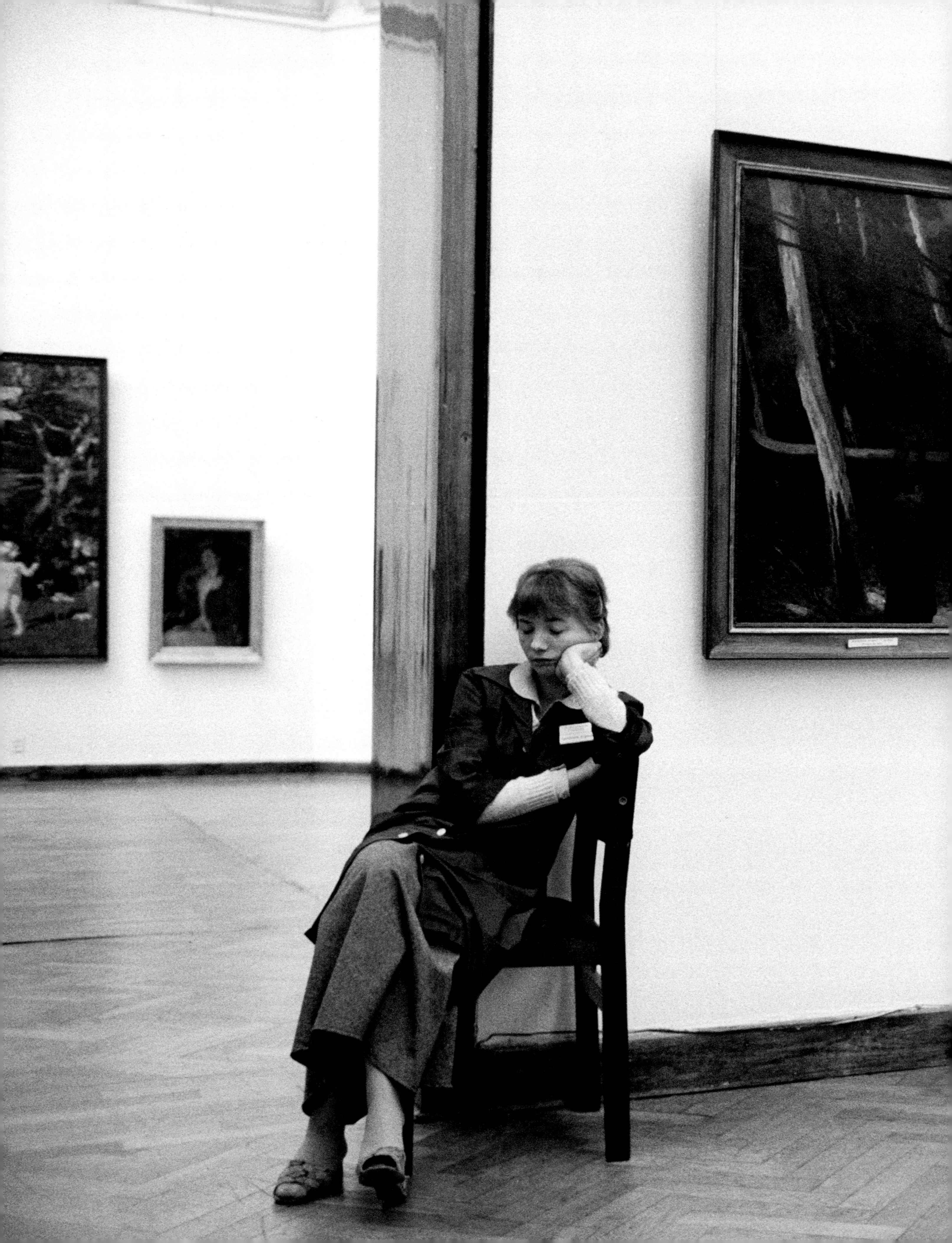

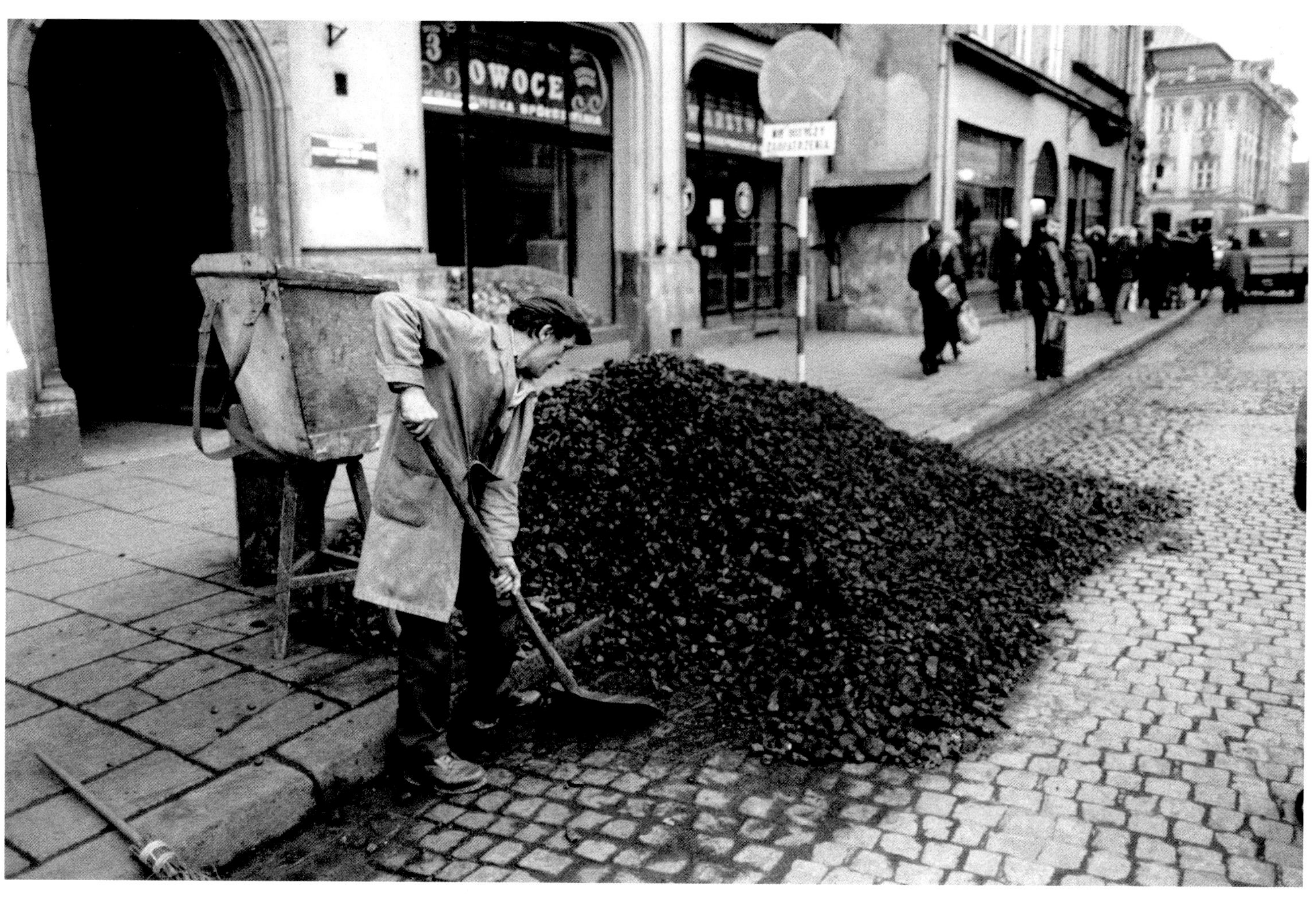
3
OWOCE

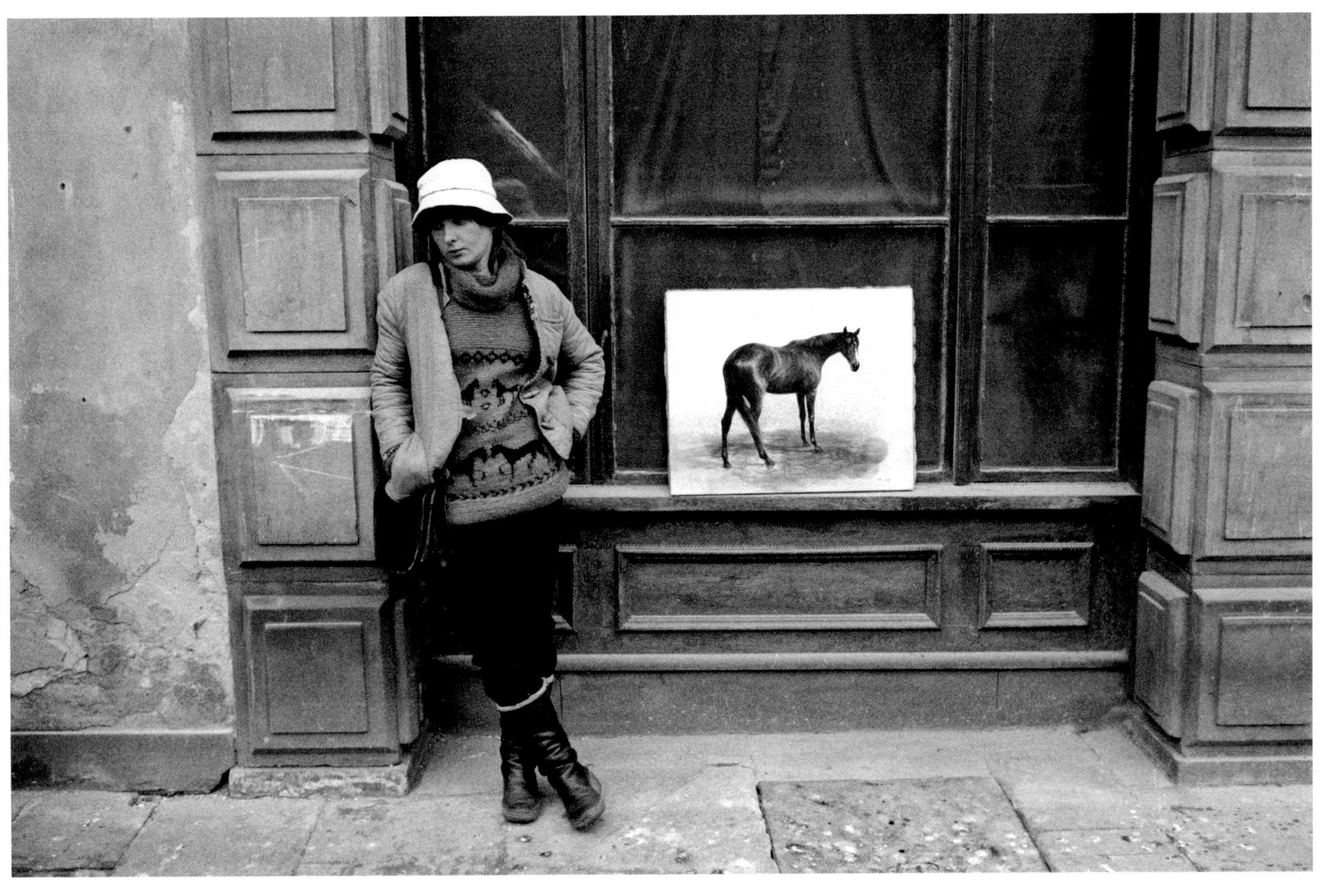

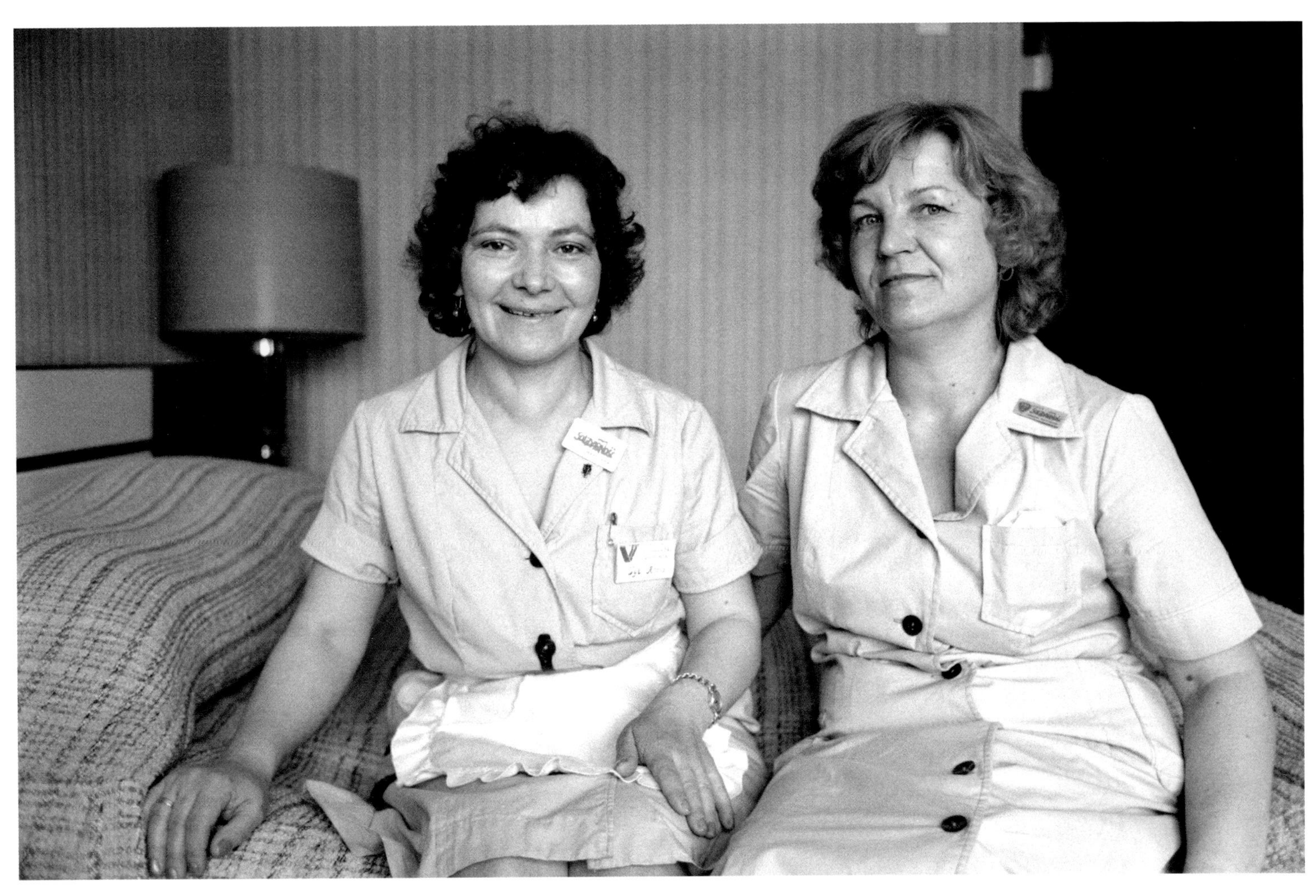

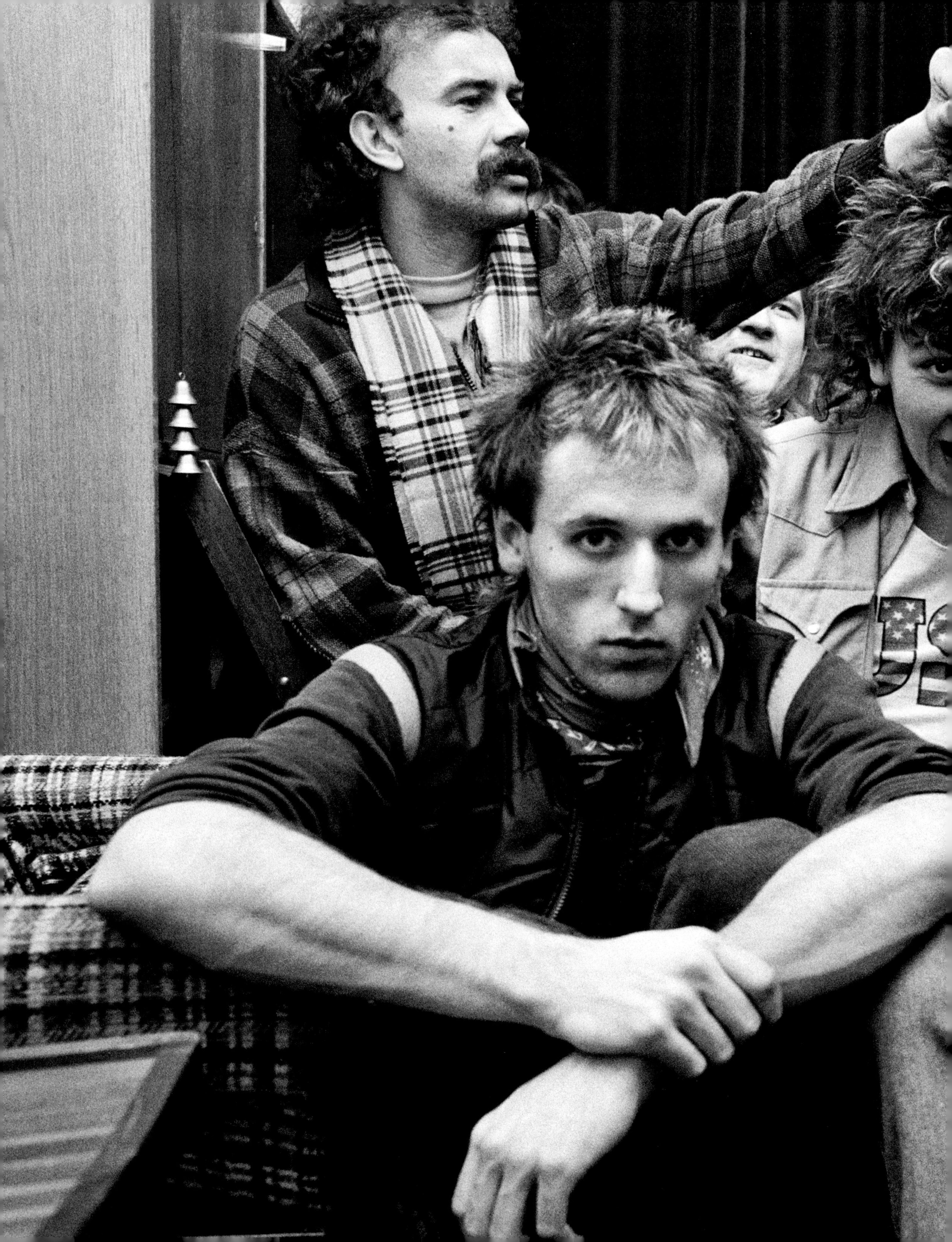

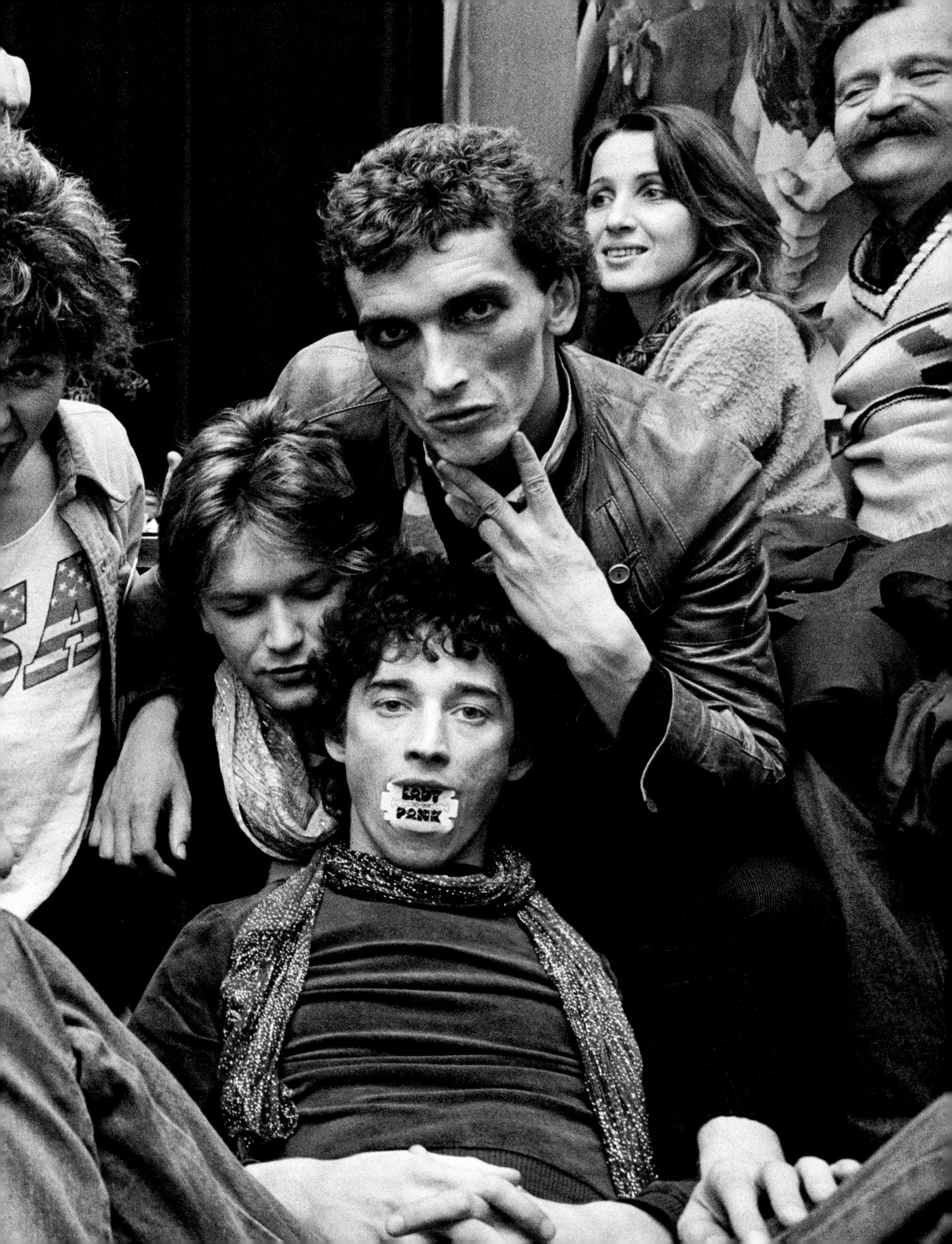

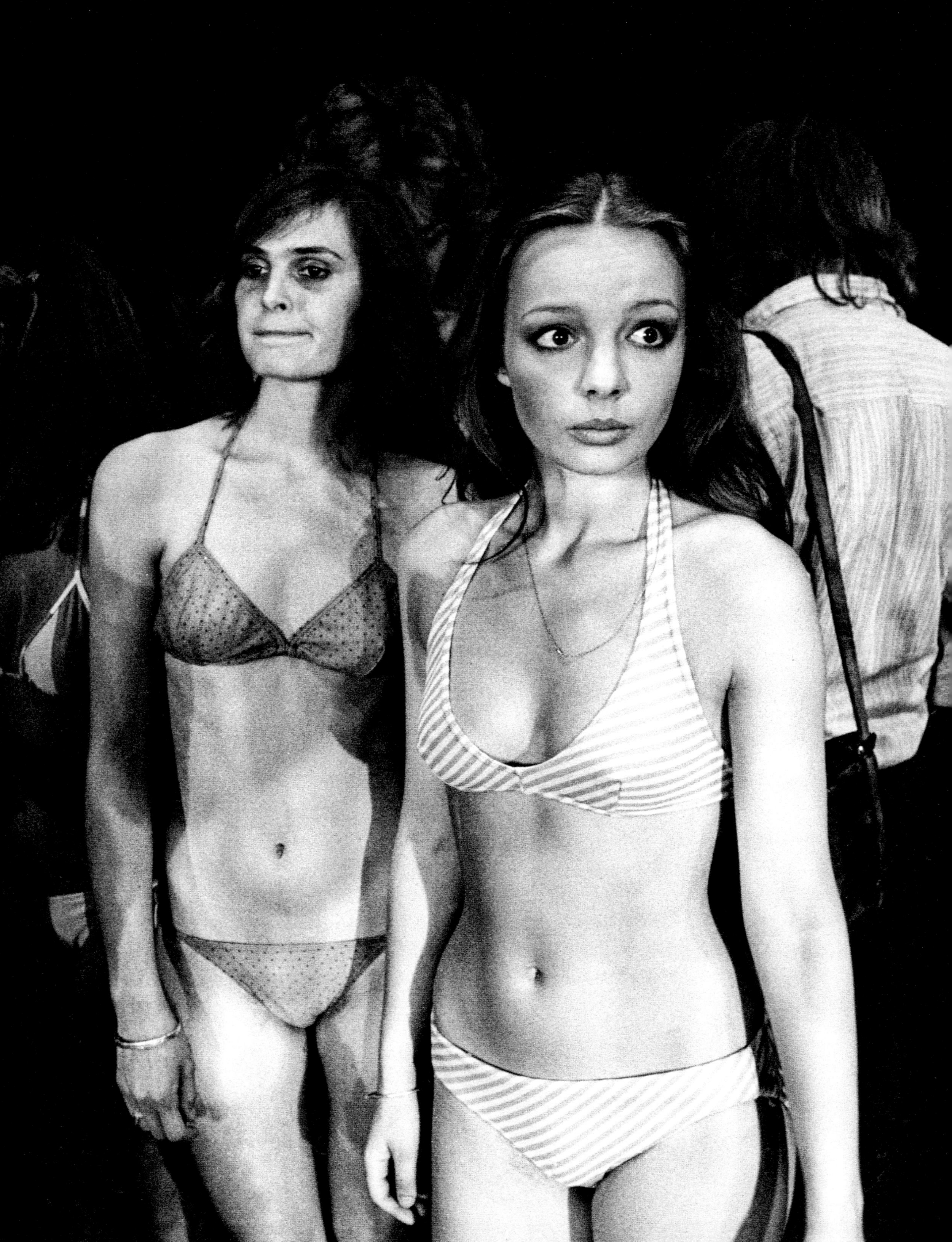

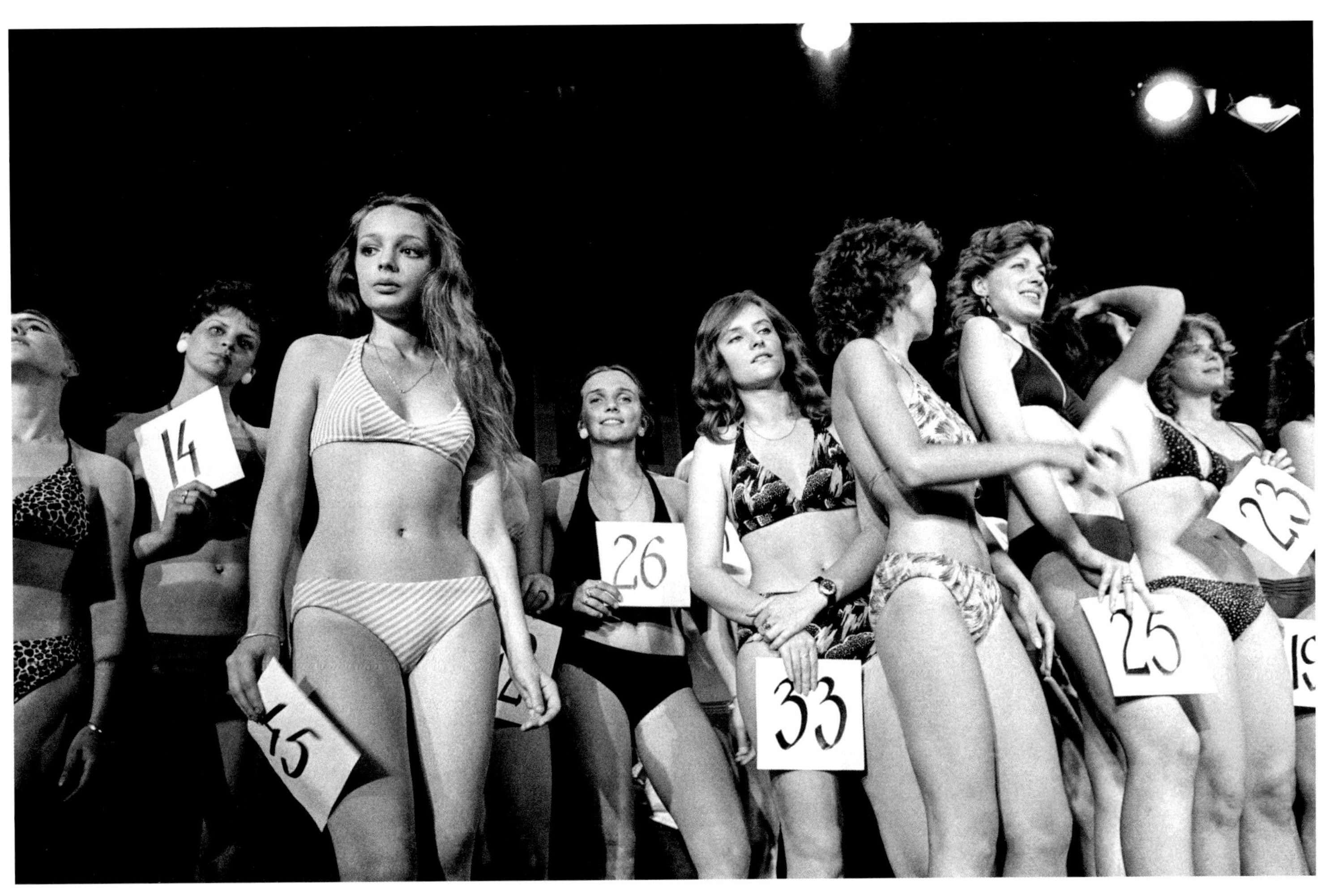
14
26
33
25
23

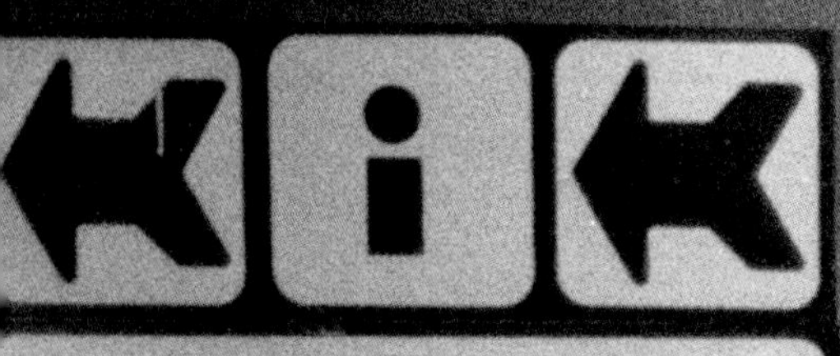
i
AKREDYTACJA
ACCREDITATION

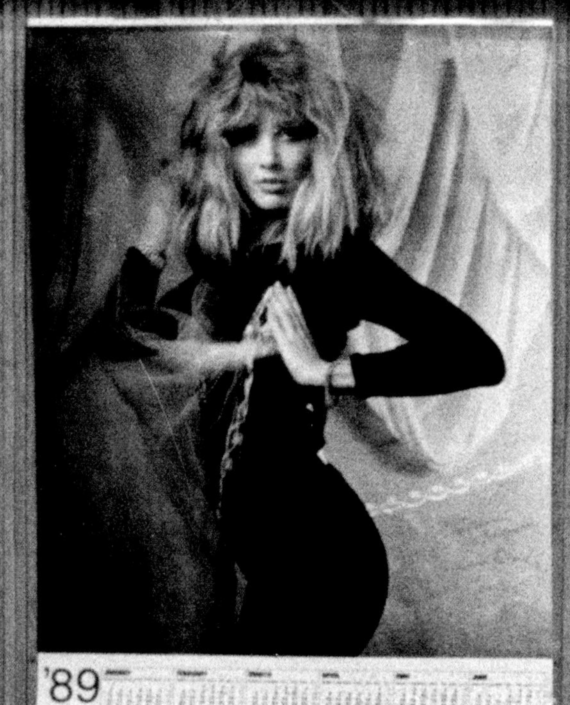
'89

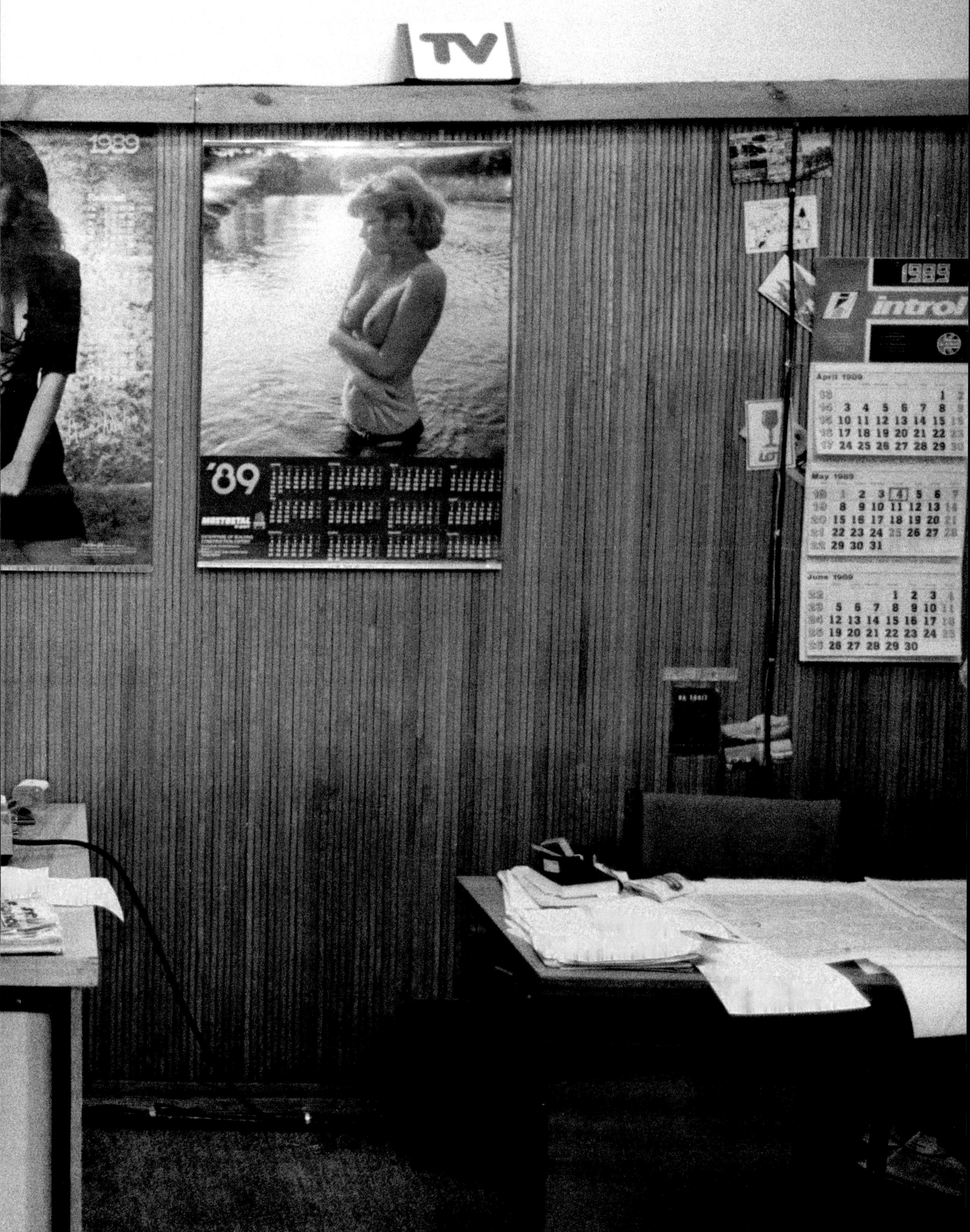
TV
1989
'89
1989
introl

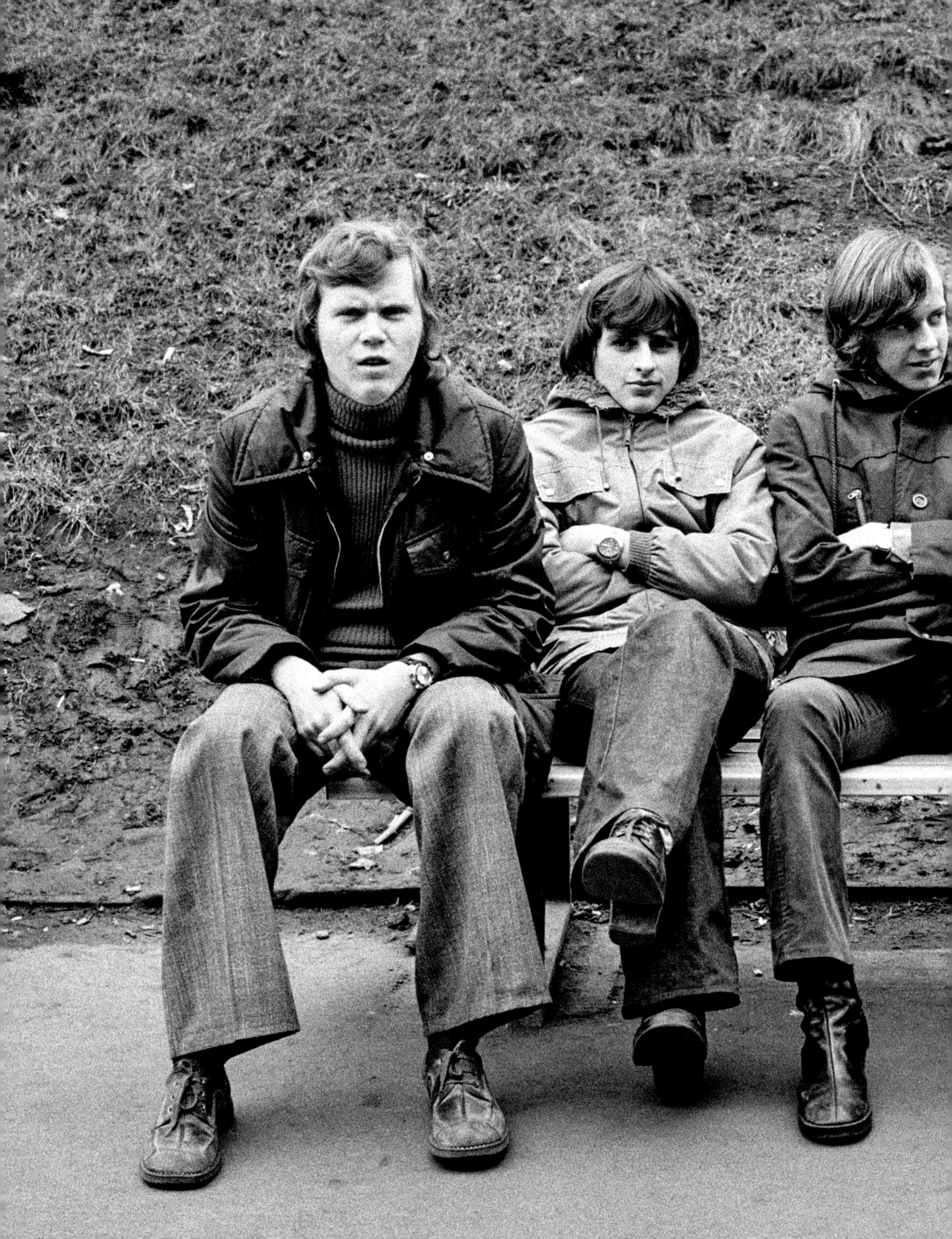

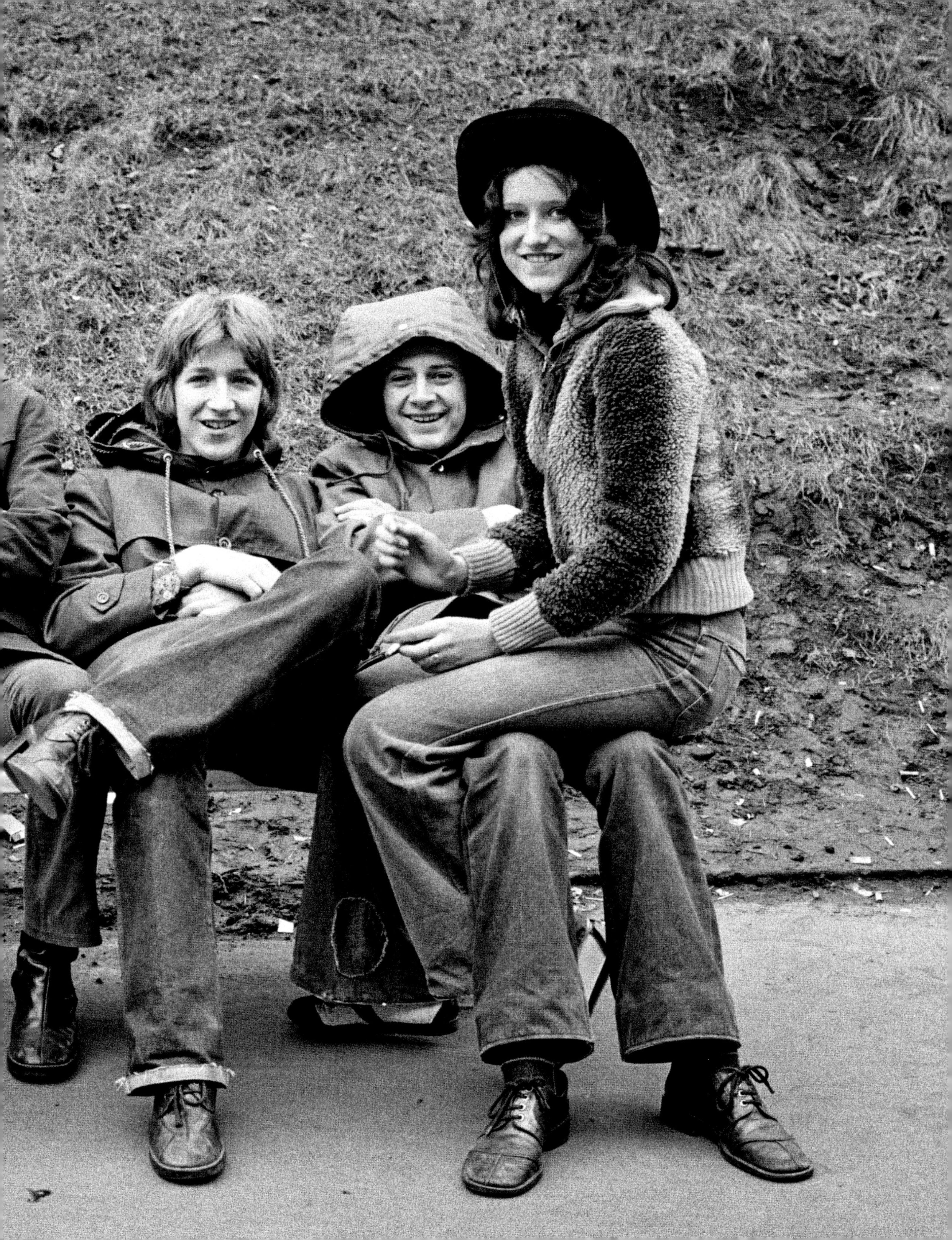

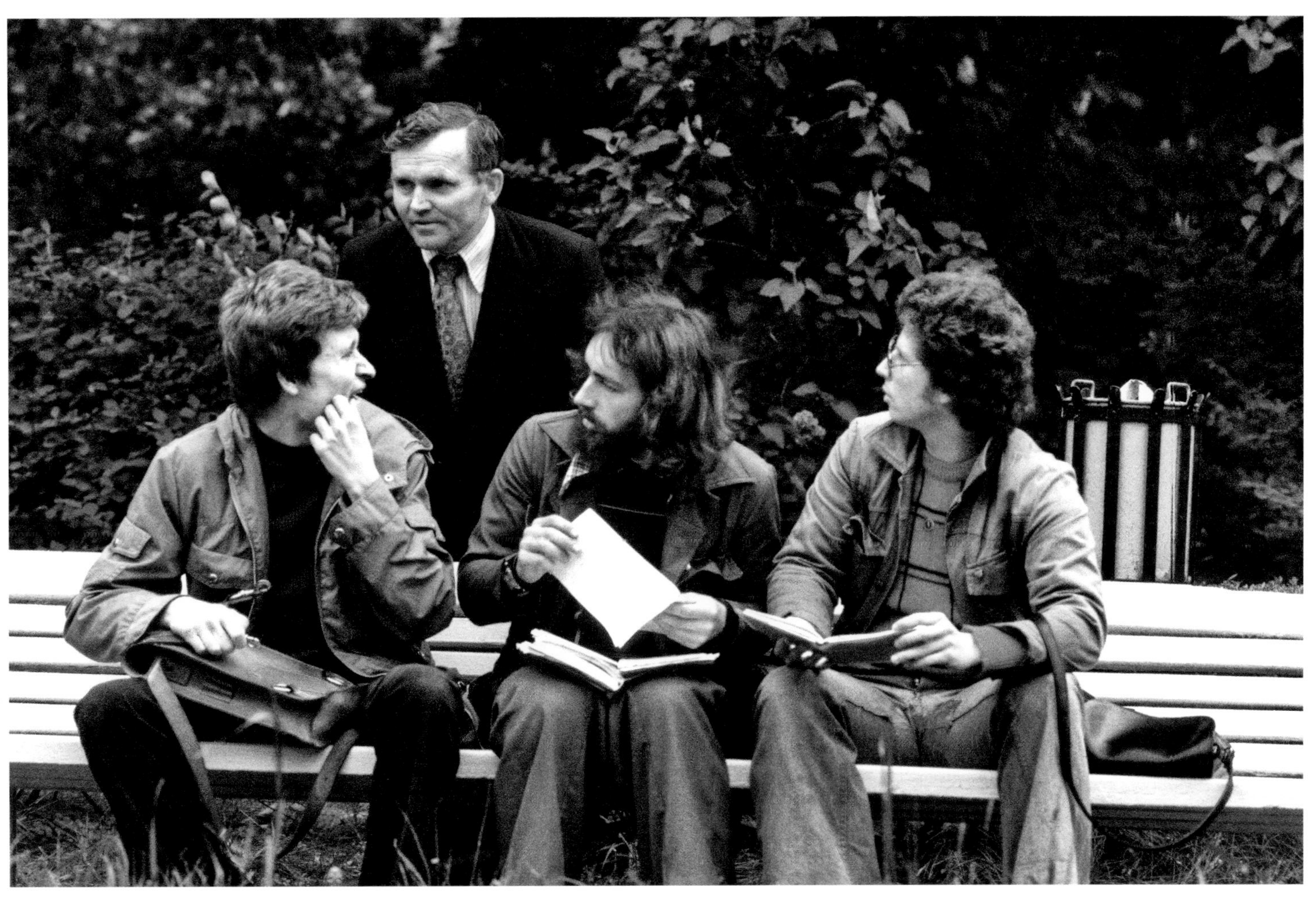

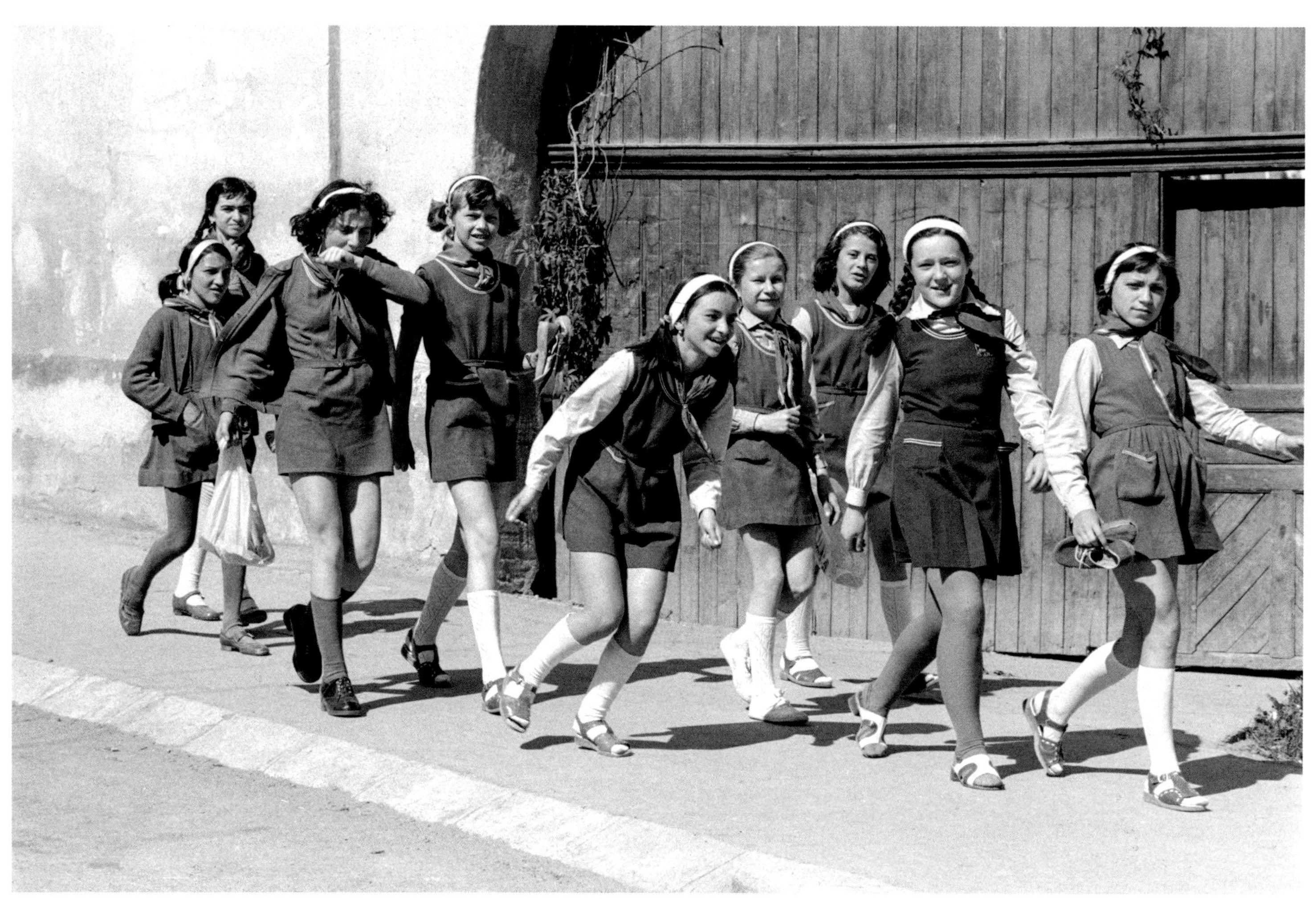

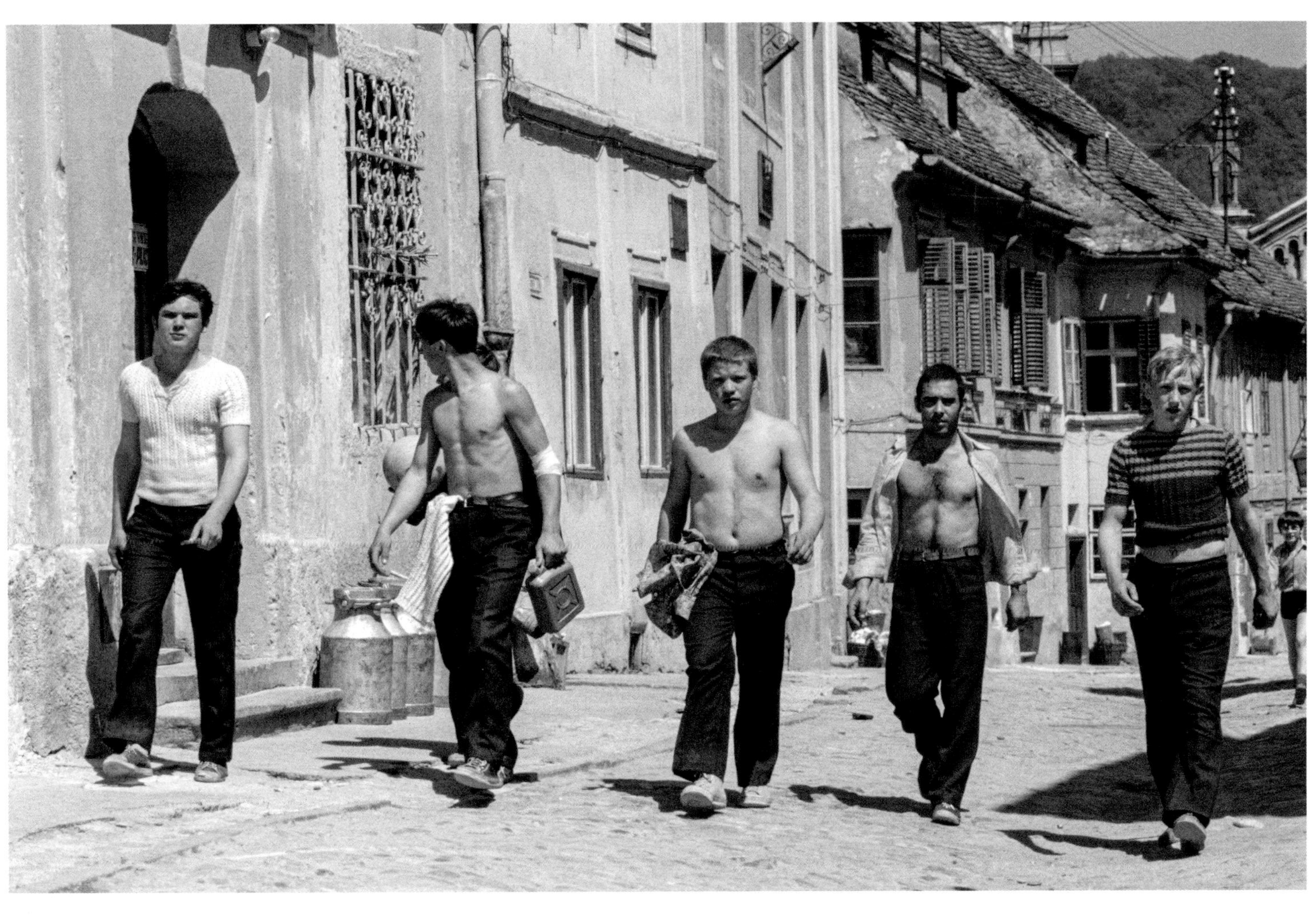

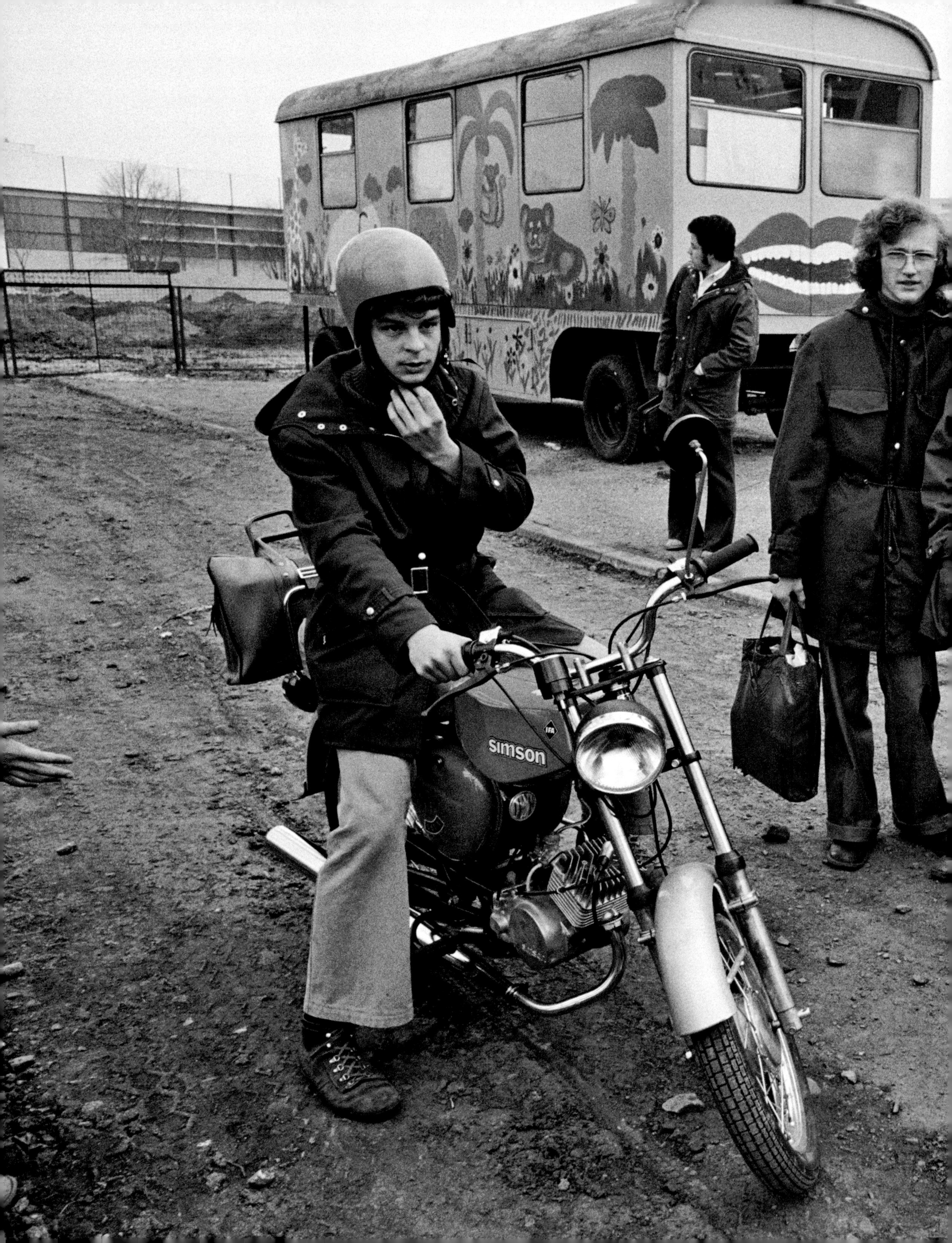
simson
IFA

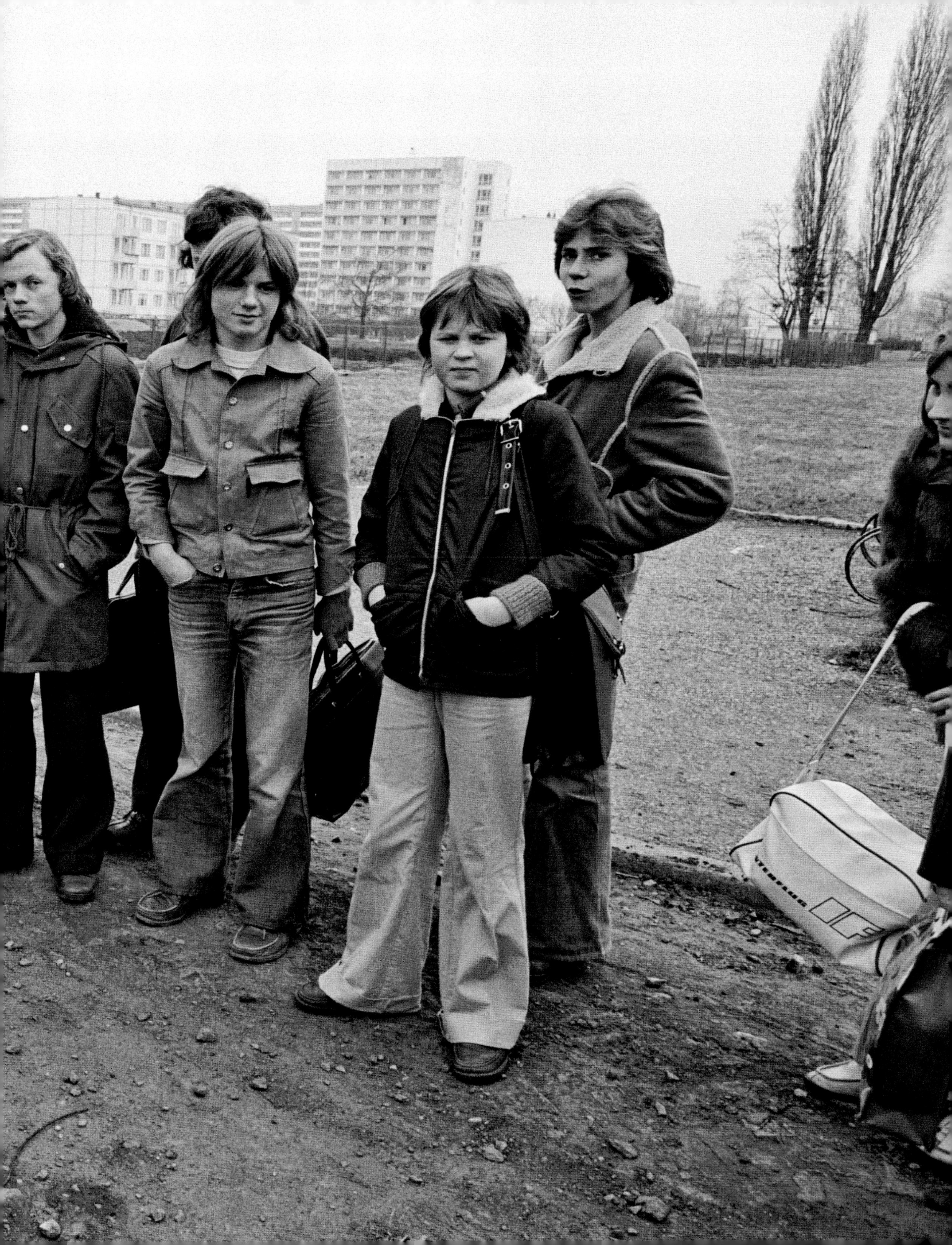

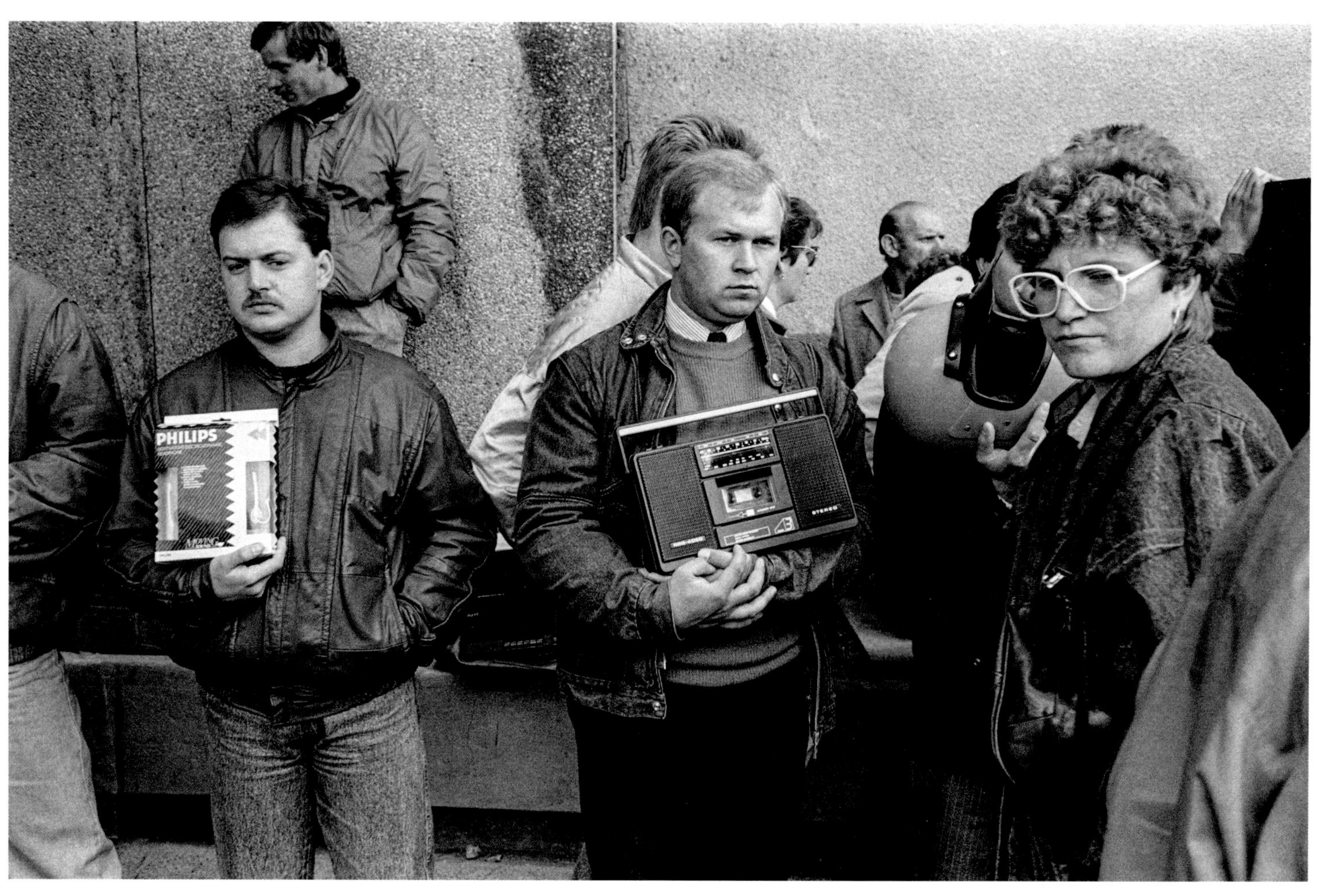
PHILIPS

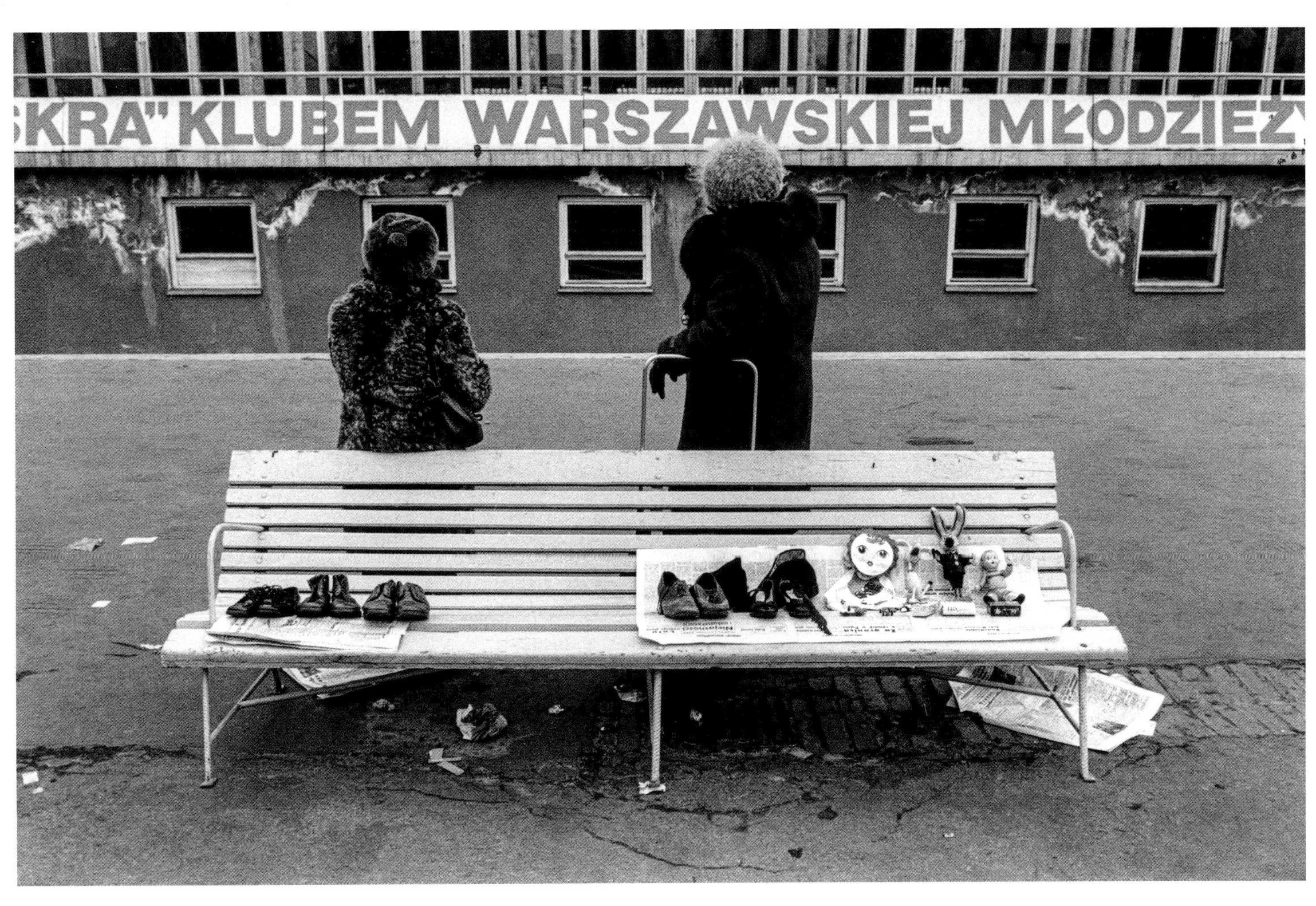
KRA" KLUBEM WARSZAWSKIEJ MŁODZIEŻ

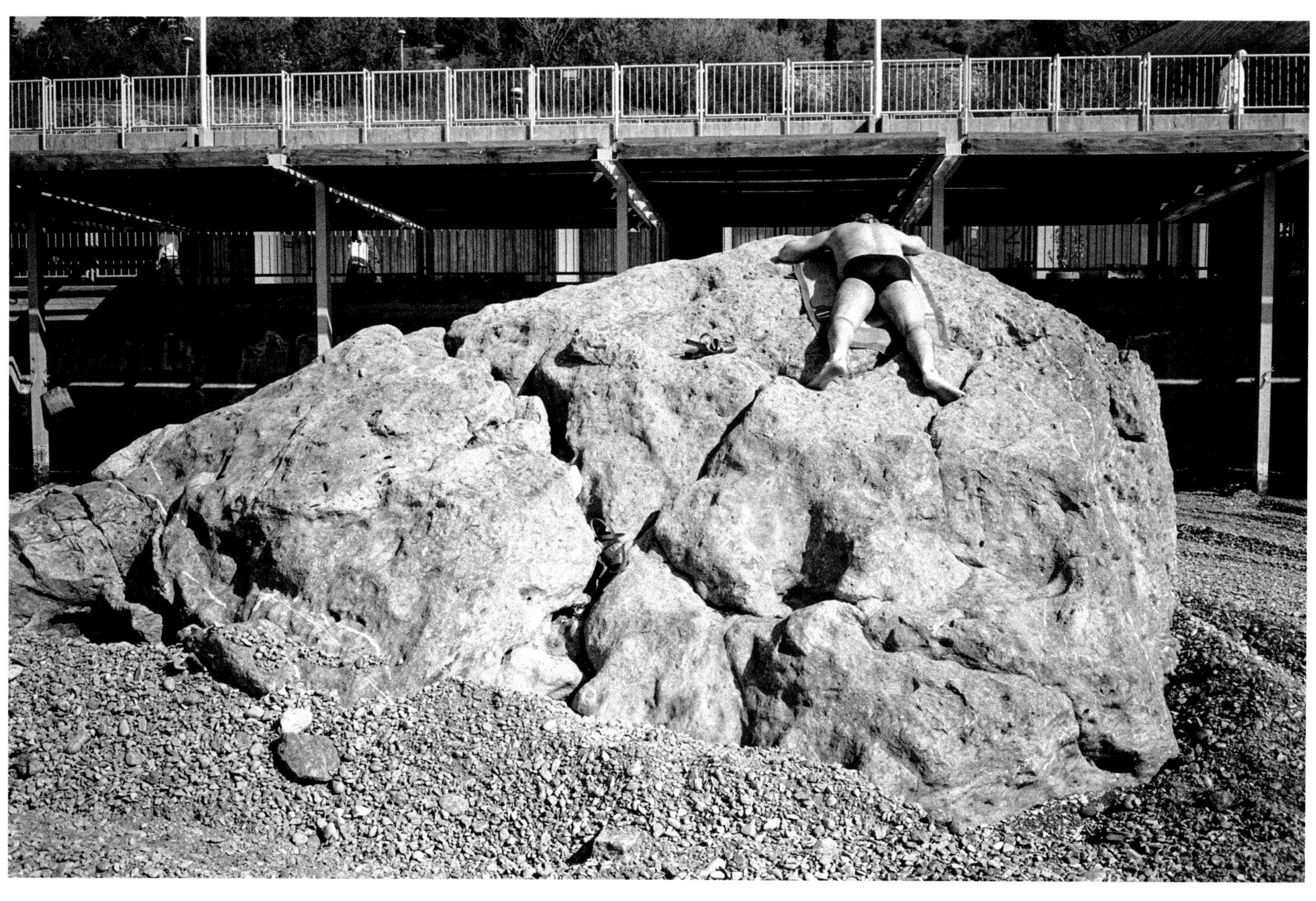

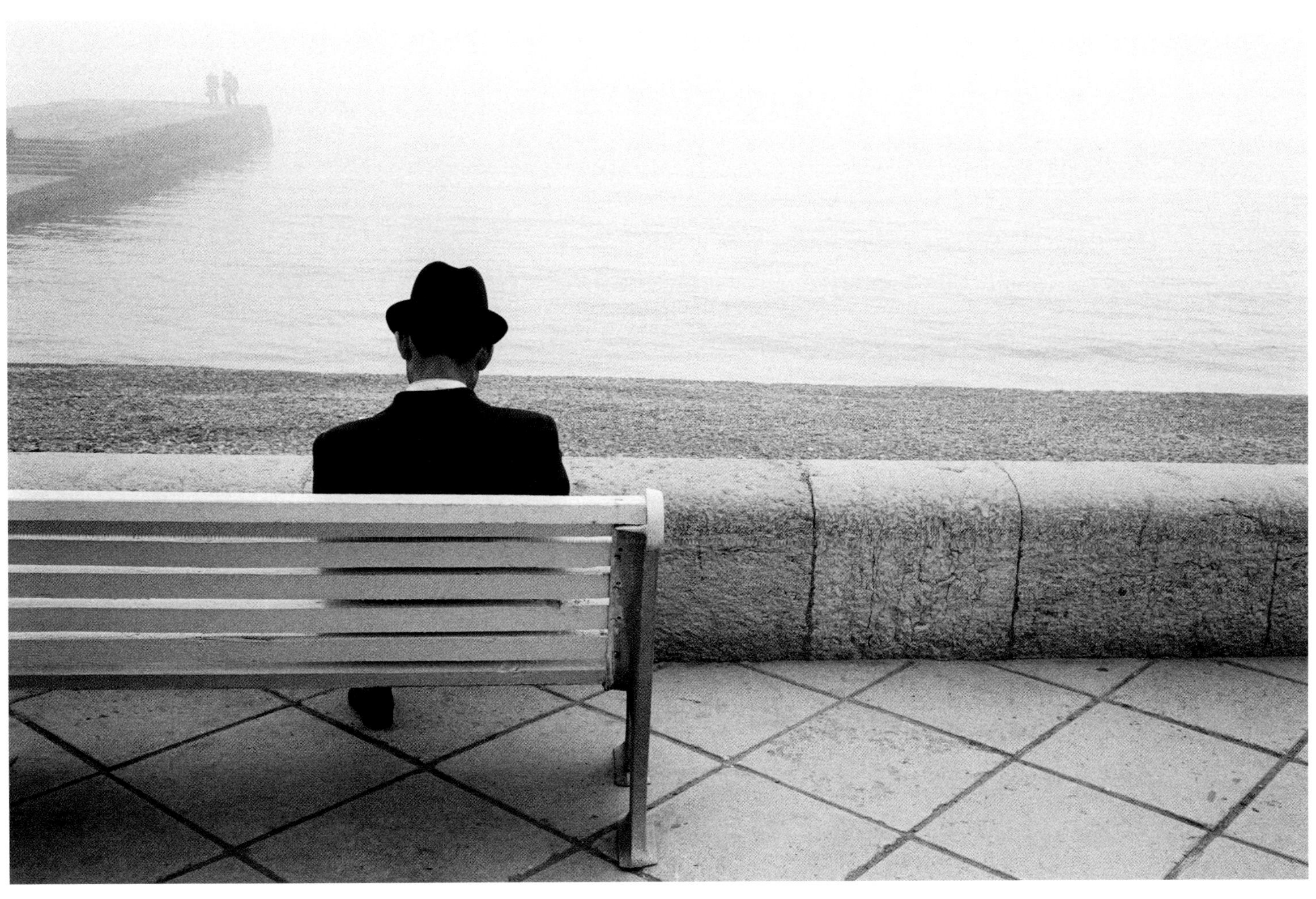

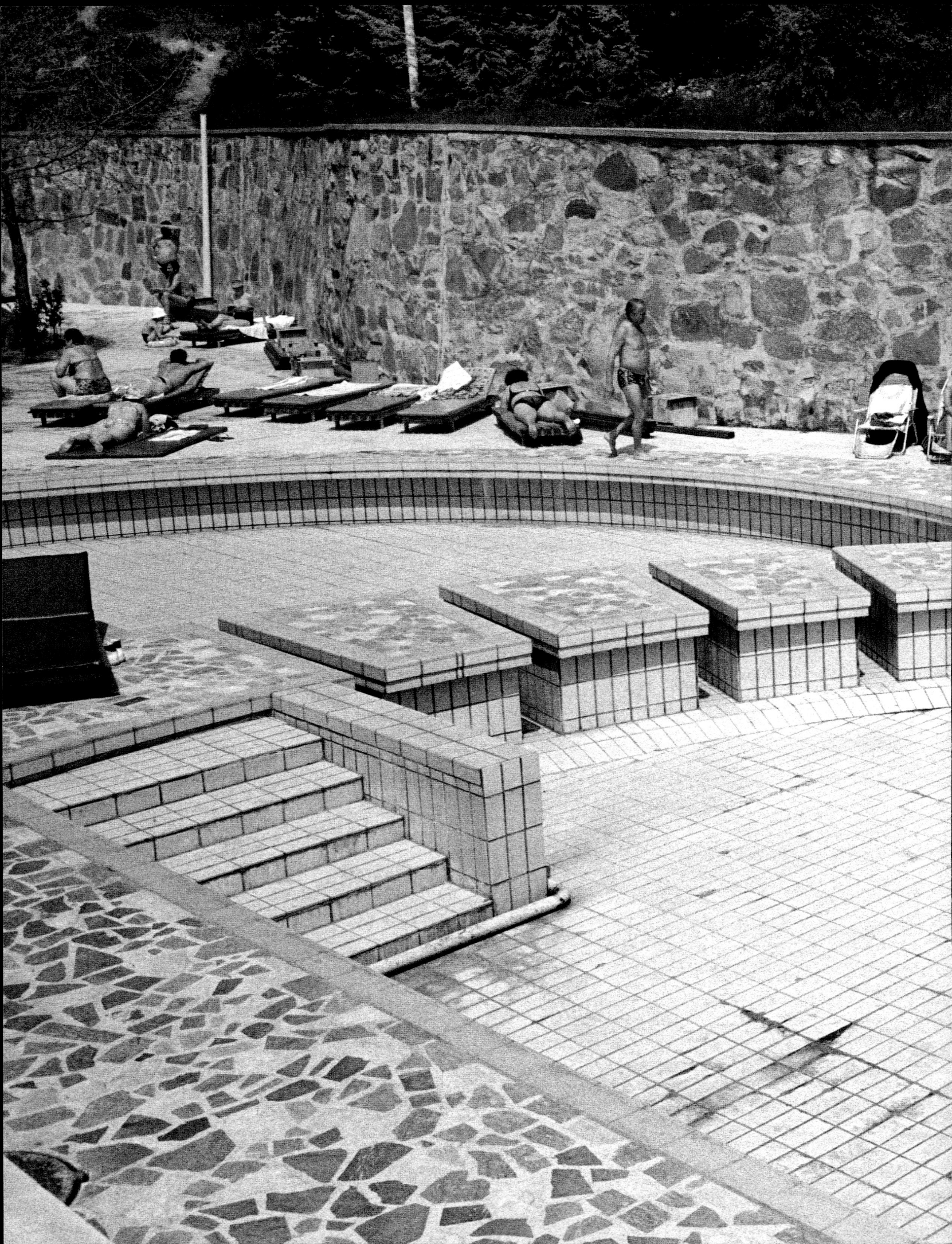

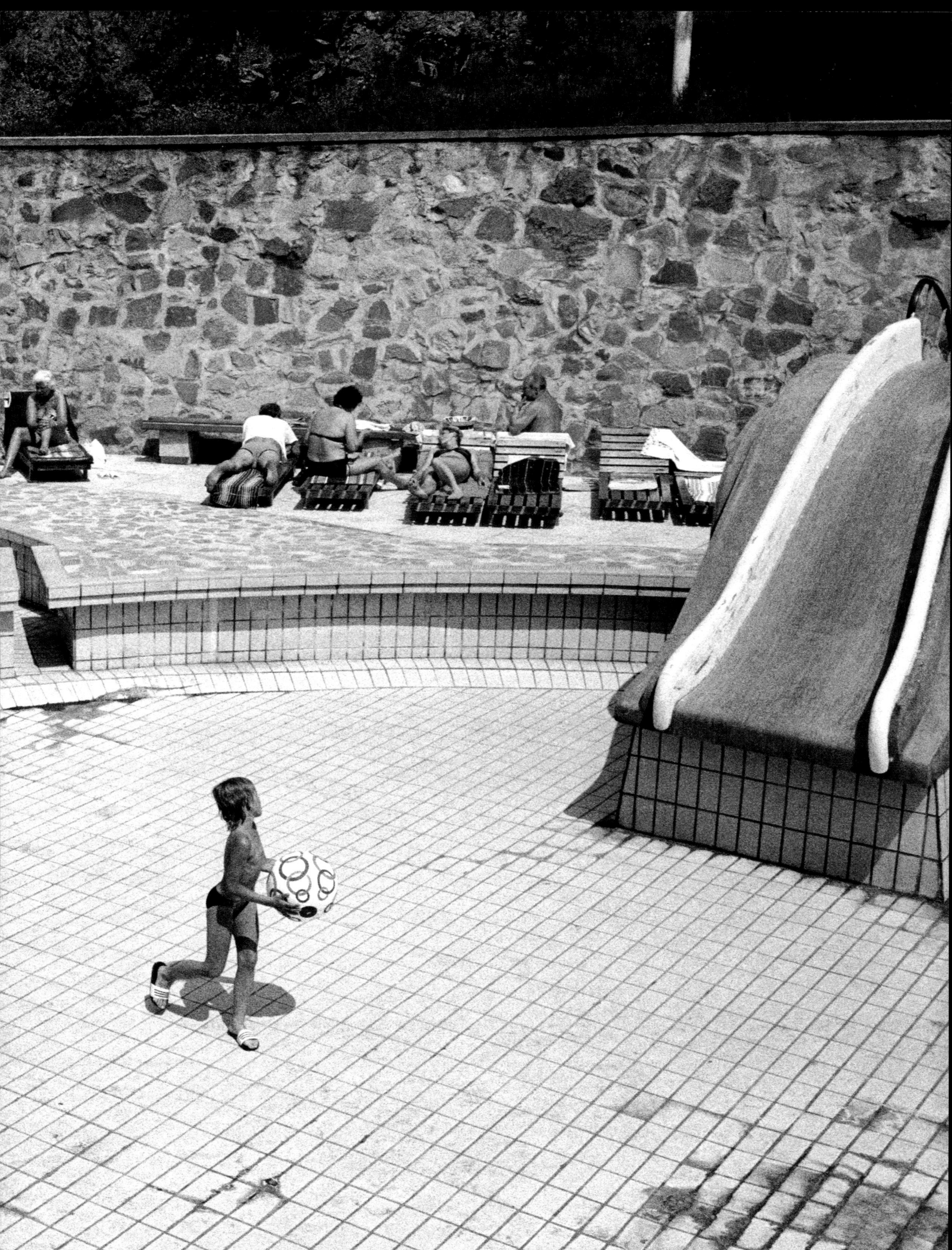

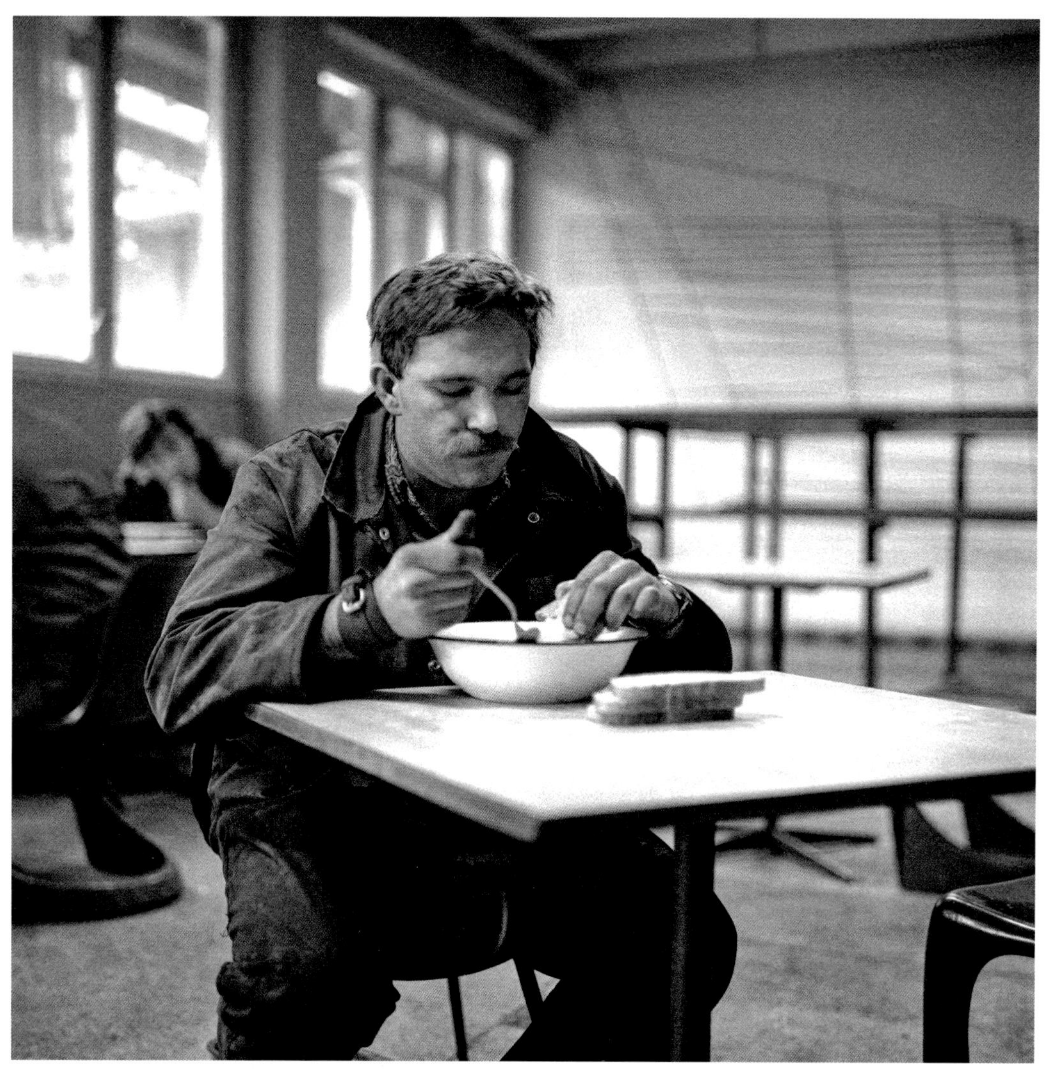

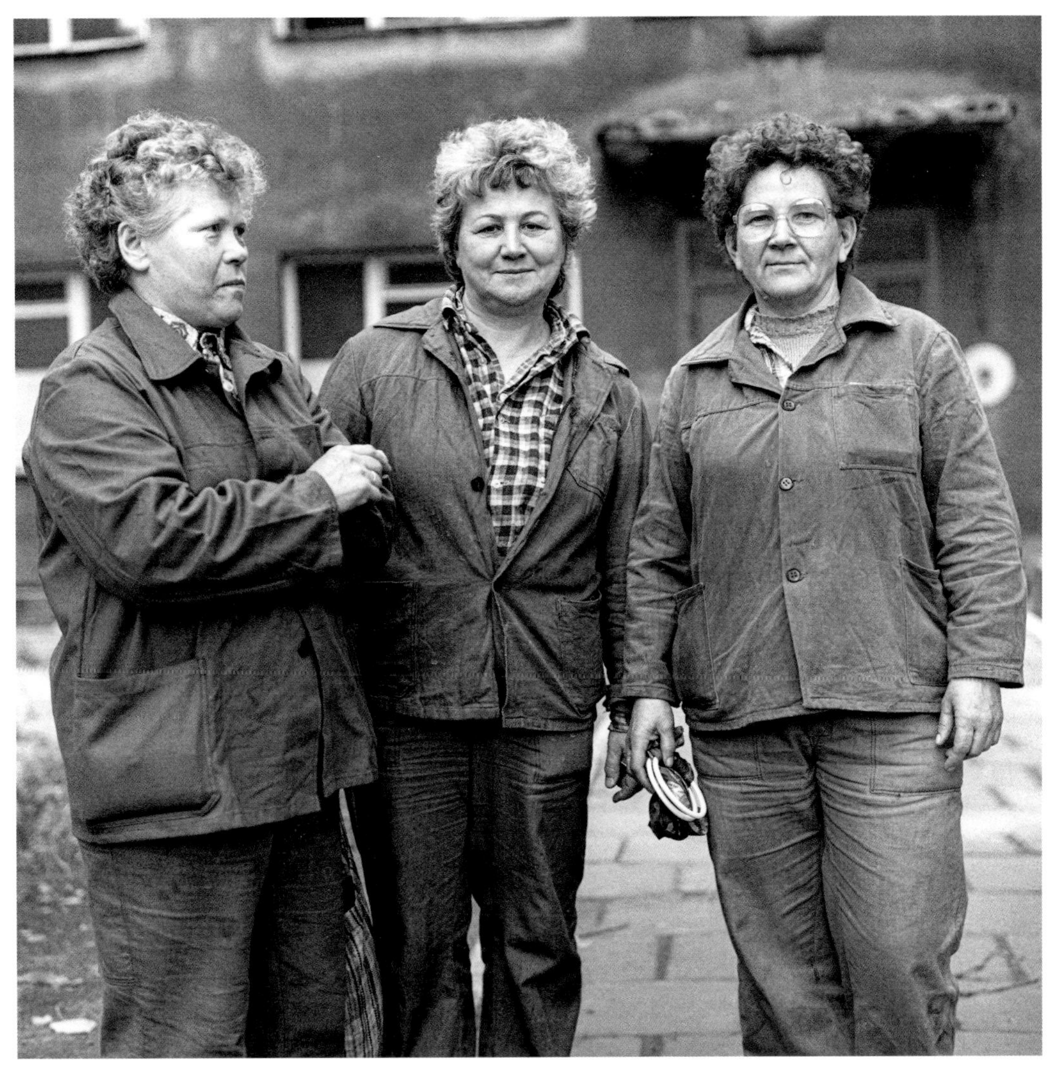

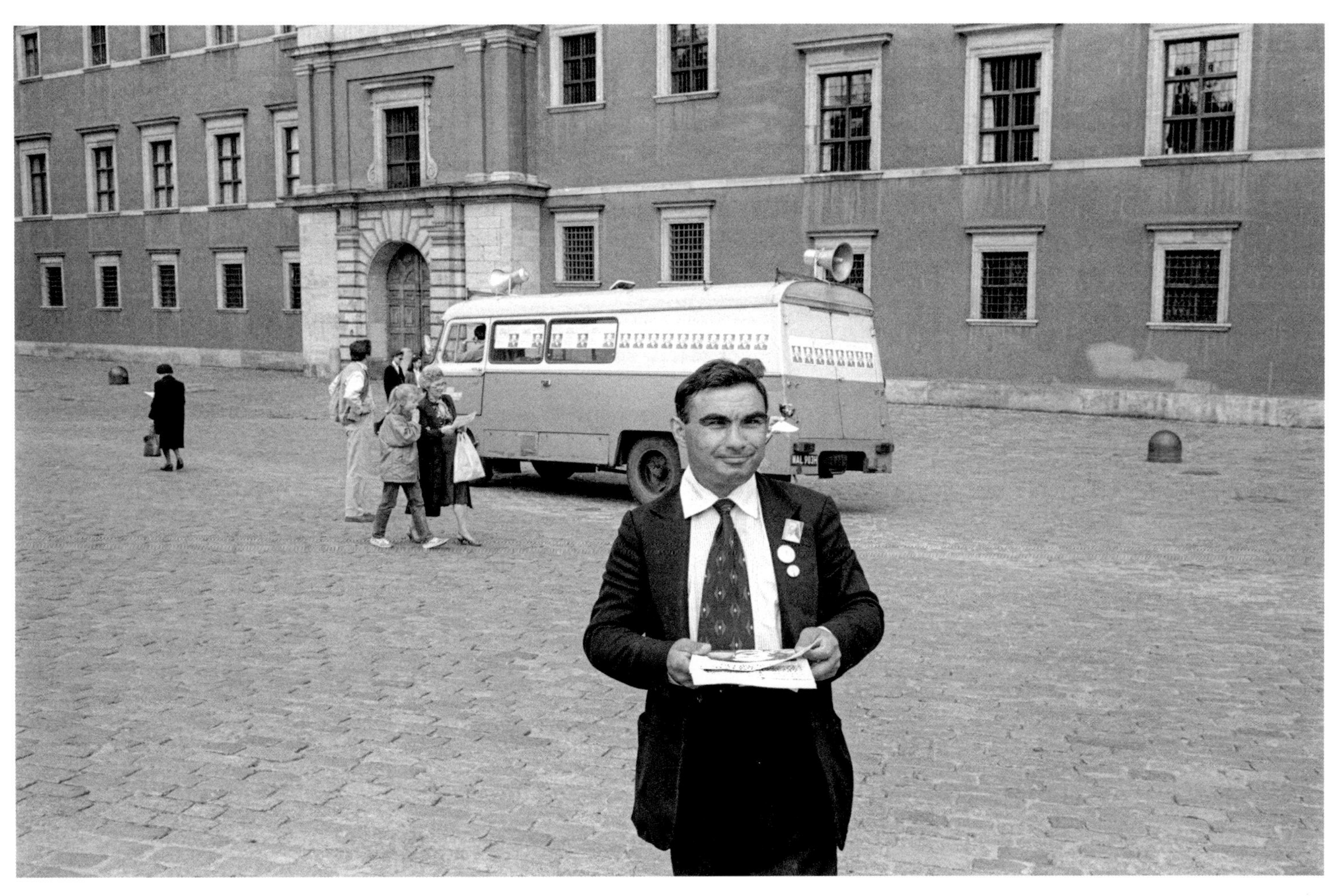

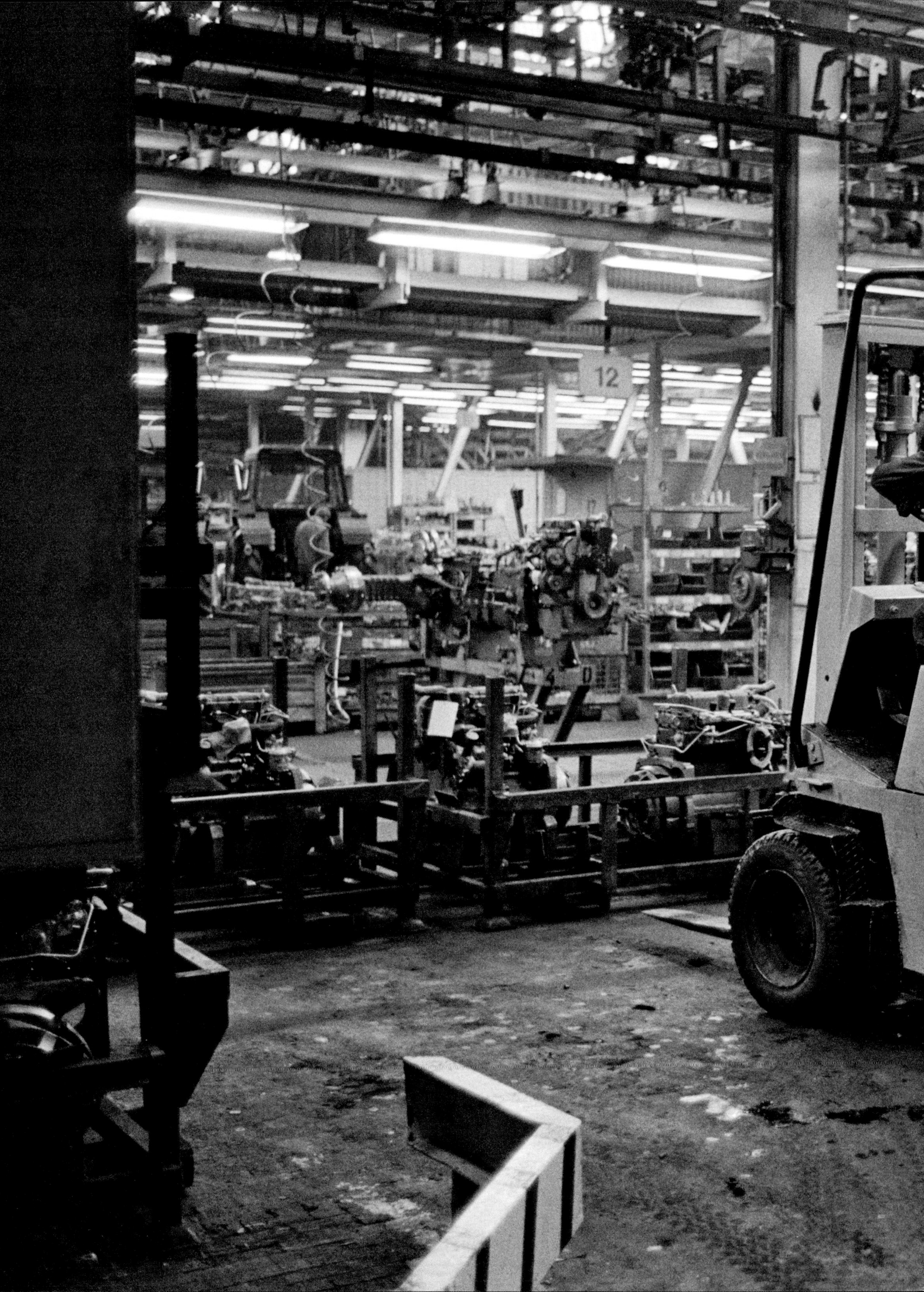
12

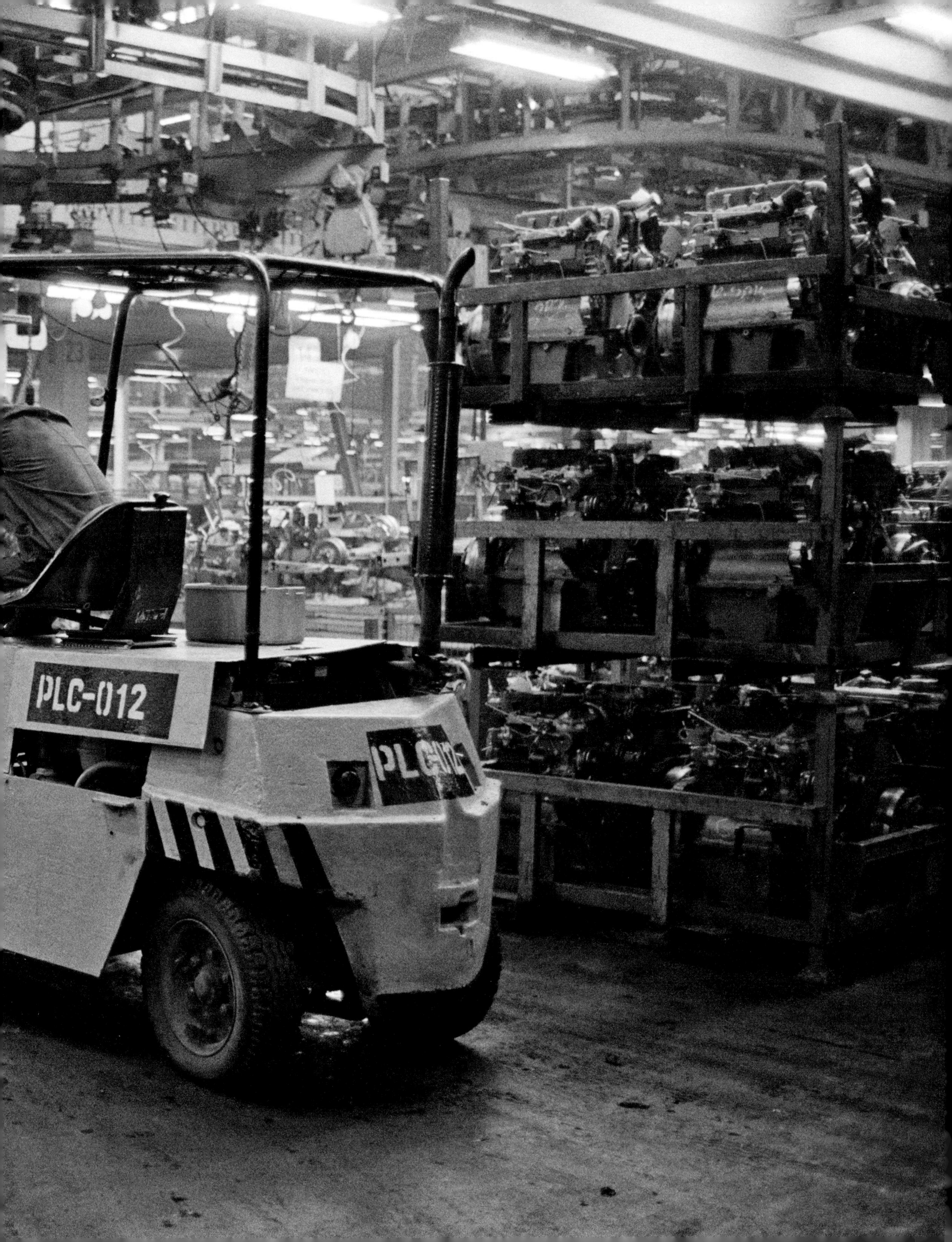
PLC-012

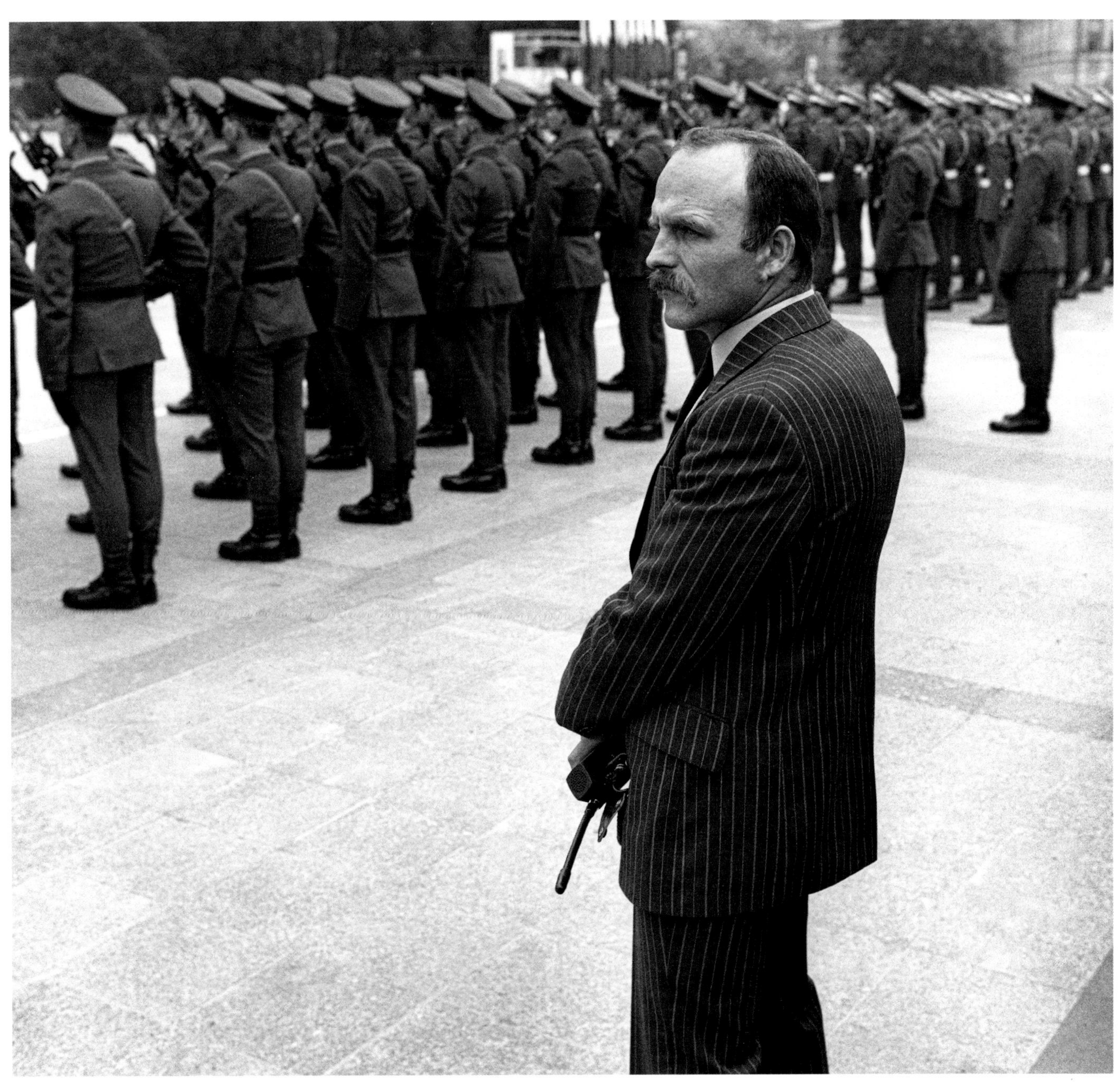

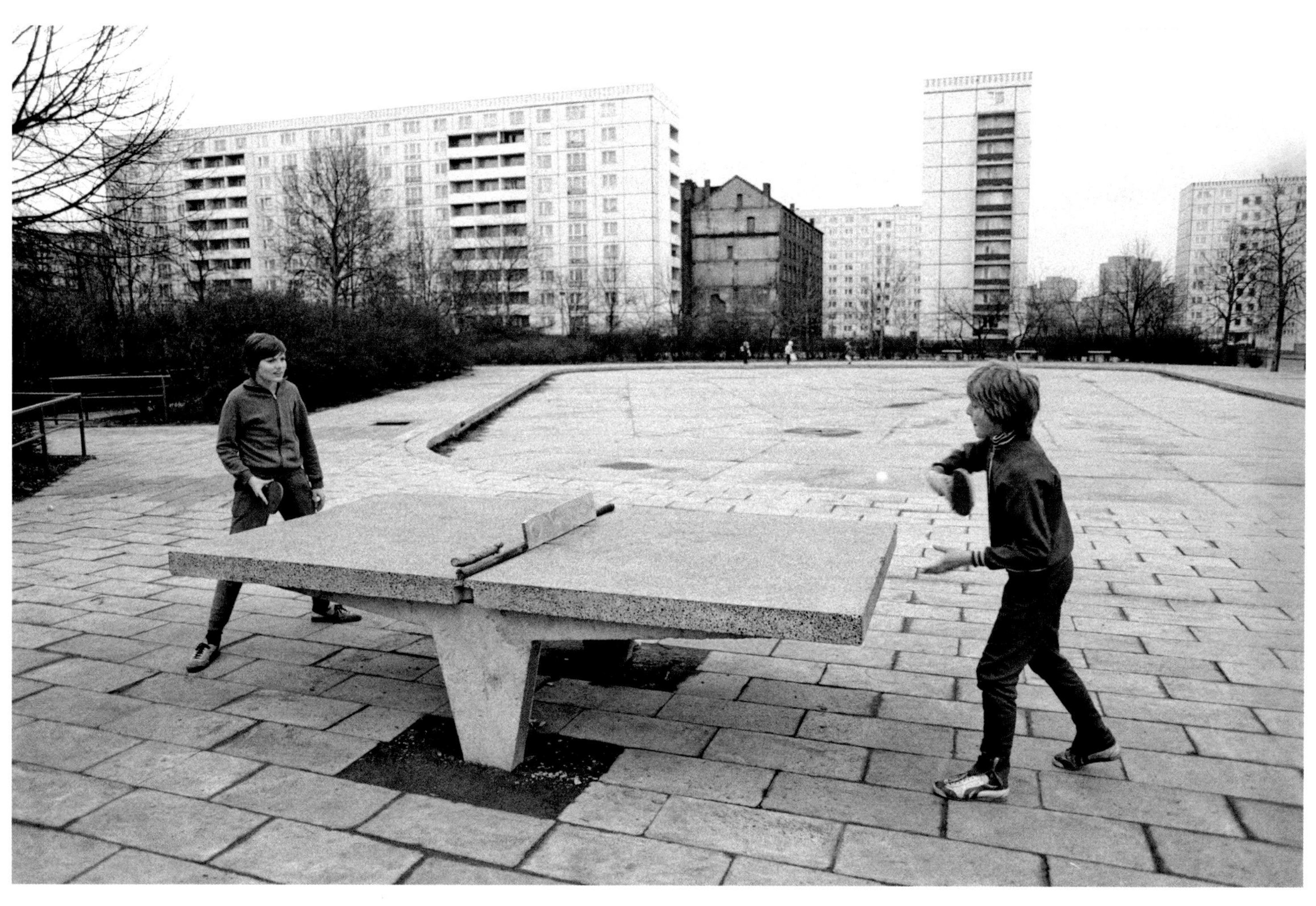

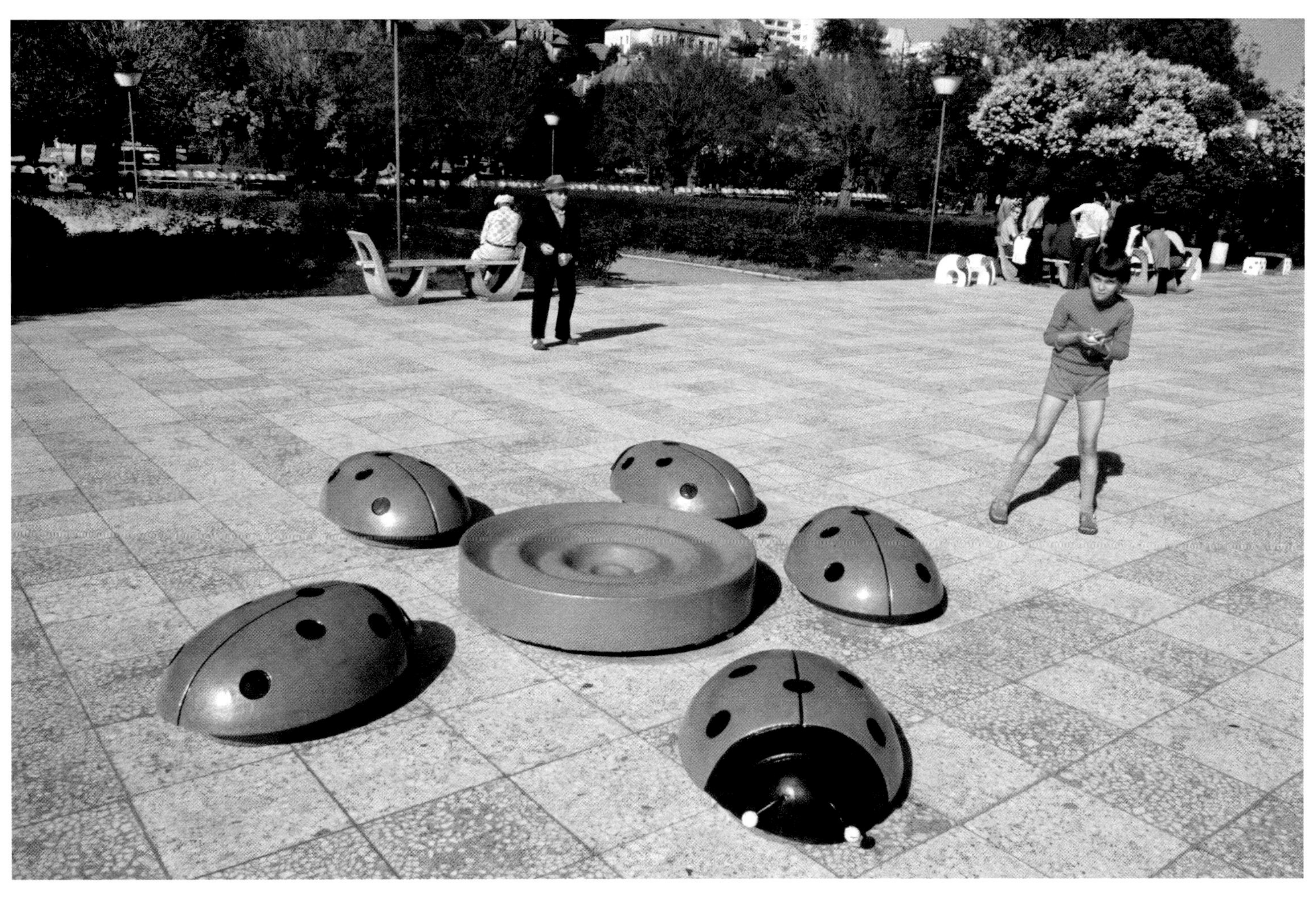

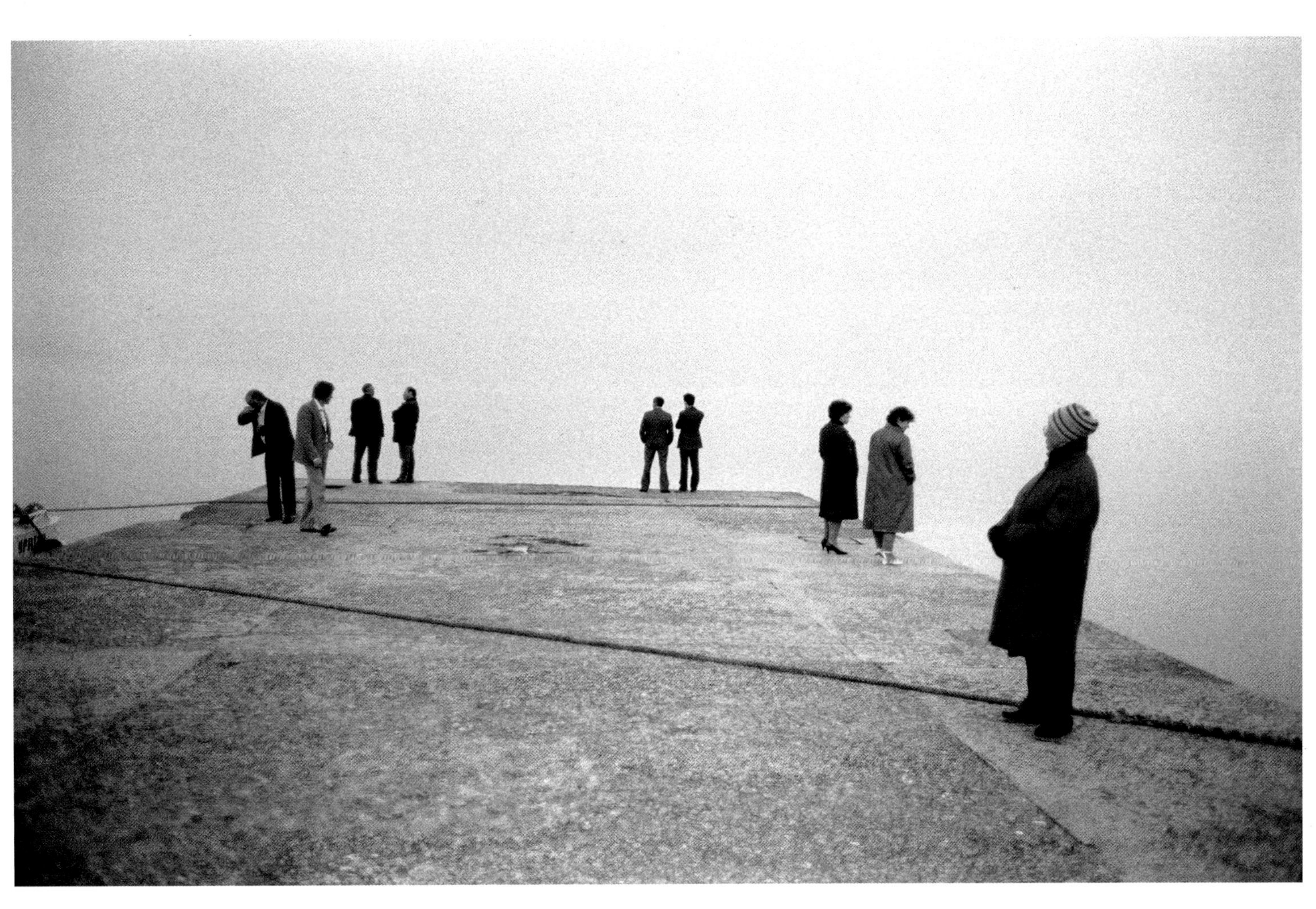

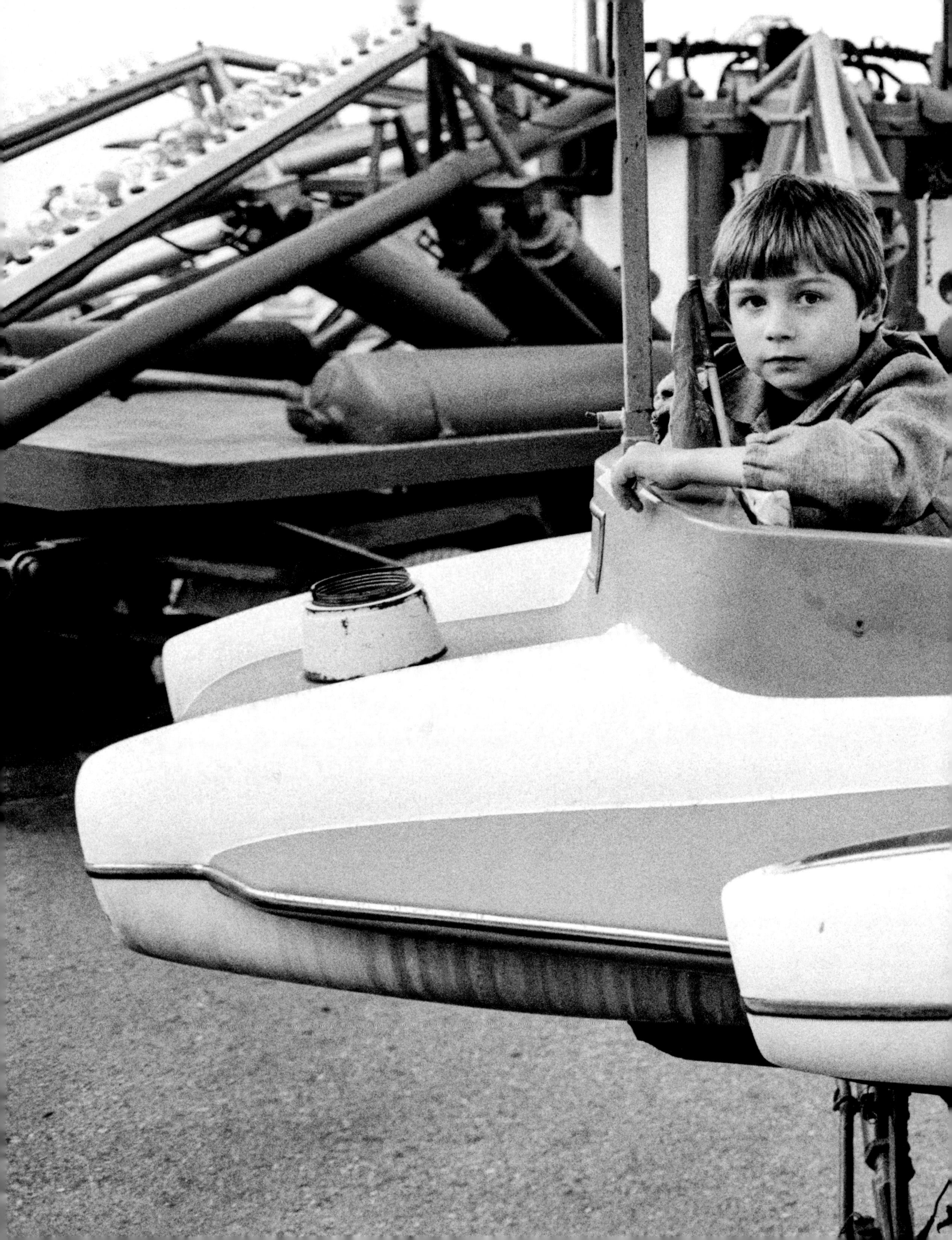

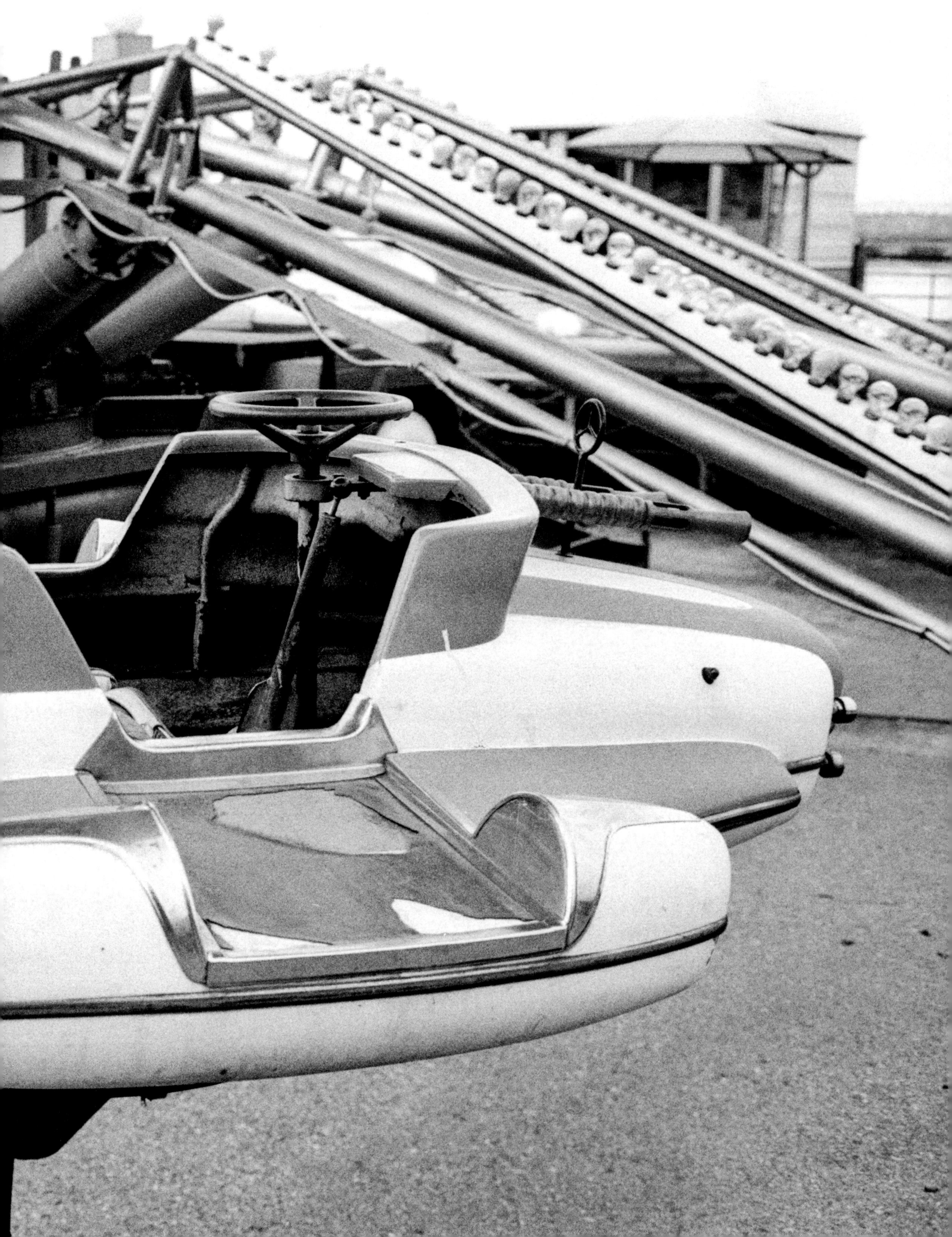

AFTERWORD

In over two decades of reporting overseas for TIME Magazine, I worked with many talented photojournalists, each of whom had a special talent in addition to the skills that are essential to be considered a true professional. Some had a knack for being in the right place at the right time; others were particularly good at getting film out of police states; still others were able to use their winning smiles to charm their subjects and gain access denied to their colleagues.

But the skill I admired most was, not surprisingly, the one needed to cover the communist regimes in which I specialized. Only a few photographers I knew had the ability not only to see through the facades so diligently erected by the propagandists who tried to control our observations, but also to capture the gritty, multi-dimensional reality those apparatchiks so desperately sought to conceal.

Arthur Grace was the best of that select lot. In both Poland in the early 1980s and China in the mid-80s, Arthur captured the visual reality that made my stories leave the page and enter the readers' minds. There is nothing simple about his images. While avoiding falling prey to the regime's propaganda of success, he also rejected the counter narrative of an oppressed, impoverished people.

His portraits are the most obvious example of that talent. Each face tells its own story, one that begins and ends with that person's inner dignity. One of the most difficult things to explain about the era covered in this book is how people who were ground down by political oppression and economic penury still managed to not just get through their daily lives but to live those lives as fully as possible. You could read volumes about that period and not gain as much insight about what it was like to live through those times as you will from exploring Arthur's photographs.

I count working with Arthur as one of the greatest strokes of good fortune I had in a career marked by much good luck – such as often being in the right place at the right time. His photographs not only elevated my articles, so too did his journalistic judgment as we discussed how to maneuver through the minefields of covering police states. That judgment is also evident in the selection and organization of the photos you will find in this remarkable book.

Richard Hornik

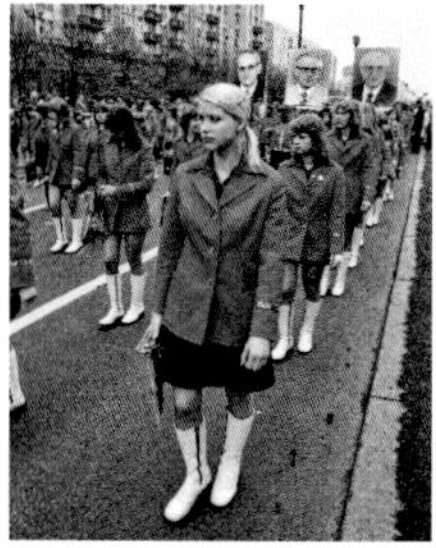

Cover:
Youthful participants awaiting the start of the annual Communist Party May Day parade. (East Berlin, German Democratic Republic, 1977)

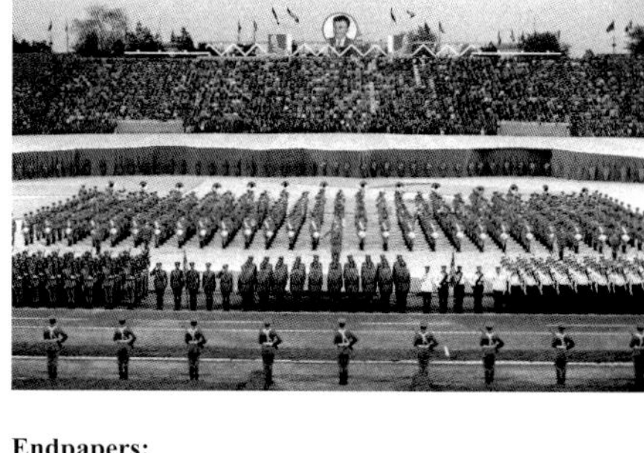

Endpapers:
The evening stadium celebration of the 100th anniversary of Romanian Independence. (Bucharest, Romania, 1977)

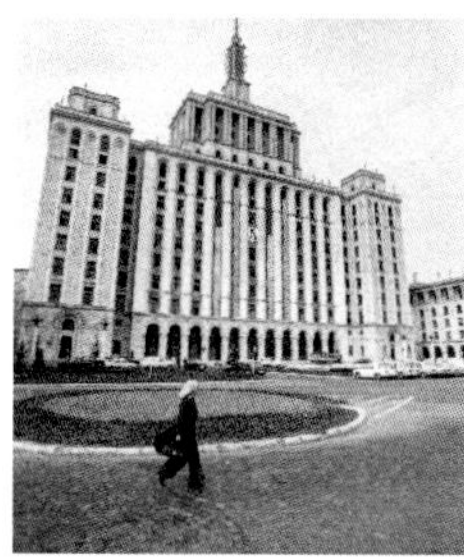

Page 5:
A woman passing a portrait of Romanian dictator Nicolae Ceaușescu outside Casa Scânteii - the massive Social Realist-designed State press building. (Bucharest, 1977)

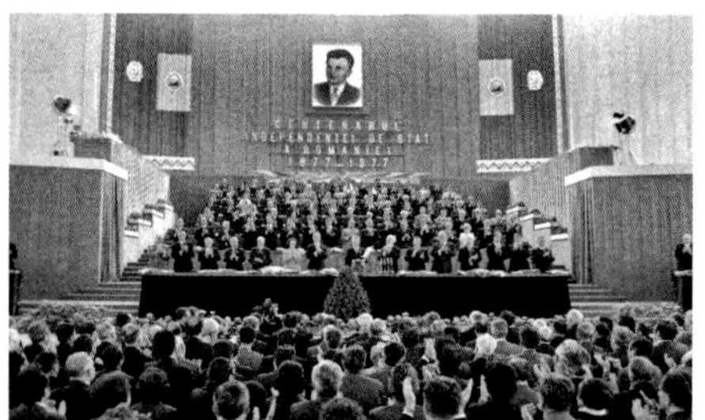

Pages 12-13:
Ceaușescu reading a lengthy speech to a packed arena of Communist Party officials, Romanian military officers, and foreign dignitaries to commemorate the 100th anniversary of Romanian independence. (Bucharest, 1977)

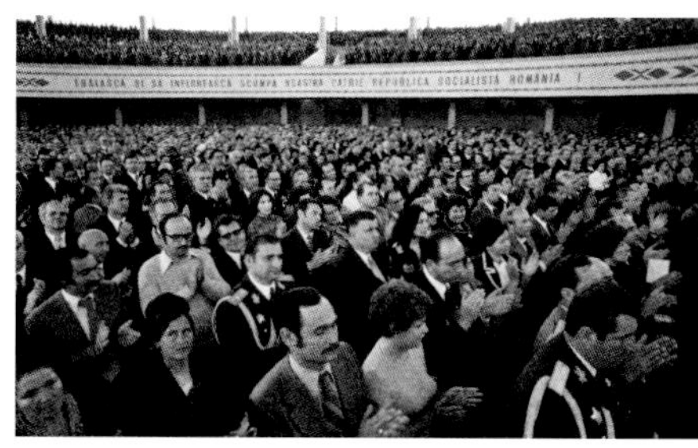

Pages 14-15:
Guests applauding Ceaușescu's speech. (Bucharest, 1977)

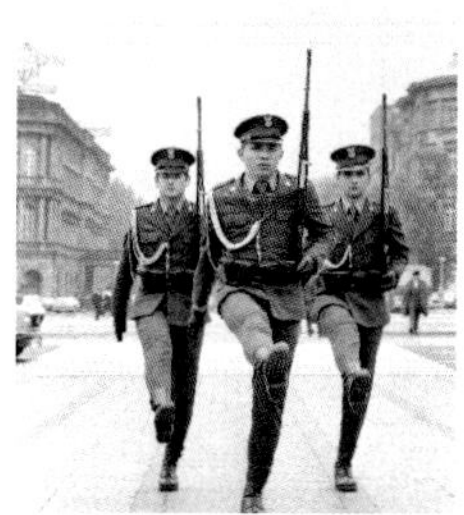

Page 16:
Polish soldiers marching during the changing of the guard at the Tomb of the Unknown Soldier. (Warsaw, Poland, 1982)

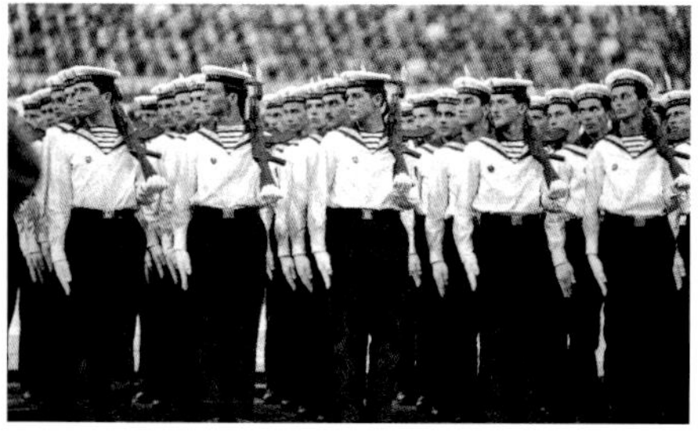

Page 17:
Sailors standing in formation at the Centenary of Romanian Independence celebration. (Bucharest, 1977)

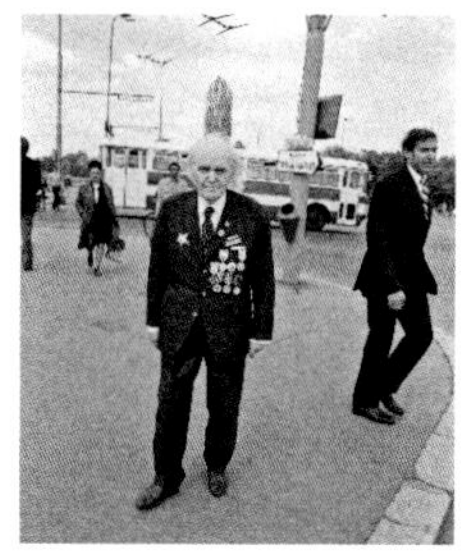

Page 19:
A decorated Romanian veteran outside the arena during the Centenary of Romanian Independence celebration. (Bucharest, 1977)

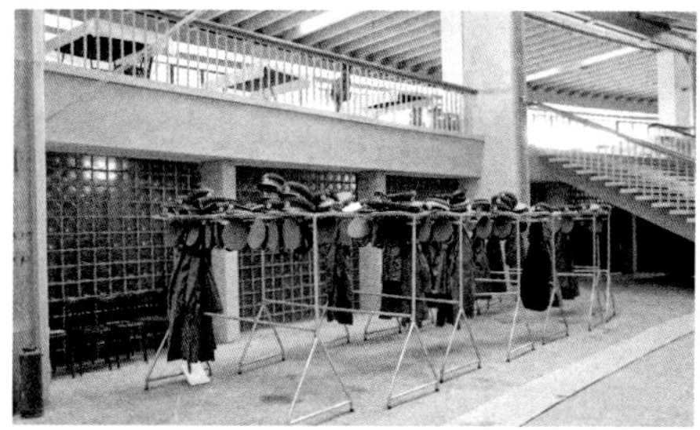

Page 20:
Military officers' hats and coats on racks at the arena during the Centenary of Romanian Independence celebration. (Bucharest, 1977)

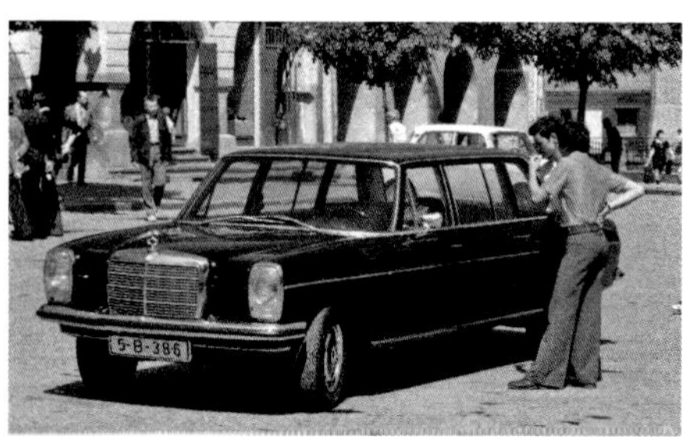

Page 21:
Romanian teens checking out a Mercedes limousine parked in the middle of the street. (Sighişoara, Romania, 1977)

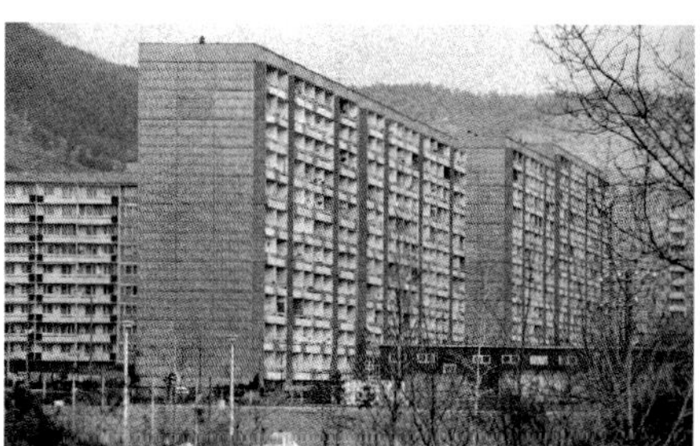

Pages 22-23:
Newly built apartment blocks. (Jena, German Democratic Republic, 1977)

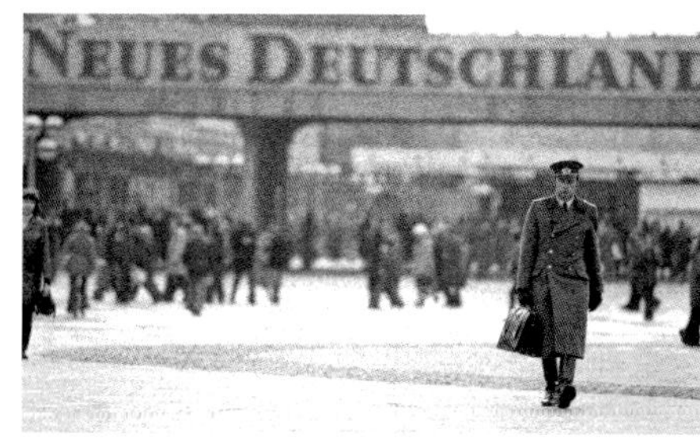

Page 25:
An East German military officer at Alexanderplatz. (East Berlin, 1977)

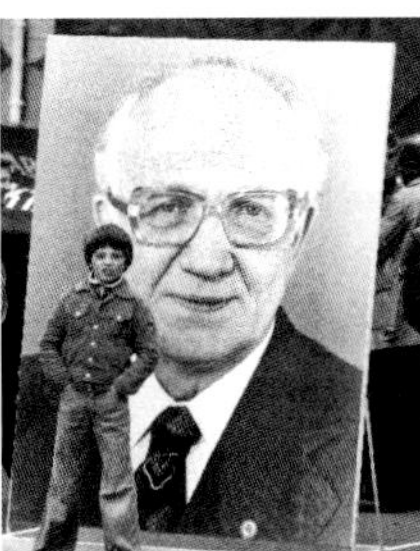

Page 26:
A young boy in front of a mobile display of former East German Prime Minister Horst Sindermann prior to the start of the annual May Day parade. (East Berlin, 1977)

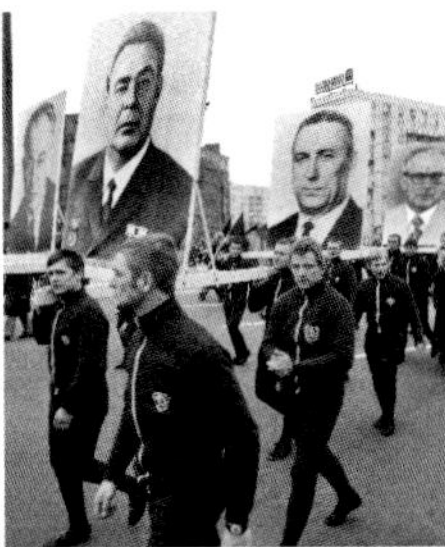

Page 27:
East German athletes marching with displays of Soviet leader Leonid Brezhnev, Polish leader Edward Gierek, and East German leader Erich Honecker during the May Day parade. (East Berlin, 1977)

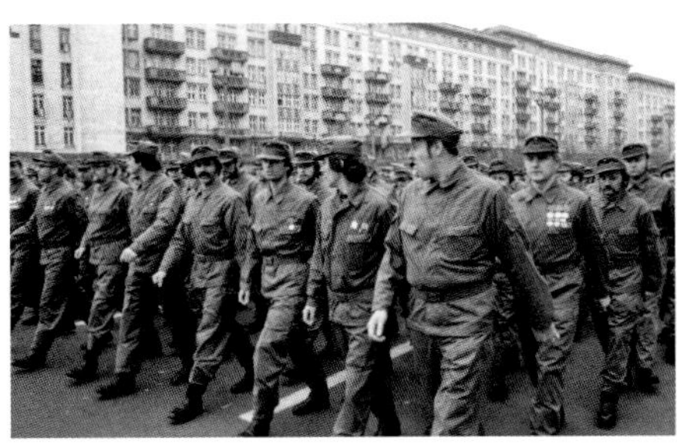

Pages 28-29:
Reservists from the East German National People's Army marching in the May Day parade. (East Berlin, 1977)

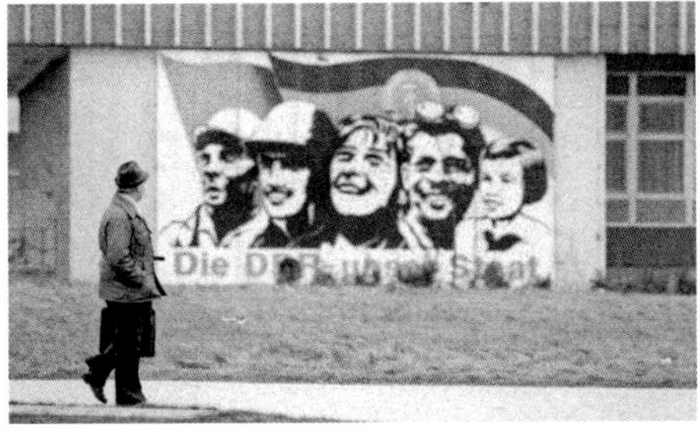

Page 30:
A citizen passing by the State propaganda mural "The GDR: Our Country." (Jena, 1977)

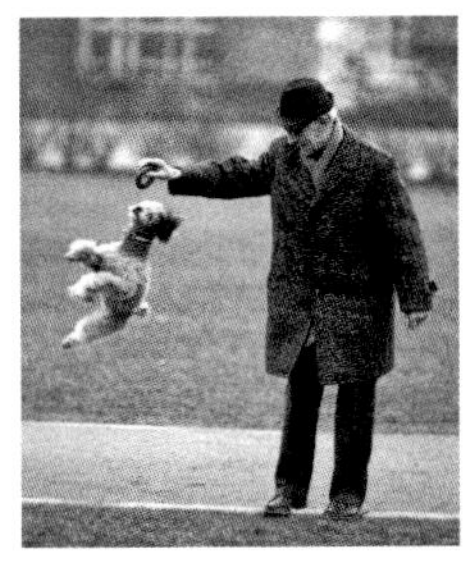

Page 31:
A man and his dog. (Weimar, German Democratic Republic, 1977)

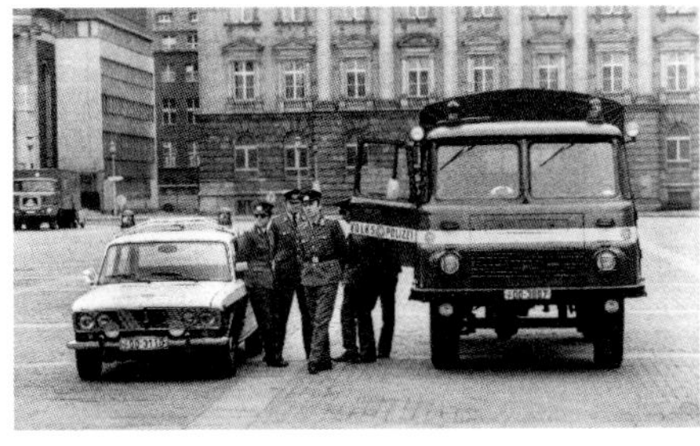

Pages 32-33:
East German police near Checkpoint Charlie. (East Berlin, 1977)

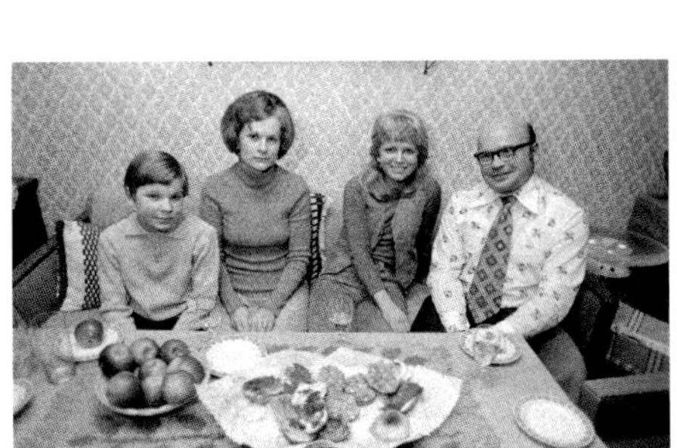

Pages 34-35:
A factory worker and family posing for a staged photograph arranged by authorities to show off a "typical" East German family. (Radebeul, German Democratic Republic, 1977)

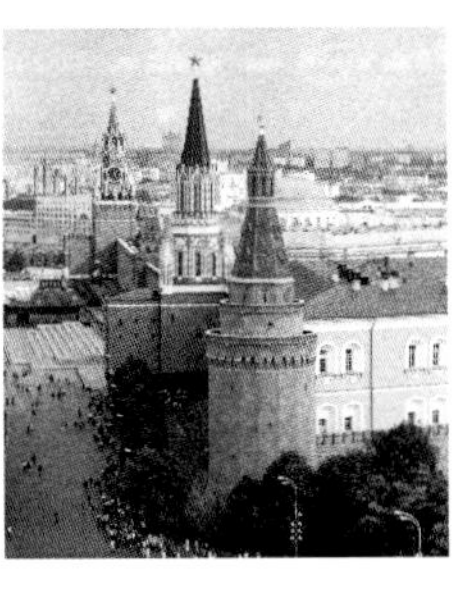

Page 39:
Red Square observed from a hotel room. The out of focus and distorted bottom portion of the photograph is due to the buckling of the poorly made window glass. This was one of my first encounters with the vagaries of Soviet quality control. (Moscow, USSR, 1977)

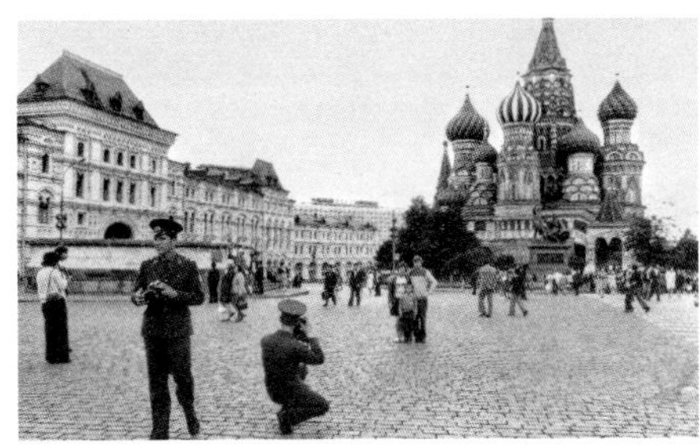

Pages 40-41:
Soviet soldiers taking photographs in Red Square. (Moscow, 1977)

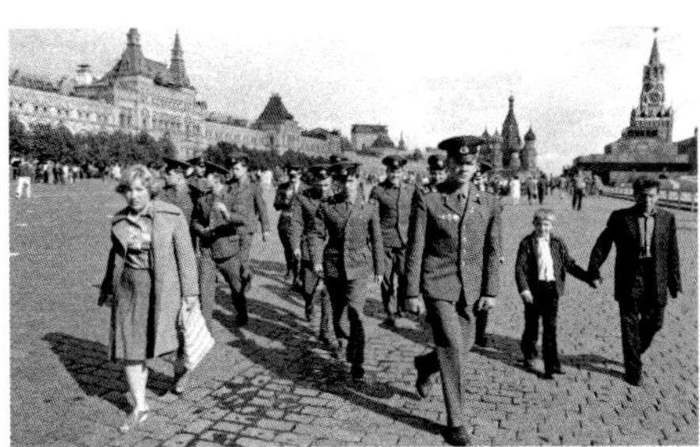

Page 42:
A group of soldiers and civilians walking through Red Square. As frequently happened during my time photographing behind the Iron Curtain, people looked with apprehension at a stranger pointing a camera at them, but always remained silent and non-confrontational. I was never challenged by anyone other than State authorities. (Moscow, 1977)

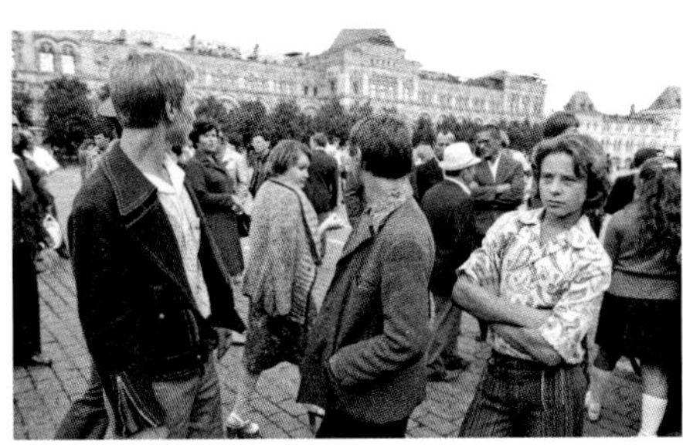

Page 43:
A group of teenage boys looking cool and checking out girls while walking through Red Square. (Moscow, 1977)

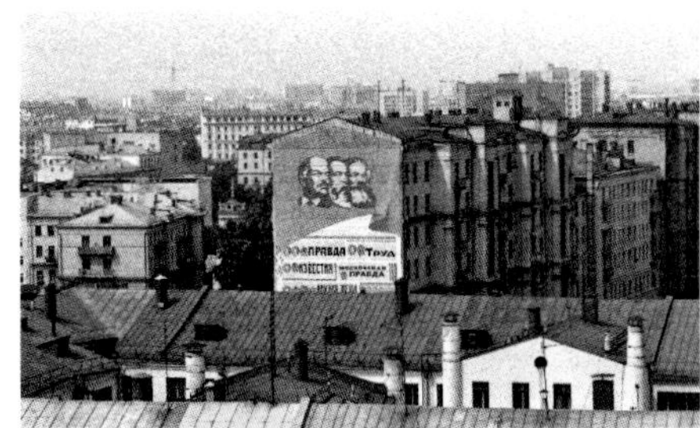

Page 44:
A prominent mural of Communist icons Vladimir Lenin, Friedrich Engels, and Karl Marx. (Moscow, 1977)

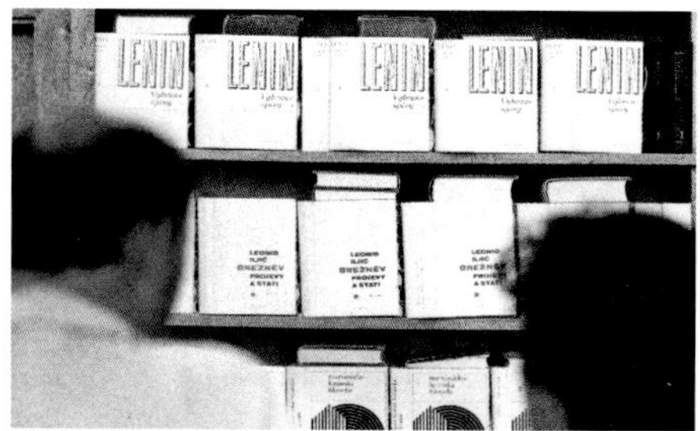

Page 45:
A bookstore's featured reading. (Moscow, 1977)

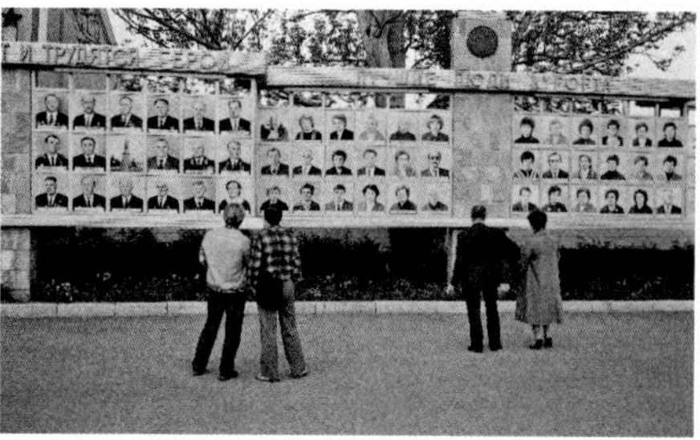

Pages 46-47:
Passers-by taking in the display of portraits of Best Employees of the Spa in Yalta's main square. (Yalta, USSR, 1987)

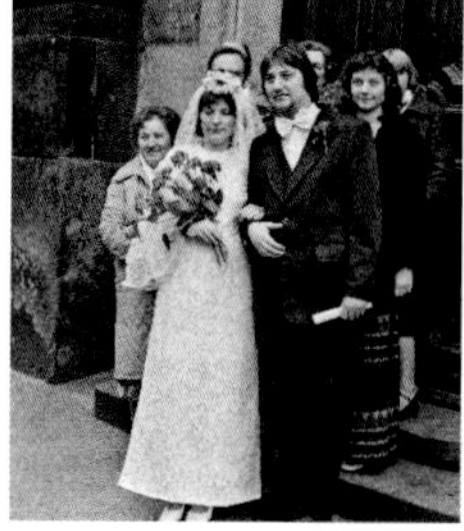

Page 48:
A wedding party posing for a local photographer. (Dresden, German Democratic Republic, 1977)

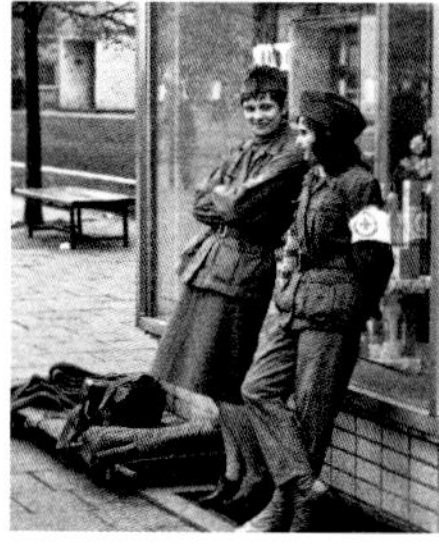

Page 49:
Two female medics keeping watch during the annual May Day parade. (East Berlin, 1977)

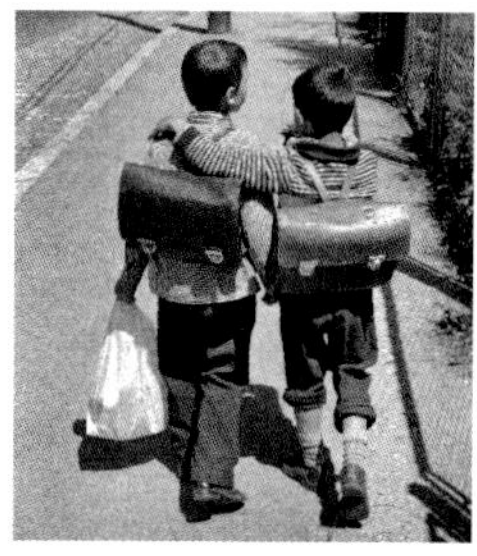

Page 50:
Romanian schoolboys walking home. (Sighişoara, 1977)

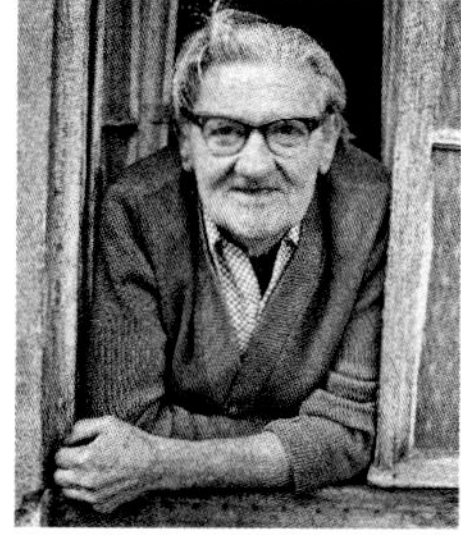

Page 51:
An East German woman at her apartment window. (Weimar, 1977)

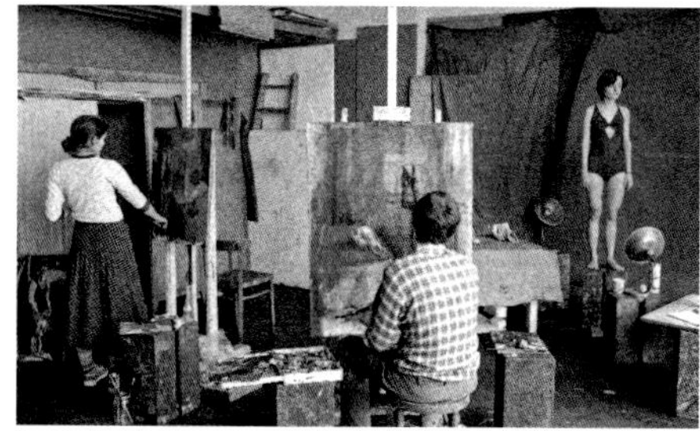

Pages 52-53:
Art school models at work posing for painting and sculpture classes. (Warsaw, 1982)

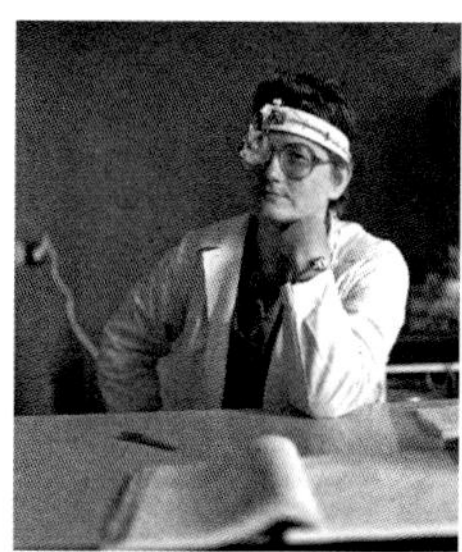

Page 54:
The factory doctor at Poland's Lenin Steelworks at her office desk. (Nova Huta, Poland, 1989)

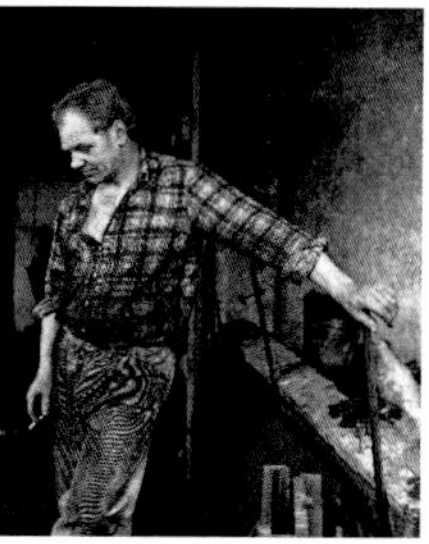

Page 55:
A blacksmith taking a cigarette break. (near Krakow, Poland, 1989)

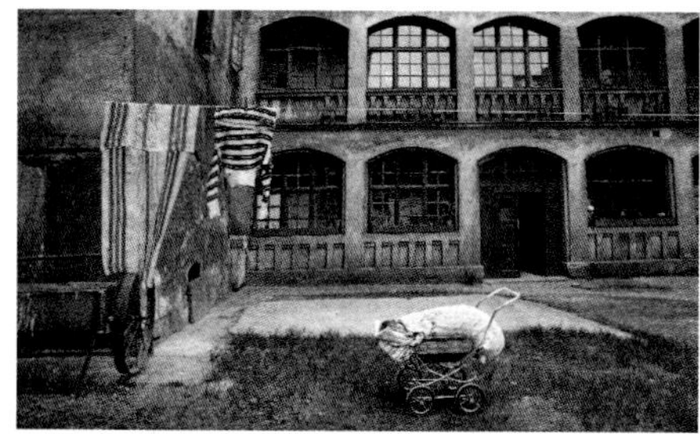

Pages 56-57:
An unattended child in a baby carriage sleeping while laundry dries outside an apartment building. (Warsaw, 1982)

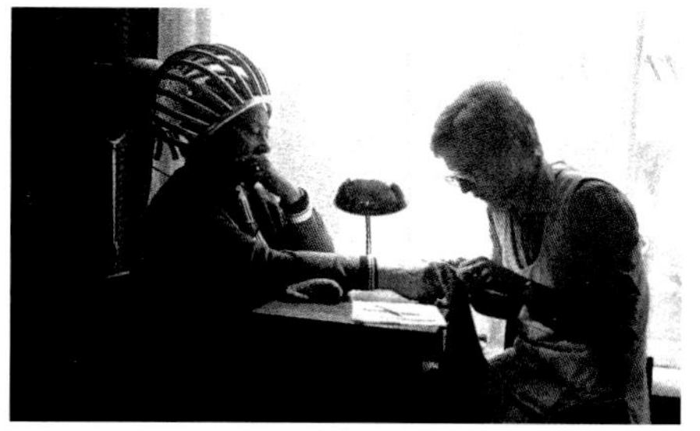

Page 58:
A customer receiving a manicure in beauty salon. (Warsaw, 1982)

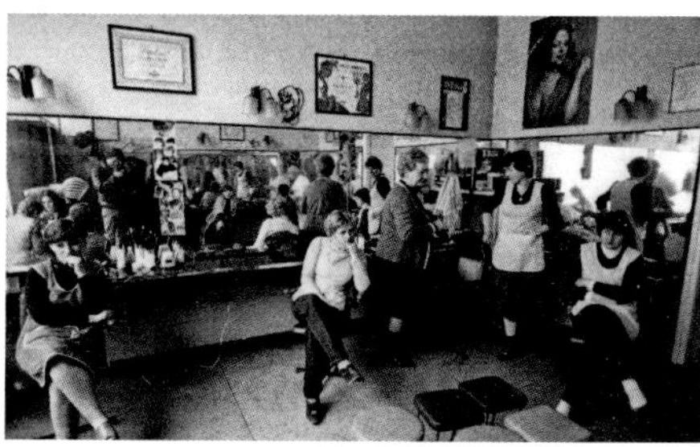

Page 59:
Hairdressers waiting for customers at their beauty parlor. (Warsaw, 1982)

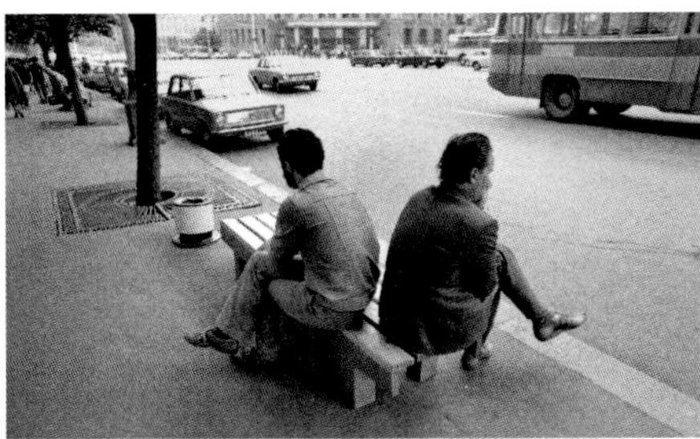

Page 61:
Men sharing a bench. (Moscow, 1977)

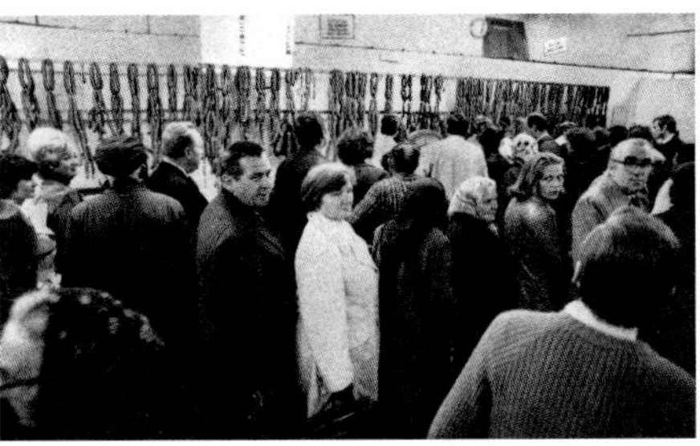

Page 62:
Customers waiting to be served at a local Butcher shop that has almost no meat remaining for sale other than sausage. (Warsaw, 1982)

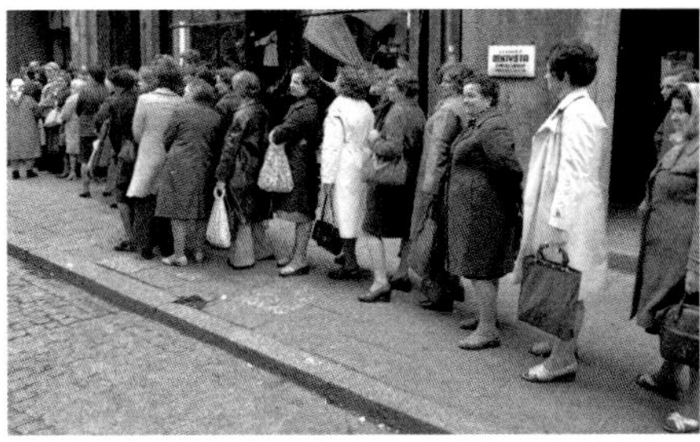

Page 63:
Women queueing for the grocery store. (Warsaw, 1982)

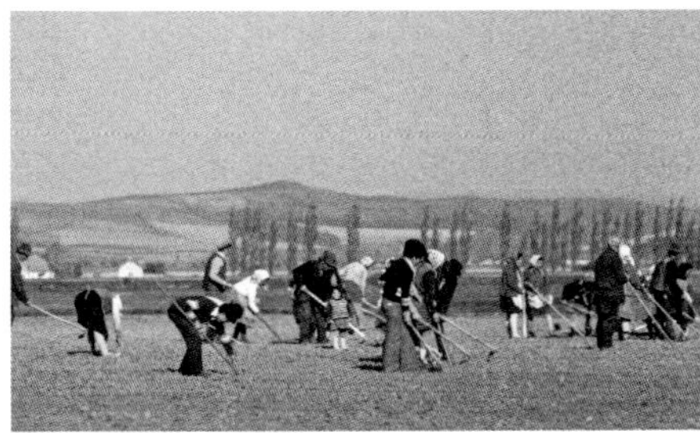

Pages 64-65:
Romanian farm workers tilling a field. (Sighişoara, 1977)

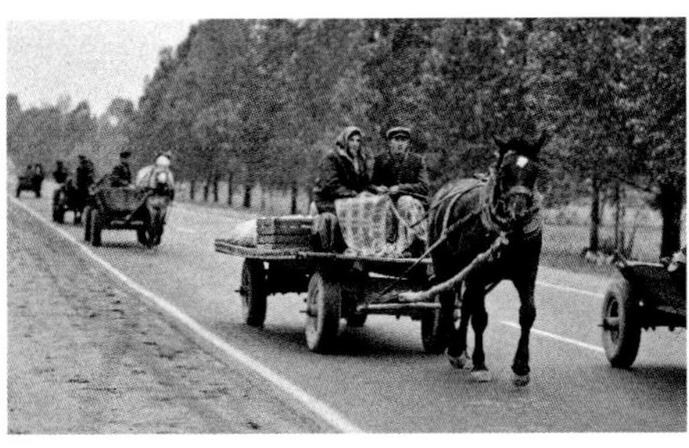

Page 66:
Horse-drawn wagons carrying produce to market. (rural Poland, 1982)

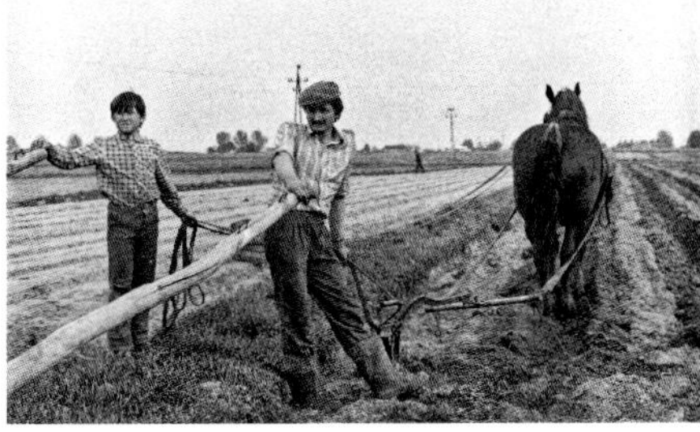

Page 69:
A farmer and his son taking a break from plowing their field. (rural Poland, 1982)

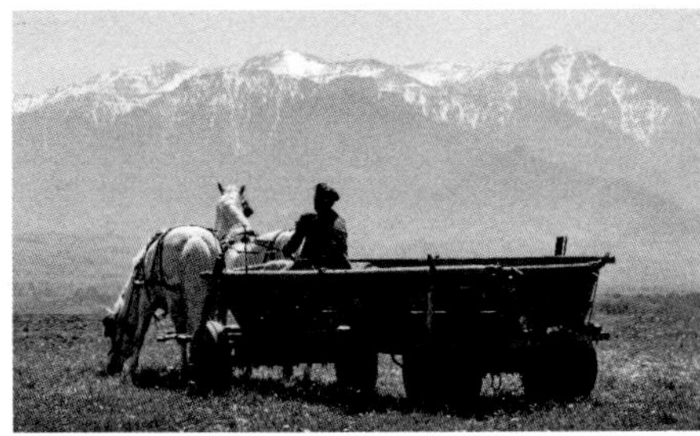

Pages 70-71:
A Transylvanian farmer taking in the view while resting his horses in a field by his home. (Transylvania, Romania, 1977)

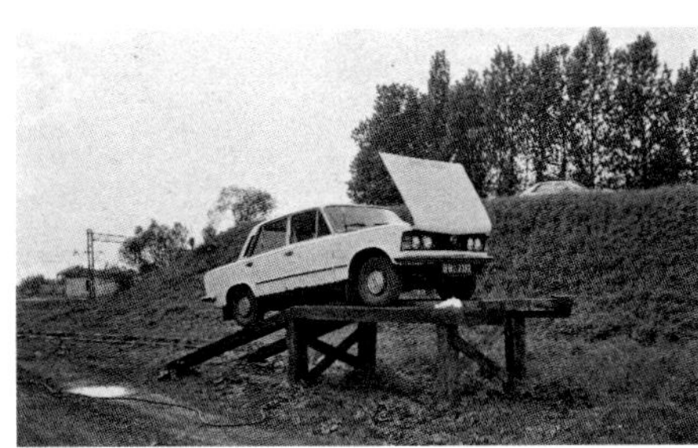

Page 72:
A wooden car lift. (rural Poland, 1982)

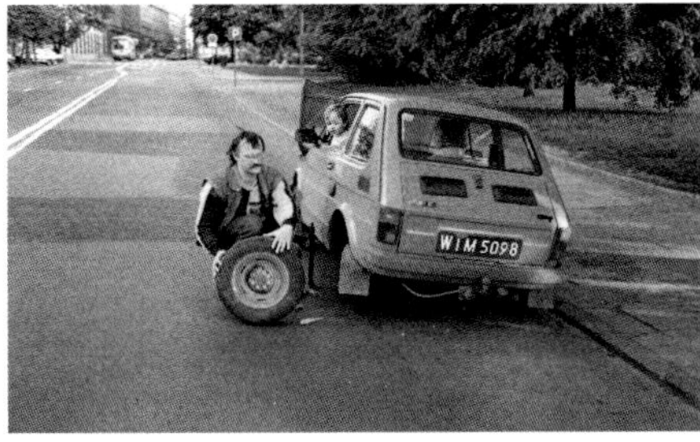

Page 73:
A father changing a tire on his Polski Fiat as his young son looks on. (Warsaw, 1977)

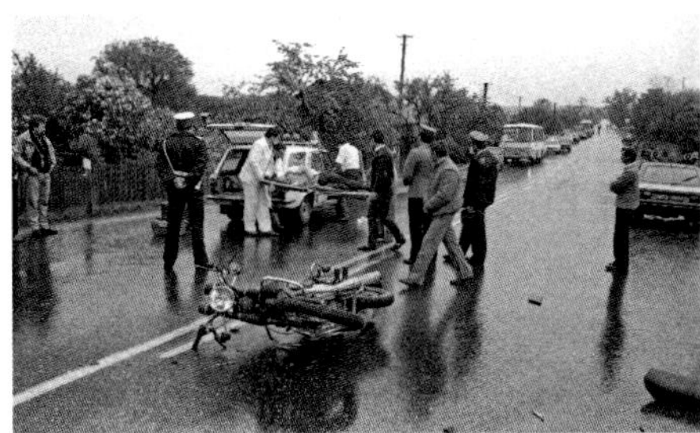

Page 75:
An injured motorcyclist being stretchered to a waiting station wagon ambulance. (Poland, 1989)

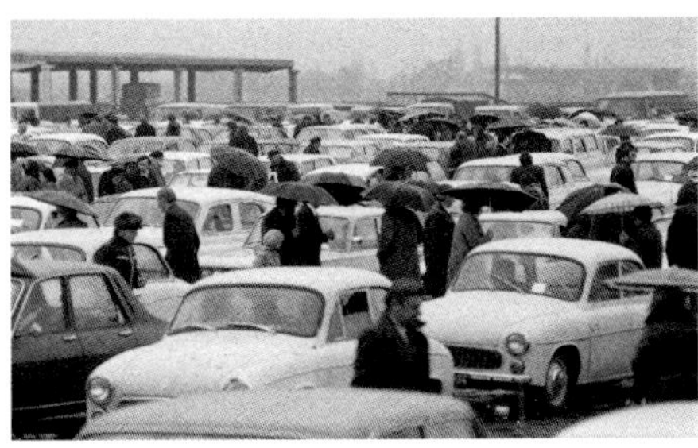

Pages 76-77:
Warsaw's weekly used car market. (Warsaw, 1982)

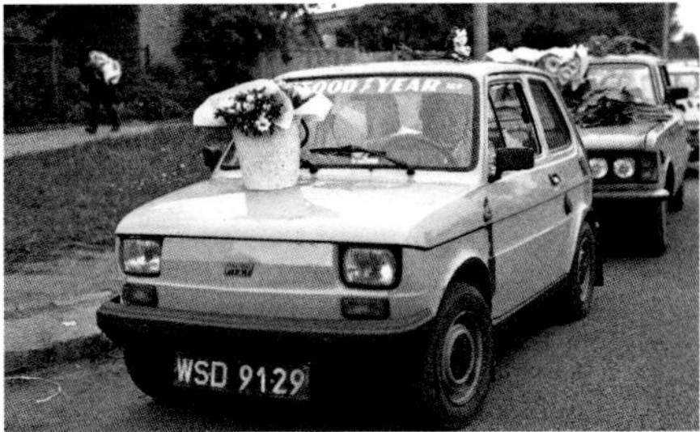

Page 79:
A woman selling flowers curbside from her auto. (Warsaw, 1989)

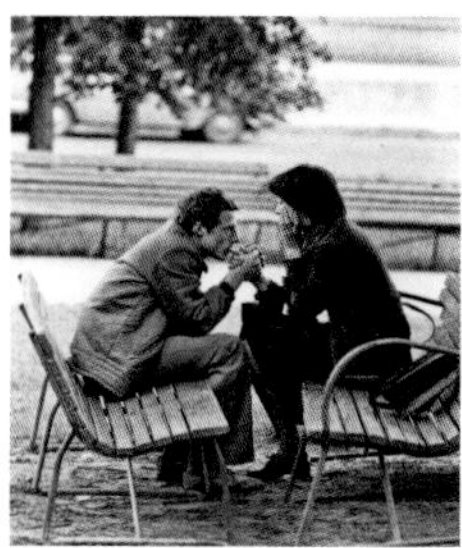

Page 81:
A young couple on park benches. (Warsaw, 1982)

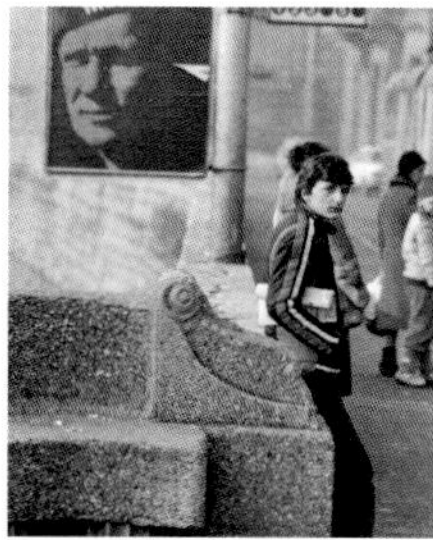

Page 82:
A teenager at a bus stop alongside a poster of the deceased Yugoslav President for Life, strongman Marshal Tito. (Sarajevo, 1983)

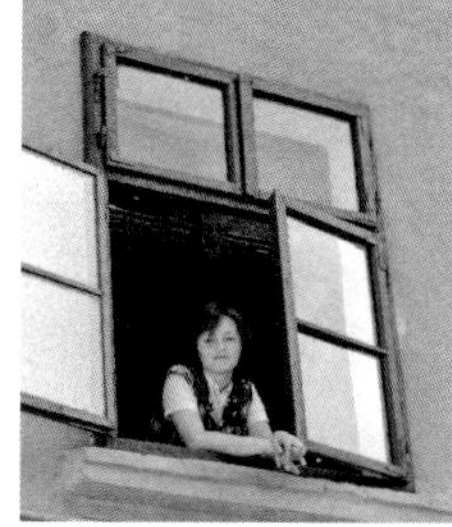

Page 83:
A young Romanian woman at her apartment window. (Sighişoara, 1977)

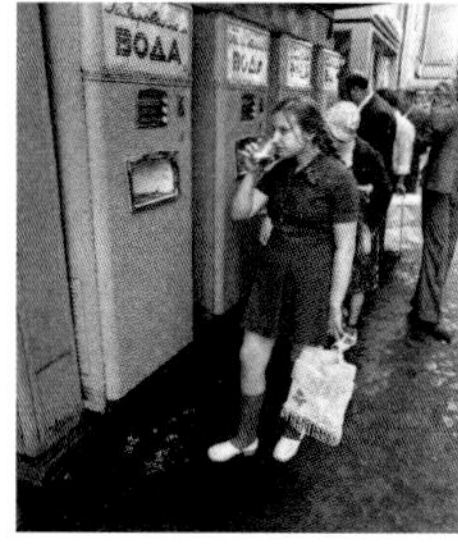

Page 84:
A girl drinking from the reusable, shared glass of a beverage vending machine. (Moscow, 1977)

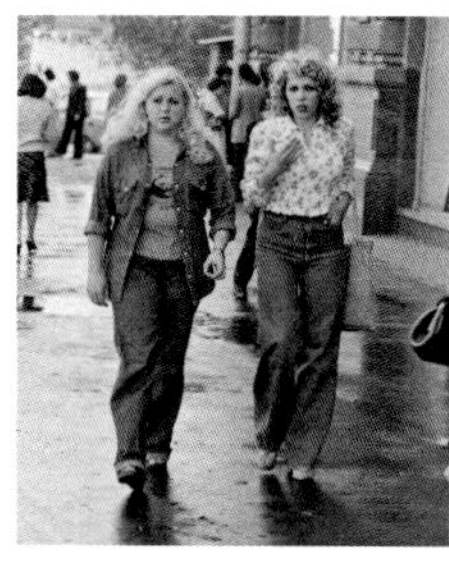

Page 85:
Two young women wearing stylish Soviet jeans. (Moscow, 1977)

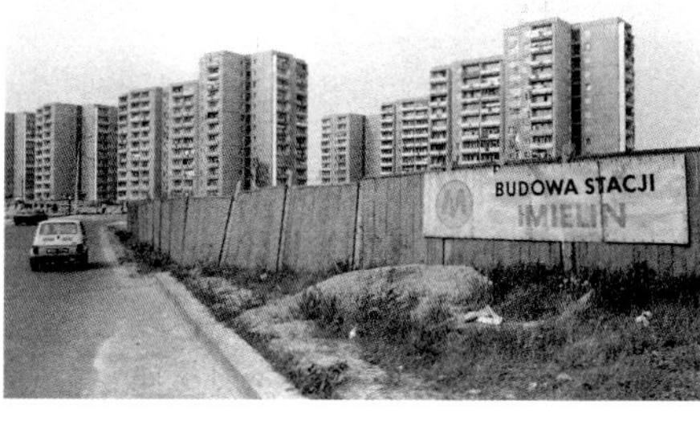

Page 87:
A cluster of apartment blocks with a sign announcing a future Metro station. (Warsaw, 1989)

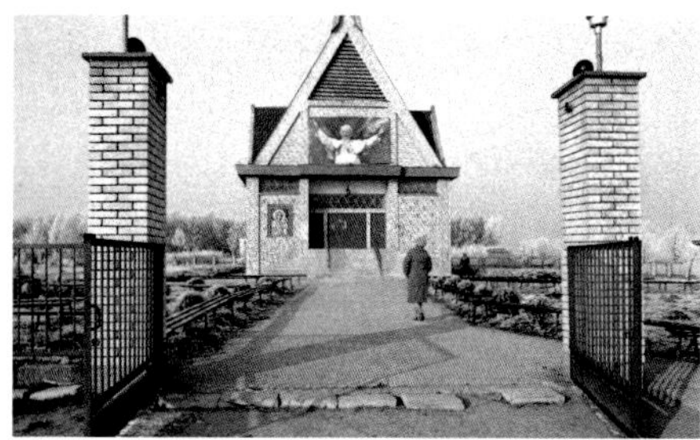

Pages 88-89:
A rural Catholic church adorned with a mural of Pope John Paul II. (Poland, 1982)

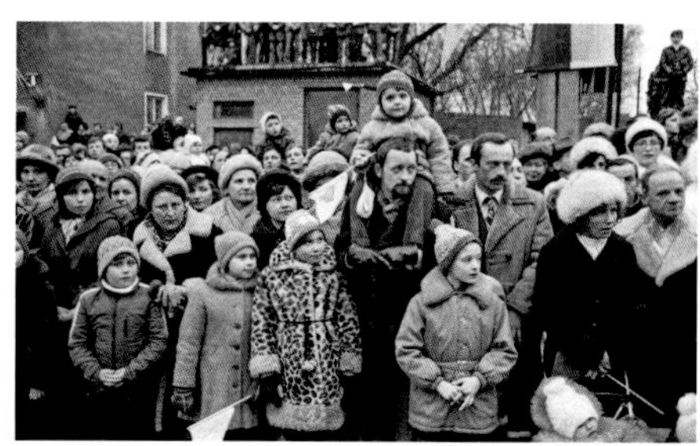

Page 90:
A crowd waiting for Cardinal Jozef Glemp, the Archbishop of Warsaw's procession to pass by. (Warsaw, 1982)

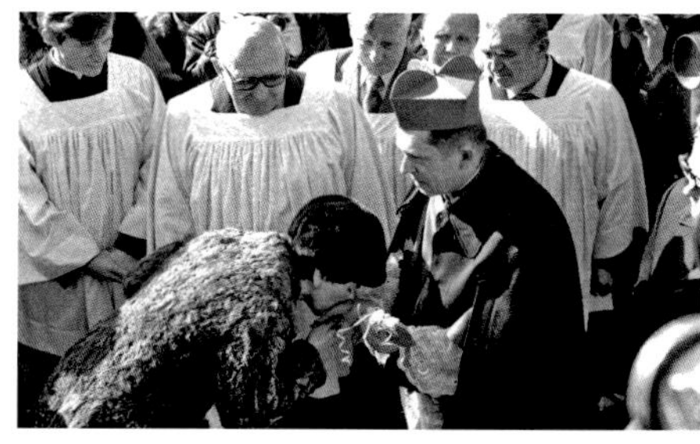

Page 91:
A woman kissing the hand of Cardinal Glemp during a religious procession. (Warsaw, 1982)

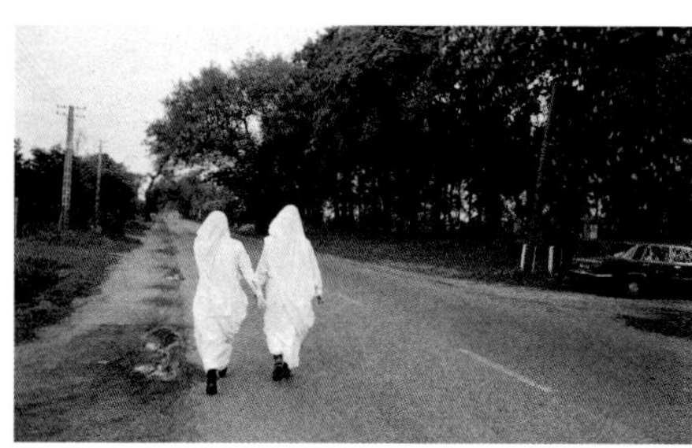

Page 92:
Two nuns walking down a country road. (Poland, 1989)

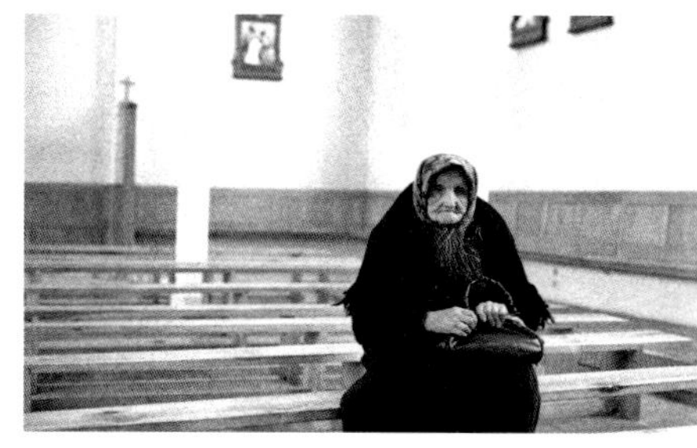

Page 93:
An elderly parishioner seated on the bench of a rural church. (Poland, 1982)

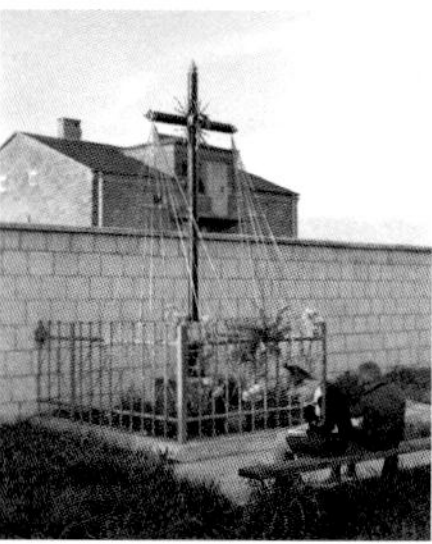

Page 94:
Two girls studying the bible in front of a religious shrine. (Poland, 1989)

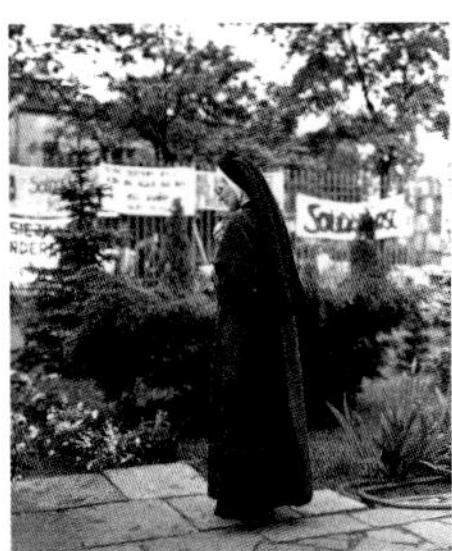

Page 95:
A nun in front of a makeshift Solidarity memorial. (Warsaw, 1989)

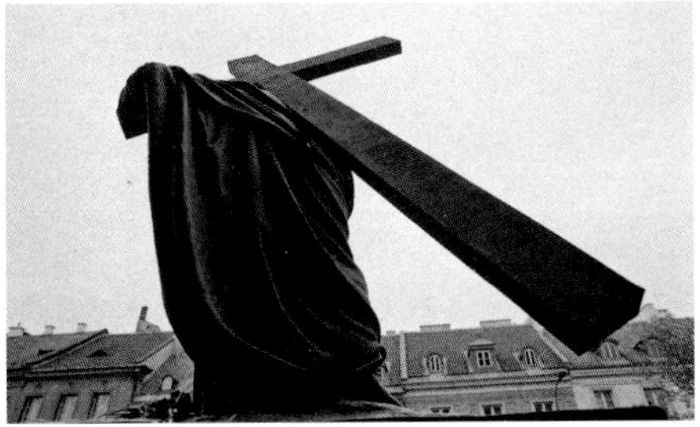

Pages 96-97:
A public statue of Jesus carrying the cross. (Warsaw, 1982)

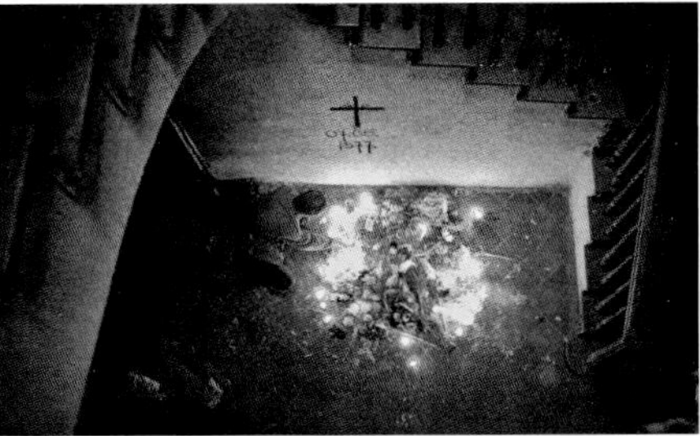

Pages 98-99:
A candle-lit memorial on the site where student activist Stanislaw Pyjas fell to his death, allegedly killed by secret police. (Krakow, 1977)

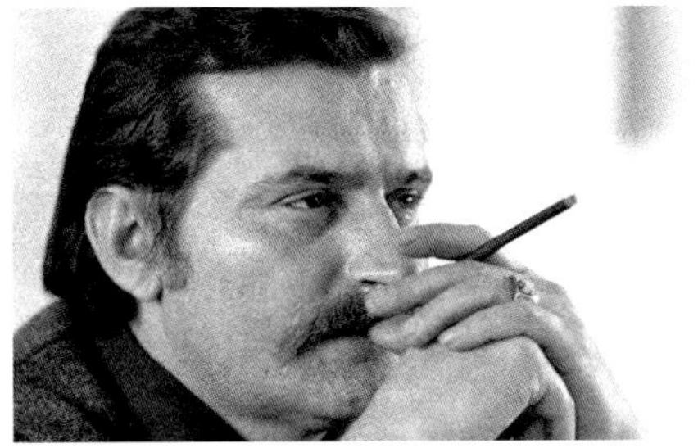

Pages 100-101:
Portrait of Solidarity leader Lech Wałęsa smoking during a committee meeting. (Gdansk, Poland, 1981)

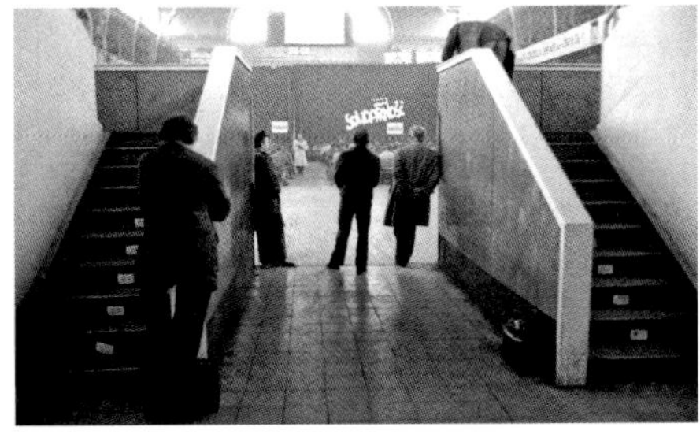

Pages 102-103:
Observers at the back of the hall during a Solidarity conference. (Warsaw, 1981)

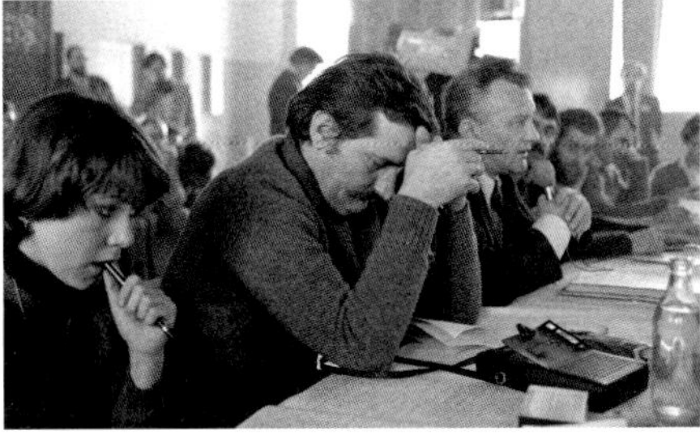

Page 104:
Lech Wałęsa during a Solidarity committee meeting. (Gdansk, 1981)

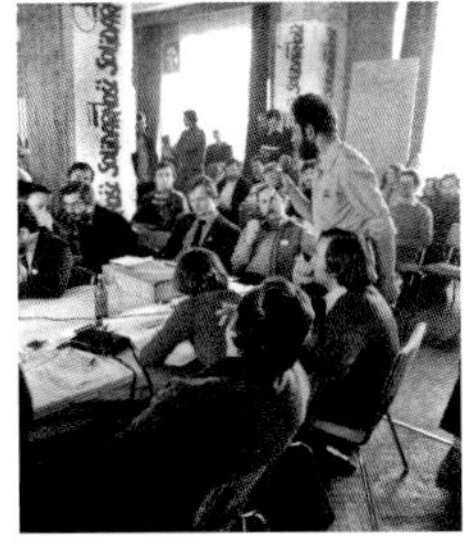

Page 105:
A committee member addressing a meeting at Solidarity headquarters. (Gdansk, 1981)

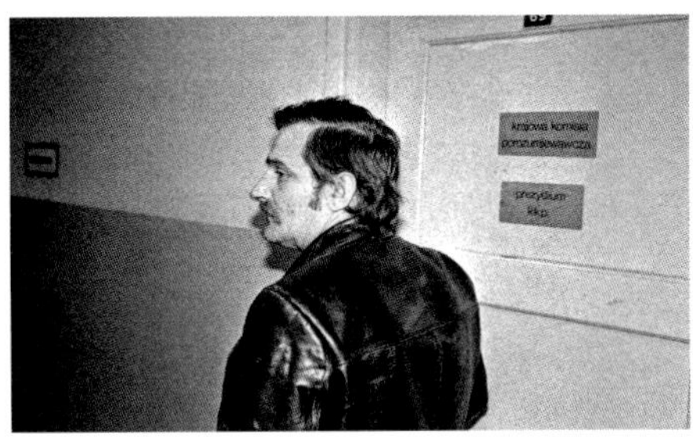

Page 107:
Lech Wałęsa leaving the Solidarity headquarters office. (Gdansk, 1981)

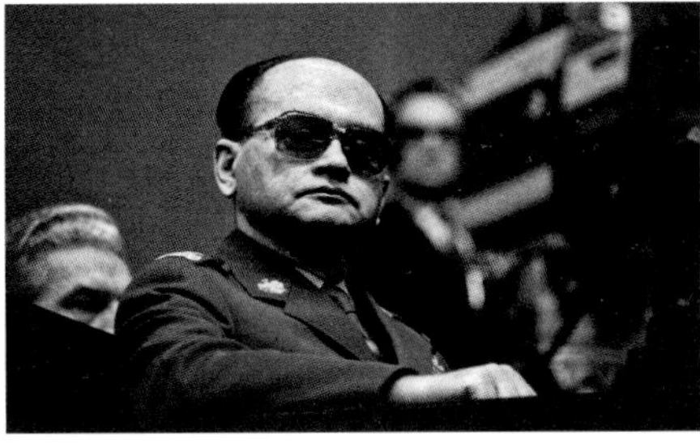

Page 108:
Polish General Wojciech Jaruzelski, who imposed martial law on December 13, 1981, seated at a session of Parliament. (Warsaw, 1982)

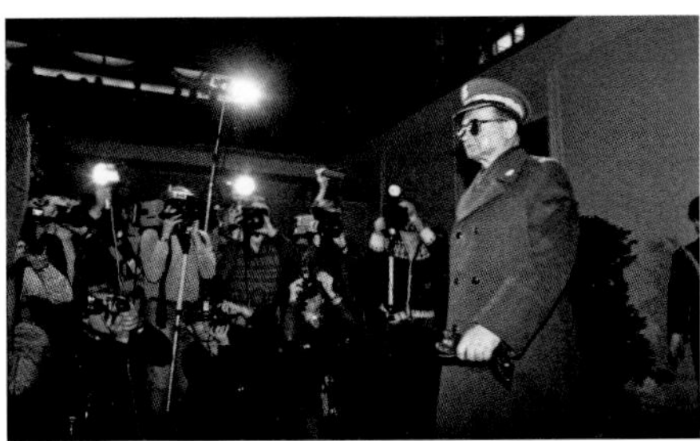

Page 109:
Jaruzelski leaving the Parliament building in front of the press after the session. (Warsaw, 1982)

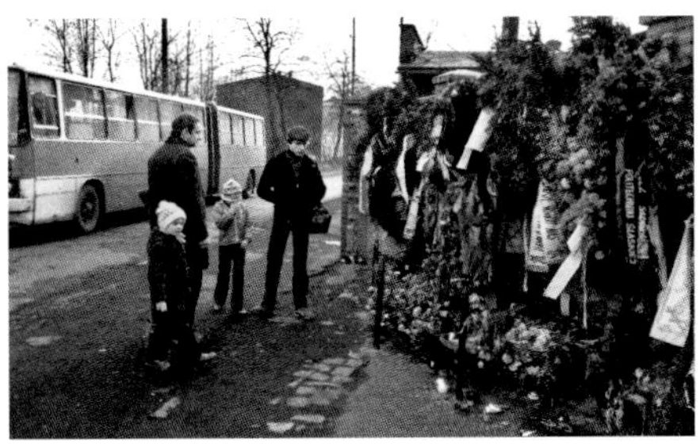

Page 111:
A family visiting a makeshift memorial for the nine mine workers killed by Polish police forces in the early days of martial law. (Katowice, 1982)

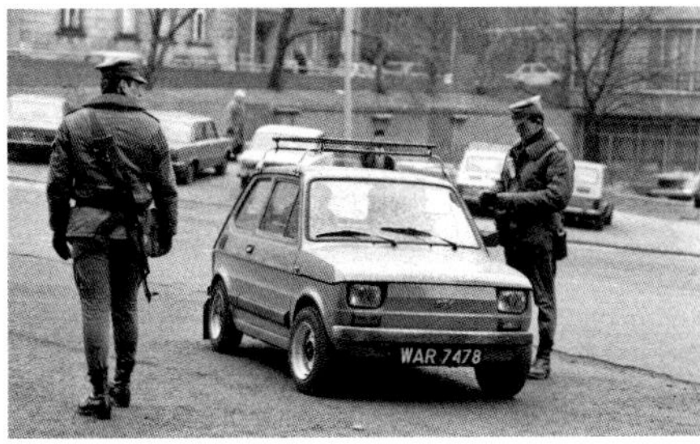

Page 112:
Soldiers checking vehicles during martial law. (Warsaw, 1982)

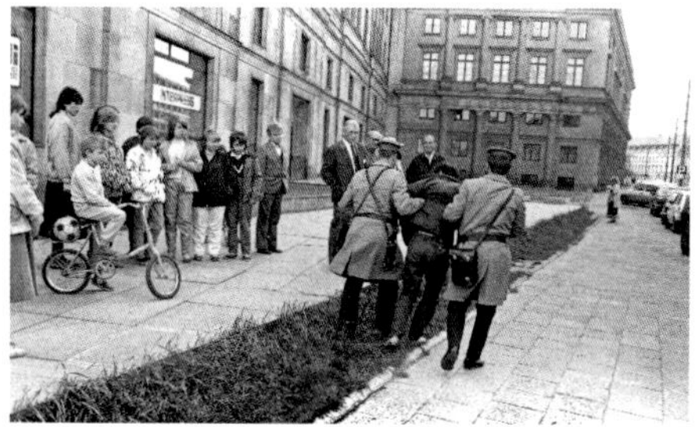

Page 113:
Police removing a drunken man passed out on the street in front of onlookers during martial law. (Warsaw, 1982)

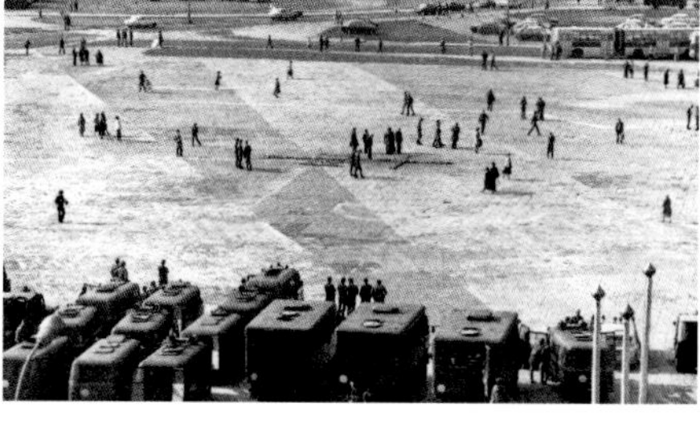

Pages 114-115:
Polish military vehicles and soldiers stationed in Victoria Square during the early days of martial law. The flower cross was created by Polish citizens in protest, and was cleared away by government workers at night. Each day it was rebuilt, and then destroyed again. (Warsaw, 1982)

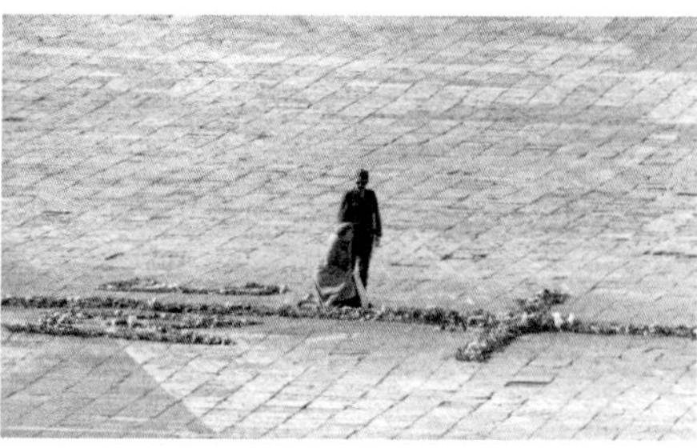

Pages 116-117:
A woman kneeling at the flower cross in Victoria Square is arrested and led away with her arms in the air by soldiers enforcing martial law. This sequence was shot with a telephoto lens from between the curtains of my hotel room window across from the square, as taking any photographs on the street would have quickly led to me being detained and my film confiscated by soldiers or the secret police who were monitoring the area. (Warsaw, 1982)

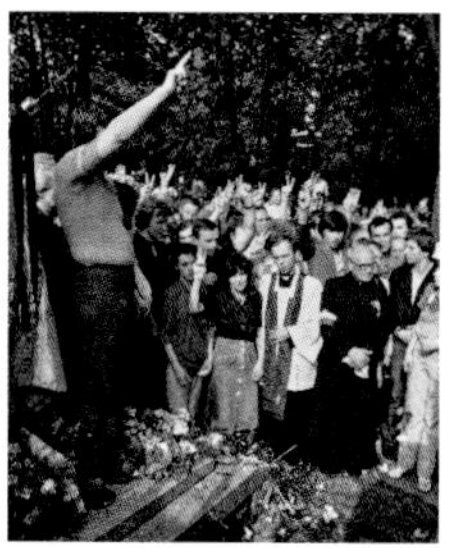

Page 119:
Mourners give the "V" sign of resistance during the funeral of a Solidarity activist who was murdered by the secret police. The clergyman standing next to the widow is Father Jerzy Popiełuszko, an activist Roman Catholic priest who was later assassinated – also by the secret police. His story was the basis for Agnieszka Holland's 1988 feature film, "To Kill A Priest." (Warsaw, 1982)

Pages 120-121:
Protesters gathering for planned peaceful demonstration against the imposition of martial law. The "V" sign was a symbol of resistance. (Warsaw, 1982)

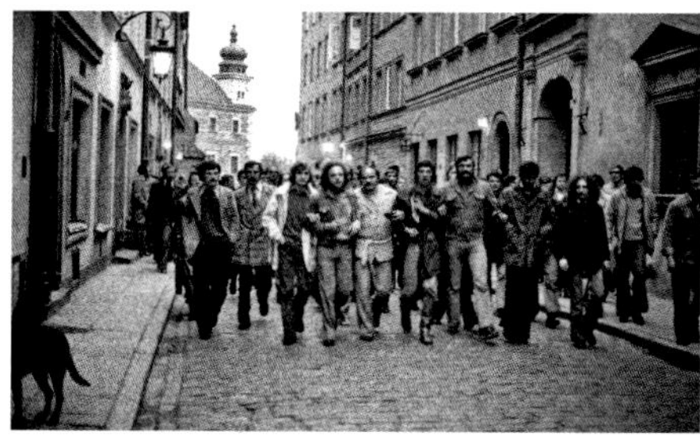

Pages 122-123:
A protest march at dusk in defiance of martial law. (Warsaw, 1982)

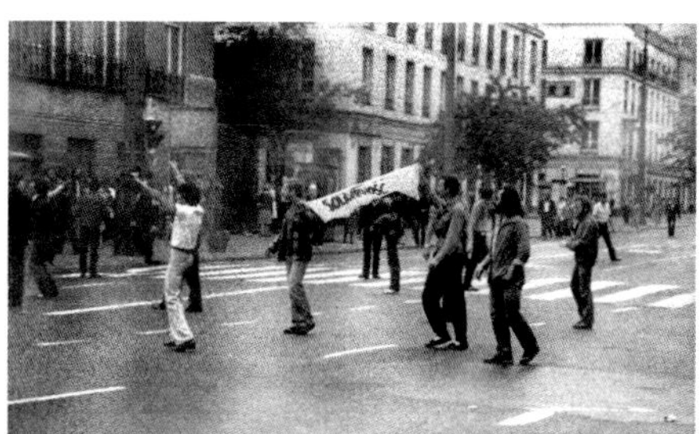

Pages 124-131:
On August 31, 1982, Solidarity leaders who had not already been arrested called for nationwide demonstrations against the imposition of martial law. These are images of what took place on the streets of Warsaw that day. (Warsaw, 1982)

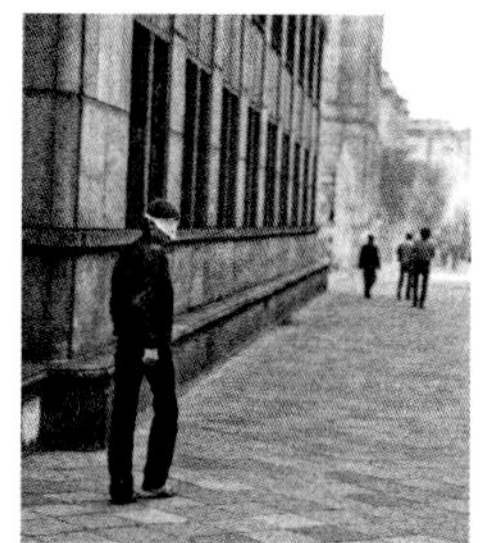

Page 132:
A lone demonstrator wearing face covering after riot police dispersed the pro-Solidarity gathering with tear gas and water cannons. (Warsaw, 1982)

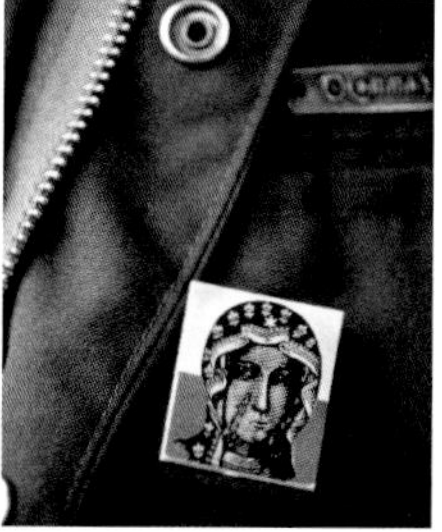

Page 135:
The Weeping Madonna pin, a symbol of resistance against the government, worn on the jacket of pro-Solidarity supporter. (Warsaw, 1982)

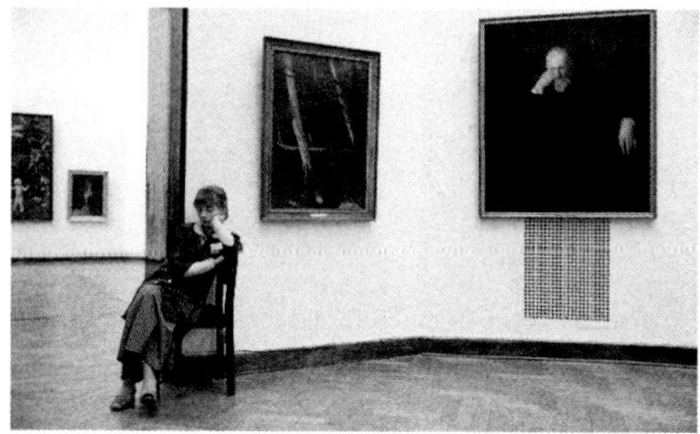

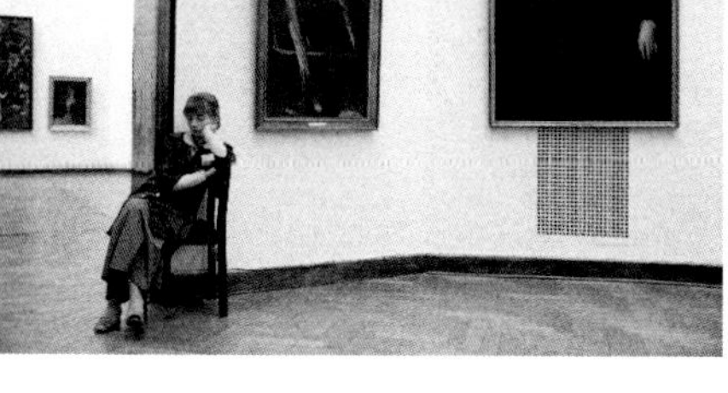

Pages 136-137:
A Museum monitor resting during her shift. (Warsaw, 1982)

Page 138:
A deliveryman shoveling coal into his carry basket. (Warsaw, 1982)

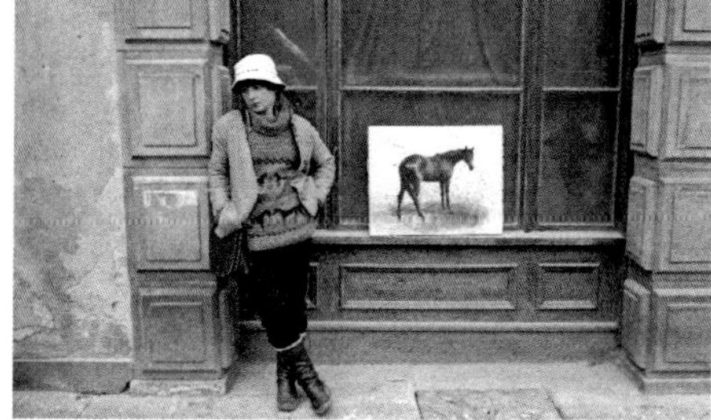

Page 139:
An artist hoping to make a sale on the street. (Warsaw, 1982)

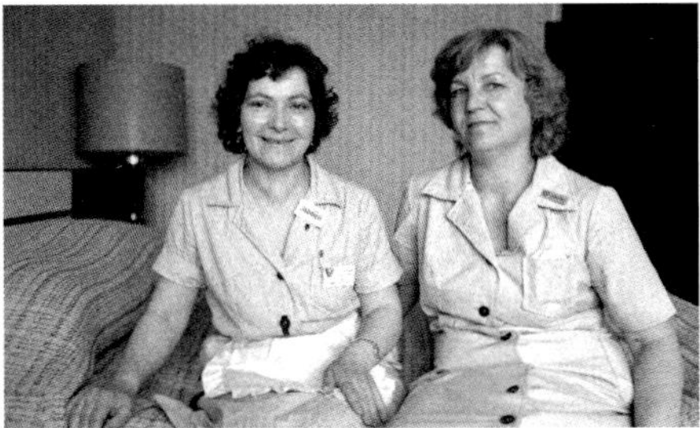

Page 141:
Two pro-Solidarity housekeepers pose for a photograph in a Victoria Hotel guest room. (Warsaw, 1982)

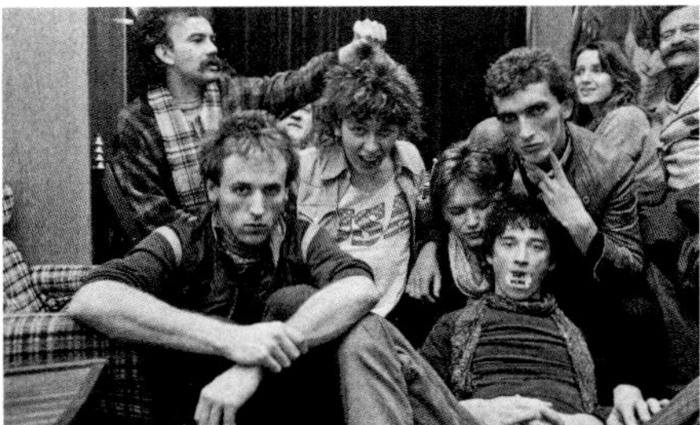

Pages 142-143:
The members of Polish rock band Lady Pank unwind after a concert during martial law. (Warsaw, 1982)

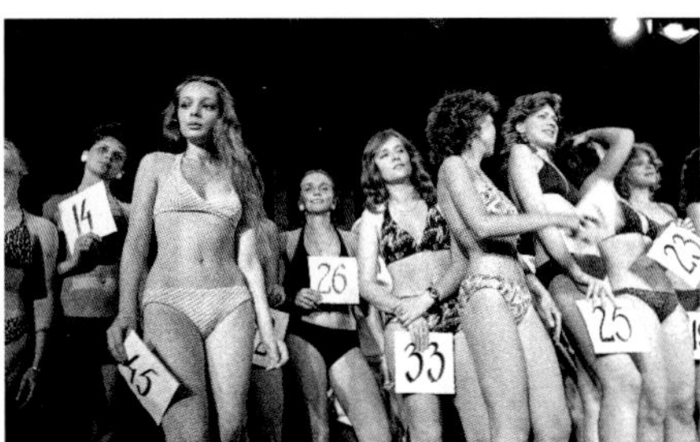

Pages 144-145:
Contestants in the Miss Poland beauty pageant waiting to be introduced. (Warsaw, 1982)

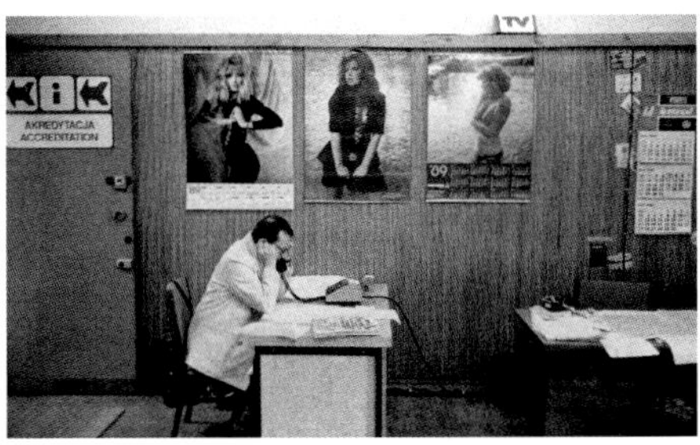

Pages 146-147:
An official of the Polish Interpress Agency, the government's organization charged with supervising foreign journalists, at his office desk. (Warsaw, 1989)

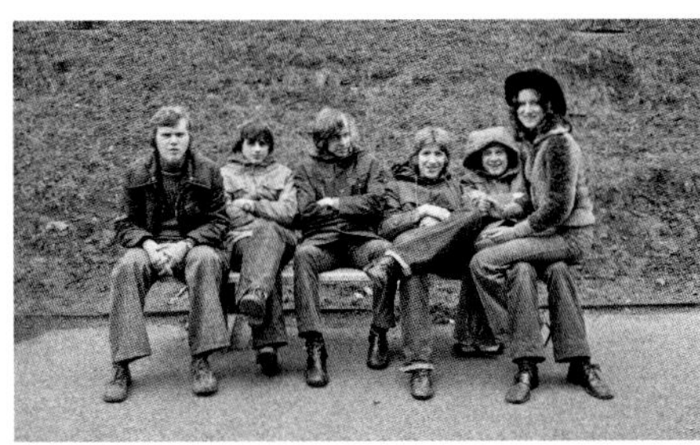

Pages 148-149:
East German teenagers hanging out in a park. (East Berlin, 1977)

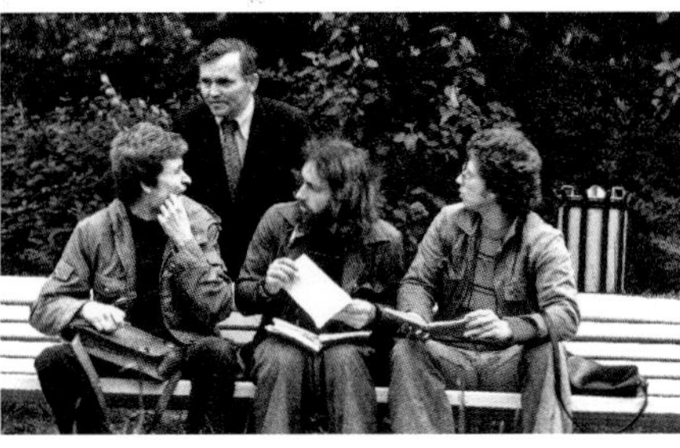

Page 151:
A plainclothes secret policeman surprises students on a bench from behind after observing them talking with a Western journalist. (Warsaw, 1982)

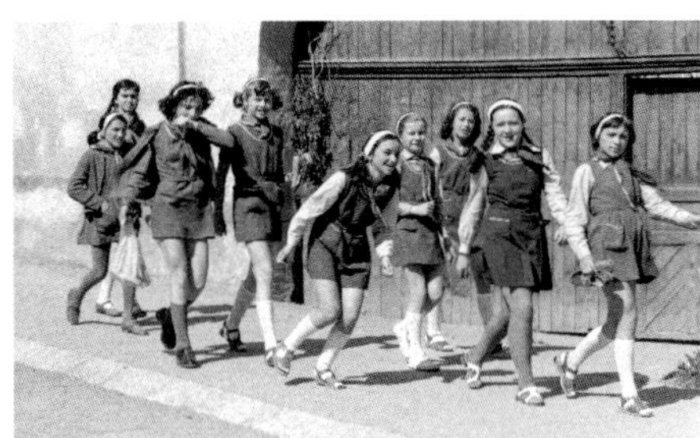

Page 152:
Romanian schoolgirls on the way to class. (Sighişoara, 1977)

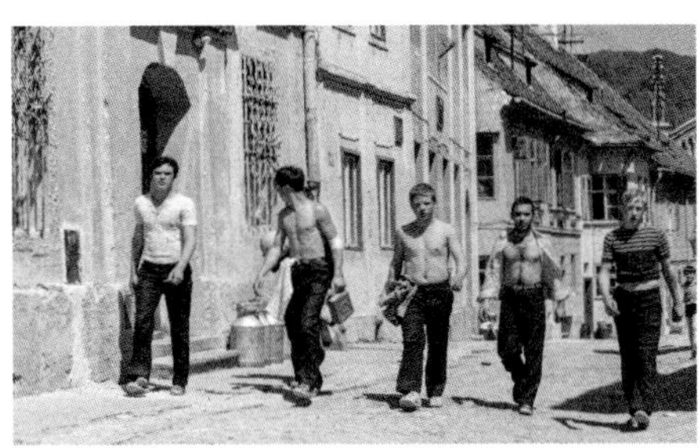

Page 153:
Romanian teenagers walking through town. (Sighişoara, 1977)

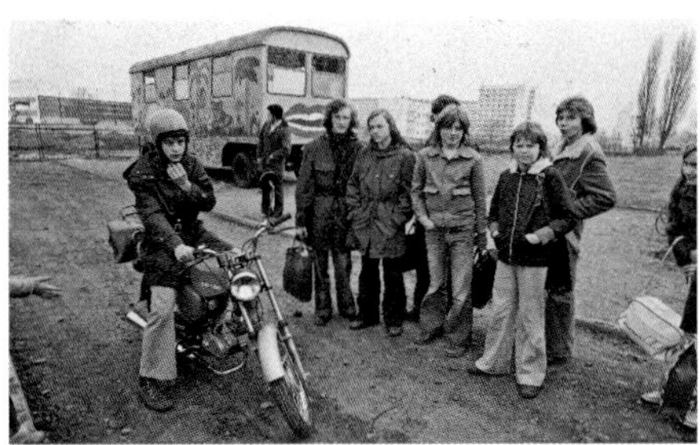

Pages 154-155:
Boys gathered around their friend's new Simson motorcycle. (East Berlin, 1977)

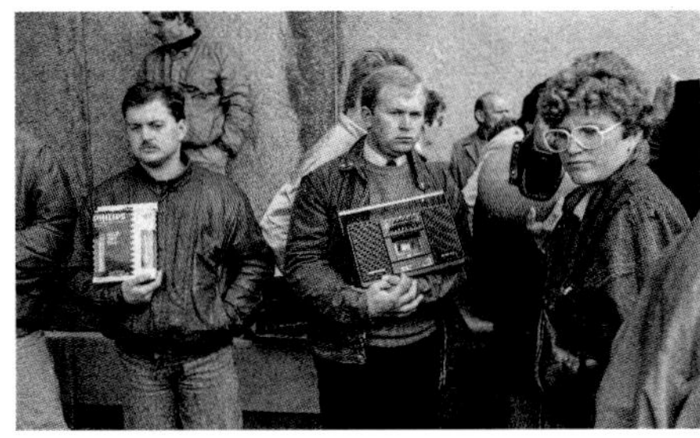

Page 156:
Men selling electronics equipment at a flea market. (Warsaw, 1989)

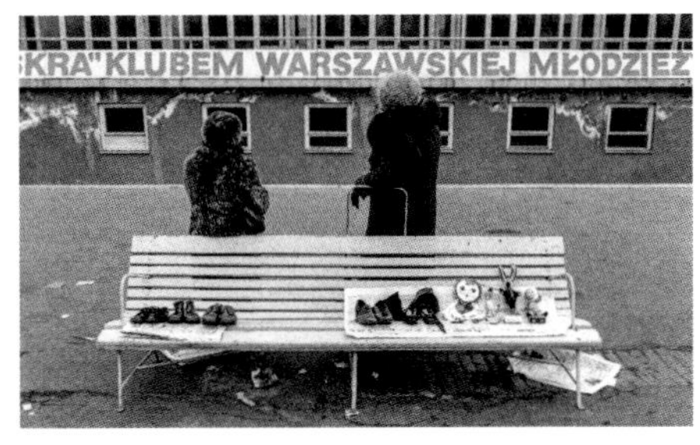

Page 157:
Women selling secondhand shoes and toys at a flea market. (Warsaw, 1982)

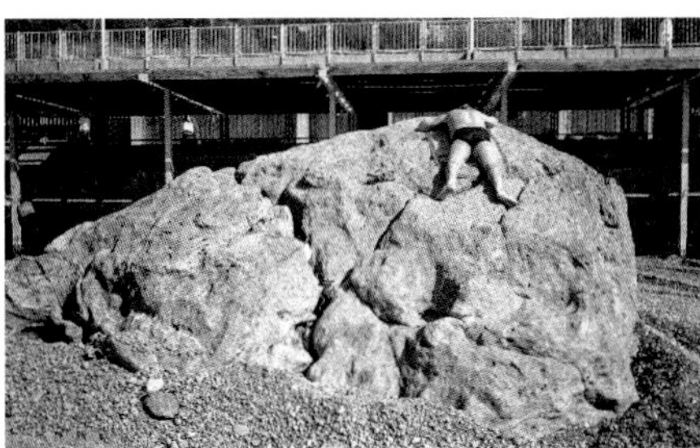

Page 158:
A sunbather on a rock. (Yalta, 1987)

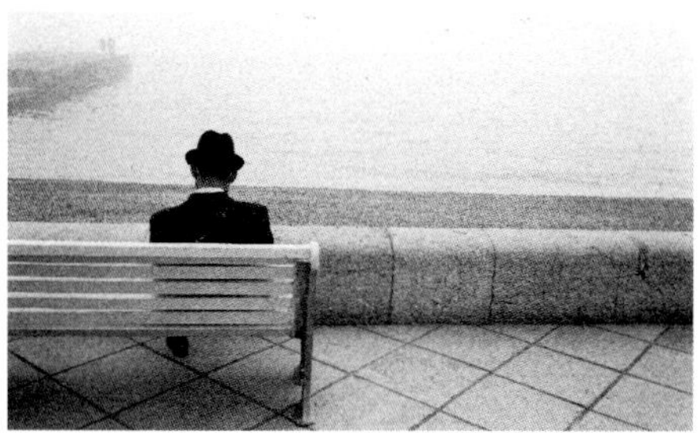

Page 159:
A foggy morning by the sea. (Yalta, 1987)

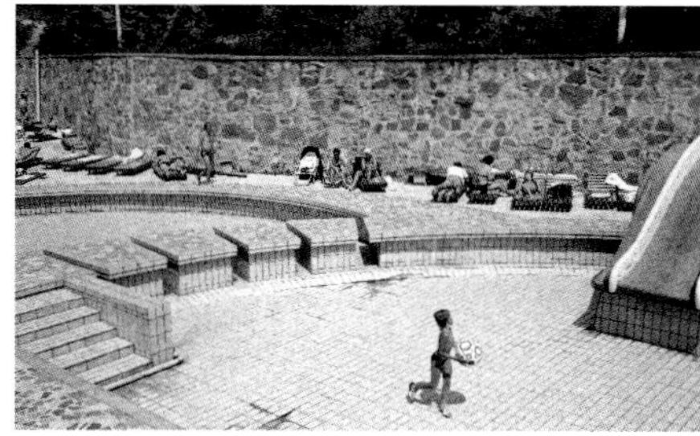

Pages 160-161:
A boy playing in the empty swimming pool of a resort hotel. (Yalta, 1987)

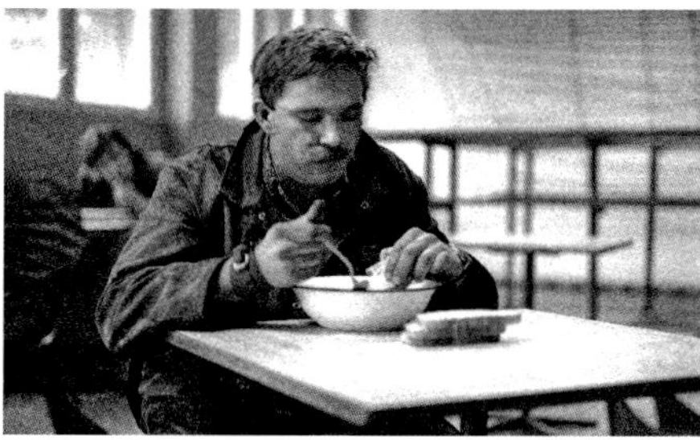

Page 162:
A factory worker having soup and bread for lunch. (Nova Huta, 1989)

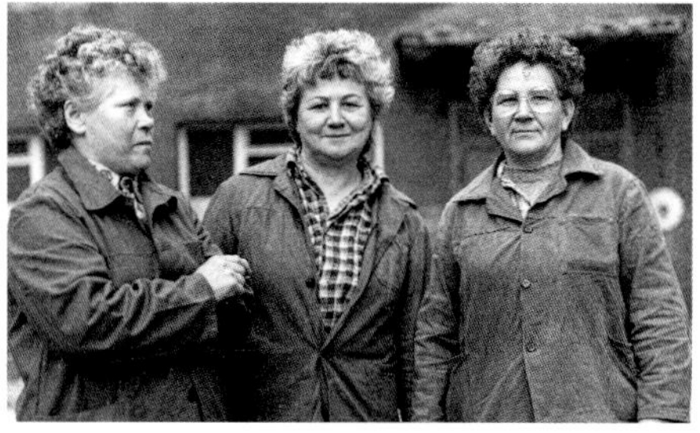

Page 163:
Factory workers on their lunch break. (Nova Huta, 1989)

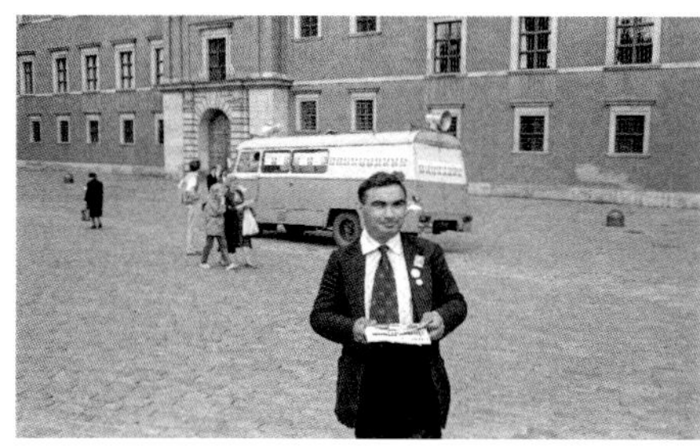

Page 165:
Campaigning for office in a public square. (Warsaw, 1989)

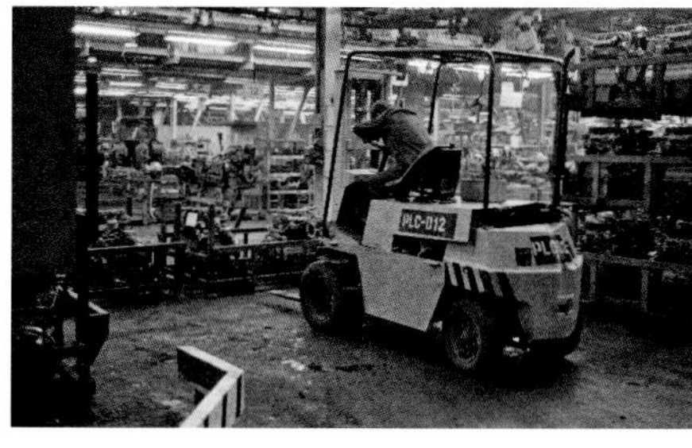

Pages 166-167:
A factory worker asleep at the wheel of his forklift. (Nova Huta, 1989)

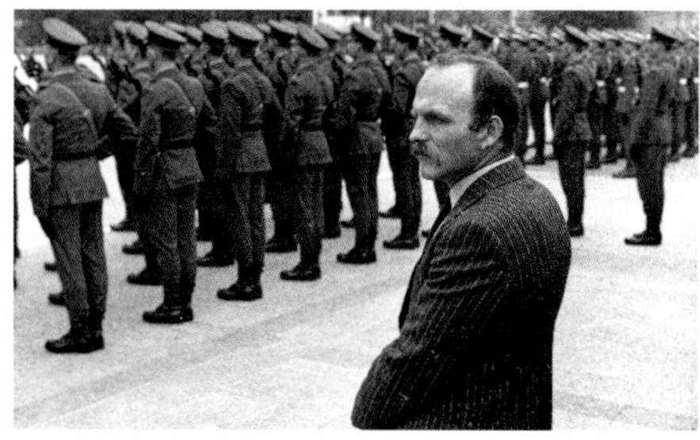

Page 169:
A security agent observing a military parade. (Warsaw, 1989)

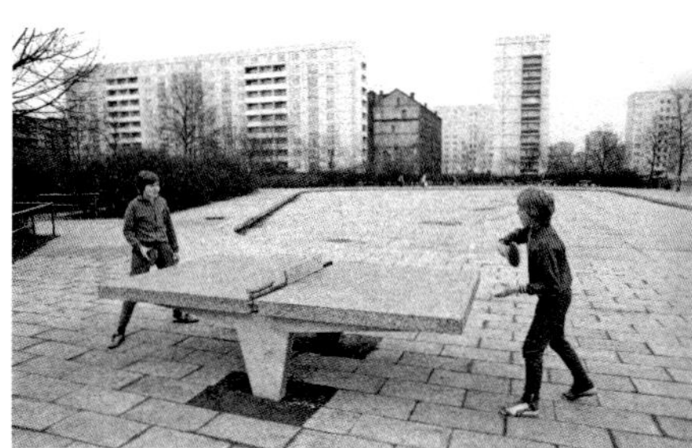

Page 170:
Boys playing ping-pong on a concrete table. (East Berlin, 1977)

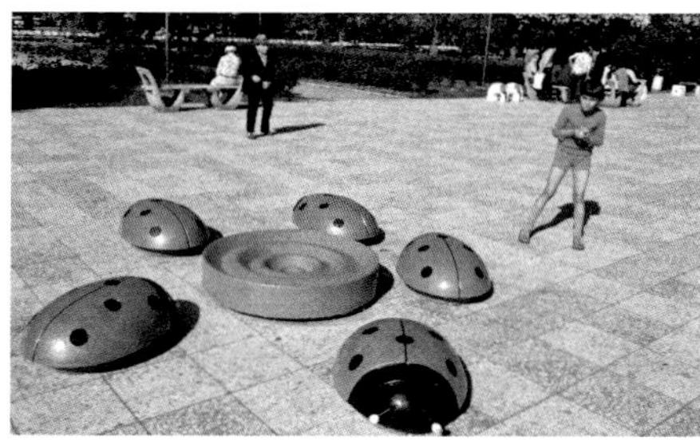

Page 171:
Toy Ladybugs on wheels at a playground. (Bucharest, 1977)

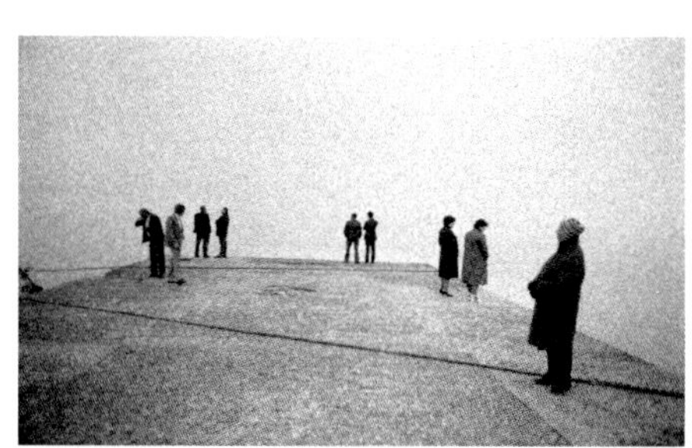

Page 173:
Early morning fog at the quay. (Yalta, 1987)

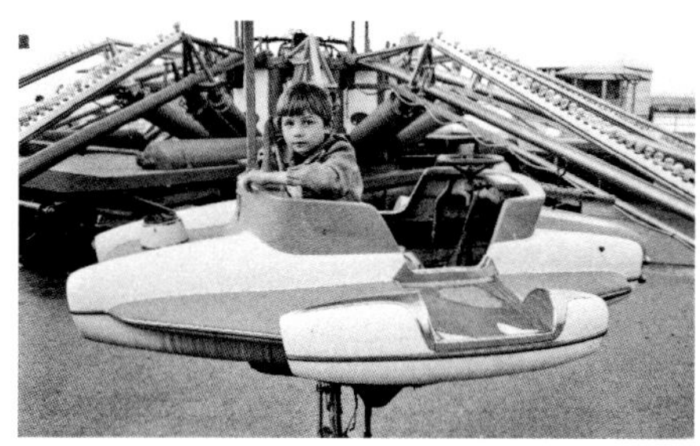

Pages 174-175:
A boy seated on a carnival rocket ride. (Yalta, 1987)

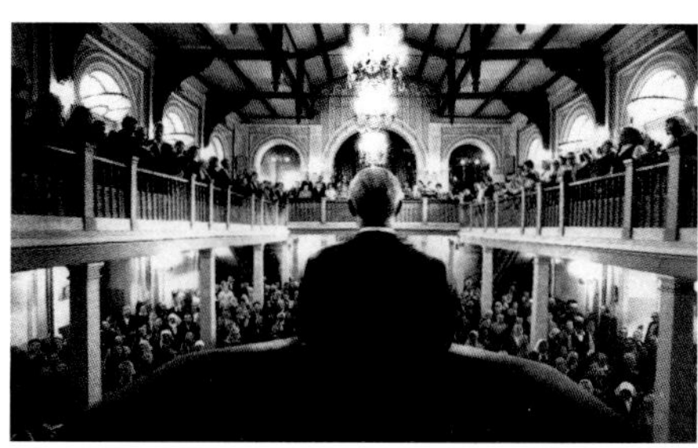

Endpapers:
A Protestant pastor preaching to his congregation. (Moscow, 1977)

ARTHUR GRACE WOULD LIKE TO EXTEND HIS GRATITUDE TO:

My wife, Debra, who kept me grounded - both literally and figuratively - during COVID-19 while I worked on "Communism(s)." It would not have come to pass without her.

The brilliant Paul Mahon, my attorney and agent, for once again bringing one of my book projects to fruition and for providing unerring advice and counsel throughout my career, (which I would never have had without him).

Richard Hornik, my former *TIME* magazine colleague, and valued friend for the past forty-one years for the cogent and insightful introduction and his invaluable overview of the project throughout.

Arcana: Books on the Arts' Lee Kaplan for his encouragement and belief in this project as well as his superb editing of both the photographs and text.

Deadbeat Club's Clint Woodside for his inspired and flawless art direction and his intuitive photo editing.

Bowhaus' Joe Berndt for his masterful digital work in preparing my images for print.

John Durniak, legendary Director of Photography at *TIME* magazine, who first assigned me to cover the Soviet Bloc in 1977.

Eliane Laffont, the savvy and indefatigable U.S. director of Sygma Photo News, who convinced John Durniak I was the perfect photographer to send to Berlin.

Arnold Drapkin, former *TIME* magazine Director of Photography, who continued to send me to cover stories in Soviet Bloc countries.

Karen Mullarkey, former Newsweek Director of Photography, for the opportunity to do a black and white photo essay on Poland in 1989.

Rick Smolan, the maestro behind the "A Day in the Life" series of photography books who sent me to Yalta in the USSR to roam freely with my Leicas and my government "guide."

Newsweek photographer Chris Niedenthal for his generosity and advice whenever I worked in Poland.

Sylvia Pesci, Eleonora Pasqui, and all at Damiani Editore for their enthusiasm in making it possible for you to now hold this book in your hands.

Edited by Arthur Grace, Lee Kaplan, and Clint Woodside
Design by Clint Woodside

Published by Damiani srl
info@damianieditore.com
www.damianieditore.com

Printed in December 2021, Italy
ISBN 978-88-6208-767-4

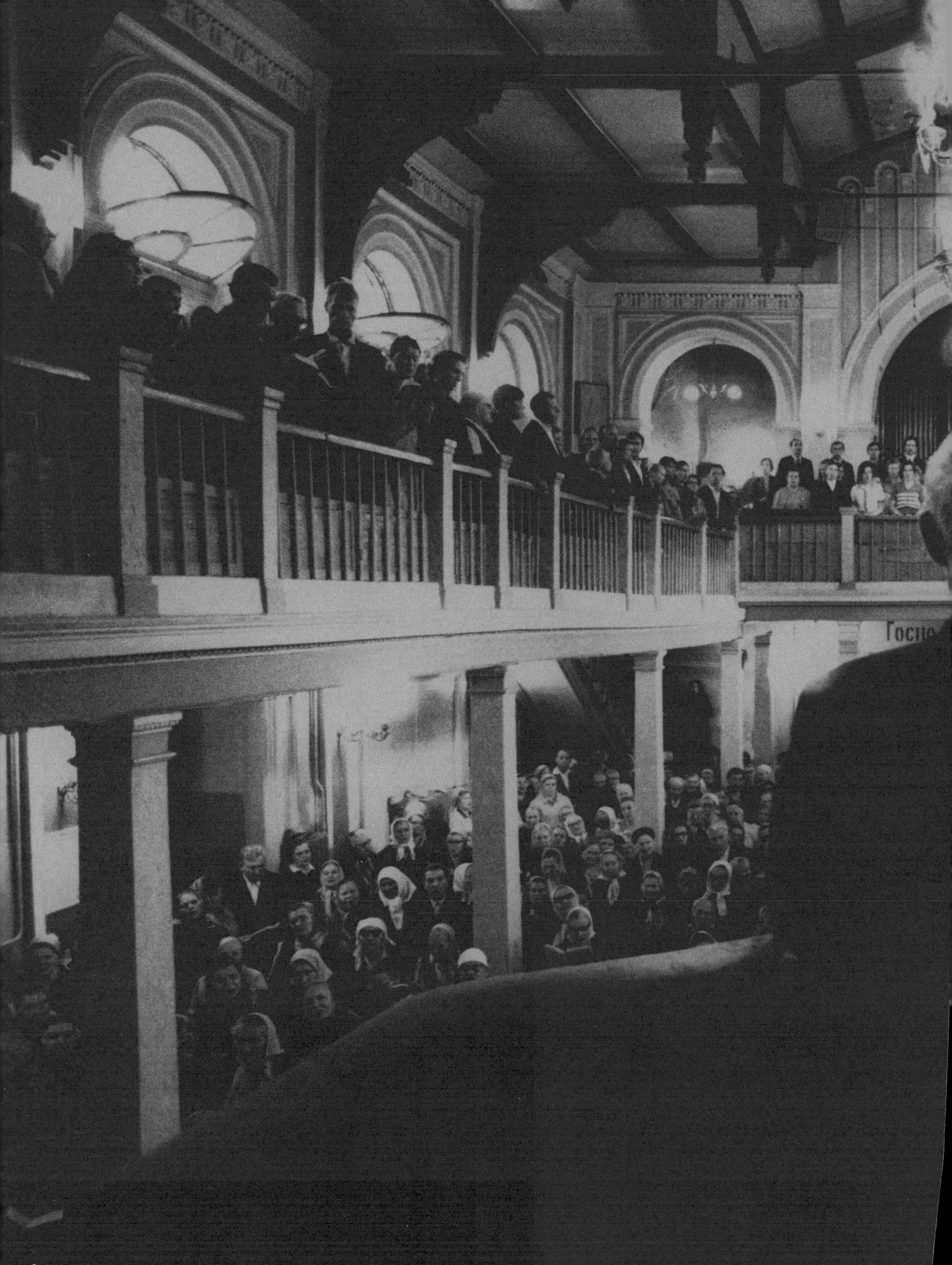